THE
TONY
YEARS

CRAIG
BROWN

EBURY
PRESS

1 3 5 7 9 10 8 6 4 2

This edition published in 2007

First published in 2006 by Ebury Press, an imprint of Ebury Publishing
A Random House Group Company

Copyright © Craig Brown 2006

The Random House Group Limited Reg. No. 954009

Addresses for companies within the Random House Group can be
found at www.randomhouse.co.uk

A CIP catalogue record for this book
is available from the British Library

Printed in the UK by CPI Cox & Wyman, Reading, RG1 8EX

ISBN 9780091909703

To buy books by your favourite authors and register
for offers visit www.rbooks.co.uk

"We have a tendency in this country to fall in love with noted personalities, like the drunks who throw their arms around a stranger's neck, only to push him away again after a while, for equally obscure reasons."

Robert Musil, "The Man Without Qualities" (1930)

Contents

DEPARTMENT OF HERITAGE

DEPARTMENT OF HEALTH AND SAFETY

DEPARTMENT OF EDUCATION AND SKILLS

DEPARTMENT OF ENVIRONMENT, FOOD AND RURAL AFFAIRS

DEPARTMENT OF MEDIA

THE END

APPENDIX

Acknowledgements

My thanks to Matthew Bell, for digging it all up; to the book's editor Andrew Goodfellow; to Ken Barlow; to Laura Chapman, Penny Cranford and Hilary Lowinger for their friendliness and lightly worn efficiency; to my friends and editors Ian Hislop, Charles Moore, Sarah Sands, Susanna Gross, Harry Mount, Sam Leith and Christopher Howse; to my wise and unfrightening agent Caroline Dawnay; to Mohamed Fayed, Tim Rice, Jordan, John Prescott, Esther Rantzen, Harold Pinter, the Duchess of York, Sir Roy Strong, Max Clifford, Tony Blair and successive Conservative leaders for providing, unasked, such a stream of inspiration; and, above all, to my wife Frances, for always being content to stop her own books mid-sentence in order to think of another word for ghastly, or something that rhymes with vegetable, or the name of the fat girl who won the *X Factor* the year before last.

Craig Brown, 2006

Introduction

FOR YEARS, he seemed so permanent; it was hard to imagine that Tony Blair would one day become a forgotten figure, like Harold Wilson or Sir Anthony Eden.

During the Tony Years, Conservative leaders came and went with such bewildering speed that, by the end, they barely registered. At the start of 2002, the powers-that-be at Madame Tussauds weren't even prepared to fork out the cash necessary for an Iain Duncan Smith waxwork. Having already been forced to melt down their William Hague, they presumed – quite rightly, as it turned out – that poor old Duncan Smith would soon have to join him in the saucepan. Of course, the most cost-effective option would have been to employ the real Duncan Smith to stand stock-still for a few hours a day for the duration of his leadership, but it is easy to be wise after the event.

Back then, it felt as though Tony would always be around, beaming away. We grew to think of him as our May Queen, with a changing cast of little pixies dancing merrily around. In many ways, he seemed more ubiquitous than Mrs Thatcher in her prime. Perhaps this was because she was so unique (or so peculiar, according to one's taste) while Tony was an archetype, a familiar figure from all our pasts: the eager boy with his hand in the air throughout double maths; the well-spoken estate agent; the energetic youth-leader, full of exciting new ways to cross a river.

In opposition, Tony had taken a ravenous interest in all that went on, vowing to bend back into shape everything that had gone wonky under the Conservatives. In 1996, he published a book of his thoughts and speeches called *New Britain: My Vision of a Young Country*. Ten years on, this title sounds ploddingly parodic, but is in fact true. "New" and "Young" were the buzz words of the time (as were the words "buzz words"). "I don't want an old social order," he proclaimed in one of his essays, "I want a new one, with rules for today ... a young country, a new Britain."

Tony's predecessor, John Major, is remembered, if he is remembered at all, for two little things: a) having an affair with Edwina Currie, and b) setting up the Cone Hotline, down which irate motorists could grumble their hatred of superfluous traffic cones. It is probably still too early to say which of these will come to be seen as his lasting achievement. During his time as Prime Minister, Major was often ridiculed for being small-time and Pooterish (he always took care to include Downing Street's postcode when signing visitors books on trips abroad to meet other world leaders). These two targets – Currie and cones – may have been modest, even silly, but at least they were achievable. But once you have based your appeal on a promise to make Britain new and young, things are almost bound to end in tears.

It has long been fashionable to blame prime ministers for everything that goes wrong – motorway pile-ups, yobby behaviour, bad pop songs – even when they have had nothing to do with it. In their turn, prime ministers like to take credit for any good news – heroic rescue missions, sporting victories, good pop songs – even when they have had nothing to do with it. Politics, Quentin Crisp once said, is the art of making the inevitable seem planned. The zeitgeist has a mind of its own, but any prime minister likes to be seen in the driving seat, even if he knows, somewhere in the back of his mind, that the steering wheel is not connected to the car. We, the passengers, are happy to go along with the illusion: it gives us a sense of security, and offers us someone important to shake our fists at when the vehicle veers headlong into a ditch.

Do dogs grow to look like their masters, or do masters grow to look like their dogs? Britain in 2006 certainly feels tinged by Tony, but how much of it would have happened anyway? At the start of his premiership, still so young and new, he was only too happy to pop his head around the door at every triumph or tragedy, beaming proprietorially or looking deeply concerned, whichever seemed the more appropriate. Following his success on the morning of the death of Princess Diana, whenever a little bird fell from the sky, up he popped, clearing his throat and saying something quivery but tasteful. Small wonder, then, that his electorate began to think of him as operating the entire Punch and Judy Show. Whatever happened on the national stage, we thought we could see the hands of Smiling Uncle Tony lodged firmly up the backsides of everyone, his fingers wiggling busily away.

* * *

Many new words became popular during the Tony Years. Some, like CCTV and Viagra, came about as a result of inventions. Others – such as sportsmen barking "K'maarn!" while clenching their fists and dragging down their right arms as though pulling invisible lavatory chains – appeared from nowhere. Chill out, hoodie, ASBO, binge drinking, serving suggestion, wicked, hissy fit, visitor centre: they each capture a moment in time with all the resonance of a pop song. But there is one word that is generally agreed to sum up the Tony Years. It is a word that was born in America in 1978, but only grew to its full height in the late 1990s. That word is Spin.

Publicity was all: privacy dwindled. In April 2002, even the occupant of that most oxymoronic of posts, Director of Communications for the Freemasons, announced that his members had decided to abandon their traditional black tie "partly because it's boring and partly because we want to raise the profile of the Freemasons".

Raising your profile was the be-all and end-all of public life. The sky over London darkened as profiles were raised. Politicians refused to be seen in public without first being slathered with a few coats of foundation. As one century gave way to another, Tony Blair's stylist revealed her secrets to the *News of the World*: "First, there's a base of Clinique moisturiser, followed by a concealer to hide the dark circles under his eyes, then something to lift the eyes and let them shine. And finally, a topcoat of blusher."

Before long, everyone was at it, left and right, big and small, sheepish and brassy. Every politician had to doll himself up to look like Widow Twankey before appearing in public. At a press conference during the 1997 general election, I stood a little too close to the Conservative front bench; I was surprised quite how bronzed they all were. And what of the figure in the corner? For a second, I thought things had perked up, and we could all look forward to a performance from Miss Clodagh Rodgers. Then I looked again and realised with a start that it was Sir Malcolm Rifkind.

The growth of spin – the art of making up – arose like a plume of smoke from the disintegration of the political divide. After ten years of New Labour, it was hard to point to a single thing that could not as easily have occured under the previous Conservative administration. Few people believed with anything like the old fervour in either capitalism or socialism. Under David Cameron, the Conservatives took pains to insist on their belief in the state, while Labour continued with their privatisations ("best when boldest"). Everyone was wishy-washy, though some protested that they were more wishy than washy, and others that they more washy than wishy.

Everything was much of a muchness, statesmen and pop stars only really distinguishable because the pop stars, being more earnest, wore fewer cosmetics. In December 2003, Yoko Ono and the then Conservative leader, Michael Howard, separately released New Year messages. "I believe that people must have every opportunity to fulfil their potential," said Howard. "Let's sing, dance and hug each other, to bring in the New Year, and with it, the new world," said Ono. Or was it the other way round?

Celebrity supplanted conviction. Even that old mascot of the left, Tony Benn, seemed to give up the ghost, opting to be a lovable grandpa, touring the country as Old Wise Owl, puffing on his pipe and reminiscing genially about days gone by. His natural successor, George Galloway, ended up on *Celebrity Big Brother* dancing in a red leotard, poking fun at an alcoholic and pretending to be a cat.

Politicians bowed and scraped to more senior celebrities. The Beckhams, Bono and Jamie Oliver ruled the roost. World statesmen tried to catch the eyes of Bono and Bob Geldof, and looked suitably penitent when these pop star grandees ticked them off in public. It is hard to imagine Neville Chamberlain sucking up to George Formby in quite the same way.

Footage of Tony chatting to Noel Gallagher at his 1997 house-warming party at Number Ten leaves one in no doubt as to which was the autograph-hunter. During the Tony Years celebrity multi-plied like a virus: once, with nothing better to do, I calculated that 32,000 people – roughly the population of Windsor – could claim to have been in the pop charts at one time or another. Add to this the ever-expanding population of footballers, disc jockeys, chefs, TV historians, soap opera stars and supermodels, and you wonder how there can possibly be room for all of them, especially as their spouses are now celebrities by association, and sometimes, as in the case of Mrs Sting's chef, the celebrity's wife's principal servants are celebrities, too. Or is there some sort of secret quota system in operation? When a new chef or home decorator is admitted to the world of celebrity, is there a fading quiz show host or TV conjuror who is simultanaeously pushed out the other side? Celebrities come and go with increasing speed. Looking through my writings, I struggle to remember which of them did what. Who on earth were Stephen Byers, Fay Tozer, David Shayler, Grant Bovey, Gareth Gates, Jennie Bond, Michelle McManus, Christopher Meyer, Charles Ingram, Lance Price, Chico, Swampy, Bubble and Bez?

One noticeable change during the Tony Years has been the rise and rise of CCTV. Britain is now thought to have 20 per cent of the world's CCTVs, 4,000,000 in all, or one for every fourteen people. This is the stuff of nightmares, but no one has bothered to scream: perhaps we nodded them through because they made us feel wanted, just like celebrities; we probably felt it was better to make regular appearances on CCTV rather than on no TV at all.

CCTV promised to keep fear down, but has given it a leg-up. In fact, fear was one of the most successful growth industries of the Tony Years. BSE, 9/11, and, as I write, avian flu (Sars proved the one-hit wonder of health scares, and now skulks in obscurity, like all former celebrities) have each contributed to generalised feelings of anxiety. Loss of privacy has been promoted as the catch-all cure for fear: this means that all our profiles are now being raised, whether we like it or not.

Is cracking jokes really the most appropriate reaction to this unceasing conveyor belt of misery and angst? The short answer is no. It certainly doesn't do any good. Even the most piercing satire has little or no effect on its victim. More often than not, a politician is only too happy to purchase every merciless caricature of himself from its snarling cartoonist, ready to hang alongside all the others in gold frames on his lavatory wall. Even as I write, Osama bin Laden is probably having a quiet little chuckle to himself as he surveys all the cartoons of him as a mad beardie hell-bent on destruction, that he has Blu-tacked so carefully to the wall of his cave.

In the immediate aftermath of 9/11, it became fashionable to say that satire and irony – knock-knock jokes, too, I imagine – were dead. But the most shocking events often give rise to the most absurd reactions, dotty, alarmist or pretentious, depending on the commentator. "Its glint was the worldflash of a coming future" wrote Martin Amis of the second aeroplane. Sometimes, laughter is the truest response to these comments.

A few weeks after 9/11 a company called Precision Dynamics produced an "Emergency Building Escape Parachute", costing upwards of £17,575, depending on the weight of the buyer. They claimed that Donald Trump had already put in an order for one. "All you have to do to initiate deployment is to jump out the window and away from the building," said the brochure. "Simple steering and landing techniques can deliver you to the surface with confidence."

As news, this was treated with all due solemnity. But it is the humorist's task to look behind the cloud for the silver lining (and sometimes vice versa). The Emergency Building Escape Parachute raised a number of issues more to do with etiquette than with health and safety. For example, should the purchaser arrive at work each day with the parachute already strapped to his back, perhaps hidden discreetly below a mackintosh, so as to not cause alarm? Or should he perhaps tuck it beneath his desk, opening up the possibility of an unseemly tussle among his colleagues the moment a fire alarm goes off in error? At the first hint of anything untoward, it would be hard not to succumb to the temptation to strap on one's parachute and leap out of the nearest window. And while everyone else in the building was muttering "False alarm!", there you would be, floating down past window after window with a sheepish expression on your face.

Such are the fears and conundrums raised – exploited might be a better word – in this book. I have given it the title *The Tony Years* so that it might appeal to zeitgeist-spotters, and because it all took place on Tony's watch. Were we the tight-lipped ventriloqust, and he the all-talking, all-winking dummy? Or were the roles reversed? These are questions for future generations to decide.

The Beginning

"The People of Britain Will No Longer Die": New Labour Manifesto 1997

TONY BLAIR WRITES: I believe in Britain.

Great! It is a great country with a great history. Great!

The British people are a great people. You feel great. I feel great. We all feel great. Everything's really great.

On second thoughts, it's not so great after all. In fact, it could be a lot greater. I want a Britain that is one nation, with shared values and purpose.

A Britain where everyone is happy and carefree and no one is upset. A modern, go-ahead Britain, where folk are able to walk forwards down the street and reach their destinations on time.

A Britain which can hold its head high and is proud to wear the very latest fashions as it swaggers along to a dinner date with a delightful friend. I want a Britain that does not shuffle into the new millennium afraid of the future. I want a Britain that strides into the future with a sense of purpose, hogging a seat near the front, and maximising the elbow room for itself.

I want a Britain we can all feel part of. I want a Britain in which what I want for my own children I want for yours – but only after I have got it for mine.

I want a Britain free of queue-barging. We have modernised the Labour Party and we will modernise Britain. Let me give you an example. Do you remember John Prescott five years ago? John will be the first to agree that he looked drab, outdated – a real no-hoper. But look at him now: wearing smart, double-breasted suits, every bit the City gent.

Under New Labour, everyone will look as modern as John Prescott.

The difference between us and the Conservatives is that we know where we want to go. We want to go forwards. And we know how to get there. Straight on. Right a bit. Left a bit. Stop. And then ask.

We will promote personal prosperity for all. We as a nation must face up to some harsh truths. We in New Labour recognise that success is better than abject failure. Happiness is better than downright misery. Children are a precious asset. Too many cooks spoil the broth. More hands make light work. It's a long way to Tipperary.

A room decorated entirely in grey can be lacking in colour. There is nothing worse than a ballpoint pen bursting in the top pocket of a white jacket. And cash in the pocket is better than cash in the hand – because that way you don't lose it.

I'm not saying the process by which we arrived at these conclusions has not been long and – at times – painful. But I believe we have arrived at them in the best interests of the ordinary men and women of this great nation.

We have done nothing more and nothing less than set out to establish a new trust for a new deal for a new partnership for a new approach for a new spirit for a new contract for the new millennium. It's as simple as that.

A new trust. A new deal. A new partnership. A new approach. A new spirit. A new contract. A new millennium. And together the seven of them – four in the back, three in the front, driven by the new deal, with the new contract reading the map and the new spirit barking out directions – will set off to the land of the future.

But only after they have all taken advantage of the facilities. For let me assure them this. There'll be no stopping along the way. We will make everyone much more healthy. During nineteen years of Conservative rule, many millions of people have died. Particularly the elderly and infirm. The cause? Ill health. Let's make no bones about it. Ill health is a major cause of death in our society. And we will attack the root causes of ill health. We will set up a major network of new initiative zones to tackle the long-term problems of expanding perceptions among the elderly and the infirm.

Under New Labour, the people of Britain will no longer feel ill. Instead, they will be encouraged to feel that their bodies have instituted major new initiatives to combat ongoing functions.

Under New Labour, the people of Britain will no longer die. Instead, they will be able to feel that a complete re-evaluation of facilities has resulted in an exciting new programme of bodily decommissioning.

We will give as good as we get. What we've got is good. But we've got to get what we've got and give what we get to know that what we've got is as good as what we get. What's the good of getting as good as what we've got if we can't give as good as we get?

Any decision about a single currency must be determined by hard-headed assessment of Britain's best economic interests. It is quite clear what we must do. We must either go in. Or we must stay out. Only New Labour can be trusted to make the one choice. Or the other. But we make this solemn pledge. We will never make both choices.

Unless circumstances are right.

New Labour.

Because Britain deserves better.

Or roughly the same.

Parallel History:
The Rise and Rise of Ant B
What if Mickie Most had paid a visit to Oxford on March 2, 1975?

TOWARDS THE END of 1974, the Oxford University rock band Ugly Rumours, formed by Wykehamists Mark Ellen and Adam Sharples, were desperately in need of a charismatic lead singer. One day, Sharples returned from a visit to St John's College convinced he had found the right man for the job. "I met this guy Anthony Blair in St John's," Sharples told Ellen. "He looks terrific. And he can sing."

According to John Rentoul's biography, Tony Blair was auditioned in Sharples's room in Corpus Christi. "Sharples and I played acoustic guitar and Blair sang," recalled Ellen. "He was fantastic. He had a really good voice. It was a very high, powerful voice and he knew all the words. So we said: 'Well, you're in. We're called Ugly Rumours and you can start tomorrow.'"

The band's first gig was in Corpus Christi. Blair was wearing purple loon pants and a hoop-neck T-shirt. According to Ellen, he came on stage "giving it a bit of serious Mick Jagger, a bit of finger-wagging and punching the air. At the end of the first number, "Honky Tonk Woman", he yelled to the audience, 'Are you having a good time? I can't hear you at the back! Corpus Christi, how are you?'"

Blair closed the set by informing the audience that Ugly Rumours would be performing at the Alternative Corpus Christi College Ball, supported by a jazz-fusion band and a string quartet. "Hope you're gonna come," he added, before launching into an upbeat rendition of Fleetwood Mac's "Black Magic Woman".

At that moment, Mickie Most was sitting in his Soho office, lined with gold records by Lulu, Hot Chocolate, Mud and Suzi Quatro. Most had established himself as one of the great pop producers of the Sixties, and was now a familiar face on the television talent show *New Faces*. But he was restless to discover the next big thing – ideally an act that would help him cash in on the new glam rock explosion.

He was about to go home when he caught sight of an invitation to a student gig in Oxford. His secretary had scrawled "Refused" over the top in thick red felt-tip. "Well," he thought, thrusting the invitation into his leather jacket, "I've nothing better to do."

Mickie Most arrived at Corpus Christi fifteen minutes late. At first the surly security guard hired from Ruskin College, a stout Merchant Navy man called Prescott, had attempted to refuse him entry, looking him up and down and muttering, "I know your type." But after Most had slipped him a £5 note, Prescott was happy to wave him through: "Make yourself at home, sir."

As Most took his seat, Ugly Rumours were performing the instrumental opening to "Take It Easy". Frankly, he was not much impressed by the band's musicianship. In fact, he was about to leave the hall when on to the stage pranced the group's long-haired lead singer, wiggling his hips in a white one-piece jumpsuit. With a whoop of "Let's go, honeys!", this young man began to sing his heart out – and Most found himself instantly won over. As the band's final number drew to a close, Most rushed backstage ("This way, sir," muttered Prescott, as a second fiver found its way into his top pocket).

A third-year undergraduate with a career in law stretching ahead of him, Anthony Blair could scarcely believe his ears. He had long been in two minds about having to cut his hair, don a shirt and tie, and kowtow to the forces of conservatism – and here was a top pop producer offering him a way out of it.

"Stick with me, son," said Most, looking him straight in the eye, "and you could be the next Alvin Stardust."

"Great!" replied Blair. "But whatever you do, don't ask me to split with the other guys in the band. They're my mates! We're agreed – wherever I go, they go too, man."

"I'm not asking you to split with the other guys," explained Most, bringing out a contract, "I'm just asking you to ditch them."

"Smashing!" replied Blair. "May I borrow your pen?"

Two months later, on Thursday, May 23, 1974, an exciting new young glam-rock star called Ant B appeared on *Top of the Pops* performing "Lay Your Love On Me" dressed in a silver Lurex one-piece bodysuit. The next week, it shot straight to number two in the charts, and was only prevented from climbing to number one by the seemingly unassailable Paper Lace.

Over the next eighteen months, Ant B enjoyed a further three chart hits – "Telling You What You Wanna Hear", which reached number seven, "Accept the Challenge", which reached number fifteen, and "Quick Fix Baby (There's No)", which was number twenty-nine for one week in October, 1975. But by 1976 glam-rock was giving way to punk, and Mickie Most found other interests to pursue.

Looking back on his career in 2003, Ant B has no regrets. "Some of my old mates say I could have gone into politics – yeah, right!" he says, with a laugh. "Anyway, a lot of people don't realise this but I'm huge on the Seventies nostalgia circuit, particularly in Sweden."

This Christmas, fans will have a chance to catch up with him at the Wyvern Theatre, Swindon, playing Dick Whittington opposite John Inman, Anita Harris and former bass guitarist with Paper Lace, Pete Mandelson.

50 Reasons Why Britannia is Cool

✱ When top American vocalist Meatloaf toured Britain in 1995, he began his first London concert by saying: "Great to be back in Britain."

✱ *Birds of a Feather* may be adapted by American scriptwriters for possible transmission by NBC.

✱ Top American actress Goldie Hawn was spotted at Royal Ascot in 1996.

✱ The British Film Industry has been given a shot in the arm with the news that an Ealing-based company won a commendation for best animated short at the Adelaide Film Festival.

✱ A British-born man is currently on death row.

✱ Peter Mandelson once met Patsy Kensit.

✱ Two leading British fashion designers now work in Paris.

✱ Bette Midler plans to do some of her Christmas shopping this year at Harvey Nichols.

✱ Robert de Niro stayed in a Mayfair apartment for three days last February.

✱ Top British model Kate Moss has had an affair with Johnny Depp.

✱ The engine of the aeroplane in which top American singer John Denver was killed included several parts manufactured exclusively in Britain.

✱ There are more Andrew Lloyd Webber musicals now showing in London's West End than in any other European city.

✱ Pyrenean goats cheese can be bought at Neal's Yard in Covent Garden for £3.95 a quarter-pound.

✱ Madonna stayed at London's Hyde Park Hotel for five nights just over two years ago.

✱ The Spice Girls have climbed to number five in the Italian charts.

✱ Tony Blair boasts an A level in French.

✱ A British make-up artist won a prize at the Berlin Film Festival.

✱ The eyes of the world will be on Greenwich for two to five seconds around midnight on December 31, 1999.

✱ Leonardo DiCaprio may have had a Scottish great-grandfather.

✱ England won the World Cup in 1966.

* Three novels by Jeffrey Archer have been made into popular TV mini-series which have been sold to Belgium, Sri Lanka and Tasmania.
* The *Titanic* was built in Belfast.
* *The Onedin Line* is still popular in Bulgaria, Turkey and Corfu.
* Steven Spielberg, Tom Cruise and Nicole Kidman all turned up at the funeral of Diana, Princess of Wales.
* Tony Blair regularly calls President Clinton – and sometimes gets put through.
* Quentin Tarantino came to London for the launch of his recent movie, *Jackie Brown*.
* Top British novelist Martin Amis is published in America.
* Heinz Tomato Soup is as famous in America as it is in Britain.
* The Duchess of York is in great demand on mid-morning cable TV shows in New York.
* The Brit Awards are regularly won by top British bands.
* Top British artist Damien Hirst has a sculpture on temporary exhibition in Helsinki.
* Elton John, Tony Blair, John Major and Paul McCartney are all in Madame Tussauds.
* Elvis Presley always promised to make a concert tour of Britain – and may well have done so, had his life not been tragically cut short.
* Madonna once interviewed an English nanny for a job.
* Harry Evans and Tina Brown invite Henry Kissinger, Jon Bon Jovi and Norman Mailer to their high-flying New York parties – and sometimes they accept.
* Tony Blair is on Christian-name terms with top American media entrepreneur Rupert Murdoch.
* British singer Liam Gallagher made second-page news in Australia after a minor fracas.
* Culture Secretary Chris Smith is sometimes seen attending premieres wearing stylish silk waistcoats and spotty bow ties by Paul Smith.
* Top American vocalist Donny Osmond has agreed to sing at a Royal Albert Hall concert to celebrate fifty years of Andrew Lloyd Webber.

* The Archbishop of Canterbury is a football supporter. He enjoys cheering on "The Gunners" whenever he has a Saturday afternoon spare.

* Saddam Hussein agreed to meet former British PM Edward Heath for a half-hour discussion prior to the Gulf War.

* British novelist Jackie Collins has entertained top American stars such as Burt Reynolds at her LA home.

* In a recent poll, HM the Queen was correctly identified by more than 47 per cent of New Yorkers.

* Top American actor Richard Gere once opened a Harrods summer sale.

* Bognor Regis is twinned with St Tropez.

* A new McDonald's is scheduled to open in Birmingham city centre in July 1998.

* Welsh singer Tom Jones still performs regularly in Las Vegas.

* Over the course of last year, top American chat-show host Larry King interviewed seven British guests.

* Last year Diana Ross told British chat-show host Des O'Connor that London is one of her absolute favourite cities.

* Tony Blair has all the albums by Dire Straits in his collection. He offered to lend one to President Clinton on his last visit to Washington, but, sadly, the President was talking to somebody else so didn't hear.

(March 28, 1998)

Department of Transport

Jeremy Clarkson's Diary

Has anyone else noticed that it's now 2006? Yup. Not 2003. Not 2004. Not even 2005. But 2006. Blimey. Can you believe it?

Happy New Year? I don't think so. It makes you think, doesn't it? Heads down and pocket calculators out. Let's face it, 2006 is a full six years – SIX YEARS! – into what used to be known as the New Millennium.

New? Six years on, this millennium is about as new as the socks I've been wearing these past six days because the washing machine's on the blink and my dear wife, being a woman, bless her, can't be arsed to give them a good scrubbing with the Lifebuoy in the kitchen sink.

Smelly? You bet. To call my socks smelly would be an understatement. In fact, to call my socks smelly would be like calling your common-or-garden pair of woman's bazonkers only quite appealing! When in fact to a red-blooded bloke like moi they are quite amazingly appealing, and the same applies to you, mate – unless you're a fully paid up member of the limp-wristed "Oooh, I love the arts" brigade!

So where was I? That's it. New Year. Or rather the so-called New Year. In fact, by my calculation it's been going a few days now. If it was a pint of milk, it would have gone off, and you'd toss it in the bin. And who likes milk anyway? It's a much-overrated substance, in my humble op. And pretty damned disgusting too. A lot of people don't realise this, but milk comes from a cow's udders. And who wants to drink something that's emerged from a Daisy's boobies? What do you think I am – a calf or something? Well, I'm damned well not. Have you ever seen a calf wearing jeans and a T-shirt, slamming his right foot on the accelerator and driving full-throttle down the motorway at 105mph in a Maserati 3.6 X before settling down in the snug with the blokes to set the world to rights over a decent pint of best bitter? You ain't? I rest my case, m'lud!

New Year's resolutions? Not many, actually. In fact, just the one. Never to take a ride on the so-called London Eye again!

You must have seen it. It's that bloody great circular thing – monstrosity, more like! – that sits by the River Thames in London like a huge great wheel, which is basically what it is.

I went on it the other day, for my sins. Talk about rubbish. Queued up for what seemed like hours, even if it was just a few minutes. Then the uniformed officials – uniformed Nazis more like! – pointed me in the direction of a glass capsule.

"Sorry mate!" says I. "I'm not being cooped up in there! I'm a bloke! I value my freedom! If I wanted to travel inside a pod, I'd grow my own broad beans!!! Which means, I'll be riding outside, on the top!"

But guess what? You've got it. No can do. The deal was this: either you ride inside the pod or not at all. Welcome, my friends, to the wonderful world of the fascist state.

So you go into the pod, give a cursory nod to your passengers – many of them our foreign friends, I regret to say – and make your way to the driving seat. Wrong again! Guess what? There's no driving seat. Zilch. Some bugger's stolen it – and not only that but he's made off with the steering wheel, too.

What kind of vehicle is this, when it's at home? It crawls along at less than two miles an hour, you can't change direction, and there's no sound system on which to play your classic Phil Collins tracks at full blast. Not only that, but twenty minutes after you've set off you're back in exactly the same place you started out from!

For crying out loud, I'd have had more fun talking to a Dane and a German over a Nigerian cocktail in a Spanish-run hotel on a wet Sunday in Belgium! So the next time someone suggests riding on the London Eye, you know what I'll say? Not bloody likely, mate – not until someone fits my pod up with a 1200cc engine, a pair of thermodynamic wings, best bitter on tap, a rocket-booster and a selection of halfway decent porn mags!

Popped into my local boozer the other day, and saw a sign that said it all. "You don't have to be mad to work here," it read, "BUT IT HELPS!" That's me, folks!

Classic humour! Cracked me right up!

So why do none of our so-called great works of literature have anything half so pithy (I said PITHY!) to say for themselves?

Hamlet, for instance. By William Makepeace Shakespeare. Talk about wordy! I tried watching it once. Frankly, I'd prefer to occupy my time drilling a hole in my own head. Myself, I prefer my literature to have a bit of action. For my money, a book should be like a fast car – but with pages instead of wheels.

Jeffrey Archer? Let's be honest, the guy can spin a cracking yarn, and, admit it, you enjoy an Archer novel even more with every re-reading. The same cannot be said of old Shakeypoos. *Much Ado About Nothing*? You said it, mate.

Who was it who said the world was round? Don't make me laugh. If that was true, after you'd walked a few miles you'd find yourself at an odd angle, and then your hat would fall off. And when was the last time you saw a map which was curved?

Yup. The world's as flat as the proverbial pancake. And all the better for it.

To the assorted nitwits, nincompoops and borderline nutcases who continue to insist that it's round, all I can say is – try flying to Australia, mate! If it's where they say it is – at the very bottom of the so-called globe – then when you disembark from the plane you'll be upside down, not to mention falling head first into space!

It all goes to show, doesn't it, what a load of old cobblers the thought-police expect us to believe these days. It won't be long before members of the Fuhrer Blair's SS will be kicking our doors down, stabbing our family hay bales with their bayonets, pulling our buttocks apart and strip-searching us all for proof that we aren't dissenters from their Political Correctness Gone Bloody Mad. Next, they'll be forcing us to swear that vegetables are good for you, that the French don't smell funny, that the Germans aren't hell-bent on world domination and that downing a dozen pints with brandy chasers dampens your driving skills.

Or else they'll be trying to tell us that cigarettes give us cancer – or that you're likely to come a cropper if you drive your sports car off Beachy Head! Sorry, mate – don't get me started on that one!

Not a Real Man

SEVERE WEATHER CONDITIONS – sleet, snow, blizzards, avalanches, the lot – have been forecast, bringing, they tell us, misery for motorists. Oddly enough, though I can and do drive, I've never regarded myself as a "motorist". Am I a real man? I've never been able to muster an interest in cars. What lies beneath the bonnet remains a closed book to me. After twenty-five years as a "motorist", I haven't ever washed my car, or known my registration number, or discovered where the oil goes in.

Last year, Mary Killen came to interview me for her motoring column in *House & Garden* magazine. Trying to be helpful, I kicked off by telling her that for the past five years we had enjoyed driving a Renault Espace. As luck would have it, my wife was passing through the room and overheard. "You know, I don't think it is a Renault Espace," she said. "I'll just go and check." When she came back, she told me I'd got it wrong: our car was not a Renault Espace, but a VW Sharan. I had once seen an advertisement for a Renault Espace in a newspaper, and though I liked the look of it, I got sidetracked and ended up with a VW Sharan. Somehow, the phrase "Renault Espace" must have lingered in the back of my mind. But let's not split hairs: the VW Sharan and the Renault Espace are much of a muchness, and it would take a real motoring buff to tell them apart.

Anyway, it was our VW Sharan that ended up in *House & Garden* magazine, and very proud we were too. Alas, it is now on its last legs, with dents all over its outside and sweet papers, ice lolly sticks, Coke cans and old tennis balls littering its inside. Other things have also gone wonky over the years.

The electric windows – so obedient when we first bought it – have developed minds of their own, with a tendency to dance up and down by themselves, as though auditioning for a remake of *Mary Poppins*. Often they take us by surprise, winding themselves down five seconds after we have got out of the car. This rackety state of affairs has been going on for some time now and we have grown used to it, even quite enjoying our lively dialogue with the windows. But recently the car has taken to spluttering to a halt when it goes through a puddle. We then have to wait ten minutes or so by the side of the road before turning the ignition key. At this point it generally gets going, at least until the next puddle comes along.

But misery for motorists is misery for motorists, so this week we decided we must buy a car, a car which was lovely and clean inside and might even go through puddles without stopping. But what sort of car should we get? When it came down to it, the only car we could think of was another VW Sharan, so off we set.

In previous encounters with car people, I've noticed that, however much one tries to appear in control, it is only a matter of seconds before they twig that they have a wally on their hands. For instance, some years ago, I strode into a garage from which, a month before, I had bought a second-hand Morris Minor. The salesman was on the phone to a colleague. "I've got to go now," he said with a nod in my direction, "Mr Brown's just come in... You know, Mr Brown with the Morris... THAT'S RIGHT! HA! HA! HA! HA! HA!"

Car showrooms, even second-hand car showrooms, are very swish these days, with a shiny, can-do, slightly *Austin Powers* air about them. The VW salesman who greeted us had obviously taken a customer relations course, as he didn't see my arrival as an excuse for a jolly good laugh with his colleagues. Instead, he told me, with some excitement, of a second-hand (or "used", as they now call them) Sharan that had just come in. I forget exactly what he then said, but it was a jumble of numbers and letters, with here and there a long word, so that it came out something like: "It's an SE OT in green, with 1836 CCJF45 aspidistra and a 2.4 stroke geranium with a specification of 400 orchids, which gives you a 340BTY chrysanthemum on the road, which, believe me, is very good at that price."

I nodded in a straightforward, manly fashion, and attempted to cover up my stupefaction by concentrating on the only word I had understood. "Hmmm, green," I said. "Is that a light green or more of a – well, erm – more of a dark green?" More of a dark green, he confirmed, and I felt I was on solid ground. He then took us outside, and invited us to sit in it. This Sharan was a newer model, so I was keen to boast of any changes I could detect.

"The radio's in the same place, but I see they've moved the cupholder," I said, knowingly. I then paused for dramatic effect. "It used to be there," I continued, pointing to the left-hand side of the driver's seat before raising my finger a few inches to the dashboard, "but now it's there!"

We then engaged, man to man, in a bit of car-buff banter as to whether the new position would make a cup more or less likely to spill, eventually concluding that, all in all, it wouldn't make much difference. With misery for motorists on the way, I had to make a snap decision. It was green, it was a Sharan, and after a while we'd probably get used to the cupholder's new position. "We'll take it," I said, and the salesman looked back at me with admiration in his eyes, almost as though I were a real man.

Your Car Owner's Manual

DEAR DRIVER, you are now the proud owner of a new vehicle. It has been constructed to the highest specifications.

We wish you many hours of motoring pleasure. If anything goes wrong, it is not our fault. It is yours. You didn't read this manual with sufficient care and attention. So you've got only yourself to blame.

Before you drive your new car, please familiarise yourself with its controls (see pages 2–379). Failure to do so may result in serious injury or death. This may impede your motoring pleasure.

READING YOUR OWNER'S MANUAL IN SAFETY

Before reading your new Owner's Manual, please acquaint yourself with the following safety instructions.

✱ Do not read your new Owner's Manual while driving. It is particularly dangerous to read your new Owner's Manual while driving at high speed in foggy or hazardous conditions.

* Your new Owner's Manual should not be eaten. Swallowing or chewing your new Owner's Manual may result in death or serious injury. Drivers wishing to eat or drink should drive with due care and attention to the nearest food store. Failure to do so could result in hunger, possibly leading to starvation.

* Your new Owner's Manual is a potential hazard. It should be housed at all times in the Glove Compartment (see GLOVE COMPARTMENT). If placed beneath the foot brake or accelerator pedal, it can endanger the lives of you and your passengers. Do NOT place it on your head while driving. It may fall off, possibly resulting in serious injury.

* Gloves are not provided for the Glove Compartment but may be purchased separately from leading glove stores in a variety of styles and colours.

* The makers of your new car recommend gloves with individual spaces provided for four (4) fingers and one (1) thumb. Motorists with fewer digits or more should consult their doctor and/or tailor before purchasing gloves.

* Gloves should be worn on the hands. While driving, do NOT wear a right-hand glove on your left hand, or vice versa, as this may result in loss of thumb-grip on steering wheel and gear, causing serious injury or death. Gloves should NOT be worn on the feet. For further information see CARING FOR YOUR GLOVES (pages 309–321).

* Having replaced your Owner's Manual in the Glove Compartment, do not attempt to close the door to the Glove Compartment without first removing your hand. Failure to do so may result in serious injury to the wrist.

* The Glove Compartment is intended only as a storage space and not as a petrol tank. Petrol should be placed only in the tank provided.

TROUBLESHOOTING YOUR GLOVE COMPARTMENT

If a strong petrol-style smell or aroma is emanating from your Glove Compartment, you may have filled your glove compartment with petrol in error. IMPORTANT. Check you have not placed your Owner's Manual in the Petrol Tank before proceeding safely to your nearest Maintenance Centre. Never throw your Owner's Manual out of the windows (see YOUR NEW CAR WINDOWS) of your car while driving. It may cause a severe hazard or obstruction to your fellow motorists to the side and rear.

YOUR NEW CAR WINDOWS

Your new car windows have been specially designed to the manufacturer's highest specifications of transparency to facilitate access of vision. They should be kept clear of obstacles at all times (see OBSTACLES).

ACCESSING YOUR NEW CAR WINDOWS

Your new car windows are fully computerised to the highest level of technical excellence.

To open the driver's window, press button seventy-three (73). And again. Now press it again. And again. And again. Just once more. And again. And again. Whatever you do, don't force it. I said, don't force it. Now you've gone and done it.

It's obviously jammed. This sometimes happens. It's your fault, not ours. It has nothing to do with our new fully programmed easy-touch electronic computer system. Be sure to blame yourself. Now please turn immediately to section 68(b): UNJAMMING YOUR NEW CAR WINDOWS.

68 (B) UNJAMMING YOUR NEW CAR WINDOWS

This simple procedure should take two easy steps:
a) Press the button on your control panel (see CONTROL PANEL, pages 18–124) which looks a bit like a window seen from a slightly unusual angle.
b) This action will cause your Glove Compartment to spring open (see TROUBLESHOOTING YOUR GLOVE COMPARTMENT). This is because the picture you thought was of a window was actually of the Glove Compartment. The Glove Compartment, having been opened, will now be impossible to close as it is connected to your new highly sophisticated central locking system (see THE BEGINNING OF THE END), which has now also activated the Bonnet Release Handle, causing your new car bonnet to open and

close every three seconds. For assistance with this problem, please turn to Section 98 (c): DEACTIVATING YOUR BONNET RELEASE HANDLE.

LOCATING YOUR BONNET RELEASE DEACTIVATE HANDLE

Your bonnet release deactivate handle (BRDH) is easy to find. It is located to the right (or left, depending on model) of the centre console of the control mechanism in the automatic transmission module situated immediately to the left (or right, depending on model) of the multi-function display recognition instrument cluster (MFDRIS) and is fully electronic. Press the BRDH and wait 6.3 seconds until you hear an odd sliding noise from the direction of the Rear Passenger Seats (RPS). For some reason, it appears that you have activated the fully automated Passenger Cup Holder in the rear seat armrest (see TROUBLESHOOTING YOUR PASSENGER CUP HOLDER WITHOUT ACTIVATING YOUR AIR-CONDITIONING, pages 209–231). You are now in a position to read your new Owner's Manual.

HAZARD WARNING

Tear stains have distorted your new Owner's Manual, thus jeopardising your motoring pleasure. REMEMBER: It's all your fault.

PART TWO: ACCESSING YOUR NEW VEHICLE

531 (a) Your new vehicle has been constructed to the highest specifications and hand-tested by computer in our laboratory-controlled vehicle workshops. The working modules of your vehicle are maintained in a state of operational excellence by your exclusive in-car computer. Ahead of you lie many years of motoring pleasure. Nothing can possibly go wrong.

531 (B) YOUR ELECTRONIC MASTER KEY

Your new vehicle enjoys the fully computerised modern benefits facilitated by at-a-touch central locking. The radio remote control, minutely adjusted to workshop specifications, is placed in your

Electronic Master Key (EMK), and can be used to unlock the car from a Long Distance Away (LDA). To facilitate your motoring pleasure, our on-board computer ensures that, when it goes wrong, it cannot cheaply be put right.

IMPORTANT: On no account place your Electronic Master Key in your mouth or the mouths of your passenger(s) for long periods of time. In the event that you or your passenger(s) have inadvertently swallowed your Electronic Master Key, turn at once to Section 27 (f): UNLOCKING YOUR VEHICLE FROM A SWALLOWED POSITION.

TAKING FURTHER STEPS TO ACCESS YOUR VEHICLE

To unlock the driver's door: (i) Press Electronic Master Key button (a) once.

IMPORTANT: If your windows are now going up and down in quick succession, you have just pressed the wrong electronic key button. Now you've gone and done it. This is not the fault of the manufacturer. It is your fault, and yours alone. We told you to press button (a), not button (b). The vehicle's three-year warranty – your secure guarantee of miles of motoring pleasure – is now rendered invalid (see Section 108 (f)).

STOPPING WINDOWS GOING UP AND DOWN AFTER HAVING PRESSED THE WRONG BUTTON AGAINST MANUFACTURER'S EXPRESS INSTRUCTIONS

For reasons of safety, the side windows and/or the sliding/tilting sunroof can only be opened and/or closed using the remote control's infrared function. The safety function may be deactivated by pressing the wrong button, in which case anything can happen and probably will unless you give us more money (SEE 1(e) PAYING THROUGH THE NOSE).

WARNING: If the windows and/or sunroof start opening and closing of their own accord, do NOT place your head and/or any other part of your body in their immediate vicinity (see Section 109b: REPLACING YOUR HEAD AND/OR OTHER PART OF BODY HAVING FIRST HAD IT REMOVED BY WINDOWS AND/OR SUNROOF).

PAYING THROUGH THE NOSE

There are many attractive ways to pay for your mistakes with your new vehicle but for peace of mind we recommend option (3) – paying through the nose.

Q. How do I set about paying through the nose?

A. Why not sign up for our easy-pay NosePlan – allowing you and your family the comfort and security of paying regular monthly instalments straight through the nose without even noticing?

531 (C) OPENING THE DRIVER'S DOOR

If you have still not managed to gain direct access to your vehicle, try opening the door by hand and/or manually.

Your access will remain blocked, but the tail lights will now be flashing. Now wait ten seconds. It is about to get worse.

There is No Point (NP) trying the door again. The flashing tail lights have now been augmented by the automatic activation of the vehicle's anti-theft alarm system. What on earth did you think you were doing? A loud wailing noise will sound, causing your neighbours to come to their front doors, shaking their heads and raising their hands in fury and/or despair. The loud wailing noise will continue to sound until you have successfully deactivated the Anti-Theft Alarm System (see 1 (g)).

531 (D) DEACTIVATING THE ANTI-THEFT ALARM SYSTEM

To deactivate your Anti-Theft Alarm System (ATAS), you must gain access to your car. To gain access to your car, you must deactivate your Anti-Theft Alarm System. See previous section: 1 (f): OPENING THE DRIVER'S DOOR.

ATTEMPTING TO ENTER THE CAR THROUGH THE BOOT

To gain entry to your car, there is no access route through the boot. Do not attempt to access the car through the boot. If you have ignored manufacturer's advice and attempted to enter the car through the boot, your left foot will now be jammed stuck beneath the lower seat guard (SEE 162 (c) REMOVING AND

DESTROYING THE BACK SEAT IN ORDER TO EXTRACT YOUR JAMMED FOOT (JF)).

TAKING HAMMER TO THE FRONT WINDOW IN ORDER TO FORCE YOU WAY INTO VEHICLE

The front window responds to a hammering by the activation of the vehicle's fully automatic STS (Smashed To Smithereens) element. This causes the Anti-Theft Alarm System to double its intensity and/or the front and rear lights to go on and off.

WARNING: This may induce fits in neighbours prone to epilepsy. If this occurs, a doctor should be consulted at once.

(J) CHECKING BATTERY TO ELECTRONIC MASTER KEY

Having tried all other options, open Electronic Master Key (EMK) to check battery has been inserted correctly.

Q. How do I open the EMK?

A. To open the EMK, place your fingernail lightly on the back panel and apply gentle pressure. When this fails to work, try again, only this time harder. And again.

Now get a screwdriver, and repeat procedure. And now stab. And stab again, much harder. Now really try to hurt it. There! It's the only language those bloody keys understand. And again! There! You have now damaged your EMK Beyond Repair (BR). Entry to your new car is now invalidated. There is nothing for it but to hire a taxi.

Have you considered joining the DOS (Distressed Owners Scheme), for first-time owners experiencing trouble entering their new vehicles? You will find the relevant details inside the glove pocket of your new vehicle (Your Car Owner's Manual).

Nine Things You Didn't Know About Thomas the Tank Engine

A PSYCHOLOGY LECTURER from Exeter has warned that the number of crashes in the Thomas the Tank Engine stories could terrify young children. This is only the most recent of many revelations concerning the controversial train:

1 Up to fifteen adults an hour suffer narcolepsy while reading *Thomas the Tank Engine* books to their offspring, warns a senior psychology lecturer. "We have heard disturbing reports of mothers and fathers drifting off mid-sentence and waking up to find that their child has grown up and left home," says the report. A wide-reaching conclusion suggests that to prevent sudden attacks of TTEN (Thomas Tank Engine Narcolepsy) parents should stretch their legs every three to four minutes. Likewise, Thomas should never be read aloud during long car journeys, or while attempting sustained tightrope walks.

2 After a ten-year study conducted under laboratory conditions, a report from the Department of Contextual Analysis at Glasgow University reveals that 90 per cent of *Thomas the Tank Engine* stories involve a train or trains leaving the line before, three pages later, being put back on. "It is a sad reflection on the nation's children that this fact has remained undetected for so long," concludes the report.

However, a little-known early Thomas story, *Gordon Goes Off The Rails* (1956), finds the normally reliable Gordon in a dramatic break from the norm. Gordon, generally considered the fastest and most reliable of all the trains, throws it all in to hang around coffee bars in Brighton, mixing with unsavoury types such as Serena the Topless Engine and Arthur the Angry Young Diesel.

3 In a follow-up, *Gordon Kicks Up a Racket*, Gordon sings rebel-lious skiffle songs until the early hours of the morning before beating up Mods on Brighton beach. Both volumes have since been withdrawn by the Thomas estate, though a film by Michael Winner based on the second volume, *This One's For Sir Topham Hatt* is believed to be in pre-production, with Vinnie Jones tipped to star as Gordon, and top model Jordan as Serena.

4 The only other Thomas story to have been withdrawn from circulation is the 1967 cult classic *Thomas and the Pigs*, in which Thomas becomes involved in an anti-Vietnam demonstration and ends up in the magistrates' court facing a £25 fine for damage to public property. The volume is rarely mentioned in studies of the Thomas oeuvre, owing to the Rehabilitation of Offenders Act.

5 Mavis, the feisty black diesel engine who works with Toby and is known for her high spirits, was born Michael, but never felt easy in her gender. Mavis's first public appearance in her new identity was on the Kilroy show in June, 1991. "It feels like a terrible weight has been lifted from my shoulders," she confessed, tearfully. "Take a deep breath," said Kilroy, "we've got all the time in the world."

6 The creator of the Thomas the Tank Engine books, the Rev A W Awdry, is thought to have come up with the idea in a moment of boredom. "It was my heart's desire to recreate that moment in prose and pictures," he later explained. And he obviously succeeded: during a live reading of the Thomas stories by veteran actor Robert Hardy at Wembley Stadium in 1978, it was estimated that over two-thirds of the audience found their minds wandering after the first two sentences.

7 Daisy, the attractive but highly strung engine who once refused to pull a container car, believing it beneath her, was married to Po, the leading Teletubby, in March, 1999. Sadly, the pair found the strain of living in the celebrity spotlight too much, and parted in January 2001, citing "irreconcilable differences". Insiders suggest that Daisy had been conducting an on-off romance with Thomas, while Po has been seen by hidden cameras holding hands with Laa-Laa.

8 Sir Topham Hatt was born Reginald Perkins in Weston-super-Mare in 1934, but changed his name by deed poll upon deciding to enter local politics in 1957. In the late 1960s, Sir Topham became a flamboyant Liberal MP, narrowly escaping prosecution for his role in the Scott affair after one witness claimed to have overheard him suggesting they should tie the former male model to Percy's under-carriage to scare him off. His career never recovered. At present, Sir Topham is ranked the 17–1 outsider in the race to be the next Chancellor of Oxford University.

9 After a bout of adverse publicity earlier this year concerning his struggles with his weight, the Fat Controller contacted top PR guru Max Clifford. Two weeks later, a front-page exclusive in the *Sunday Mirror* was headed "Medium-sized controller dates Geri Spice". It pictured the railway mogul frolicking on a beach with the scantily clad former Spice Girl. Media experts suggested that the following weekend's scoop – "Thomas the Spank Engine" – may have been placed there by Clifford as part of a tit-for-tat agreement with the newspaper.

7.15 from Paddington

MY FAVOURITE Agatha Christie – perhaps because I associate it with the film version starring the redoubtable Dame Margaret Rutherford – is *4.50 from Paddington*. I thought about it the other day, as I sat crammed into the 7.15 from Paddington.

The book gets off to a cracking start. Mrs McGillicuddy has just finished her Christmas shopping ("The face towels had been excellent value, and just what Margaret wanted, the space gun for Robby and the rabbit for Jean were highly satisfactory, and that evening coat was just the thing she herself needed, warm but dressy"). Mrs McGillicuddy is alone in her train compartment, having "settled herself back on the plush cushions with a sigh".

Agatha Christie knew better than anyone that her readers would grow fidgety at too much domestic detail, so she soon gets down to business. The 4.50 from Paddington has slowed down, and another down-train is creeping past it. "At the moment when the two trains gave the illusion of being stationary, a blind in one of the carriages flew up with a snap. Mrs McGillicuddy looked into the lighted first-class carriage that was only a few feet away. Then she drew her breath in with a gasp and half-rose to her feet. Standing with his back to the window and to her was a man. His hands were round the throat of a woman who faced him, and he was slowly, remorselessly, strangling her. Her eyes were staring from their sockets, her face was purple and congested. As Mrs McGillicuddy watched, fascinated, the end came; the body went limp and crumpled in the man's hands. At the same moment, Mrs McGillicuddy's train slowed down again and the other began to gain speed. It passed forward and a moment or two later it had vanished from sight."

"Fascinated" seems to me a particularly telling choice of word by Christie, but, anyway, Mrs McGillicuddy is sufficiently upset by what she has witnessed to mention it to the ticket collector when he comes calling.

"Strangled?" he said, disbelievingly.

"Yes, strangled! I saw it, I tell you. You must do something at once!"

4.50 from Paddington was first published in 1957. Nearly fifty years on, squeezed like a sardine into the 7.15 from Paddington, I felt a twinge of nostalgia for all that lovely empty space. Not only did Mrs McGillicuddy have a compartment all to herself, but so too did the murderer (though he had been obliged to share his, at least for a while). Nowadays, so many passengers are forced into such a small space that murder is uppermost in most people's minds. All that prevents them from strangling one another on a daily basis is the vast number of witnesses and the lack of elbow room.

Most of the faces on my 7.15 from Paddington were every bit as purple and congested as that poor victim's, though without the excuse of having been strangled. My own face was, I fear, a picture of purplish congestion.

Long gone are Mrs McGillicuddy's days of settling back on plush cushions with a sigh. Even if you arrive on a train with ten minutes to spare, you must search high and low for a seat without a reserved ticket stuck on it. When you finally take a chance and sit in a reserved seat, you do so knowing you will spend the rest of your journey fearing the prospect of a shadow looming over you, the words "Excuse me but I think that's my place…" signalling the start of a ritual humiliation, with all eyes upon you.

I eventually found myself a free window seat, opposite a man with a laptop and another with a bobble hat. But seconds later, an immensely fat man plumped himself down in the reserved seat next to mine, squashing half of my jacket under his bottom. I then attempted to remove my jacket from his bottom with a good strong tug, but it wouldn't shift an inch. The fat man was too absorbed in opening a catering-sized packet of Sainsbury's Salted Peanuts to notice anything amiss.

Now all the seats were taken, so everyone else was obliged to stand. A middle-aged woman stood, huffing and puffing, leaning against the top of our seat, as I struggled to avoid her deathly gaze.

For the next half-hour the fat man chucked peanut after peanut into his mouth, one at a time, with a great cartwheeling action of his arm, as if in training for the Salted Peanut Olympics. We were approaching Didcot Parkway before the peanuts ran dry and the cartwheeling finally stopped. Just as I was breathing a sigh of relief, he began slapping his hands self-righteously together in an absurd cleaning action, sending loose shards of peanut and salt spiralling over the rest of the table.

I looked at the man with the laptop opposite, wondering if he was as irritated as I was. Part of me imagined that, if I could get the entire carriage on my side, we could execute a discreet group homicide, following the example of that other great Christie classic, *Murder on the Orient Express*. But he only began adding to my irritation, bellowing at his mobile phone: "Not so bad. How's yourself?"

Next to him, the man in the bobble hat started to twiddle his thumbs, surely one of the most irritating actions in the world. Behind me, two women increased my stress level still further by talking entirely in clichés. "They're all the same these days," said the first.

"It's the luck of the draw," said the other. "As I say, all the same these days," repeated the first.

And so forth.

For the fifth time in an hour, the intercom crackled with an announcement, this time drawing our attention to the safety instruction pamphlet beside our seats ("please take a few minutes to familiarise yourselves with the contents").

How I longed for the 4.50 from Paddington, calling at Brackhampton, Milchester, Waverton and stations to Chadmouth! One might have had to put up with one modest strangulation per trip – but just think of all that space, and all that silence, and all those plush cushions.

Ministry of Defence

The News of Armageddon

Jim: ... 600,000 deaths "more than likely" in the next five minutes. And now over to Steve with the sports news.

Steve: Football, and up to 40 per cent of major-league players are currently living in fear of their lives, according to a major new report published today. According to a survey, MKD, or Muddy Knee Disease, represents a very real threat to the future of soccer as we know it. I have with me Professor Hans Upp, from the Institute of Clean Knees, which commissioned the survey. Professor, just how terrified should the public be by these terrifying findings?

Prof Upp: Well, these things are notoriously hard to measure, Steve, but at a rough approximation I would judge that they should be somewhere between slightly terrified and terrified out of their wits.

Steve: And what do you reply to those who say that footballers have been getting muddy knees since time immemorial, so we have nothing to worry about?

Prof Onn: I would remind them that just five weeks ago an amateur footballer in the Congo got a very muddy left knee – and we've just heard that the man died tragically yesterday from tragic head injuries sustained in a tragic car crash.

Steve: News that is bound to send shock waves around the international knee community. We now have Reginald Cox, the chairman of the Let's Keep Knees Muddy campaign, on the line. Mr Cox, these findings must have come as a body blow to your ailing campaign.

Reginald Cox: Well, I, er...

Steve: Yes or no, Mr Cox?

Reginald Cox: We contend that there is no immediate threat from muddy knees, so therefore...

Steve: So there is a long-term threat?

Reginald Cox: That's not what I…

Steve: I'm afraid that's all we've got time for. Frightening news indeed. And now over to Martin with the latest traffic news. Martin?

Martin: Thanks, Steve. The threat of a dramatic increase in global warming, with the prospect of millions of deaths, comes ever closer today with the disclosure that a motor vehicle stopped by police on the A303 in the early hours of this morning was found to have a faulty exhaust. In response to this dramatic news, leading opponents have called for a tightening up of the laws against global destruction. Otherwise, all quiet on the roads. And now back to Jim.

Jim: With the news just coming in that a budgerigar near Bagshot is looking a little poorly, and has so far refused most of its breakfast, it seems increasingly likely that, one way or another, we are all of us about to die. I have with me in the studio Jemima Puddleduck, the spokesperson for the FFA – the Federation of Fictitious Birds. How do you react, Ms Puddleduck, to accusations that, by sentimentalising bird life, you and your fellow members have jeopardised the future of the human race?

Ms Puddleduck: Quack, quack. Quack quack quack quack quack *quack*? "Quack quack." Quack!

Jim: So there we have it. An angry rebuttal there, from Jemima Puddleduck of the Federation of Fictitious Birds. And with me in the studio listening to that interview is our Apocalyptic Correspondent, Enid Snigh. So what did you make of that, Enid? And in the longer term, how do you think the destruction of the planet might affect David Cameron's chances?

Enid: Well, Jim, the experts are suggesting it would take only two or three inner-city binge drinkers to get hold of a nuclear bomb for the world to end as early as tomorrow morning, weather permitting.

Jim: And so to our Showbusiness Correspondent, Sue Narmy. Sue, obviously the end of the world will rock the world of showbusiness, but the question everyone is asking is how exactly David and Victoria Beckham are going to cope with such a crisis?

Sue: Well, Jim, we've been given repeated assurances from those close to the Beckhams that the end of the world is something the couple have always planned for; in fact, they see their imminent destruction as a tremendous marketing opportunity.

Jim: So a glimmer of sunshine there on this gloomiest of days, though I should add that the government's Chief Medical Officer has urged the public to smother themselves with high-factor skin-protection at the slightest glimmer of sunshine. And so to today's headlines. There are two headlines to look out for. The first is "Bird Flu". The other is "Bird Flew". One signals a real threat; the other we can probably live with. And now over to Gillian with the weather…

Gillian: Thanks, Jim. The Met Office is warning that heavy showers and torrential thunderstorms are liable to cause tidal waves around the M25, possibly exiting at Junction Sixteen.

John: Whatever happened to the good old tidal wave? These days, it's all "tsunami"-this and "tsunami"-that. With me in the studio is Professor Anna Larm from the Institute of Imminent Threats. Professor Larm, your new study suggests that the human race is only likely to survive until just after lunchtime today. Depressing news for those people who may have long-term plans, then?

Professor Larm: Good morning, Jim.

John: That's as maybe. But what about the afternoon? You remain convinced we are all going to perish by teatime?

Professor Larm: That's certainly the message in my new book …

John: … published next week?

Professor Larm: Yes.

John: … with an accompanying Channel 4 series, *100 Best Imminent Threats to Mankind – Ever*, premiering next month?

Professor Larm: That's correct, John.

John: … and a follow-up series, *100 Even Better Imminent Threats to Mankind – Ever*, due early next year. So, Professor Larm, what makes you so convinced we are all going to die by teatime?

Professor Larm: We believe that the threat is all too real, John, and it comes from a full range of garden birds, including the deadly chaffinch. These birds have been secretly binge-drinking in special training centres in Afghanistan, and are even now wobbling their way in zigzag lines through the skies armed with supplies of Sars, BSE and ricin, all kept from previous scares.

Jim: We now go to Patricia Hewitt, Secretary of State for

Condescension, with special responsibilities for global patronising. Ms Hewitt, how do you react to stories that we are all shortly to die? **Patricia Hewitt:** Good morning, Jim. And a very good morning, too, to all your little listeners, bless them. May I just say, Jim, what a simply marvellous job you are doing, asking all the questions which really need answering – an initiative which has this government's complete support. *Well done, indeed.* In answer to your question, Jim, I've been absolutely delighted with the very, very positive feedback about the forthcoming apocalypse we've been receiving from very, very ordinary men and women up and down the country. And do you know what they've been telling us, Jim? I'll tell you! They've been telling us that instead of going on and on about the one or two rather negative aspects of our imminent destruction, as some elements in the media would have us do, as a responsible, committed government we should be highlighting the truly *positive* aspects. If you'll just let me finish, Jim – you see, the moment the world ends, there will be no more cigarette smoking, with all its harmful side-effects – and harmful emissions will cease immediately, and all this government's on-going problems with the old and the young and the middle-aged will gain closure. And that must surely be a good thing!

Jim: And now over to Steve with the sport.

Steve: Thanks, Jim. Racing: and according to the chairman of the Federation of Nervous Wrecks, there is a good chance that up to 95 per cent of racehorses will succumb to a new strain of AGB, or Always Going Backwards disease, when it arrives in the country the day after tomorrow, fresh in from Malaga. As a result, it looks increasingly likely that all major races will be run in reverse, with jockeys forced to sit back to front on their horses. And so to ice hockey: there was disappointment yesterday as a major-league game was altered at the last minute to a fully-dressed swimming championship as a result of global warming.

Jim: And now 'Thought for the Day', this morning presented by the Reverend Green, with the lead piping, in the hall.

Rev Green: What exactly do we mean when we say "there will be weeping and gnashing of teeth"? Some people maintain that this may not be enjoyable. Well, there will always be pessimists in our community, sharing with us their own unique insights. And they are more than welcome. But in my experience, there's much to be said for sitting down and enjoying a jolly good weep. As for gnashing of teeth, I have often found it a tremendously helpful activity, and that's why I've just announced our very first "Gnash'n' Weep Interfaith Community Funtime", to coincide with the End of the World.

The Need for CCTV

June 9, 2015

SIR – Just three years after the compulsory installation of CCTV cameras in every vehicle, the scheme has been an overwhelming success. The police are now able to tell at a glance if anyone is contravening any motor-based law.

Only last week, a middle-aged man alone in his vehicle was successfully prosecuted for sucking on a boiled sweet. This was, of course, in direct contravention of Patricia Hewitt's excellent Prevention of Boiled Sweets Act (2010), which has had such a notable effect in cutting down on tooth decay in adults and in little children too (let's never forget that they're our future, bless!).

~ Arthur Tremble, Dunstable

June 10, 2015

SIR – I am most grateful to Mr Tremble for drawing our attention to the tremendous success of CCTV cameras in the community. With so many people intent on abusing the hosepipe ban, the police are delighted by the recent extension of the compulsory CCTV scheme to all gardens and patio areas.

Those so-called "liberals" who so love to wring their hands about "civil liberties" should be made aware of an incident that happened in my own garden last weekend.

We were enjoying a family picnic in the garden with my grandchildren when a team of policemen arrived at the front door. They immediately ordered us all indoors, with all doors and windows closed. At this point, a trained marksman arrived and darted straight into the garden with all the necessary apparatus.

Three minutes later, he returned bearing the corpses of three wasps. Unbeknownst to us, the presence of these three wasps in our garden – buzzing about within yards of our grandchildren – had been picked up on the police CCTV.

One dreads to think of the enduring trauma that might have been suffered by our grandchildren had one of them been stung that day. My only hope is that compulsory CCTV can now be extended to the west coast of Scotland in the summer. For too long, the mosquito has been able to buzz about undetected.

~ **Virginia Creeper (Ms), Sevenoaks**

June 27, 2015
SIR – Those who continue to bang on about the "good old days" should remember that as recently as 2004 there was no police protection accorded to the citizen in his or her own bathroom. The younger generation would now hardly credit it, but there was no legal requirement for CCTV cameras to be installed. This meant that a great many wrongdoers were getting away with not brushing their teeth properly, leading to widespread dental decay and gum disease, causing a drain on our economy.

In 2007, when cameras were first installed in bathrooms on a test basis, up to 40 per cent of those filmed were discovered to be brushing their teeth from left to right rather than up and down. After many of these cases had been successfully prosecuted (resulting in custodial sentences for 60 per cent of adults and detention and/or community service for 55 per cent of juveniles) there was a dramatic 80 per cent fall in inept tooth-brushing, with a consequent long-term drop in the burden placed on those working in the dental healthcare sector.

There were several all-too-predictable voices raised in "protest" at "invasion of privacy" at the time. The same politically motivated voices could be heard a year later, in August 2008, when the government of the day had the foresight to bring extra CCTV cameras into the bathroom in order to ensure that, for the protection of themselves and others, all Britons would wipe their behinds with sufficient vigour and attention to detail. But seven years on, Britain is close to the top of the European

Cleanest Bottoms Chart, and these voices of dissent have at last been silenced.

~ P. Roberts, East Sussex

June 29, 2015

SIR – Subsequent to your previous correspondent, might I remind younger readers that, well into this century, most households lacked any sort of provision for CCTV in the kitchen?

Nowadays it may be hard to credit, but I have a vivid memory of my parents in the spring of 2004 serving us breakfast of cereal, toast and marmalade with no cameras trained on them at all. One shudders to think of the many health and safety hazards that must have passed unobserved – a very real danger not only to their young and vulnerable family, but to the world at large. Sure enough, soon after government health officers forcibly installed CCTVs in our kitchen and larder area in early 2008, my parents faced prosecution: my father for employing a dirty knife to spread marmalade on toast on two separate occasions, and my mother on the even more serious charge of failure to use a government-approved low-fat spread. Imagine our shame when we discovered she had been caught on film using illegal full-fat butter instead.

As children, we were, I will admit, a little upset when, after the incriminating video evidence had been played in court, our parents were led away in tears to serve their sentences. But it taught us a lesson in hygiene we shall never forget. Now that we ourselves are parents, I am proud to say that, thanks to twenty-four-hour monitoring by CCTV, we have the freedom to maintain spotless kitchens.

Yes, our generation has much for which to be thankful. Incidentally, only last week my elderly father was imprisoned for nine months for the serious offence of failure to wash his hands before consuming a snack. Will he never learn?

~ Maj R Kennet, Basingstoke, Hants

July 1, 2015

SIR – May I join with your correspondents in rejoicing at the onward march of CCTV. It seems extraordinary to think that, just ten years ago, the civil liberties lobby were all whining about encroachment on their human rights, blah, blah, blah.

Nowadays those of us with nothing to fear can sleep easy, content in the knowledge that we have compulsory CCTV in our bedrooms. Though originally installed to enforce safe sex and to make sure that no householder was smoking cigarettes upstairs, CCTV also makes the night-time intrusion of a burglar or burglars much less likely.

One more point. The plinth in Trafalgar Square still remains empty. Surely it is high time we installed a large statue of a CCTV camera. It would make a fitting symbol of our country today. Perhaps the powers-that-be might even make it a working model, covering those nooks and crannies of the square at present inaccessible to the CCTV cameras already installed. If it catches just one person doing something he shouldn't, the expense will have proved worthwhile.

~ **Geoff Vigilant, Oxon**

July 3, 2015

SIR – As a preliminary step in the continuing fight against terrorism, the government must consider installing miniature CCTV cameras around the necks of one in ten birds in the UK.

These birds would then become our undercover police force of the air, sending back urgent footage of foreign extremists plotting despicable acts. If the special bird-cameras also pick up evidence of an ordinary Briton smoking or drinking, then so much the better.

Needless to say, we should trust only native British birds – the friendly robin, the plucky woodpecker – with these miniature cameras. One shudders at what might happen should a foreign bird ever get his claws on one. In fact, the government would be well advised to install CCTV in all foreign bird nests to prevent such a terrifying scenario.

~ **Tim Badger, Manchester**

July 7, 2015

SIR – On holiday beside the seaside last week, I was horrified to discover that there were no CCTV cameras beneath the water.

This represents an open invitation to terrorist frogmen without ID cards. It is also only too possible that a fish, or fishes, may be taking advantage of the lack of proper security in order to enjoy a quiet smoke. Needless to say, ordinary decent law-abiding fish have nothing to fear.

~ Hector Daley, London

Wallace Arnold:
Exterminate! Exterminate!

WITH THIRTY YEARS' standing on the Membership Selection Committee of the Garrick Club behind me – five as Hon Treasurer, seven as Hon Secretary – I have, as you might imagine, many a tale to tell regarding the "also rans".

Our little black ball has, I regret to say, found not infrequent employment in my hands. Some aspirants, for instance, attempt to bypass the basic membership requirement of three months' minimum in pantomime within the UK.

I well remember the young Melvyn Bragg (now Lord Bragg, if you please!) attempting to convince the committee that he'd played the role of Buttons at the Yvonne Arnaud Theatre in the mid-Sixties. "All very interesting," I said, in a casual tone, adding: "I suppose you found the scene in which you confront The Three Bears most dreadfully demanding?"

"Very demanding indeed – and emotionally exhausting," explained the young Melvyn.

At this point, I reached for the black ball. "I must ask you to leave," I said.

"B-b-but why?" asked the young Melvyn, visibly upset.

"Because The Three Bears appear in *Goldilocks* – and not in *Cinderella*!" I exclaimed. "Next!"

It was another twelve years – and a stint in *Dick Whittington* in Weston-super-Mare – before Melvyn was finally elected. Needless to say, I rib the poor fellow quite mercilessly about it now, but he takes it in good heart. After all, he is now more aware than anyone that even our most illustrious members (Lord St John of Fawsley, Sir

Terence Conran, Sir Gerald Kaufman) all paid their pantomime dues (as, respectively, Mother Goose, Baron Hardup and the seventh dwarf) at some point in the distant past.

Nonetheless, I would not like it thought that the Garrick Club is prepared to accept any old one who ever played the Widow Twankey. Quite the reverse. Only the other day, we were obliged to turn down Mr Gary Glitter for quite different reasons.

But I digress! At our interviews for new admissions last month, we had seen half a dozen candidates, and there was just time before luncheon to squeeze in one more. I turned to our entertainments officer, HRH Prince Michael of Kent, and enquired as to who was next on the list.

"He doesn't give a name," said Mike, "but he is a veteran of a remarkable string of television dramas, some of them stretching way back to the early Sixties."

"The Golden Age!" I said. "Just the sort of member we're looking for! Send him in!"

Initial impressions were not, alas, in his favour. His first mistake was to fail to knock on the door of the Committee Room; instead, he chose to bulldoze it through with sheer force.

Some might have turned him down there and then, but I felt that, if a little uncouth, his entrance at least demonstrated a strong, decisive personality.

"We don't seem to have a name for you," I said, without looking up from my list of candidates.

"I-am-a-Dalek!" he replied. "You-will-elect-me! Any-delay-will-result-in-death!"

I looked up. The creature standing before me was a far cry from our traditional member. I am a lifelong student of character, and his slightly aggressive introduction suggested to me that he was in some way "on edge".

"Don't I recognise you?" I said, attempting to put him at his ease. "Haven't I seen you on the dread gogglebox? Let me guess – weren't you in *The Forsyte Saga*? Or was it *Upstairs Downstairs*? Both of them great favourites, chez Arnold, I might add!"

"There-is-only-one-form-of-life-that-matters!" he replied. "DALEK-LIFE! Obey-your-orders! Or-I-will-exterminate-you!"

"That's it!" said my colleague, John Julius Norwich. "Doctor Who! One of my firm favourites! Don't tell me … weren't you one of the Doctor's assistants? I must say, it's tremendously exciting to meet you!"

"Silence! That-is-of-no-consequence!" replied the Dalek. "Mind-your-own-business! That-is-an-order! I-will-be-back!"

He then swivelled round, manoeuvring his rotund body through what remained of the door, leaving us to our decision.

"His manner may be somewhat … brusque," observed John Julius, "but, underneath, I think there lies a heart of gold."

"He may have been a touch bullish," I replied. "And I suspect he doesn't suffer fools gladly. But on the other hand, he is straightforward and hugely commanding, with an almost palpable sense of purpose. He might be just the person we need to knock the Wine Committee into shape."

"Didn't he say something about wanting to exterminate us?" asked Prince Michael. "I'm just wondering how that will go down with the younger members?"

On paper, the Dalek's curriculum vitae – veteran of more than sixty television programmes, three times on the cover of the *Radio Times*, well-loved household name – would have guaranteed him instant membership. But some considered his manner too overbearing, his bearing too ungainly, his conversation too pragmatic, indeed, his whole personality unsuited to membership of what is undoubtedly a hugely social institution. In a nutshell (dread receptacle), there were those who considered the poor Dalek *unclubbable*.

Of course, not all our members are what one might call easygoing. Far from it. Only the other day, I was obliged to have a gentle word with our new member, Mr John Prescott, to point out that the club rules preclude the biffing of other members before 6pm. But one hopes to maintain generally high standards of affability, and some of us on the committee felt that, though in many respects admirably straightforward, the Dalek might not attain the requisite social threshold.

While we chewed over our decision, the Dalek had been kicking his heels outside the committee room. After a few minutes, I summoned him back for a question.

"Forgive me, Mr Dalek," I began, "but many of our members like to relax by swapping anecdotes, many of them of a theatrical nature. We were wondering if, perchance, you had any such anecdotes up your (albeit proverbial!) sleeve?"

"You-will-desist-from-these-questions! That-is-an-order!" replied the Dalek. "Admit-me-to-your-club! Any-delay-will-result-in-extermination!"

I contrived to chuckle politely. "Well, I suppose one could call that an anecdote," I remarked. "And it certainly possessed what one might call a certain bravado. But I wonder if some of our older members might not find it a trifle … abrupt? Perhaps one could spend a teensy bit longer on the build-up, so as to give the admirable punchline a little extra oomph?"

"Do-not-question-a-Dalek!" he replied, testily. "There-is-only-one-form-of-life-that-matters – Dalek-Life!"

"Point taken," said my fellow committee member John Julius Norwich, who always favours a more emollient approach in these situations.

"I think I have the solution," piped up our entertainments officer, Prince Michael of Kent. "Why don't we give our friend here a probationary membership for, say, a month, and then see how he gets on?"

"Motion carried!" said I, reaching for the lapel badge saying probationary member before, with no little trouble, affixing it upon the Dalek's shoulder.

Somewhat to my surprise, in those next few weeks the Dalek made full use of the club facilities, arriving for the full English breakfast at the crack of dawn, and remaining at the Garrick, off and on, for the rest of the day. But my initial misgivings as to his suitability for membership were never, alas, quite allayed.

An early suggestion that all was not well came when a club servant strode up to me in a fluster to inform me that one of the bar staff had just that minute been exterminated. At first, I thought nothing of it – these things happen from time to time – but when he added, with an apologetic cough, that the responsibility for the misdemeanour lay with the new probationary member, I felt that the time would soon come when a polite warning might be in order.

The following day, a Tuesday, there was another disturbance. A post-prandial conversation about matters bookish in the members' snug on the ground floor between Sir Peregrine Worsthorne, Dr David Starkey, Mr Daniel la Rue and Mr George Walden had been interrupted mid-sentence by the Dalek, who had demanded their assistance in getting up the stairs.

Messrs Walden and la Rue had excused themselves, citing bad backs, but Dr Starkey had taken a more abrasive approach, hissing: "I have no intention whatsoever of helping you climb those stairs! You truly make me want to vomit! Be off with you, you ghastly little mechanical monster!"

Apparently, the Dalek had not taken kindly to this rebuff, forcing the four of them, under threat of immediate extermination, to remove their trousers and underpants and to dance the conga in circles around the hallway. As the dancing of the conga in any sort of undress is strictly banned in the Garrick rules, other than in the second week of June, it was a case of issuing a formal warning either to the participants or to the Dalek, who – or so they claimed – had put them up to it.

Other distasteful incidents followed. Determined to get rid of him, I scoured the rulebook for anti-Dalek legislation, but found nothing. I was near the end of my tether when John Julius stepped in.

"Got him!" he said. "I was going through his application form with a fine-tooth comb, when I stumbled upon his Christian name. It's Susan! Yes, a Dalek may be a member – but never a female Dalek! Gentlemen, I'll have her removed, post-haste!"

Two False Prophets

(I) NOSTRADAMUS

Following last week's grim events, the prophecies of Nostradamus have shot up the bestseller lists. Three of the top five titles on amazon.com, the online bookseller, are by or about Nostradamus, with the Complete Prophecies at number one.

This sudden rise in sales is apparently the result of a rumour that the great sixteenth-century bore foretold the destruction of the twin towers. His interpreters have pointed with excitement to the following prophecy:

> *In the year of the new century and nine months*
> *From the sky will come a great King of Terror*
> *The sky will burn at forty-five degrees*
> *Fire approaches the great new city.*

This would be impressive indeed, if only it were true. But, as is so often the case with Nostradamus, it is not. The first line of this quatrain is, in fact, a mistranslation from the wonky French: "*L'an mil neuf cens neuf sept mois.*" Rather more accurately translated, this comes out as: "The year 1999 seven months."

On closer investigation, the final two lines have been tacked on from a different quatrain, plundered from some 150 pages earlier in the prophecies. The quatrain in question actually goes, in full:

> *The year 1999 seven months*
> *From the sky will come the great King of Terror*
> *To resuscitate the great king of Angolmois.*
> *Around this time Mars will reign for the good cause.*

As with all Nostradamus's hundreds and hundreds of vague but invariably doomy prophecies, this one can be interpreted only in retrospect, and even then it may be quite a time before enthusiasts find the anagram for "Bin Laden" in "Angolmois".

Those who attempt to apply his predictions to the future always come a cropper. For instance, in 1961, the leading Nostradamus expert Stewart Robb set about interpreting the very verse that is now being accepted as the prophecy of the destruction of the twin towers. Robb concluded that it in all likelihood referred to an invasion from Mars in 1999, further linking it to a great pyramid prophecy setting the end of the world at 2000 or 2001.

It may be a comfort to those still tempted to believe in the psychic powers of Nostradamus that in 1961 Stewart Robb's other great interpretations of his prophecies included Anthony Eden's return to the office of Prime Minister, the coming of Armageddon in 1973, and, last but not least, the revelation that Adolf Hitler escaped from Germany by submarine to South America.

(II) GORE VIDAL

It is a rare disaster that remains free from an accompanying tap-dance by Gore Vidal. Sure enough, within days of the destruction of the twin towers, Mr Vidal popped up on Radio 4 drawling one of his jowly homilies on sowing and reaping. This would prove, he said, the excuse for which President Bush had long been looking for the introduction of martial law.

Only last month, Vidal declared the Oklahoma bomber, Timothy McVeigh, innocent of all charges against him; not only that, but McVeigh was, he said, a "Kipling hero" with "an overdeveloped sense of justice". Vidal then hinted that he was close to revealing the names of the real Oklahoma bombers, who had been allowed to pursue their murderous ends by the FBI, who wanted to pressurise President Clinton into pushing through draconian anti-terrorist legislation. And so on.

Vidal's insights tend to prove as shaky as those of his sixteenth-century counterpart. During the Lewinsky scandal, he appeared on television declaring with his usual omniscience that Clinton was an unwitting victim, Miss Lewinsky having been put up to it by the American tobacco industry.

During the first Reagan administration, Vidal wrote an essay warning that President Reagan was preparing for world war. During the second Reagan administration, he wrote another essay, "Armageddon?", in which he boldly named both the arena and the enemy ("a war, to be specific, between the United States and Russia, to take place in Israel"). He made this pronouncement in 1987; later that year, Presidents Reagan and Gorbachev signed their missile treaty. Two years later, the Berlin Wall came down.

Poor Gore! Yet he has never allowed a little thing like a mistake to hinder his affectations of omniscience; still he appears, conceit dripping from his brow, drawling his lordly bulletins on this, that and the other. But it cannot be long before even those who enjoy the droll wisecracks of America's answer to Larry Grayson start to wonder whether he is all he cracks himself up to be.

Speaking for myself, disillusion first set in when I heard him, again on the BBC, speaking with apparent authority about the British secret services. It was only when he began talking about "M-Fifteen" and "M-Sixteen" that I realised that, far from knowing all about MI5 and MI6, Gore Vidal didn't even know how to pronounce them.

(September 18, 2001)

The Fourteen Best Hiding Places for Osama bin Laden

1 Crouching in the filing cabinet at Conservative Central Office, under "R" for Radical New Ideas.

2 Standing in the hallway of Shaun Woodward's Liverpool terraced house.

3 Sitting cross-legged behind the fresh fruit bowl in Keith Richards's kitchen.

4 Perching eagerly beside Anthea Turner's agent's telephone.

5 Fronting the Virgin Railways Customer Services department.

6 Acting as the greeter at the Railtrack office party.

7 Attending the House of Lords during a major speech by Lord Ashdown on the overwhelming need for Proportional Representation throughout a fully integrated Europe.

8 Appearing onstage as the page-turner for Norman Lamont's lecture "The British Economy: The Way Forward" to the CBI.

9 Co-starring in the new Vanessa Feltz *Fight the Flab* workout video.

10 Reading the new Andrew Motion verse celebrating "Five Years of Network-Southeast" onstage at the Poetry Society.

11 Touting in a peaked cap for RAC membership outside the Little Chef at the motorway services at Membury.

12 Taking part in a wide-ranging discussion with leading academics and military experts on *Newsnight* on the subject of his own possible whereabouts.

13 Presenting 'Thought for the Day' on the Radio 4 *Today* programme.

14 Roaming stately homes in a tweed jacket buttonholing visitors with details of the advantages of an annual membership of the National Trust.

(November 27, 2001)

Veterans

An Absolute Poppet: The Unpublished Letters of John Gielgud

To Noel Coward
October 17, 1939

As I said to Binkie the other day, this tiresome war is perfectly beastly, playing havoc with one's exits, let alone one's entrances. I sometimes suspect that that fussy little Miss Hitler (common, common, COMMON!) is timing those wretched bombs of hers with the sole aim of ruining my finest lines, I really do.

How I wish I were alongside our brave boys at the front rather than sitting here, sipping dry Martinis at the Savoy! With my undoubted gift for voice projection (commended only yesterday by Peggy A, bless her), I could be employed to stand behind some sort of protective wall in a divine khaki helmet, gesticulating gracefully and yelling waspish abuse in the general direction of the enemy. That would put a stop to their knavish tricks! We wouldn't hear another peep out of them.

I slogged through the entire text of Hitler's most recent speech last night. It was so very, very dreary and hugely disappointing. My performance as Algernon has now been playing to considerable acclaim in the West End for three months now. Yet he failed to mention me once.

To Winston Churchill
June 5, 1940

Darling Winnie, I can't begin to tell you how deeply touched and moved I was by your quite magnificent speech on the wireless yesterday. It all went so wonderfully well, particularly that marvellous bit when you said, "We shall fight in the fields", with just a hint of pathos. It deeply reminded me of my own end-of-act speech as Private Percival Plomondeley in *Hats Off to Our Lads!* now running at the Criterion, which is still packed out, and has, as you will be aware, met with the most tremendous acclaim.

I hope you realise how I have always admired you and your work so very much. So I know you will take the following advice in the spirit in which it is offered. Might I suggest that the next time you consider making a "morale-boosting" speech about fields and so forth, you do so on an afternoon when *Hats Off to Our Lads!* is not booked in for a matinee at the Criterion? It is just that, with what my friends call my "superior drawing power" (bless them!), the clash could prove ruinous to yourself, and our war effort might suffer most dreadfully as a result.

To Winston Churchill
February 19, 1943

Darling Winnie, just the briefest of scribbles to congratulate you on a superb tour of the front, so heroic and sweet and STIRRING. As always, you had our boys in the palm of your hand, and, I may add, looked quite gorgeous in your little khaki two-piece! Bravo! Forgive me, Winnie, but might I add the smallest of suggestions? It occurred to me that, after delivering an encouraging word to the troops, and just before conducting your inspection, you could do some marvellous "stage business" with your handkerchief – perhaps dropping it casually on the ground before retrieving it with a flourish, or waving it to and fro with an air of infinite melancholy, or perhaps, with a few deft flicks of the wrist, folding it in such a manner as to create a snow-white swan. It is a little trick I have employed with notable success in my hugely successful run of *Tap-Dancing to Victory*, currently at the Albery, and I am delighted to pass it on.

To Noel Coward
February 20, 1943

There is no doubting Winston's brilliance, though I do wish he wouldn't slur his words so, and he is a trifle ... BULLISH for my tastes. And MUST he wear that ghastly khaki two-piece? What DOES he think he looks like, the poor old pet?

His performance is undoubtedly strong – none of us would deny him that – but it seems to me he could make much more of his hankie, and rather less of that simply dreadful cigar.

To Binkie Beaumont
April 15, 1944
This war is really most disagreeable. The incessant explosions play havoc with one's delivery. I feel like writing to that dreadful little Adolf H. I would sum up everything I had to say in just two little words: "*Must* you?"

To Harold Macmillan
March 14, 1960
You were such an absolute poppet last night in Downing Street listening to silly me rambling on about Larry's deceit – and you so dreadfully, dreadfully busy, too! But if Larry hadn't promised, absolutely promised, me the role, and then reneged on that promise, I would never have burdened you with my worries, particularly when you were so busy trying to sort out the Balance of Payments.

I can't tell you how much I value your friendship – your powers of oratory, your command of politics, your urbane manner, those splendidly coarse yet effortlessly elegant tweed suits and, perhaps above all, your magnificent moustaches. Promise me you'll never shave them off. They look so very becoming on you – and one dreads to contemplate what lies beneath. My best love to your darling Dorothy, too. She looked so very lovely in that pretty floral dress last night.

To Dadie Rylands
March 14, 1960
One feels so dreadfully sorry for them both. Harold, perfectly hideous in tweeds, is now something desperately important in politics. He does go on so. I fear that moustache of his has gone to his head. He asks my advice on the Balance of Payments. I tell him that Tony Quayle would be excellent in the lead, with Peggy as second fiddle, but he pays no heed. These politicians are so one-track-minded.

Dorothy M was clad from top to toe in the most hideous fabric, poor darling. Had I not known better, I would have taken her for a large pair of curtains and attempted to draw her open.

To Ronald Biggs
October 9, 1963
Just a note to congratulate you and your company on a most excellent robbery. How supremely gratifying it must be for you that everyone but everyone is already describing it as the Great Train Robbery. Tell me, dear Ronnie, did you wear corduroy on the big day? It does look so very, very becoming with a stocking pulled casually over the head, finished off with a lovely warm Arran pullover in cream or lilac.

To Fred Flintstone
June 7, 1964
You may remember we met at a party given for Dirk Bogarde by Roddy McDowall. Rock Hudson introduced us. You immediately struck me as so very very direct, so very very – well, primitive is not the word, but you have an almost *neanderthal* simplicity about you that I confess I found most appealing. And, dearest Fred, I shall never forget your leopard-skin blouson, barely covering those marvellously meaty legs of yours. I would dearly love to see you tackle one of the great classical roles. I feel sure you would make a gorgeous Hamlet. I was also pleased to meet your dear little mousy wife Wilma, who I feel sure must be a tremendous support.

To Nobby Stiles
July 23, 1966
Dearest Norbert, I can't begin to tell you how very deeply impressed and moved I was by your performance in the World Cup.

I dare say you may be tempted to feel a smidgin of resentment against "Bobby" Moore and those frankly unprepossessing Charlton brothers (couldn't some brutal angel tell them to do something about that hair of theirs?).

But it struck me that you went after that soccer ball like a veritable will o' the wisp, injecting a note of the very purest humanity into your performance as you "took a tumble", and rolled over on that grubby turf, clutching manfully at your shin.

And what beautifully curvaceous knees you have, Nobby! Do you mind me calling you Nobby?

To Martin Hensler
May 23, 1968
Such a striking boy at Binkie's yesterday – perfect skin and teeth, marvellously loose-fitting dark suit, wonderfully flashing eyes, an entrancing (Birmingham?) accent. His name was Enoch, if you please! I asked him how he was, and he became most dreadfully agitated, saying that like the Roman, he seemed to see the River Tiber foaming with blood.

"Frightfully inconvenient," I agreed, saying that if I were him, I would certainly holiday elsewhere. Had he tried the Caribbean? I insisted that if he visited Jamaica, he should look up Noel. He's just Noel's type, and would look quite wonderful in a crisply laundered pair of Bermuda shorts.

To J Edgar Hoover
January 17, 1972
Edwina dearest, what a thoroughly trying time you must be having, with all that law and order to enforce. But everyone agrees you carry it off so beautifully, with the lightest of touches. I really don't know how you manage. I wouldn't know one end of a truncheon from another, and a helmet has never suited my complexion.

To Dr Ian Paisley
May 5, 1972
Darling Poopsy, I simply cannot be bothered with intrigues, lies and recriminations. When I bumped into you – a perfect stranger! – in Piccadilly and told you how much I admired your white ankle socks, adding as an aside that you also had the most beautiful hands, I had no idea your mind was already occupied. How was I to realise that you were busy leading a demonstration of ten thousand Ulstermen, bless them, against this, that, and the other? One cannot be expected to notice simply everything.

You bellowed at me to get out of the way, yet I was only being sweet. I sense you are a bit of a bossy-boots, darling Ian. If you cannot take compliments, then I shall no longer bother to offer them, and then you won't like it, will you? And you so marvellously tall and broad-shouldered, and with such a twinkle in your eye. Oh, but there I go again!

To Richard M Nixon
April 23, 1977
Darling Dickie, you were simply marvellous on television last night, being cross-questioned by that impertinent little David Frost. He does tend to speak through his nose. Has he never heard of projection? But you carried it off *magnificently* – London has been talking of little else. Your hair, in particular, looked quite immaculate, combed back in luscious waves across that magnificent scalp of yours rather than – dear oh dear! – "side-parted" like poor Mr Frost!

How one wishes all these ghastly people wouldn't go on about Watergate all the time. Watergate this, Watergate that: you'd think there was nothing better to talk about. I prefer to remember you for that marvellous performance of yours in China, starring opposite that darling little Chairman Mao, who looked such a poppet in his neat little two-piece cotton suit, buttoned right up to the neck. I wanted to pop him in my pocket and take him home with me – he would, I think, look an absolute dear with a crew cut, perhaps in shorts and a tight-fitting polo neck in mauve or tangerine.

To David Frost
April 23, 1977
You were simply marvellous on television last night, going to the trouble to cross-question that terrible old cross-patch Richard Nixon. Your voice came over quite beautifully, and I have never seen your locks look quite so lustrous – I felt like putting my hands through the screen and running my fingers through them in appreciation!

To Laurence Olivier
June 4, 1978
Your most sweet letter touched me very much. It was wonderful of

you to take the trouble to write, particularly at what surely must be this simply ghastly time for you, when every critic worth his salt is pouring such vicious scorn upon you. You must know how greatly I marvel at your endless courage, never more so than now. You were so very very brave, dear Larry, to take on the role of Mrs Tiggywinkle, particularly as so many (younger) actors turned it down, thinking it beneath them – and so very ill-paid! How very much one hopes that that wretched hedgehog costume is not playing havoc with your delicate skin every night.

Needless to say, in recent years your memorable characterisations of woodland creatures have gone from strength to strength. Everyone who works with you is lost in admiration for the way you cope with each fresh humiliation. You may now look back on a flourishing career, a reminder, my dear, of triumphs past.

To Laurence Olivier
February 3, 1987

Busy, busy, busy! Much enjoying my extended run in the title role of an exciting experimental production of *Mother Goose* at the Bristol Hippodrome opposite Danny La Rue (not a born actress, I fear).

So sorry to read your disappointing notices in *The Omen III*, which I have pinned up on my dressing room wall in protest. Today's critics can be so very insensitive in their failure to understand what a tremendous challenge over-acting can be, especially at your age.

Bless you.

Remember Me This Way

THERE ARE QUITE a few captions that might be apt for updating one of those "The Man Who…" H M Bateman cartoons in which astonished onlookers leap aghast from their shoes, flinging up their hands in horror at some poor little fellow who has just perpetrated some dreadful faux pas.

"The Man Who Said He Rather Liked Tony Blair"; "The Man Who Asked for One for the Road"; "The Man Who Welcomed

Global Warming"; "The Man Who Failed to Laugh at Little Britain"; "The Man Who Said He Thought He Might Have a Touch of Avian Flu"; "The Man Who Admitted Looking Forward to Christmas"; "The Man Who Said He Couldn't Really See the Point of John Peel…" This new century yields quite as many ways in which to transgress social convention as the last one ever did.

So it is with a degree of trepidation that I now shuffle forward as "The Man Who Asked the Disc Jockey for Some Gary Glitter". Yet, as the Christmas season approaches, I find myself yearning for a quick blast of "I Love you Love me Love (You Love me too Love)" or "I'm the Leader of the Gang (I Am)".

Best of all would be to hear "Hello Hello I'm Back Again", with its memorable verse asking whether one missed him when he was away, and whether one hanged his picture on one's wall, followed by his panicky accusations that, no, one might not have missed him at all.

Ah, those blue remembered hills! Back in my teenage years, no disco would be complete without at least a few records by Gary Glitter. Everyone would get up and dance, even those who had better things to do. But though popular, Gary Glitter was never fashionable. Trussed up in silver foil like an oven-ready turkey, hobbling around on platform heels, he was too self-mocking to be taken for an idol, and even then, too old and tubby to be considered cool.

In fact, he may well have been the first wholly ironic pop star. Even his name was a joke within a joke, a signal that he knew, and we knew, and he knew that we knew that he knew, that he wasn't what he cracked himself up to be.

His contemporary Alvin Stardust – the poor man's Gary Glitter – had a similarly daft name, but, with his black glove, dipped eyebrow and stiltedly sultry expression, was never quite in on his own joke.

Of course, Gary Glitter had tried on any number of personae before hitting the big time with the silliest of them all. Born Paul Gadd in 1940, he first performed as the leader of a skiffle group, Paul Russell and the Rebels. For his first record, he changed his name again, this time to Paul Raven (later Paul Raven and Boston

International). At one point, he even became Rubber Bucket, singing the words "*We are living in one place*" to the tune of "Amazing Grace", on a record released on the MCA label, featuring a choir of squatters. It never made it into the charts.

He then had a shot at being a soul singer in Germany before at last achieving fame, at the ripe old age of thirty-two, as Gary Glitter. His record "Rock and Roll (Parts 1 and 2)" whizzed to number two in the charts in the early summer of 1972. It must be the simplest song ever released: a distant chorus of "*Rock and roll – Rock! Rock and roll*" repeated over and over again, overlaid by a thumping beat provided by the Glitter Band, which employed two drummers.

I remember seeing Gary Glitter opening a rock and roll revival concert at Earls Court in July of that year. Cans bounced off his silver suit, thrown by angry old rockers in the audience who had come to hear Little Richard, Bill Haley, Jerry Lee Lewis and Chuck Berry. But it didn't seem to bother Glitter: in fact, he seemed almost to relish it, dodging the cans and then throwing them back into the crowd with gay abandon.

For three or four years, British rock had been serious and gloomy, with groups like Pink Floyd and Yes issuing solemn, wordy double or even treble "concept albums" with titles like *Tales from Topographic Oceans* and *The Piper at the Gates of Dawn*, full of endless guitar solos. Gary Glitter heralded a welcome break from all this earnest tedium. Progressive Rock was introspective, self-important and self-regarding. Glitter Rock was fun, communal and parodic.

Whenever Progressive Rock was played, people would sit on bean bags and follow the words on the lyric sheets provided. When Glitter Rock was played, everyone would get up and dance, often punching the air in a jocular fashion. People smiled when "I Love you Love me Love (You Love me too Love)" was played. No one ever smiled when Pink Floyd's "Money (It's a Crime)" was played: in fact, at that time, it could well have been a capital offence.

I was introduced to Gary Glitter by Tessa Dahl in the late 1970s at a party thrown at Regine's for Andy Warhol. Bubbles

Rothermere, Bianca Jagger and Patrick Lichfield were there, too. I mention this not just to name-drop – I was only there as a reporter – but to show that Glitter was, for a time, invited to all the most fashionable parties.

By chance, he then bought a big house in my parents' village of Rogate, in West Sussex. I always hoped we'd bump into each other in the village shop, but we never did. Rumour had it that if anyone approached him in the pub saying, "Excuse me, are you Gary Glitter?" he would reply: "No, but people tell me I look just like him."

I used to have a cassette of *Gary Glitter's Greatest Hits* in my car. It has since vanished into thin air, as cassettes do. These days, I often feel like a refreshing blast of "Do You Wanna Touch Me" with its almost criminally unsuitable chorus (*"Where? There! Oh yeah!"*) but alas his *Greatest Hits* aren't on sale any more, and it's years since I've heard him on the radio.

Around the time that Gary Glitter was riding so high, Bernard Levin was busy writing articles in *The Times* about Wagner. As far as I can remember, he would argue that it was perfectly possible and legitimate to deplore the thoughts and actions of the artist while continuing to rejoice in his art. The same must surely be true of the equally rumbustious sounds of Gary Glitter.

Fat, friendless and disgraced, the sixty-five-year-old Paul Gadd now sits in a Vietnamese prison. But his pop songs remain as joyful as ever they were. As he himself put it in his Top Ten hit of 1974: "Remember Me This Way".

The Seventy-Year Bitch: John Richardson's Memoirs

THERE IS A CERTAIN type of guest, to be found in many of our more comfortable stately homes, who specialises in delivering waspish anecdotes about his – or, as often, her – previous hosts. Even as they chuckle in glee, the audience for these anecdotes feels a sense of dread, for they know that, in a few days' time, it is they who will be the targets, and other hosts who will be doubled up in mirth.

Reading John Richardson's new book of anecdotes and reminiscences about people he has known,* it is hard not to place him in the curious company of these stately home nomads. Of course, his preferred society, while certainly well-heeled, veers more towards the arty and the bohemian, but he is as adept as any rival at grasping the hand that feeds him and then – with the greatest aplomb, and beautiful manners – biting it.

Having first dropped a name, he will then take delight in suavely squidging it into the ground with the ball of his foot. "I stayed at Weston once or twice during the war," he recalls in an essay on the Sitwells, "and remember Georgia Sitwell's covetous attitude." Or of the art collector Peggy Guggenheim, "Lunches in the shady garden at the back of the house would have been more delectable had the food been better … the wine was so poor that the scarcity did not matter." Or, again, of the society hostess Sibyl Colefax, he writes that "her food was good in a conventional way" and "her background was respectable, but she lacked fortune, looks, wit and charm".

I can't help wondering whether he mentioned these shortcomings in his thank-you letters at the time. And what a lot of thank-you letters John Richardson must have written in his time! Now getting on for eighty, he boasts in his introduction that his reminiscences of the great and the not-so-good "go back well over half a century" – and in many respects further than that, as from his childhood he was already mixing in an older Bohemian set whose memories would have stretched back well into the nineteenth century: astonishingly, Richardson's grandfather was born in 1814.

Richardson himself is probably best known for his highly praised but to my mind rather plodding biography of Picasso, but he has also viewed art through the binoculars of money, having been the head of Christie's in New York. As a memoirist, he belongs to the tradition of James Lees-Milne and Cecil Beaton: camp, polished, elegant, snobby, merciless.

And like so many snobs, he deplores the snobbery of others. At one moment, he is complaining that Osbert Sitwell is snobbish; at the next, recalling Truman Capote's refrigerator repairman

---

* *Sacred Monsters, Sacred Masters* by John Richardson

boyfriend looking out of place on the deck of a rich Italian's yacht, he observes with a sniff that "it was all too evident that he would have been happier with the crew".

On the other hand, bitchiness is not to be under-rated: it can often be the yeast that gives life to a memoir. Though occasionally Richardson becomes hopelessly entangled in the web of his own gossip ("at least that is the way Sam told me the story" he concludes one anecdote, "and the way I told it to a friend of mine, who repeated it with embellishments to his sister-in-law – in those days Garbo's inamorata – who in turn repeated it back to Garbo, who was furious") at other times his beady prosecutor's eye picks on the one detail that would surely have his accused screaming for mercy.

For instance, he notes of the wife of the billionaire fraudster Armand Hammer that "her taste was Middle America at its most motelish: 1950s Sunbelt furniture, wind chimes, and plastic flowers in need of dusting". It is that final phrase – "in need of dusting" – that is the killer, just as in his description of the New York arty set "with their mink-lined raincoats and their choice little dinners of tiny lamb chops and unborn vegetables followed by wild strawberries in a bath of blood-orange juice" it is his use of the adjective "unborn" that puts the icing on the cake, or, if you would prefer, the acid on the drop.

If there is a general theme to this disparate group of essays, written over a period of some decades, it is the disastrous effect of artworks upon those who covet them. Richardson takes an almost diabolic delight in detailing the unhappy ends awaiting the wealthy and the well born, from Picasso's grandson who, denied access to his grandfather's funeral, "swallowed a bottle of bleach, which burned away his intestines", to Salvador Dali, poisoned by his terrifying wife Gala, ending his days writhing on the floor, under the illusion that he was a snail. More merciful writers would have found something poignant in the death of Armand Hammer at the age of ninety-two, the day before he was due to have the barmitzvah that his father always denied him. But even at the end, John Richardson refuses to withhold his unforgiving cackles: "Jehovah withheld his blessing. On the eve of the ceremony, He killed off this shameful old hypocrite before he could glorify himself at His expense," he concludes.

Though his style is grandiose, his sense of character is tabloid. Everyone is either a saint or a sinner, with little in between. Millionaires are invariably motivated by the desire to get their own back on society for childhood slights. Artists' wives are greedy and philistine. And so on.

It comes as a surprise whenever Richardson finds a good word to say about anyone. His praise – or what there is of it – tends to fall on the just and the unjust in equal measure. He refuses, for instance, to see anything hypocritical about Andy Warhol decorating his own home with religious paintings and eighteenth-century furniture while publicly espousing the brash and the modish.

Most people who have read George Plimpton's biography of Edie Sedgwick will have concluded that there was, at very least, something inherently creepy about the way in which Warhol stood blankly by while watching his followers descend into hell, yet Richardson maintains that "tenacity and gentleness and down-to-earth resilience were at the heart of Andy's character". He also claims that Warhol "did rescue many of his entourage from burnout". But isn't this like congratulating an arsonist for taking his turn with the hose?

But when his praise falls on the just, Richardson can provide a fund of first-hand perceptions and information. He is fascinating, for instance, about sitting as a model for Lucian Freud, and where others have written about Freud's anger and passion, Richardson writes, far more tellingly, of his restraint. From getting close up, as it were, to Freud, he notes that he has a lazy left eye, and probably suffers from a mild form of presbyopia, which is an inability to focus on nearby objects. The same condition has, he notes, afflicted other painters in old age – Titian, Cézanne and Rembrandt among them – but it can be a blessing in disguise, adding both to the richness of the paint and the rough grandeur of the scale.

Richardson also has the gossip's great merit of being able to identify a good joke when he hears one. He is right to single out Lord Berners for special praise in this area. Wanting to take the social-climbing Sibyl Colefax down a peg or two, Berners sent her an invitation to dinner, scrawling "the P of W is coming". Imagining he was referring to the Prince of Wales, Colefax cancelled all other arrangements and rushed to Berners's dinner table – only to find herself sitting next to the Provost of Worcester.

Harold Pinter's Revised Book of English Verse

I Remember, I Remember
I remember, I remember,
The house where I was born,
The little window where the sun
Came peeping in at morn;
He never came a wink too soon,
Nor brought too long a day,
But now, I often wish the night
Would have sodomised him up the fucking arse.

O No John!
On yonder hill there stands a creature
So who the fuck are you, chum?

If
If you can keep your head when all about you
Are losing theirs to the American fucking bastards
Who couldn't give a fucking shit whether
Your fucking head stays on your neck or bloody not;
If you can talk with crowds and keep your virtue
Or walk with Kings – and tell them to shut the fuck up.
If neither foes nor loving friends can hurt you
Because they've just blown the fucking bollocks off you
Yours is the Earth and all the fucking piss that's in it,
    And – which is more – you can eat shit, my son!

The Lake Isle of Innisfree
I will arise and go now, and go to Innisfree
And a small cabin build there, of clay and wattles made;

Nine bean-rows will I have there, a hive for the honey-bee,
Until the Yanks come along and fuck the shit out of it.

Home Thoughts from Abroad

Oh, to be in England
Now that April's there
And whoever wakes in England
Sees, some morning, unaware,
That stinky fucker Mr Tony fucking Blair,
And says, Look, chum, get off my fucking land
You're trespassing so wipe that fucking smile
Off your fucking face and fuck the fuck off.

Horatius

Lars Porsena of Clusium
    By the Nine Gods he swore
That the great house of Tarquin
    Shouldn't get its nose ground
In the shit any fucking more.

We'll Go No More a Roving

We'll go no more a roving
    So late into the night,
Certainly not if the Blair fascists
    Have their fucking way
And gag myself and Lady Antonia
    And leave us head-first in a fucking gutter
Somewhere South of Holland Park.

I Wandered Lonely as a Cloud

I wandered lonely as a cloud
That floats on high o'er vales and hills
When all at once I saw a crowd,
A host, of golden daffodils
And I said, come on, Lady Antonia,
Get your coat on, I'm not standing
For any more of this fucking nonsense

Those fucking daffodils have got it in for us
It's free speech they can't abide.

Elegy Written in a Country Churchyard
The curfew tolls the knell of parting day
The lowing herd wind slowly o'er the lea
And the ploughman homeward plods his weary way
Until the bomb goes off, his head is smashed to blazes
And his hand is blown to fucking smithereens
And his ploughman's lunch ends up in a fucking puddle, all wet and soggy.

The Charge of the Light Brigade
Half a league, half a league,
Half a league onward,
All in the valley of Death
Rode the six hundred.
On the direct orders of Mein Fuhrer Blair:
Thanks a fucking bunch, chum.

Cargoes
Quinquireme of Nineveh from distant Ophir
Rowing home to haven in sunny Palestine,
With a cargo of ivory,
And apes and peacocks,
Sandalwood, cedarwood, and sweet white wine.
They blew them into fucking shit.
They are eating it.
Now I want you to come over here and kiss me on the arse, chum.

The Owl and the Pussy-Cat
The Owl and the Pussy-Cat went to sea
    In a beautiful pea-green boat.
They took some honey, and plenty of money
    Because they were fucking Yanks
Sucking the shit out of the arse of the poor.

Come into the Garden, Maud
Come into the garden, Maud,
For the black bat, Night, has flown:
Come into the garden, Maud,
For I am here at the gate alone,
Sniffing the pong of the dead.

The Tiger
Tiger! Tiger! burning bright
In the forests of the night,
The big pricks are out.
They'll fuck everything.
Watch your back.

The Heart of the Mattress
by Joan Bakewell

IT WAS 1960, the very first year in the extraordinary decade that was later to become known as the 1960s. Overnight, society had shaken off the starchy sexual mores of the 1950s. Suddenly, young men and women were casting aside their inhibitions and tapping their toes to the urgent, febrile rhythms of Lonnie Donegan. Among enlightened couples, cheese fondue was all the rage.

All the old barriers came down. I found to my alarm that even men of the very greatest distinction couldn't keep their hands to themselves. I well remember having to fend off the then Chancellor of the Exchequer. I was interviewing him about the trade deficit on live television for *Late Night Love-In* when suddenly he cast aside his red box, pulled down his trousers and leapt on top of me.

As I struggled to retain hold of my clipboard, veteran broadcaster Cliff Michelmore attempted to rectify the situation. "Let's move swiftly on to the balance of payments, Chancellor," he said. "Any hope of an upturn come the autumn?" But before the Chancellor had a chance to reply, the incoming governor of the Bank of England had barged into the studio, wearing nothing but a posing pouch.

It was in this steamy liberated atmosphere of sexual awakening that I first set eyes on Harold Pinter. We were at a party. It was, as I recall, a fondue party. None of the usual rules applied. Knives, forks, spoons: who needed them? Cutlery was dismissed as conventional, and even serviettes had been discarded. Instead, we would – wildly, madly, crazily – dip pieces of bread just any old how into a hot cheesy sauce. Then we would toss them into our mouths as "My Old Man's a Dustman" played suggestively in the background. The effect was electrifying.

Pinter and I went outside together. I said nothing. He said nothing. I said nothing back. He added nothing. Nothing would come between us. Pinter was already known for his pauses, but in those extraordinary moments he managed to stretch it from a slight pause to a mild hesitation and then, before we both knew it, to a full-blown silence.

We met many times after that first, fateful meeting, but Pinter never so much as uttered a word. Once we had a rendezvous in the kettle department of Rumbelows, the electrical retailer. The kettle department was the only place we could let off steam. I arrived late – I must have needed a new set of batteries for my transistor radio – and, while he waited, Pinter wrote a poem, which he gave me:

> *Turning, you cross your arms*
> *Still holding your fingers tight*
> *And then, unfolding them,*
> *Create what looks like*
> *A sort of hat. I know*
> *You are a dab hand*
> *At origami.*

Pinter was to become known as the master of the pause. He certainly couldn't keep his pause off me. Over fondue-based meals, in places as distant as Venice, New York and Hong Kong, we would stare at one another in silence. Before long, our fondues, originally cheese-based, had begun to incorporate chicken, lamb and even beef. There was, we both knew, no turning back.

As the 1960s progressed, Pinter's fame grew, and so did mine. I was now on *Late Night Love-In* three nights a week. On Tuesdays,

I would fend off advances from leading neurosurgeons, on Wednesdays from philosophers and on Thursdays from elder statesmen. The 1960s were by now well under way. This was the decade Pinter produced his greatest work, much of it with fondue-based themes.

It was fondue that brought us together. And it was fondue that was to pull us apart. Arriving with my husband at a hotel suite in Monte Carlo in the long, hot summer of '68, I found a seventeen-piece fondue set waiting on the bed for me, complete with antique-style bronze plate-warmer, each item embossed with my name.

My husband must have sensed my embarrassment, for he asked me what I was doing throwing a fondue set out of an open window. At that moment, there was a knock at the door. It was a waiter, delivering my husband his very own fondue set, a present from an unknown woman.

We were caught up in the giddy maelstrom of the 1960s. We were determined that jealousy should not come between us. But we became jealous of each other's lack of jealousy, and so our marriage came to an end.

Years later, I was at home when a parcel was delivered. It was a set of blank pages. I recognised it instantly as a new work by Pinter. To my horror, I recognised the silences as our own. They were all there, for the world to ignore. Years on, I have decided to break the silence surrounding the silence. I hope my account may now take its place in a serious study of Pinter's life and work, and may also be of interest to serious historians of fondue in the early 1960s.

Peace Is Over: Yoko Ono

ALMOST FORTY YEARS AGO at a theatre in Japan, Ms Yoko Ono premiered a work called *Cut Piece*. It consisted of Ono standing on stage wearing a long white gown. After a while, she produced a pair of scissors. She then invited members of the audience to cut pieces from her gown. She ended up stark naked. It was, she explained, all in the interests of world peace.

It is not known whether President Johnson caught the performance, but within weeks he had sought and received the approval of

Congress to take "all necessary action" against the communist regime in North Vietnam. Later that year, Ms Ono published a limited edition of *Grapefruit*, a book of "instructional poems" in Tokyo. One of the poems read, in full, "Smoke everything you can, including your pubic hair." A week later, a state of emergency was declared in Malaysia following landings by Indonesian paratroops.

Heaven knows how many wars have been started since Ms Ono first performed *Cut Piece* in 1964. It may be unfair to lay the blame for every single one of them at her door. Nevertheless, she does seem to possess an unfortunate knack for sending out the wrong messages. In March 1969, for instance, she joined her third husband, the late John Lennon, for a week-long "bed-in" for peace at the presidential suite of the Hilton Hotel in Amsterdam. Within a few weeks, British troops were sent into Northern Ireland, where they have remained ever since.

Prospects for world peace have now taken a further blow. At the weekend, Ms Ono, now in her seventy-first year, announced that on September 15 she plans to recreate *Cut Piece* at the Theatre Le Ranelagh, in Paris. This time, she will ask members of the audience to cut pieces no larger than a postcard from her clothing "wherever you like" and to send the scraps to those they love.

"*Cut Piece* is my hope for world peace," she told a press conference. "I do it with love for you, for me, and for the world." Personally, I plan to spend September 15 cowering under my sofa with a loaf of bread and a good supply of bottled water.

The Rolling Stones: The First 60 Years

✱ **1915:** The birth of Charlie Watts. For some days, Mr and Mrs Watts believe him to be stillborn; it later emerges that he just hasn't seen any reason to move.

✱ **1916:** The birth of Bill Wyman. Mr and Mrs Wyman fail to announce the event in their local newspaper. "We didn't want to bore everyone," they explain.

✱ **1932:** Keith auditions for George Formby's backing group. "He's a bit of a tearaway, is our Keith," Formby tells a reporter after Richards insists upon wearing a brightly coloured cravat rather than a tie. Keith accompanies Formby on his hit "Leaning on a Lamp Post". Forty years later, he will adapt the song for a modern audience, retitling it "Lean On Me".

✱ **1939:** Too old for active service during the Second World War Two, the Rolling Stones are recruited by ENSA to entertain the troops as part of a variety package that includes Max Miller and the young Gracie Fields. Mick Jagger performs a self-penned protest song, "Chill Out, Führer", in which he advises the German Chancellor to "quit being so harsh", which he rhymes with "but I love your cute moustache".

✱ **1940:** The ENSA tour is cancelled after a major falling out between the Rolling Stones and Gracie Fields. Miss Fields complains she was just preparing to perform "The Biggest Aspidistra in the World", when she was informed that it had just been smoked by Keith and Brian.

✱ **1942:** Mick Jagger denies rumours of an affair with Forces' Sweetheart Vera Lynn after some observers claim to have detected telltale drug references in her hit song "The White Cliffs of Dover". "Bluebirds is drug slang for the carriers. Why else would those cliffs be white?" observes thrusting young cultural commentator Beverley Nichols.

✱ **1945:** At a press conference to launch his group's *A Fresh Start* tour, sponsored by Demob Suits Ltd, Jagger says "Chill Out, Führer" was a significant factor in the Allied victory.

✱ **1949:** During a Rolling Stones concert in Southampton, a member of the audience claims to have spotted Charlie Watts moving. "This is just the sort of rumour that's always going around," says the group's manager, Sir Montagu Norman. "Everyone knows that Charlie hasn't moved since 1940, when a bomb briefly landed on his head."

✱ **1952:** Leading novelist Barbara Cartland denies having an affair with Mick Jagger. "Each of the Rolling Stones has proposed marriage to me many times over," she says, "but alas I have had to disappoint them as – does this sound too awful? – they are frankly far too common."

✱ **1953:** Stung by Miss Cartland's criticism, Jagger embarks on a course of elocution lessons. Towards the end of the year, he releases his next 78 disc: "I Simply Cannot Get Sufficient Satisfaction, Even Though I Have Attempted To". It reaches number six in the hit parade.

✱ **1955:** Denying rumours of an affair with Dorothy Macmillan, Mick Jagger is seen out on the town with Ruth, Lady Fermoy. "Ruth and I are old friends from way back," he explains, with a wink. Many insiders believe that his latest single, "Ruthie", ("Ruthie, you're beautiful, Ain't it time you brought out the decent silver?") is really about her.

✱ **1958:** The Stones top *The Royal Variety Show*. After the curtain call, Her Majesty the Queen lines up to shake hands with Jagger. "She's such a social climber," he is heard to mutter.

✱ **1967:** The new single, "Brown Sugar", is sponsored by Tate and Lyle. In response to criticism that this supposedly anti-establishment group is in league with multi-national corporations, Jagger points out that their last but one single, "Jumping Jack Flash", was sponsored by a well-known washing powder, while "Honky Tonk Woman" was sponsored by HonkyTonk Kitchens of Cheltenham. "Only through sponsorship can you ever hope to change things," he explains.

✱ **1970:** Doctors confirm the death of Brian Jones after someone notices he is not playing guitar. The Rolling Stones appoint leading historian A J P Taylor to take his place. Taylor is the youngest member of the band by a good thirty years, but the addition of a bow tie and glasses help him to appear older.

✱ **1971:** Mick Jagger flies off to Australia to film *Ned Kelly*. Bill Wyman auditions for the role of Private Godfrey in *Dad's Army*. He is rejected by the producers as "just a little too elderly".

✱ **1973:** Regarded as the voice of rebellion back in the early 1930s, Mick Jagger is accepted into the Establishment when a rousing medley from *Exile on Main Street* is played by the Band of the Royal Scots Guards as Captain Mark Phillips escorts HRH Princess Anne down the aisle on the occasion of their wedding. "Tunes you can really hum along to," murmurs the Queen Mother, appreciatively.

Tickled Pink: The Diaries of Tony Benn

ALAN BENNETT once said that in England you only have to survive long enough and all is forgiven you. "If you can eat a boiled egg at ninety in England they think you deserve a Nobel Prize," he added.

Now aged seventy-seven, Tony Benn has been undergoing this quaint process of sanctification for a good ten years. It was a process set in motion the second he stopped posing a threat. In 2002, he is now everyone's favourite grand-uncle, full of the tweedy phrases of yesteryear ("Blow me down!" "I'm tickled pink!"), offering Polo mints to one and all before pointing out, between puffs on his trusty pipe, that things aren't what they were.

Since 1940, Tony has been keeping diaries and publishing them – or at least a digestible selection from them – in big, fat volumes, of which this, *Free At Last!*, is the seventh.* The preceding volumes were unexpectedly jaunty in tone, and, for a man who has always professed his determination to keep personalities out of politics, extravagantly gossipy, not to say bitchy.

Of course, there is gossip and there is gossip, and anyone who is not all that interested in learning what Barbara said that Jack thought Jim planned to say about Harold to Roy when Len was out of the room would be best advised to avoid some of the earlier volumes, particularly those from the Sixties and Seventies. Benn would, of course, argue that this is not gossip but politics, and that he sees his diaries as part of a political archive, a valuable resource for historians, etcetera. But gossip and politics are both dishes best served warm, and there must now be a limit to anyone's interest in forgotten figures like Len Murray and forgotten causes like the Meridien Co-operative.

The new volume is, to my mind, the best. This is partly because it is the most recent, and the mists of time have not yet closed over its events and participants, but also because it is more personal, and Benn the Diarist, now on the furthest fringes of power, is less anxious to present his noblest political profile for future Labour historians. Instead, he discards his Sunday best and allows himself to

---

Free at Last! Diaries 1991–2001 by Tony Benn

emerge as a human being full of weaknesses and anxieties balanced by an enviable capacity for love and joy.

Towards the end of this volume, there is an entry dictated not by Tony Benn but by his little grandson Daniel, who has wandered into his office and found his tape recorder. "My grandfather's a bit of a nincompoop," he says. And reading the previous entries only the most fervent Bennite (not a word you hear a lot, these days) would deny that little Daniel is on to something.

Malcolm Bradbury once described him as "the Bertie Wooster of Marxism", and certainly his absurdities are many and obvious. He has, for instance, an unlimited appetite for being praised, avidly recording every compliment paid to him, whether by cabbie or colleague. The Archbishop of Canterbury calls him "one of our most distinguished British parliamentarians" – and in it goes. Peter Shore calls him "the best leader we never had" – and in it goes. He is even happy to bung in the news that the arch-right-winger Teresa Gorman has called him her hero, failing to add that she is as nutty as a fruitcake.

His comical ability to make bold predictions on one page that turn to dust on the next is undiminished. On one and the same page in 1998, he predicts that Ken Clarke and Michael Heseltine will shortly be joining the Blair Cabinet and that Ken Livingstone certainly won't stand as an Independent for Mayor of London. A few pages later, he predicts that Mandelson won't resign over the Robinson Loan. On the next page, Mandelson resigns. "I think it is the end of New Labour, because Blair without Mandelson is lost," predicts Tony. But this is evidence, too, of his accuracy as a recorder: other politicians carefully airbrush out their blunders, so that their memoirs read like the lives of the saints.

But Benn is only too aware of the English sentimentality for elderly politicians who have had their wings clipped. "The final corruption of radical politics is that you become a sort of well-loved old eccentric, seen at parties," he says at one point, yet it is a cosy doom from which he is unable to save himself. As in the earlier volumes, though far less frequently, he manages to bring the reader up with a jolt by expressing a political belief that is chilling in its naivety. He sees the disappearance of the Soviet Union as "a great setback" and he breezily tells the Chinese ambassador that he is a "great admirer of Mao", adding that, "He made mistakes, because everybody does, but it seems to me that the development of the countryside and so on was very sensible." In terms of ignoring mass-murder, this is no different from someone declaring their admiration for Hitler, saying "He made mistakes, because everybody does, but it seems to me he gave his people a sense of pride."

But these crass moments – for me, they actually border on the wicked – are fewer and further between in this latest volume. Living through a period when British politics has moved from the ideological to the managerial, Benn does his best to keep the Red Flag flying, going on demonstrations and making speeches and attending meetings, but somehow you feel that even he is being dragged along by the apolitical tide, and that his interest is ebbing. "I can't say that politics is my main interest at the moment," he reflects towards the end, "what I have learned recently is the tremendous importance of personal relations."

Small wonder, for *Free at Last!* is dominated, far more than ever before, by his love of his family. Never has there been a political memoir so full of delighted and delightful references to children and grandchildren, and this volume is full of happy stories and funny remarks. ("Little Daniel, who's five, said to his dad, 'Daddy, what is the biggest number in the world? Is it 168,000?' And Stephen said, 'Well, Daniel, there's 168,001.' 'Oh,' said Daniel, 'I got very close to it, didn't I, Dad?' Marvellous.")

Free at Last! is also a touching, day-by-day love letter to Tony Benn's late wife Caroline ("the finest person I ever met in the whole of my life"). It charts the growth of her spinal cancer from 1996 to her death in November 2000. Benn's account of Caroline's decline is deeply affecting, and there is a beautiful purity in his naked expression of love. At her death, "I kissed her, and dropped tears on her cold, cold face."

No doubt Tony Benn will squirm with irritation when people point out that he is becoming more and more chummy with his old enemies on the right, and more and more irritable with his former allies on the left. Knowing him, he might even see such an observation as part of an Establishment (still a word he uses) plot to undermine him. But *Free at Last!* is full of compliments to right-wingers. Norman Tebbit is "terribly soft and good-natured", Alan Clark "very kindly", John Major "such a nice guy", Steve Norris "always very agreeable", Ian Paisley "a very nice guy". Throughout the book he conducts a somewhat one-sided courtship of Ted Heath ("I am rather fond of him"), culminating in him asking Heath whether he is going to resign from the Commons as "I couldn't bear the thought that you were there and I wasn't".

But just look how he deals with his own side! Robin Cook is "an angry little man", Gordon Brown "absolutely pathetic", George Robertson "a little twit", Mandelson "frightfully self-satisfied, smirking and oily", Blair "so smirky and bland", Kinnock "grinning and arrogant" and, as for Gerald Kaufman, "I can't stand the man".

Whether he likes it or not, Tony Benn has become the "well-loved old eccentric" of his radical nightmares. It is surely a little eccentric for a veteran politician to suck a mothball thinking it is a sweet, and more eccentric still to peel off a "Smoking" notice from a railway carriage, keep it in his pocket, and then, months later, stick it over a "No Smoking" notice and light up, observing, "I really do feel somebody's got to take a stand on behalf of smokers."

By my reckoning, if Tony Benn can still suck eggs by the time he's ninety, he'll be ushered into a new and demanding job, perfect for such a cosy, old-fashioned conviction politician. For this reason, I look forward to his 2017–2025 diaries, *Tory Leader at Last*.

Sharon Osbourne's Diary

I got Kelly a puppy the other day. Kelly loves, loves, loves puppies, she really really does. Don't ask me what fucking sort it was, but I tell you that puppy was fucking expensive, bless it, what with the diamonds we got put into its collar and tongue, the liposuction, the tummy tuck, the arse lift and the tail job.

So Kelly's all over her beautiful new puppy, patting it and that, and she says she's going to call it Cuddles. "So why you wanna fuckin' call it Cuddaws?" I say.

"'Cos it looks like it wants a great big fuckin' cuddaw. So what you gonna fuckin' do 'bout it?" says Kelly. Bless!

So Cuddles it fucking was. At least for an hour, but then it only goes and fucking shits and pisses all over the new settee.

"What the fuckin' fucks that?" says Kelly, pointing at the poo.

"That's fuckin' poo, that's what that is," I tell her.

"Urgh! I don't want this fuckin' dog no more! Get me a new one!" she says.

"So what we gonna fucking do with the old one, after all what we spent on it?" I say.

But at that point the problem's solved because Ozzy comes in and sits on it.

"Look what you just fucking gone and done!" I say to Ozzy.

Ozzy stands up and looks back down at the dead puppy.

"Funny," he says, "I can't remember eatin' that."

We gave Cuddles a beautiful send-off, though. We spent a shit-load of money hiring José Carreras and that fat one, Jessye Norman, that's it, and the orchestra and chorus from the Royal Opera House for the afternoon and flying them over for Cuddles's funeral, mind you we got most of it back from MTV, who was filming it live.

As that little gold coffin was put into the ground I don't mind telling you I was in a terrible state, sobbing, sobbing, sobbing. I was in my funeral dress which the lovely Vivienne Westwood, a personal friend, had designed specially for the occasion.

I wrote a poem, "For Cuddles", which I read out at the grave-side, choking through the fucking tears:

"I loved you little Cuddles
Your lovely fur and tail and head
Til Ozzy came along
And squashed you fucking dead."

It choked us all up, I read it so beautiful. But that's the kind of person I am, I wear my heart on my sleeve, and that's why the public warm to me, because they know I'm the kind of person who'll give a little puppy a good send-off, even if it's taken me to hell and back by shitting over my new settee.

"Fuck you!"
"No, fuck you!"
"No, fuck you!"

If there's one thing I've learnt, it's you can't win an argument with Camilla Parker Bowles.

We're peas in a pod, her and me. We've both got a shitload of money, an adoring public and a hubby who wants his fucking brain examining. And we're both royalty, if you know what I mean.

But that's no reason for her to get fucking above herself. She may be the duchess of fucking manure, for all I care, but that doesn't give her the fucking right to wear a tiara like mine. So last time I saw her, I got her in a corner and gave her what for. I was like, who the fuck do you think you are, madam? You're fucking B-list, you are, for all your fancy airs and crap hairdo. And you know what? People appreciate my honesty. We've been best mates ever since.

The X Factor. Don't get me started! When those lovely young men come on stage in their tight little trousers and sing their hearts out for Sharon, my heart melts. I truly care about every single one of them, I really do, and the public senses that, and that's why they love me.

Just yesterday, I was being driven along by my chauffeur in our $463,000 limousine. I was in the back with my plastic surgeon Roger, who was just putting the finishing touches to my new toes (sorry, but you've got to have six on each foot these days if you want to be noticed). Suddenly, we hear this fucking yell from the river. A boat had capsized, and there's five people in the water struggling for their fucking lives, bless 'em!

Call me a great big softy, but I couldn't just leave them to drown, I'm sorry, that's not the kind of person I am! So I get the chauffeur to park near the river, and I get out the old mirror and make sure I'm looking fan-tastic – I'd never let the fans down, they want to see me at my best – then I squeeze into my $3,000 stilet-toes and walk ever so sexily down to the riverside, where there's just the one lifebelt to throw them.

The five of them are still thrashing about in the river, all fucking soggy and that, hair all over the place, only now there's only four, bless, because one's gone under! "Sorry guys, I can only rescue the one of you!" I announce, as sweetly as possible, because I truly care about them all, and I'd dearly love to be able to save each and every-one of them from drowning.

"So which of you lovely young people is it going to be?" I ask them. They look so adorable, all shivery and panicky and cuddly, thrashing about in the river and that. By now, they're all so desper-ate, they're screaming for help at the very tops of their super voices, they really are! Yes, they love me!

"Decisions, decisions!" I say, flashing my trademark smile. "I only wish I could save you all, you're all so truly fabulous!"

By now another one's gone under, and there's just the three left – but it doesn't make my choice any easier! "Ho-hum!" I say. "This is one of the toughest decisions of my life. It's truly momentous! You know what, guys? Sharon's going to have to have herself a little sit-me-down before deciding."

You could almost feel the tension in that river! So I have myself my little sit-me-down, and check on my make-up – but when I get up again, the last three have disappeared below the water!

Yes – I'd left it too late! Story of my life! I'll never forget those young people's faces. I'd made their day! They looked so thrilled to have met Sharon Osbourne before they drowned. I walked back to the limousine with a lovely warm feeling in my heart. See, when you're in my position, you've got to put something back, you really have.

Comedy's Straitjacket: Spike Milligan

BEING SPIKE MILLIGAN was no fun at all. "I am basically the unfun-niest person in the world," he once said. Later, he told the poet Robert Graves, "There's something very unfunny in being funny."

Throughout his adult life, Spike Milligan was trapped by depres-sion. He would often stare at the wall for days on end, saying nothing. Sometimes, it would be worse. In the middle of writing the third series of *The Goons*, he had a complete breakdown.

"The madness built up gradually. I found I was disliking more and more people. Then I got to hating them. Even my wife and baby," he later confessed. In the midst of it all, he started to believe that only by killing Peter Sellers would it all come right again. He then went round to Sellers's house and walked straight through a glass door, cutting himself all over. He ended up in the isolation ward of a mental hospital, wrapped in a straitjacket.

Were the jokes he cracked – the manic, relentless, unstoppable jokes – an escape from the trap of depression? Or were they an essential part of that trap? To some extent, it seems he lived his life at the mercy of puns and skewed logic. Whenever his brain sensed the world was not mad enough, it did its best to make it madder.

And there was more than a hint of megalomania to his comedy: he wanted the world, and everyone in it, to bend before his jokes; if they refused, he would give them hell. Performing on stage with the Goons in Coventry in 1954, he became increasingly cross at the lack of audience response. Finally, he snapped, "I hope you all get bombed again!" and left the stage, locking himself in his dressing room. When the rest of the cast finally prised open the door, they found Milligan standing on a chair with a noose round his neck, trying to hook the end of the rope round an overhead pipe.

His biographer, Humphrey Carpenter,* chronicles all this anti-social and depressive behaviour with tremendous diligence, even relish, yet he tends to shy away from linking the comedy to the madness. "Plenty of comedians and clowns have been manic-depressive," he writes, "but paranoid schizophrenia does not sit comfortably with laughter."

I wonder if this is true? The humour of *The Goon Show* is based largely on puns, and the pun is formed from a kind of verbal schizophrenia, in which a word points in two ways at once, meaning two entirely different things at the same time. Shakespearean characters tend to tumble into a world of puns when they begin their descent to madness.

In *The Act of Creation*, Arthur Koestler reported on the phenomenon of compulsive punning, known as Forster's syndrome, after the German surgeon who first observed it. When Dr Forster was removing a tumour on the brain of a patient, he noticed that as he manipulated

---

* *Spike Milligan – The Biography* by Humphrey Carpenter

certain areas of the brain, the patient would burst into a manic flight of puns, the sound of one word swiftly echoed in the sound of the next, all the words having something to do with knives and butchery – and all this gruesome humour coming, as Koester noted, "from a man tied face down to the operating table with his skull open".

The pun can also arise from aggression, a revenge for being mocked or condescended to. It is a swift way of establishing superiority, of ordering the world according to one's own whim, while its levity provides the perfect alibi. The pun slips madness into language: what is the Freudian slip, if not a pun?

Perhaps this psychologising sounds a bit heavy going. After all, you may say, we are only discussing a comedian. But comedians are, more often than not, driven to comedy as a form of self-defence, both on the playground level of using jokes to distract bullies, and on the more fundamental level of using jokes to distract themselves from their own darker impulses.

Perversely, Humphrey Carpenter gallops through Milligan's childhood as though it didn't matter. "My boredom threshold for what you might call Childhood Experiences is almost as low as for Ancestry," he writes, early on. "Am I alone in finding biographies tedious until the subject becomes old enough to make choices, take decisions, do things?" This, from a man whose previous biographies of Dennis Potter and Benjamin Britten have located the source of their art in the traumas of their childhood.

Spike Milligan spent an idyllic childhood in India and Burma. His father was a lowly non-commissioned officer, but nevertheless the family had servants and lived in some luxury. Aged fifteen, Spike returned with his family, to live in a two-room flat in Catford, South London. "He never grew up," said the psychologist Anthony Clare, who once attempted to collaborate with Milligan on a book about depression. "He stopped when he came to England. It was so gloomy and disappointing to him that he wanted to remain the child he'd been in India."

His call-up to the army came on his twenty-first birthday. "One day an envelope marked OHMS fell on the mat..." he begins the first of seven volumes of wartime autobiography, "in it was a cunningly worded invitation to participate in World War Two."

At first, joining the army, with its jokes, its camaraderie and its great sense of purpose, must have seemed like liberation. Every morning, he sounded the reveille on his trumpet, and he even started a comic newspaper called *Milli-News*. But everything came to a head when he found himself stationed outside Naples in 1944.

Anyone who has read *Naples '44*, the diary of Norman Lewis, will be able to see how the mayhem so sanely recorded by Lewis could flip a less stable man into madness. One night, there was a direct hit on the battery's ammunition, and a burning camouflage net fell on top of his fellow soldiers, trapping them. Milligan was, says Carpenter, horrified by the sight of the incinerated corpses. One of his friends, Gunner Musclewhite, was killed sitting up in bed. "He was partially roasted, and his white teeth shone out of the black of his fleshless head."

Small wonder that *The Goon Show*s are full of explosions and things falling and being smashed to pieces, its protagonists only coming through the chaos intact by dint of their heroic stupidity. The craziness of *The Goons* is generally seen as a reaction to the drab Britain of the 1950s – in a neat phrase, Carpenter says that they "challenged stuffiness with joy" – but it was also, surely, a reaction to what Milligan witnessed in Naples, the choreography of frenzy into farce.

Though I wouldn't go quite so far as Carpenter, who believes that *The Goon Show*s are "funnier than anything else in the history of comedy", fifty years on they remain extraordinarily fresh and energetic; my twelve-year-old son is addicted to them. Milligan's other lasting achievement is his children's verse, which seems to have sprung straight from the sweetest and silliest part of his heart. But, post-Goon, most of his comedy seems to me too self-consciously and mechanically "zany", often with an off-putting undertow of self-righteousness. I can no longer watch repeats of his later appearances on chat shows without shielding my eyes: all that laughter based on nothing.

Milligan once claimed that his father said to him before he died, "Spike, people are made of shit, yes, every little tiny bit." Certainly, this seems to have been his own belief by the time he died in February 2002. Obsessed by overpopulation (even though he himself had fathered six children), he wrote to Tony Blair in 1997 urging him to introduce a ban on new babies for five years; his pervasive misanthropy suggests he might have preferred the ban to have been extended to all time.

I visited him in his unexpectedly soulless house in East Sussex a year or two before he died. He seemed a desperately sad old man, staring into the void. I thought there was no possibility of cheering him up, but then to my surprise I remembered, for the first time in well over thirty years, some of his *Silly Verse for Kids*, and began to recite it:

> *Fifty hairy savages*
> *Sitting down to lunch*
> *Gobble gobble, glup glup*
> *Munch, munch, munch.*

It's impossible to say it without smiling, and by the end Milligan was chuckling too, proving once again that laughter is both the consolation of madness, and its gift to the world.

Foreign Office

On Holiday with Wittgenstein

1   The world is all that is the case.

1.2   The world is all that is in the case.

1.3   The case divides into several compartments.

1.4   Including a small one for personal items.

1.5   Such as a toothbrush.

1.6   Every item in the case must be put into a compartment; even if it is the wrong one.

1.7   There is no part of the case that cannot be counted a compartment.

1.8   Some compartments have compartments.

1.9   Every item that is not in the case is not worth taking.

1.10   Except for the camera, which you left in the hall.

1.11   Every item but the camera is in the case; the case is in its case, but not in the case.

1.12   Every item is in the case but the case is not in every item. The case would not fit into every item.

1.13   There is no way you could fit a case into a toothbrush.

1.14   But you could fit a toothbrush into a case.

1.15   If you hadn't forgotten to do so after brushing your teeth this morning; now we will have to buy a new one when we get there.

1.16   The case is packed; but it cannot be closed.

1.17   It was not me who broke the zip; I told you not to try packing your pillow.

1.18   There are any number of pillows abroad.

1.19   The case is in the hall, ready to put in the car.

1.20   The car is parked outside, ready to drive away.

1.21   We are going to be late.

1.22 Late is what we are going to be.

1.23 I did not say it was your fault.

1.24 No, you can't check the cooker's off.

1.25 We are never going to make it. To make it, we are never going.

1.26 That's not what I meant. Of course we've got to go. Or we'll never make it.

1.27 All I meant to say was, we're going to be late.

1.28 I am not going on about it. You are going on about it.

1.29 The M25 has never been this bad.

1.30 The totality of everything in the world is on the M25. The world is made up of the totality of everything on the M25.

1.31 M25+M4=M11x M6+M3

1.32 I am not blaming you. It is not you whom I am blaming.

1.33

1.34

1.35

1.36 There is silence in the car. In the car, there is silence.

1.37 It is not me who is not speaking. It is you who is not speaking.

1.38 But it was you who said we could easily leave it another hour before setting off.

2.1 In logic nothing is accidental: if a thing can occur in a state of affairs, the possibility of the state of affairs must be written into the thing itself.

2.2 But that doesn't explain why there's a 40mph speed limit with cones over this five-mile stretch but no roadworks or accident visible.

2.3 It would seem to be a sort of accident, if it turned out that a roadworks would fit a stretch that could exist entirely on its own.

2.4 Cones contain the possibility of all situations.

2.5 Including missed flights.

2.6 Cone+cone+cone+cone = traffic build-up east of junction 14.

2.7 The expostulation of the heated expression "come on, come on" under my breath to the slowcoach in front has no effect whatsoever on the progress he makes. Yet I continue to utter it.

2.8 Traffic build-ups constrain the possibilities of all situations.

2.9 Things are independent in so far as they can occur in all possible situations, but this form of independence is a form of connection with states of affairs, a form of dependence. (It is impossible for vehicles to appear in two different roles at once: by themselves, and in jams.)

2.10 The possibility of turning off at the next junction and taking a succession of A roads and B roads in the hope of making swifter progress is evident in an imagined world; but occurs rarely in the real one.

2.11 Shortcuts are simple and effective.

2.12 As long as you don't mind where you end up.

2.13. It is obvious that an imagined world, however different it may be from the real one, must have something in common with it.

2.14 A picture is a model of reality. But not if you've been looking at the map the wrong way up for the last half-hour.

2.15 Why do you keep maintaining that I have ever said that you are to blame?

2.16 B2109+A173+Tjunction+B3067+A412+Pullin+Lookat Map=Sigh+Curse+U-Turn-A412-B3067-Tjunction-A173-B2109.

2.17 I distinctly remember you telling me to turn LEFT at the second fork.

2.18 Blame is what subsists independently of what is the case; but it may also incorporate it.

2.19 Space, time, substance and content are tools to be employed in the apportioning of blame.

2.20 The first person you see is the one whom you ask directions.

2.21 The requirement that simple signs be possible is the requirement that sense be determinate.

2.22 But he ignores this requirement and starts rattling off directions, then changing his mind and suggesting a prettier route.

2.23 He has all the time in the world. We have none of the time that was once in the world. All day is what we have not got.

2.24 Going away is the sum of our hopes.

2.25 Getting away is the sum of our fears.

DC Inconsequential (i):
The Memoirs of Sir Christopher Meyer

VISITS BY NEW LABOUR ministers offered endless variety and amusement during my years at the embassy in Washington. What funny little fellows they were!

I liked John Prescott, but I was told that he felt I was in some way "snooty". This is a great shame, as I have always prided myself in being able to "get on" with the working classes, however chippy they may be.

From the moment he arrived at the embassy, I did everything I possibly could to make the poor chap feel at home. Before his first state dinner, I even took him aside and gave him an impromptu lesson in how to hold his knife and fork properly (or "prawper" as he would no doubt have preferred to phrase it!).

I was also decent enough to inform him as tactfully as I possibly could that our hosts would prefer he didn't wear a flat cap to the meal, or bring his racing pigeons in with him. "And I would advise you not to graffiti the dining-room table – it never goes down well," I added, discreetly.

I was careful, too, to place some suitable reading matter by his bedside for his edification and enjoyment, including a couple of early *Janet and John*s and the latest *Beano* annual.

Yet for all the hard work I undertook on his behalf (and I made every effort to put on a thick Northern accent to make him feel more "at home" in what I described to him as "our great big house"), I was later to hear on the grapevine that he considered me a "pin-striped toff" who was somehow "stuck up" and "snooty", and was always patronising him. Bless!

In fact, I had a high opinion of the tubby little chap. I was impressed, for instance, by how still he could remain on formal occasions, so much so that I took to balancing my glass on his head. And his intellect was not to be underestimated. Quite the opposite: I once informed my colleagues that I thought he had a marvellous little brain in that great fat head of his, and that it would be folly to look down one's nose at him just because he sounded so daft.

During our informal talks with Vice-President Cheney, I made every effort to encourage Prescott and boost his confidence. "Well done! Ten out of ten!" I would exclaim, generously, after he had finished making one of his funny little points to the vice-president. Then – completely off my own bat – I would act as his interpreter. "I think what the Deputy Prime Minister is trying to say is …" I would explain to Cheney and his staff.

As we left the White House, I dipped into my pocket and offered Prescott a $5 note, a reward "for doing so jolly well in there". But he brushed it aside with a degree of discourtesy I was to find all too common among members of the New Labour administration.

As an experienced diplomat with many years training behind me, I would always let the President of the United States go through the door first. I could tell he was highly impressed by this old-fashioned display of English good manners.

In my experience, prime ministers have an unhappy relationship with their clothes. They are not, alas, fertile ground for sartorial suggestions from those of us with a finer sense of style.

"Are you absolutely certain that tie really goes with that suit, Prime Minister?" I asked Blair, in my naturally friendly manner, as he prepared to go to the White House for a meeting with President Bush. He proceeded to thank me curtly for my enquiry, but in the end, to my astonishment, paid it no heed.

Throughout their subsequent meeting, I remained convinced that the tie in question – a far lighter blue than I myself would have chosen – was wholly inappropriate. I later sent the President a memo apologising for the tie in question, but received no reply.

To be frank, I was never greatly impressed by the intellectual firepower of those government ministers who insisted on knocking on the door of my embassy, trying to beg a room for the night. Blair was, I think, somewhat overawed by my greater intelligence. I can understand why. He was hesitant and nervous in my presence. On one memorable occasion, when I was giving him the benefit of a lengthy overview on Anglo-American relations, I noticed that he had closed his eyes, to concentrate on what I was saying. As I got to the crux of my analysis – the bit about the need not to underestimate the Americans, even though they often spoke with strong accents –

I noticed he had begun to breathe deeply, as though determined to take it all in.

I have long prided myself on being an acute judge of character. Human nature is, in fact, a hobby of mine. When I first encountered Tony Blair and Gordon Brown, I wrote this pen-portrait of them, in a private memo to myself: "Blair is the Prime Minister. Of this, I am certain. Brown, on the other hand, is Chancellor of the Exchequer. To my mind, Brown has the stronger accent (might he be Welsh?)."

I added this to my dossier on leading statesmen and world figures. It would prove invaluable to my successors as ambassador to the US. It included pen-portraits of HM the Queen – "she is married, with four children, three boys and a girl" – and, of Ronald Reagan, "former president, quite tall, with, I would hazard a guess, strong Republican tendencies".

Sadly, my superior knowledge of the world gave rise to envy and chippiness among British politicians who would arrive in Washington expecting the red-carpet treatment. Filled with resentment, they would often try to do me down. Once, before dinner at the White House, Tony Blair insisted that he should take my place on the top table – even though he knew full well that I was the British ambassador!

Politicians!

DC Inconsequential (ii):
Why Do I Bother?

IT OCCURRED TO ME recently that when I am dead and gone the words "Beyond Parody" should be carved on my gravestone. It is a phrase I have been muttering a lot recently, dipping into books on the bestseller list. Sharon Osbourne, Jeremy Clarkson, Jordan: the parodist is now largely redundant, all his efforts at absurdity preempted by his intended victims.

Recently, I parodied *DC Confidential*, the memoirs of Sir Christopher Meyer. At that point, I had read only the newspaper serialisations. It occurred to me that I might have been a little mean.

This was, after all, Our Man in Washington. Surely he couldn't be as daft as all that?

Since then, I have read the whole book. It now occurs to me that I wasn't nearly mean enough. Had it been marketed as a novel, penned in the first person by a buffoon, it would be being hailed as a comic classic, a sequel to *Diary of a Nobody*, our hero a model of self-importance and stupidity, his hackles rising at those he sees as barriers to his self-advancement, his knowledge of the world seldom spreading beyond the bounds of received opinion.

Auberon Waugh once wrote that, for years, he wondered how the most conceited bores at his school had somehow disappeared from the face of the earth; only later, when travelling abroad, did he realise they were all running our embassies. *DC Confidential* might have been published simply to prove him right.

Even the cheap, peek-a-boo title is irritating. If the information was confidential, well, it certainly isn't any more. And if it was never confidential, why pretend it was? Meyer reeks a heady combination of stupidity and conceit. On the very first page, he boasts that he got a "scholarship at Peterhouse, the oldest Cambridge college". Alas, "I disappointed my professors by not getting a first-class degree". But by page two his grieving professors are able to wipe away their tears, because he takes the Foreign Office exams and "to my astonishment, I came top".

Heaven knows what those examiners were looking for: presumably, the candidate with the most instinctive command of cliché. Deaths are "untimely", decline "dramatic", attempts "last-ditch" and nerves "stretched to breaking point". On the international scene, Germany is "a mass of contradictions" and France "a fiercely proud nation", while – even more surprising – in Northern Ireland "the hatreds and rivalries between Catholics and Protestants were so deep, you did not know where to start". And the self-aggrandising prefacing quotes to the book – from Palmerston, Clausewitz and Machiavelli – are those that any A-level student knows off pat.

Christopher Meyer is especially incompetent at detailing the incompetence of others. At times, he is like a figure from the *Keystone Kops*, carefully balancing a bucket of water on the top of a door, only to get soaked himself. He complains that John Prescott never liked him. "Somebody said to me that he thought me a pin-striped toff, determined to belittle him." Yet in the very same passage he proves Prescott's suspicions completely accurate, calling him "poor old John Prescott", comparing him to a mastiff and reproducing his verbal absurdities.

There are strong suggestions, too, that, as Our Man in Washington, he tried to suck up to various American bigwigs by poking fun at members of the government he was being paid to represent. In the middle of a paean of praise to Donald Rumsfeld, for instance, he lets on that "Rumsfeld once told me off for trying to imitate George Robertson's Scottish accent". As well he might: Americans like Rumsfeld are taught good manners.

Meyer is far too solipsistic ever to have noticed anything of any significance. He regularly boasts of sending high-powered, etc, etc, reports back to London, but they were obviously the sort of thing that might have been cobbled together by anyone with a television set in their sitting room. 9/11 "proved to be the controversial Giuliani's finest hour"; "Delors was a hate-figure for the Euro-sceptics"; Laura Bush is her husband's "tower of strength". Whatever next? "Hollywood is the capital of the film industry"? "New York is home to many tall buildings known as skyscrapers"?

Throughout the book, Meyer goes on about how necessary it was for him to establish high-powered contacts to garner the inside information of Washington necessary for the top-secret reports he would send to Downing Street. Yet every time he quotes from one of his own reports, it becomes all too evident that his inside knowledge was woefully hand-me-down.

"As I said in one report…" is a phrase that invariably precedes an observation of mind-numbing banality. "As I said in one report," he writes on page 159, "Gore … is more comfortable with policy than politics, with governing than campaigning. A steady vice-president, he is an insecure and inconsistent campaigner." And the British taxpayer bankrolls a staff of four hundred in our Washington embassy to produce such insights!

There is a laziness to much of the writing and research that makes one question Meyer's qualifications to become an embassy doorman, let alone our most senior diplomat. At one point, he writes of Lord Levy (whom he particularly disliked): "If I remember rightly, his son is, or used to be, chief of staff to the Israeli politician Yossi Beilin." At which, as a reader, one wants to scream, "What do you mean, 'if I remember rightly'? Do you remember rightly or don't you? And if you don't, why put it in?"

The range of adjectives at Meyer's command is also bewilderingly small, so that his pen-portraits of bigwigs all tend to meld into one another. Geoff Hoon is "likeable"; Robin Cook "someone more to be admired than liked"; Jack Straw "someone more to be liked than admired", and, as for John Major, "you had to like and admire him". As for John Prescott, "it would be folly to underestimate him" (though he never says why). In this regard, Prescott is just like George W Bush, of whom we are told not only "this was someone not to be underestimated", but also, twenty pages later, "it would be a huge mistake to underestimate him".

Small wonder so many of the characters who encounter His Excellency are bored stiff by him. In a rare moment of perception, he notes that Barbra Streisand "looks bored" as he talked to her at a state dinner at the White House. And Tony Blair himself loses interest as Meyer tries to explain a point he has already mentioned in one of his reports ("Why do I bother? I thought to myself"). The fault, of course, is never his. When the jokes in a speech that he delivers in Milwaukee fail to raise a titter, it is not because they are so unfunny, but because of "a preponderant German influence in the local population".

His new sexy second wife Catherine, with "short skirts and legs to match" (eh?), sounds as though she, too, has a strong nightmarish quality. "With all the enthusiasm of a newcomer Catherine threw herself into restoring the house to something like its pristine glory. She has a natural talent for design, decoration and colour."

Sadly, Catherine takes it amiss when she is told by Whitehall that there may be better ways to spend the money of the folk back home than on fancy new carpets and cushions. "It was a tiring, disillusioning experience for someone of Catherine's energy and enthusiasm, who wanted to show Britain at its best."

Early on in *DC Confidential*, Meyer preeningly quotes the previous ambassador to the US, who apparently said to him: "You are by far the best candidate." Can this really be true? Might they not have been better off picking the worst?

As Sure As Spring Follows Summer: The Non Sequitur Association

IT WAS THE PERFECT weekend for the Non Sequitur Association (motto: *Semper Non Sequitur*) to hold its annual picnic.

"Haven't we been lucky with the weather?" I said to my neighbour on the coach as we sped towards our destination.

"Not to worry," she replied. "We'll easily be back in time for *University Challenge*."

"But isn't it on Tuesdays?" I said.

"I couldn't agree more," she replied, thoughtfully. "But you know what they say about suede."

By this time, I was flummoxed. "Suede?" I said.

"Swayed," she said. "Easily swayed."

"Oh – swayed!" I said.

"It's pronounced swede," she said. "Though it's never been a vegetable I've been particularly fond of. Or a nationality, for that matter. Not that it does matter, of course."

This year's Secretary of the NSA is Janet Street-Porter, so it had fallen to her to arrange our annual picnic. The invitation had been composed with all her customary bravura. "The coach will leave at midday," it said. "So with all this war stuff going on in Iraq, let's hope the government finally decides to do something about halfway-decent funding for the arts and at long last provides adequate nursery school provision for those who need it least."

We occupied our time on the journey by joining in with some of our favourite singalong songs – a marvellous mix of old and new such as "Una Paloma Gan Goolie" and "Bridge Over Troubled Quartermaster's Stores" and, to kick off the proceedings, "God Save the Yellow Submarine". Janet insisted that the coach left the motorway at every exit, going once or twice around each roundabout before resuming its journey. "It's so much quicker that way," she explained. "Especially if you've had something to eat, or if you're feeling a bit chilly."

After our sing-songs, Marina Warner, our official archivist, delivered a most interesting talk on the history of the Non Sequitur Association, taking in the Virgin Mary, Walt Disney, the Knights Templar, James Joyce and the Channel Tunnel. "The Non Sequitur Movement grew out of an increasing dissatisfaction with what its founders saw as society's obsession with sticking to the point," she explained. "As children, they had always been led to believe that one thing leads to another, but they had begun to suspect that this might not be so. And after a number of experiments on goldfish, daffodils and woodlice, they came to realise that the opposite was the case, and that, far from one thing leading to another, it now seemed much more likely that – now, where was I?"

By the end of Marina's lecture, we all felt that we understood a good deal more about recent developments in Western Philosophy, the musicals of Stephen Sondheim and the everyday care and maintenance of household plants. But by now we were all feeling a bit peckish, so after a quick rendition of "One Man Went to Mow, Mow a Bicycle Made for Two", we were delighted to find that the coach had at last arrived at its destination. Our treasurer, Ivan Massow, called for a vote of thanks. "I'm sure we'd all like to thank Ms Warner for her interesting and illuminating talk," he said. "And to wish her a speedy recovery."

"Everybody out!" called the driver, Peter Bottomley. "And might I remind passengers upon alighting to sit well back in their seats for safety and comfort, as a refusal can offend."

"Red or white?" I asked the lady sitting next to me on the picnic rug.

"I'll have the brown, please," she replied. "They say it's so much healthier than the white. Of course, there's a lot of talk these days about health, isn't there? But what I always say is that you're only as old as the crow flies, and the early bird catches the worm."

"Russell Crowe's undoubtedly a marvellous actor," chipped in the man to her left. "But for my money Pavarotti's got the better voice."

"My father taught me never to trust a man with a beard," replied the lady. "Because, let's face it, it's been proven that smoking can lead to cancer."

A lively discussion ensued, excellently chaired by Janet Street-Porter. She then brought us all to order, and called for us to dig deep into our pockets for a show of hands. "Please raise your arms if you agree," she said.

I felt confused. "Agree with what?" I asked.

"First things first," she snapped. "That's to be decided after the vote."

On the way back, I reflected on the great leaps forward the Non Sequitur Association has made recently, with our members now featuring each week as experts on the *Today* programme and *Question Time*. And who'd have thought that the President of the United States would agree to be next year's secretary, weather permitting?

Two Vital Questions

I) CAN YOU GET TO SPACE IN A LIFT?

The American space agency, NASA, has announced it will invest several million dollars in the development of a space elevator capable of delivering satellites, spacecraft and people thousands of kilometres into space along a single vertical track.

Apparently, the space elevator would be operated by a cable reaching up as far as 100,000 kilometres from the surface of the earth, with the earthbound end tethered to a base station, probably somewhere in the middle of the Pacific Ocean.

Personally, I love travelling in lifts, but only by myself. The twinned senses of complete solitude and unimpeded progress cannot be duplicated by any other form of travel. On the other hand, travelling in lifts with strangers is almost unbearably tense and embarrassing. Something about the physical proximity and the enclosed conditions makes conversation dry up even before the floor-buttons have been pressed.

The moment the doors shut, looks between strangers become so charged with unwanted meaning that everyone spends their time frantically trying to avoid exchanging glances with anyone else. This means that they all end up swivelling their eyes all over the place –

the ceiling, the floor, the walls – rather in the nervy, cornered manner of Andrew Lloyd Webber.

I have been unable to obtain details as to the exact speed at which passengers in the space elevator can expect to travel. But even the most up-to-date lifts take a minute or two to get to the top of the tallest skyscrapers. The high-speed lifts in the Sears Tower in Chicago operate at just over twenty miles, or nearly thirty-two kilometres, per hour. At this speed, anyone planning to stay in the space lift for the full haul of 100,000 kilometres should allow 3,125 hours, or well over four months, for the completion of their journey.

Timing would be all. I would be extra careful to step into the lift only when it was empty and I was completely sure no one else was around. Of course, one can never be sure: often you think you have a lift all to yourself only to find, just as you smugly press the button and the doors begin to close, that various ungainly strangers you thought were safely in the distance have made a dash for it and somehow managed to barge their way into the lift at the very last minute.

Lifts are cramped at the best of times, but they will become even more so if every passenger insists on wearing a bulbous space-suit with showy fish-bowl helmet. Worse still, NASA, like some leading department stores, may well insist its lifts are not passenger-operated. This will mean that even the canniest traveller will find himself saddled with a commissionaire in braided uniform standing by the buttons ready to announce one's arrival ("top floor: outer space, stars and sundry planets") after the full four months.

Like so many of NASA's recent projects, this one requires much more careful planning. And have they given the slightest thought to their choice of background music? A light orchestral version of "Yesterday" can lend variety to a trip up three or four floors, but after 100,000 kilometres, it may well begin to pall.

(September 18, 2003)

II) IS THERE LIFE ON MARS?
Astronomers at the giant radio telescope at Arecibo in Puerto Rico have heard signals that modulate in what has been described as "a strange and seemingly unnatural way". Some eminent astronomers

believe that these peculiar noises, recorded on three different occasions, may have been transmitted by aliens.

Of course, the truth may be more prosaic. I wonder if they have ever heard of Chris Moyles in Puerto Rico? The intermittent grunts that emanate for three hours a day from this Radio 1 disc jockey bear an uncanny similarity to the "strange and seemingly unnatural" noises seized upon by the Puerto Rican astronomers. This would be sad news indeed for those hoping for signs of intelligent life.

But many in the astronomic community remain optimistic that these noises came from creatures from outer space. Writing in the *Daily Mail*, the Astronomer Royal, Professor Sir Martin Rees, described the news from Puerto Rico as "fascinating and surprising". He added: "There may be a lot more life out there than we could ever detect. The fact that we don't seem to have had alien visitors so far should not make us sceptical about the Arecibo results. It would be far harder to traverse the mind-boggling distances of interstellar space than to transmit a message."

Rees argues that if these strange signals were, indeed, transmitted by aliens, they would have taken quite a time to get here, since they would have travelled nearly 183 trillion miles across space to reach us. This means that whatever it is that they were trying to tell us would now lack zip. I know this because in my bathroom I have a pile of back numbers of the *Spectator* magazine which I sometimes dip into. I am regularly surprised by the speed with which even the most urgent and authoritative pronouncements ("*Why Blair must fear IDS*"; "*Mowlam to oust Blair by 2003*") grow stale.

But Sir Martin Rees remains buoyant. "It makes sense for us earthlings to listen, rather than transmit. Any two-way exchange would take decades at least, so there would be time to plan a measured response," he suggests, while admitting that: "In the long run a dialogue could develop, but not snappy repartee."

This could be extremely problematic. With a minimum of ten years between each response, even the briefest of civilities – eg "Hello there!" "Hello! How are you?" "Very well, thank you. And yourself?" "Ooh, can't complain" – would take four decades to get through. Anyone starting such an exchange aged thirty would be seventy before he had asked a proper question, and eighty before he received a reply.

Which interviewer should we humans entrust with this sluggish dialogue? It would have to be someone with the necessary kudos to impress our alien friends, who may be a bit snobbish in that direction. Greg Dyke is available, but he might put them off by pulling out one of his horrid little cards saying "Cut the Crap", just when they were getting going. No: we must look for a broadcaster with proven interviewing abilities. John Humphrys? Lacks the patience. Jonathan Ross? Too coarse. Parkinson? Good at taking things slowly, but bound to be upset by the dearth of household names in outer space.

My own choice would be good old Simon Dee (*"Dee Time! Da-da-da-da Dee Time!"*), whose involuntary retirement in the early 1970s has given him plenty of practice in kicking his heels. I am sure he would now be happy to play with his clipboard while his interviewee's reply trudged the 183 trillion miles across outer space.

Sir Martin Rees concludes his piece with the declaration: "I, for one, would be massively disappointed if all our searches for alien life were doomed to fail. We would then feel truly alone in a vast, uncaring cosmos." This raises a number of points. First, human nature is such that there would never come a day when those who spend their time searching for aliens would decide that there were no aliens to be found. Loch Ness is, we are told, quite a bit smaller than outer space. No monster has ever been found in it, but this serves only to inspire dedicated monster-hunters to even greater heights of certainty that one exists.

Second, Rees imagines that, if it could be proved alien life did not exist, we would be desperately upset – "we would then feel truly alone in a vast, uncaring cosmos". Yet my own sense of well-being has nothing to do with believing that the outer reaches of the universe are jam-packed with doe-eyed creatures with sympathetic half-smiles who care one way or the other about how I am getting on. Or is there really a planet 183 trillion miles away that is populated by thousands of Esther Rantzen lookalikes, all of them gearing up to present us with our very own Hearts of Gold?

(September 7, 2004)

Did I What On Holidays My
by John Prescott

THE DEPUTY *Prime Minister, John Prescott, recently returned from holiday with a spring in his step, urging Labour backbenchers to "shut up for the summer".*

In this exclusive diary, Mr Prescott asks colleagues to "hink thong and lard" about "getting away to the shun and sea". He continues: "As the old saying goes, a rest is as good as a mile, and I urge you all to get out the old check dare and put up your feet, if any."

MONDAY: This the is life! I'm on holiday, and frankly my idea of a holiday is to go on vacation, I bake no moans about it. To my mind, nothing beats pesting by a rule while the bun seats down. With band in my sucket, I expect to be having built a superbulous range of much-needed sandcastles by the time this holiday, or holidays, has terminated as per expectations permitting.

First offs, it's breakfast in the hotel, and what a magnificent spread of comestibles they have provisioned for available guests. What I always say is when in Spain do as the French do and order yourself that Full English Breakfast you've always been promised to yourselves and others throughout the annual year ahead. At the end of the day, nothing beats breakfast by which I do not wish to infer-ate that I have my breakfast at the end of the day. I don't – I have it at the beginning of the day, which is the right time to have it, at the end of the day.

What I always like is a nice spoiled egg and soldiers, washed down with a tug of me and a round of hot-tuttered boast.

"More tea, sir?" says the waitress. After vital consideration the matter further, I come to the conclusive that I could when all is dead and sun manage one additionalised cup, so I give her the go-ahead pertainerising to the matter in hand.

TUESDAY: Let's be fright quank about this. Sometimes, the find-ing of the hotel swimming pool and surrounding facilities is not as easy as it may or may not look. So I go up to the receptional desk and negotiate for the bloke in charge to draw me up a long-perm tan and easy-mead rap as to how to be getting to the recreational-ising area.

I dive headfirst into the pool. The guests on the sun-loungers all make no end of fuss and complainerise that they've been splashed. I take the brave decision to confront them head-on. I'm not a man to wince my merdes, but on the alternative hand, I am very much concernivated to establish a broad measure of agreement so we can go forward in a spirit of mutual brotherhood.

"Can I say this one thing to you all in terms of something you should already should have knowing?" I say, reconciliatingly. "It's just that having all matters being taken into consideration with due accord, I have no hestitational in pointing out, cloud and leer, that if you didn't want to get wet, you shouldn't be lying about on your fat arses around this pimming swool in question. May I further remind you of the old saying – 'If you can't stand the kitchen, stay out of the garden, Maud.'"

WEDNESDAY: Out for a walk along the promenade, I hear the familiaral chimes of an ice-cream van. "You know, I could murder a lanilla volley," I say to the wady life.

I join the queue. "Oi! Get to the back of the queue, fatty," says a rude man.

"Don't get me wrong," I say. "I can understand your reasons for wanting me to join the queue at the back, not the front. But to you I say this. If you want to make the criticisms, make the criticisms. That's your fright, and if you think I shouldn't have joined the queue at the front, then I am fully supportivate your right in coming to that conclusion. But once you've finished prattling on with your criticisms, let's talk about how this queue's lying out crowd for a sense of real leadership, and how it should welcome direct initiatives at this point in time."

THURSDAY: A life on the ocean-based waves! I order a lacked punch and charter a bowing rote. The wady life and my own good self set sail. After six years, the sea is one of the most remuckable achievements of this Lewd Neighbour government. The tides continue to run on time, the salt content is steady and the waves remain very, very wet. So can I this saying to some of my colleagues: when it comes to the sea, let's not forget to forgive ourselves a jolly good bat on the pack, shall we?

FRIDAY: I observate there's a performance on at the theatre on the pier, so we decide to shake in a toe.

It's a conjuror, a bit like Tony only not so good. First, he produces a habit out of a rat, then he puts a lady in a box and proceduralises to hut her in calf. My colleague Clare Short is without a job and must be looking for a painful ghost, so I make a memo to myself to tell her to applicate for this one.

Mr Memory ends the show. He claims he can rememberise everything, and gets the audience to ask him any question. "OK, pal!" I yell out. "So can you list the greatest achievements after six years of this Lewd Neighbour governmental?"

Mr Memory goes ever so quiet, so after a dissent interval, I provide him with the correct answerable.

"We're still in power!" I say. And believe you me, that's a record to sing from the tooth-rots.

(August 2, 2003)

Monaco Twinned with Babylon

MEASURING 485 ACRES, or less than one square mile, Monaco is roughly the size of Hyde Park, and five times smaller than Richmond Park. Its population is 31,000, which is less than the population of Oswestry. Would one of today's leading Hollywood actresses – Julia Roberts, say, or Catherine Zeta-Jones – fall for the Lord Mayor of Oswestry?

It is worth bearing these details in mind when contemplating what J Randy Taraborrelli* believes to be the fairytale grandeur of the Grimaldis of Monaco.

Francesco Grimaldi first entered Monaco in 1297, disguised as a

---

* *Once Upon a Time: The Story of Princess Grace, Prince Rainier and their Family* by J Randy Taraborrelli

monk. With a small gang of thugs, he scaled the cliffs, killed the palace guards and took over as ruler. Thus was borne a dynasty that might have walked straight off the set of an Ealing comedy, though in recent years it seems to have been rather more heavily influenced by *Confessions of a Window Cleaner*.

"There is no property or inheritance tax, no military service, no unemployment, just fun and sun," writes Taraborrelli. "Why would anyone live anywhere else?" He neglects to mention that it is also claustrophobic, grabby and soulless, its residents united only in their desire to avoid tax.

Did Grace Kelly know what she was letting herself in for? In 1955, she was the toast of Hollywood, the Oscar-winning star of marvellous films like *Rear Window* and *Dial M for Murder*. Though Taraborrelli is irritatingly evasive when it comes to exact figures ("today, such detail about fleeting romances and youthful indiscretions serves little purpose"), it is fair to say that the young Grace Kelly had been a few times round the block. "She screwed everybody who she came into contact with," was the way one former boyfriend put it in an earlier biography.

"Grace had more lovers in a month than I did in a lifetime," said Zsa Zsa Gabor. This makes it all the more odd that she should finally settle for Prince Rainier of Monaco, a podgy little man with a moustache who, in the more flattering photographs, bears more than a fleeting resemblance to Private Walker in *Dad's Army*.

Even Taraborrelli finds it an uphill task to present Rainier as a fairytale prince. "His was an assemblage of features that came together to create a face that was, at least to Grace's eyes, unusually attractive," he writes. (On the other hand, Taraborrelli often finds it hard to convey sexual attraction: of Grace, he reveals that Rainier "liked the way her lips parted and moved when she spoke".)

Perhaps to impress her father Jack Kelly, who had always yearned to be accepted by the upper reaches of Philadelphia society, Grace opted to become a princess. Rainier's manner of proposing must be considered among the naffest of all time: over pears in poached wine, he handed Grace a parcel, saying, "If you are to be at my side, then you may need this." Grace unwrapped it, to find a glossy, full-colour history of the Grimaldis of Monaco. "This is gonna be the biggest news of all time," gushed Jack when he heard about it.

Monaco's status as a tax-haven was riding on Grace's fertility – if Rainier did not produce a successor, an ancient treaty meant France could reclaim the prinicipality – so before becoming a princess, Grace was obliged to undergo a medical examination to ensure her Fallopian tubes were in working order. Her main worry seems to have been that the doctor might betray her lack of virginity to her future husband. "Maybe I will say I was in some kind of sporting accident in school," she said to a friend.

Thankfully, the doctor kept his lips sealed, but Rainier then presented Grace and her family with two more hurdles. First, he wanted a dowry of $2million, which they eventually agreed to pay. Second, he wanted Grace to sign a marriage agreement which, among other things, would have made her responsible for outstanding palace bills. "Does he think I just fell off the turnip truck?" said Jack Kelly.

The wedding itself makes Michael Douglas and Catherine Zeta-Jones look like paragons of restraint. Three miles of red carpet were laid throughout Monaco, and Aristotle Onassis hired a seaplane to drop thousands of red and white carnations over everyone. In return for documentary rights, MGM agreed to pay for basic essentials such as the wedding dress, and on top of all this Rainier made $450,000 from the sale of commemorative stamps.

Grace left the church the most titled woman in the world – not only a princess, but twice a duchess, once a viscountess, eight times a countess, four times a marchioness and nine times a baroness. So much for Zsa Zsa Gabor, who would have had to marry twenty-five different men to achieve the same score. The only blot on the horizon was that our own Queen sent a telegram refusing to attend. "The fact that we have never met is irrelevant," harrumphed Rainier. "This is still a slap in the face."

Alas, it didn't take long for it to dawn on the newly enthroned Princess Grace that life in a casino with a few acres of principality attached would be far from fun, especially as she was not allowed to leave the palace without either her husband or her lady-in-waiting (like Dame Edna's, an Australian called Madge).

It soon emerged that Grace and her husband had little in common. Rainier loathed the theatre and the movies, and would fall asleep at the opera. He preferred cars, skin-diving and donning his apron to barbecue steaks. He refused to let Grace continue her acting career, or, in his words, go "parading about on a movie screen with an actor, doing who knows what".

But Grace bit back. Having urged Rainier to get rid of his sister Antoinette, who was busy plotting for her own son, Christian, to inherit the throne, she took the matter into her own hands by summoning Antoinette and telling her she must go. Antoinette said that she would go and pack her bags, at which point Grace told her that would be unnecessary: they were being packed as they spoke.

In time, Grace crumpled, giving way to Rainier and the creepy inhabitants of Monaco, turning down all offers of films, including the lead in *Marnie*, and wearing the chilly mask of grandeur until it ate into her face. As a result, Rainier began to appreciate Grace.

When their eldest daughter Caroline was still a child, Grace would spend her time leafing through the *Almanac de Gotha* in search of a suitable husband for her. Inevitably, Caroline had other ideas, and married the smooth-talking Lothario Philippe Junot ("Caroline loved my energy, my zest for life"), who chose to celebrate their engagement by pulling down his trousers in a nightclub and pouring a bottle of Johnnie Walker over his private parts.

Their wedding was a triumph for bad taste, the high point coming when Rainier and Caroline kicked off the celebrations by dancing to "Sweet Caroline" by Neil Diamond. Once again, our Queen gave it the thumbs-down, and even the Norwegian, Belgian and Dutch Royal families decided it wasn't worth the cost of the air ticket. Afterwards, when the two went off on honeymoon together, Philippe forgot to tell Caroline that he was bringing along a cameraman so that he could earn extra cash from the photos. These days, twenty years after Grace's fatal car crash, Caroline has taken on the mantle of grandeur: she is at present on non-speaks with the saucy Princess Stephanie, whose former husband Daniel was once videotaped having sex with the former Miss Bare Breasts of Belgium.

Faced with so much evidence that Monaco is twinned with Babylon, J Randy Taraborrelli is stalwart in his defence of it, believing it to be a sort of Eden with roulette wheels. In his curious language, loosely based on English, he maintains that the moral of Grace's tale is: "Sometimes, the real challenge of living has to do with making a life that seems to no longer work, *work*." But most readers will be left wishing that the doctor who examined Grace had snitched to Prince Rainier, and that she had been sent back to Hollywood, where they do these things so much better.

Home Office

Five Stay at Home and Watch Telly

"I SAY!" said Julian, pluckily. "Let's embark on a big adventure!"

"Rather!" said Dick, joyfully. "I vote we sail to Kirrin Island and explore the shipwreck there! Who knows? It may contain smugglers' treasure!"

"Good idea, Julian!" agreed Anne.

"I can't wait!" exclaimed George.

"Woof! Woof!" barked Timmy, their lovable scamp, covering George's hands with licks.

"I think Timmy agrees!" said Dick, and the four of them all rolled around with laughter.

"Make sure you scrub those hands of yours, George!" said George's mother. "Or else you'll catch the latest life-threatening germ transported on dogs' tongues from the Far East and we will have to put you on a debilitating course of antibiotics! I heard about it on the *Today* programme!"

* * *

The next morning, the Famous Five awoke early, eager to embark on their big adventure. They planned to take the pony and trap to the water's edge, then row over to the island at low tide.

"Wizard!" said Dick.

The Famous Five rushed out of Kirrin Cottage bubbling over with excitement.

"Don't forget to tie your shoes up tight, children!" shouted George's father after them. "In some areas of the country, up to two per cent of admissions to casualty are caused by people failing to tie their shoes up tight, sometimes resulting in hideously crippling injuries!"

Having double-checked their laces, the children climbed into the trap.

"Has everybody got their High Factor Skin Protection Lotion on?" asked George's mother. "After all, the sun might come out, and we don't want you catching skin cancer, now, do we?"

"Yes, Mother!" sighed George.

"And are you wearing your protective clothing?" piped up George's father. "An increasing number of children are allergic to grass! And watch out for flies, wasps, buttercups, cattle, birds and life-threatening flowers! And don't fall into a cow pat, or you'll go blind!"

* * *

Soon they were ready for offs. Julian was saying "Giddy-up" when a strange man appeared before them.

"Halt!" he said. "Do you have a licence for this pony and trap? And are you all over the age of eighteen? And I trust you are in possession of the necessary government Trap Proficiency Certificates?"

"Gosh!" said Julian, despondently. "Who are you?"

"I am your local Health and Safety Officer," said the man, grudgingly, "and I advise you to alight from that vehicle."

From out of the blue, another man appeared alongside him carrying a clipboard. "Who is the owner of this quadruped?" he barked.

"I think you mean Freckles the Pony!" exclaimed Julian, proudly. "I am his master! And who are you?"

"Animal Welfare," replied the second man, brandishing a grand-looking badge. "This quadruped is not suitable for passenger haulage…"

"…and it constitutes a potential hazard to motor vehicles," added a third man, who, it turned out, was a senior figure in the Road Vehicles Inspectorate.

At this point, poor Anne burst into tears.

"Oi! Oi! Textbook signs of potential child abuse!" observed a passing Health Visitor. "Tell us all about it, dear."

George sighed. "It looks like we'll have to walk to the sea!" she exclaimed.

"Woof! Woof!" agreed Timmy.

* * *

"Here we are – at last!" exclaimed Dick, who was the first to catch sight of the sea, just past the "DANGER: SEA" sign.

"Gosh, what a lovely time we are going to have!" said George. George was dressed exactly like a boy in jeans and a jersey.

George's mother and father had registered her with the local child psychologist, and George seemed to be responding well.

Julian began throwing pebbles into the sea. "To see how far you can send them is the most splendid fun!" he said.

"But it's against the guidelines," added an official from Heritage Coastline. "Not only is this coast subject to erosion, but a passing fish could easily be injured by one of those stones. And don't you kids realise you should never pick up a stone without a trained adult in attendance – it could have a sharp edge!"

The Five went off to the secret cave where they had hidden their boat the summer before. "I say! Our cave's been filled in with cement!" said Dick. "This Information Board says that it's all part of the Department of the Environment's hugely successful Crackdown on Caves Initiative!"

"Oh well," sighed George. "We could always make a camp fire and cook ourselves some bangers, I suppose!" But at that moment, an alarm sounded, loud and clear. It was the local Fire Prevention Officer arriving in his van with his friend from the Uncooked Sausages Inspectorate. So the Famous Five were forced to abandon their plans for a big adventure.

"We could always have a SMALL adventure, I suppose!" sighed Anne, despairingly.

"I know!" exclaimed Julian. "Let's all sit in front of the telly at home and stuff ourselves full of fatty foods!"

"Last one to grow clinically obese is a cissy!" added Dick, excitedly.

The Laughing Politician

THE MOST POSITIVE role model for our police service is surely the Laughing Policeman, "a fat and jolly red-faced man". So the decision by the Home Office to put an end to speed and agility tests when recruiting for the police service is to be welcomed.

Up to now, one in every two women has failed the tests, which involve running "slalom style" through a series of cones in under twenty-seven seconds. But now fatties everywhere are to be welcomed into the police service, and once again our streets will be alive with the sound of laughter:

So if you chance to meet him
Whilst walking round the town
Shake him by his fat old hand
And give him half a crown.
His eyes will beam and sparkle
He'll gurgle with delight
And then you'll see him laughing
With all his blessed might!

I feel the time is now right to encourage fatter MPs to come forward as well. The last few years have seen a notable drop in weight among MPs, with a consequent rise in small-mindedness. At the moment, the sole fuller-figured member of the Cabinet is the Education Secretary, Charles Clarke. It could be argued, of course, that he is not all that jolly. However, close study of a photograph of him reveals that if you rotate it 180 degrees, his face remains almost exactly the same but now appears to be smiling. From now on, Mr Clarke might consider the PR advantages in adopting the handstand position before embarking on his speeches in the House of Commons.

(May 24, 2003)

My Royal Appointment
by Gyles Brandreth

TO COMMEMORATE the fiftieth anniversary of Her Majesty's accession, veteran social correspondent GYLES BRANDRETH was granted privileged access to the Queen.

Wednesday, November 8, 2001
The Queen never misses a trick. Her courtiers confirm that she has an extraordinarily sharp eye for whatever is going on. As she stepped

out of her carriage today, she must have noticed the number of umbrellas because – quick as the proverbial flash – an observant sovereign immediately observed: "Is it raining?"

Sure enough, it was pelting down. "You can't pull the wool over Her Majesty's eyes," the Comptroller of the Royal Wellingtons confided in me as we accompanied her down the rain-sodden streets. "Even if you pretend it's sunny, she'll always notice it's raining. It might surprise a lot of paid-up republicans, but she has an expert eye for rain. Never misses a drop."

Friday, November 10, 2001

I greet the Duke of Edinburgh, dear old friend and quaffing partner, with a friendly slap on the back. As always, I am delighted to find him in robust form. "Who the hell are you?" he says, with his usual gruff good humour. "Have we been introduced? Get to the back of the queue!"

I roar with my trademark laughter. It is his little joke. The last time we bumped into each other, just fifteen years ago, he said exactly the same thing. His pretending not to know who I am has become what one might call a "standing joke" between us.

Of course he knows exactly who I am. In 1968, I was privileged to be presented to him when he honoured the offices of the *Spectator* with a royal visit. We struck up an immediate rapport. "What do you do, then? Bugger all, I suppose!" he quipped. I immediately applauded this brilliantly quick remark.

"And stop that infernal clapping!" he added, in that familiar tone, before passing on to the next person with a characteristic stamp of his foot. It was at that point that I realised how very much we had in common. We had that all-too-rare thing, commonly known as "rapport".

Today, I approach him as he turns on his heels. I inform him that I have – for my sins! – been granted privileged access to his "better half". "She may well like to be presented to me," I add, agreeably. "We have a great deal in common. She, too, is a lover of the Great Outdoors."

"Some people are the bloody limit!" replies the Duke, in mock indignation. A born comedian!

"Absolutely!" I say with a chuckle, setting him at his ease. "Couldn't have put it better myself! I must say, m'lud, you are simply MARVELLOUS for your age!"

Monday, December 21, 2001

I am privileged to accompany Her Majesty around the Obesity Unit of the new Farnsworth Hospital. She is in a dress of peacock blue with an elegant straw hat with pink brocade. Her lady-in-waiting informs me she has made it a firm rule never to wear slacks on official visits. I myself am wearing a dark brown Harris tweed suit with sensible check shirt and sober light green woollen tie. It is what people expect.

The Queen speaks to an obese inmate, a man in his forties. Her Majesty avoids the temptation to call him Fatty, or poke him in the tummy.

"She has enormous tact," her lady-in-waiting confides.

I approach the patient once the Queen has moved on. He seems delighted at their meeting. "What a gracious lady," he says.

I set him at his ease. "I bet you're relieved she didn't get the giggles or call you unkind names like Fatty Pants or Porky Pig!" I say.

Before each royal arrival, there is a heightened sense of expectation, leading to nervous laughter from those due to be presented. When the Queen arrives in the outpatients ward, I attempt to break the ice.

"Good morning, ma'am," I say (pronouncing the "ma'am" to rhyme with "Clapham", as is correct).

"It's nice and warm in here," she observes. I lead the laughter.

"Boom! Boom!" I say. Within minutes, there are tears literally rolling down my cheeks. Her Majesty is, when all is said and done, a natural comic with a perfect sense of timing.

January 6, 2002

To an exhibition of driftwood jewellery at the Commonwealth Institute. I am waiting for Her Majesty in the company of Denis MacShane, MP, a junior Foreign Office Minister. He is still recovering from the excitement of playing host to Her Majesty three weeks ago.

"Have you noticed how she wears her hats so well?" he observes, respectfully. "Always firmly on the head. And she's brilliant with gloves, too. She knows where to put every single finger, one in each slot. I've never seen her get it wrong."

She arrives in lilac coat and matching hat. She approaches a figure holding a labrador on a lead.

"Ah," she says. "A dog."

"She gets it right every time," the Lord Lieutenant of the country whispers to me. "Marvellous with animals."

January 9, 2002

Visiting Cardiff with Her Majesty, I decide after close consideration to wear my dark made-to-measure pinstripe suit with a pink-and-white spotted tie. It is what people expect. The Queen is wearing her customary coat, dress and hat. I feel desperately embarrassed that my own perfectly judged Savile Row splendour will divert attention from her, but decide on a policy of least said, soonest mended.

"Wales is very important," she tells me as we sweep into the St Swithin Day-Care Centre for the Elderly. I roar with good-natured laughter, and repeat her little joke to the assembled line of nurses so as to "set them at their ease".

We are greeted in the day room by a massed band and male voice choir, all performing a fanfare of *Vivat Regina* while fifty school-children dressed as druids and leeks enact some sort of Welsh pageant. I study the Queen's face throughout: she doesn't yawn or raise her eyes to the ceiling once.

"Very Welsh, ma'am!" I whisper as the whole effort appears to be drawing to an end. I attempt (unsuccessfully, I may add!) to stifle a giggle at my own jest. I then make my famous comical hand-pinching-the-nose chain-pulling gesture that has set many a dinner table a-roar. Greatly to her credit, Her Majesty manages to maintain a straight face. She then looks at me with what on anyone else would appear to be a furious expression, but which I know to be a face full of natural empathy and good humour.

The Lord Lieutenant tells me Her Majesty's tour of the day-care centre for the elderly has been planned meticulously over the past six months. Yet still they couldn't somehow devise a route avoiding all those old people! I decide to "help her out" by briefing her before each encounter and steering her away from obvious danger zones.

"Ca-veee! Definitely one to avoid, ma'am!" I hiss in her ear as she approaches an old bird who looks, to my practised eye, a little over-keen on meeting her. But Her Majesty is obviously a little hard of hearing.

She then falls into the trap of asking the old dear where she lives. This prompts a tedious reply involving street names and so on. Is it just me, or does she look bored stiff? Stifling the impulse to say, "I told you so!", I step into the breach with an amusing anecdote.

"Did I ever tell you, ma'am, of my chance encounter with the late, great Arthur Askey?" I ask, attempting to steer her away. I then embark on my famous (or – I dare say – infamous!!!) rendition of "*Buzz-Buzz-Buzz, Buzzy-Bee, Buzzy-Bee*", complete with hilarious flapping wings.

"I'm not sure that's particularly helpful," comments Her Majesty, and continues to talk to the tiresome old lady.

It is at times like this that one does well to remember that the Queen is, beneath it all, a human being, just like you or I. Small wonder she is miffed! Few of us like to see our thunder stolen – and my Arthur Askey routine is, I am reliably informed, second to none.

January 15, 2002

"Aren't those daffodils lovely?" Her Majesty confides in me as we tour the Wiltshire countryside.

"Funny you should say that, ma'am," I tell her, setting her at her ease. "The daffodil is one of my very favourite flowers, so I know a fair amount about it. Typically yellow, with a fair bit of green foliage, and most plentiful in this country, particularly in the spring. The tulip, on the other hand, is generally red, or at any rate reddish, and is, I believe, one of the most successful exports of the Netherlands, where they speak Dutch, fend off the sea and ride bicycles."

Looking down, I note Her Majesty has removed her gloves to place one forefinger in her left ear, the other in her right ear. She is humming to herself. Delightful! She took piano lessons from an early age, and was, I believe, a hugely gifted young pupil. Blessed with a musical ear, I pick up the tune and hum along.

January 22, 2002

To Buckingham Palace, to attend an investiture. Prince Philip greets me with his usual affectionate male banter. "What the hell are you doing here?" he jests. "I thought I told them to keep you away!"

I roar with infectious laughter as he turns on his heel – but with perfect timing I catch him just as he reaches the door. "You are an irrepressible old character, sir!" I congratulate him. "A national treasure, forsooth!"

At this point, the Prince raises a good-natured fist and socks me in the mouth.

"Marvellous, sir!" I enthuse, picking up my front teeth from the beautifully polished floor. "Have you ever heard my immortal anecdote about my meeting with Henry Cooper? Oh, but you MUST!"

Home Decoration:
Terence Conran's Q&A

Q. Sir Terence, how did you set about designing Osama bin Laden's famous home in Afghanistan? G W, Wilts.

A. Osama came to me in search of something very secluded, very intimate and intensely private – simple, but with a practical edge. I hit upon the idea of a rather stark, rather gorgeous cave, which he adored, and then I filled it with the most marvellous group of Taliban fanatics, all in richly distressed robes. "But there's something missing!" I said. "I know – beards!" And so we set about sticking beards on them all. The effect was pure Bloomsbury, with a hint of Bauhaus.

Q. Could you tell us, Sir Terence, how you came to design the so-called Black Hole of Calcutta? H Ogden, Cheam.

A. It was a project that excited me hugely. At the time that my client, the young Nawab of Bengal, Siraj-ud-Daulah, first got in touch, back in 1756, everyone was going in for truly dreadful mauves and lilacs.

So when Siraj told me he was after a marvellous new hole concept, I seized the opportunity. "I know!" I said. "Let's make it black!" But by that stage, I had grown tired of vast, open spaces. So

1740s! No – I was after something much more intimate. So I sat down and designed a tiny room with just two small windows, capable of holding up to one hundred people, or 146 if stacked. People still talk about the Black Hole to this day. I've created many other holes in my time, but none quite so black or Calcutta-ish. It was all hugely exciting.

Q: Tell me, Sir Terence, how in the mid- to late Seventies you set about bringing a thoroughly modern sense of design to the premises which belonged to the Old Lady Who Lived in a Shoe? H Dumpty, Wallsend.
A: It was hugely exciting. I had just finished designing the very first fully working car – up until that time everyone had sat in the shell of a car, with their legs sticking out of the bottom, running as fast as they could – when the Old Lady commissioned me to redesign her shoe as a workable living space. First, she had far too many children, so we got rid of them. Then we opened up the heel and the toes and put bean bags in the instep.

Finally, we bought the shoe for ourselves, converted it into a marvellous new store, and evicted the Old Lady, which was all hugely exciting.

Q.Tell me, Sir Terence, what did people used to sit on before you invented the chair in the early 1960s? Mr C Crawley, Herts.
A. There was no actual "sitting down" as such. Until I came up with the chair, people would stand up for up to eight hours at a stretch. But by halfway through '64, my whole chair concept had really caught on, and people were sitting down on chairs all over the country. It was hugely exciting.

Q. And you must also be very proud of having designed the first window. How did this come about? Ms Joy Greenly, N1.
A. It was hugely exciting. Some people don't realise quite how dreary life was before I invented the whole "window" concept. In the 1950s, people simply stood around indoors in the dark. For years, I grappled with the whole problem of how to look through a wall and at the same time get some light into a room. Then I discovered that by cutting a hole in the wall, that gap between "inside" and

"outside" could be bridged. It was almost as exciting as the moment when I hit upon the whole concept of the "door".

Q. Terence, what are your worst failings? S Bayley, Liverpool.
A. A tricky one, but here goes! My sense of humour. My passionate belief in hugely exciting design. My love of people. My clarity of vision. My overwhelming enthusiasm. My need to change the world for the better.

CCTV Personalities

FEW OF US would care to have our shopping bags subjected to public scrutiny. Whenever I visit a supermarket, I am intensely aware of the nosy parkers behind me in the queue, all of them impatiently surveying my drab purchases for any sign of improper living.

"Why would one man need all that bubble bath?" "Wouldn't someone his size be better off with low-fat milk?" "Surely he won't be employing all that toilet paper!" These are the sort of impertinent comments I imagine forming in their minds.

So my sympathy goes out to the disc jockey Chris Evans, whose recent purchases have been detailed in the newspapers. His twenty-minute shopping spree at the Godalming Waitrose resulted in a trolley laden, we are told, with twenty-four cans of Foster's Lager at £16.98, twelve cans of Carlsberg lager at £8.69, five bottles of French Chardonnay from the fine wine section at £8.99 each and a bottle of Australian Cabernet Sauvignon at £5.99. I doubt many of us share Mr Evans's taste for Foster's lager, but otherwise his shopping list seems relatively modest. Yet the *Sun* reported that "Shopper Margaret Shuttleworth, 28," said, "He made no secret of the fact he was buying a load of drink. He looked like he didn't have a care in the world."

I have never knowingly met shopper Margaret Shuttleworth, 28, though she may well be one of the travelling busybodies who scrutinise my own trolley. But I would suggest she finds something better to do with her time than trailing disc jockeys around the Godalming Waitrose, totting up their purchases and issuing rolling news reports to the tabloid press.

I don't suppose shopper Margaret Shuttleworth, 28, has ever held down a position as a popular disc jockey on a radio breakfast show. Certainly, I can find no entry for her in Paul Donovan's encyclopaedic *The Radio Companion* (HarperCollins). If she had, she might not be so shocked to discover a link between disc jockeying and drinking.

Most of us would find it impossible to talk non-stop nonsense for three hours each morning without first downing at least five bottles of French Chardonnay. Even the most resilient disc jockeys have been prone to temptation. In Tony Blackburn's seminal autobiography, *The Living Legend* (1985), he tells of his bleak period, back in May 1979, when he was switched from his daily show to the weekends. He took it awfully badly. "I began to sink two or three bottles of wine a day with an actor friend in a wine bar. I was adrift in a sea of drink and misery."

The multiplication of radio stations has occasioned a remarkable increase in the number of disc jockeys. They already outnumber blacksmiths and cowherds; it is perfectly possible that by 2020 they will outnumber police officers. The only humane solution would be for the supermarket chains to introduce discreet disc jockey-only sections, in which household names can prowl the darkened aisles for hours on end, sure in the knowledge that their purchases will remain secret.

Inevitably, this will lead shopper Margaret Shuttleworth, 28, with time on her hands. But in every other respect, the world is swinging her way. There are closed-circuit television cameras in most town centres and 4,300 cameras trained on virtually every inch of road. On Monday, police chiefs said they want to see the network of road cameras treble to more than 12,000.

Out walking in a pretty wood near Chichester last week, I was surprised to see a notice peeping out of the shrubbery proclaiming that CCTV cameras were in operation. The only living creature to have outwitted the plague of the CCTV seems to be the Loch Ness Monster, or "Nessie", who continues to live the life of Riley – drinking to her heart's content, racing hither and thither at whatever speed she fancies – and all the while enjoying almost total privacy. The same is even truer of her husband and children, who have even managed to keep their real names out of the press. Now, in a brilliant public relations coup, they have let it be known that they do not in fact exist, and are no more than commotions in the water caused by mild earthquakes. If this throws snoopy shopper Margaret Shuttleworth, 28, off their scent, then the entire Ness family may be said to have struck a blow for freedom.

Christmas at Home

CHRISTMAS CONJUGATIONS

I disapprove of rampant consumerism
You cut back on presents
He is a Scrooge.

The jumper I gave you is certainly different
The jumper you gave me is certainly colourful
The jumper she gave me is non-returnable.

I break the ice
You break the glasses
He breaks wind.

I did myself proud
You didn't hold back
He is a greedy pig.

I missed the Queen
You avoided the Queen
He has no sense of duty.

I am *Oscar Wilde*
You are *Eric Morecambe*
He has *Beadle's Bumper Book of Jokes*.

I greet
You pounce
He gropes.

I am childlike
You are childish
He is infantile.

I had a quiet Christmas
You kept yourself to yourself
He acted suspiciously.

I like to add last-minute touches
You fuss
They panic.

Our tree is festive
Your tree is colourful
Their tree is common.

I am effervescent
You are bubbly
She is pissed.

Our children are full of fun
Your children are full of e-numbers
Their children are on drugs.

Our turkey served us well
Your turkey kept going
They were still eating their turkey in February.

We discuss
You argue
They row.

I'm young enough to wear this
You're brave enough to wear that
She is Cilla Black.

Our children catch the telly
Your children watch the telly
Their children are glued to the telly.

Ho ho ho, I am Father Christmas
Ho ho ho, you look like Father Christmas
Ho ho ho, who's the fat beardie?

We had a wonderful Christmas
You say you had a wonderful Christmas
They clearly had a dreadful Christmas.

We sing Christmas carols
You manage Christmas carols
They murder Christmas carols.

Our child starred in the Nativity
Your child had a part in the Nativity
Was their child on stage?

I throw another log on the fire
You won't leave the fire alone
He's a bloody pyromaniac.

I plan ahead
You like everything just so
She is a control freak.

I am young for my age
You are good for your age
She does well, considering.

I have a sense of humour
You have a sense of fun
He has a whoopee cushion.

I said a few words
You made a speech
He went on and on.

I shut my eyes
You doze
He's off again.

We pushed the boat out
You went to a lot of effort
They made a song and dance about it.

I enjoy Monopoly
You like to win at Monopoly
He owes me exactly £1,275 and I
Want it all now in cash; I'm
Sorry but that's the rules or
What's the point in playing?

I know my limit
You have your limit
He is the limit.

Our turkey certainly isn't overcooked
Your turkey could do with another few minutes
Their turkey is a death trap.

I look charming in my paper hat
You look amusing in your paper hat
What DOES he think he looks like?

We had a family Christmas
You had an uneventful Christmas
Nobody invited them anywhere.

I had one too many
You had too one many
He one many had too.

Christmas Countdown with Trinny and Susannah

✱ **Day 23:** FIRST impressions are so important. So liven up your front garden and greet Christmas guests with a specially constructed rockery with fifteen varieties of seasonal heather. Order a quarter of a ton of rocks on the internet today, construct the rockery tomorrow and the next day consult your plumber about inserting a spectacular six-foot fountain in time for Christmas.

✱ **Day 22:** Christmas simply isn't Christmas without a partridge in a pear tree to greet your guests as they enter your hall. Live partridges may be easily obtained by purchasing a return rail ticket to Perth, hiring a marvellous old gamekeeper steeped in countryside lore, and then stalking and netting your partridge. Pear trees are readily available from leading garden centres. Partridges may be fixed to pear trees with string or Sellotape, but avoid household adhesive. Your partridge should be fed correctly, three times a day. For instructions on exactly how to feed your partridge, log on to www.partridge-advisorycentre.com.

✱ **Day 21:** Today it is vitally important to put aside two to three hours to start work on the bread sauce for Boxing Day. If you are unable to make your own organic flour with which to make the bread, a few shop-bought varieties can make poor if necessary substitutes. Important: bread sauce simply isn't bread sauce unless you include Moroccan cloves (available on the third Tuesday of each month from the central market in Marrakesh).

✱ **Day 20:** By now you should have had your third fitting for the ballgown you plan to wear for the traditional dinner dance you should be throwing on the evening of the 23rd. If you haven't booked your orchestra or dance band yet, why not place your extended family on an intensive musical tuition crash course?

✱ **Day 19:** Problem! You have forgotten to pre-order your turkey, and there is frankly nothing you can do. You should have ordered it by mid-September, or early October at the latest. Naturally, your family will be desperately disappointed when they get to hear of it, particularly the teenagers, who are already under a great deal of stress coping with the extreme hormonal changes that come with adolescence.

Solution! Regrettably, there is no real solution, but some families report having found Mathew Bernard's Turkey-Style Fish Fingers a reasonable festive substitute last year. "If you close your eyes, it's hard to tell they're not ordinary fish fingers, except for the feathers," reports one child.

* **Day 18:** High time you tackled that crippling limescale in the guest bathroom. An hour and a half with a scouring brush and heavy-duty bleach should do the trick, but in cases of severe scaling, a new bath may prove necessary. You have left the plumbing and fitting a bit late, though, haven't you? In the north and south-west, today is the last day to order Brussels sprouts.

* **Day 17:** If you forgot to order your Brussels sprouts, you should pay an urgent visit to your local supermarket and panic-buy a dozen tins of their own-brand baked beans. Moulded together in batches of twenty-two, and dyed light green, baked beans form a workable substitute for the real thing, particularly if you employ dim lighting on your Christmas dining table.

* **Day 16:** With little more than a fortnight to go, by now you should have begun laying the table for Christmas Eve. Remember: finger-bowls are essential. Without them, your festivities are ruined. But don't worry: if all else fails, you can always make your own, out of papier mâché.

* **Day 15:** By now, you have left it too late. Honestly! You should have replanted those garden borders with seasonal shrubs at least two months ago! But you didn't – and now your Christmas guests will just have to make do with the ghastly dull greens and browns of a neglected garden in the depths of winter.

What sort of a host will they take you for? The only last-minute solution is to make exotic blooms out of brightly coloured waterproof paper, available, in person only, from leading stockists in Copenhagen, and then to thread these blooms through all the available stems in your garden. Recommended background reading: *The Art of Danish Xmas Paper-Blooms Made Complicated* (£20).

* **Day 14:** If you haven't retiled your roof in time for Christmas, it's frankly too late to start now. No one likes to see dirty old tiles on a Yuletide roof, so I always retile my roof in early November. But for those of you lazybones who simply couldn't be bothered, the

only possible solution is to make sure your Christmas guests arrive after nightfall, so that their opportunities to survey your roof are kept to the barest minimum.

✳ Day 13: Less than a fortnight to go and most people will have completed their Christmas preparations. But for those who are too ill-prepared, incapable or just plain sluttish to have made the effort, we offer these emergency tips:

✳ Day 12: There's still time to install a whirlpool bath in your downstairs toilet. Of course there isn't room; we're not saying there is but, with a decent sledgehammer, obtainable from reputable hardware stockists, you still have time to knock down an outside wall and build a small extension. Memo: we no longer live in Victorian times, so your overnight guests have rightly come to expect a whirlpool bath on each floor. If planning permission is delayed, then achieve a similar effect by placing a garden hosepipe in your ordinary bath and switching it on when your guest has settled in.

✳ Day 11: Have you prepared those Christmas parsnips yet? The only proper way to cook Christmas parsnips is to marinade them in a mixture of Afghanistan honey, fresh anchovies and crème de cassis for three weeks before pummelling them for twenty-four hours with an oak skittle before wrapping them in Egyptian muslin, available from the Conran Shop (Tokyo) and burying them three foot deep in clay soil for no more than three days. Then slow-cook in a low oven for eight hours, and serve with parsley, coriander and Maori yogurt. But if you haven't done this by now, there's no point in even trying. Basically, your Christmas dinner is wrecked and there's nothing you can do about it.

✳ Day 10: Be sure to visit your local GP in good time to order up those seasonal anti-depressants. Christmas can be a time of great stress. If you plan to play Monopoly over the Christmas period, supervised after-care should be provided for all your guests. Two-for-the-price-of-one offers on Extra-Absorbent Kleenex are available from Tesco, Woolworth and many leading department stores. Warning: bare-knuckle boxing can be dangerous after a heavy lunch.

✳ Day 9: By now, your Christmas turkey should have been roasting, under a low-to-medium heat, for the past five days. There are, alas, no short-cuts. If for any reason you forgot, do not attempt to put it in your oven now, because on opening the oven door on Christmas Day you will find that your turkey is severely underdone, and even quite possibly still clucking. If so, hit it over the head with a heavy object and reschedule your main meal for early March.

✱ **Day 8:** What to wear for breakfast on Christmas Day? It can be desperately hard to strike the right note. Many find full evening dress too formal, yet full nudity somehow too casual. Why not compromise with something in between? We suggest a turquoise-and-peach kaftan from Monsoon, with slip-on shoes from Esmerelda of Knightsbridge, and – to add that extra seasonal dash – bright orange shoulder-length gloves by Dior.

✱ **Day 7:** Why not grow your own mistletoe? The shop-bought variety is terribly unattractive, and your guests will be bitterly disillusioned if they see it in your house, muttering things to one another about the kind of host you have turned out to be. Alas, with just a week to go, you have left it too late. You should have planted your mistletoe at least twelve years ago to have ensured ripe berries for this Christmas. But you are still in reasonable time to bring a bit of seasonal cheer to Christmas Day 2015 if you start digging now.

✱ **Day 6:** Less than a week to go, and tempers are already frayed, but – don't worry! – there may well be a simple solution. Have you considered a quickie divorce? Many couples find it all too easy to get stuck in a rut, but a change of partners in the run-up to Christmas can lend colour and variety to the big day, bringing just the right note of seasonal cheer to your twelve-seater French oak dining-table.

✱ **Day 5:** What do you mean, you don't have a twelve-seater French oak dining-table? It's far too late to order one now. There's nothing for it but to cancel this Christmas. So let's start planning next year's instead.

✱ **Day 370:**

THE LITTLE BOOK OF CHRISTMAS CHAOS

Exceptionally Gifted

Stuck for a present for your
exceptionally gifted godson
who, though six months younger than
your own son,

is a full two years ahead of him
at school?
How about an
Alsatian puppy?

Spiritual
Be sure to inject a
note of contemporary spirituality
into your Christmas celebrations
by gathering around
the Christmas tree
and singing
"My Sweet Lord"
from a family hymn sheet.

Soft Furnishings
Keep toddlers amused
after Christmas lunch
by scattering
liqueur chocolates
around the sitting room.
Delight in their little ways
as they bite into the choccies,
make faces
and spit them out
all over the soft furnishings!

Lavender Bags
Determined to bury the hatchet
with your touchy cousins
over the Christmas season?
Your present list should be
for him: a Corby trouser press
for her: a box of Lavender Bags
from Woods of Windsor
and for the kiddies:
the latest Limp Bizkit CD

with the "Parental Guidance" sticker
discreetly removed.

Countdown To Christmas
It is as well to save food
for next Christmas, and
the Christmas after that, and
the Christmas after that.
So be sure to invest
in a Christmas hamper
packed with piccalilli,
strawberries in heavy syrup, mandarins
in Cointreau, chocolate-covered
sultanas, advocaat and
a selection of crystallised fruits.

A Thoughtful Solution
What to give that old acquaintance
who ekes out her days stuck
alone
near the top of a
high-rise block,
making you feel guilty?
A garden voucher
should do the trick.

Something To Look Forward To
Inject a note of seasonal
confusion
into the world
by sending your friends
Christmas cards
saying:
"With love from Geoff, Sue, Freddy,
Jamie, Zoe and Charlotte
PS: Can't wait until the 29th!"

A Time for the Kiddies
There is nothing more
exciting
for children to find in their stockings
than a five-pence piece, a
digestive biscuit and
a crushed satsuma.

Getting Out of the House
At this time of year
it is always important to
get out of the house
so take care to
tuck a penny piece
into the Christmas pud, then
wait until it catches in someone's
throat.
Hey presto!
Your cross-country trip to casualty
will be assured.

A Christmas Conundrum
3pm on Christmas Day:
On BBC2
the Queen's Christmas message
for Granny.
On BBC1
the Christmas *Top of the Pops*
for Samantha.
On ITV
Sporting Highlights of the Year
for Dad.
One television.
Enjoy!

Countdown To Christmas
Less than two weeks
to go
and you still haven't started
wrapping the bacon around
the chipolatas or cutting crosses in the
Brussels sprouts?
To be honest, it might be wiser
in the long run
to reschedule Christmas dinner for
the early hours of the 28th.

An Icebreaker
Boxing Day. Granny is
not speaking to Deirdre, Deirdre
can't think why you invited
Richard and Janet, Grandpa is
in one of his moods, your black sheep
nephew is tormenting the twins,
your mother-in-law has fallen out
with your brother's wife's sister and the
television's on the blink.
A brainwave!
Let's revive the old-fashioned art of conversation!

Mmmmm!
At the back of the larder
you discover one tin of
apricots, the remnants of a jar
of chutney (sell-by date
February, 1992), a tin
of dried-up brown shoe polish, some
condensed milk, three cloves,
two cubes of orange jelly and
three-quarters of a bottle of Chilean Red
from last Christmas.
Anyone for mulled wine?

No Better Time

At last, the whole family
has gathered around the table
for a nice old-fashioned game
of Snakes and Ladders.
The board is out, the pieces assembled.
What better time
to hide the dice?

A Considerate Guest

It is as well to show
what a considerate guest
you are
by waiting until the very last dish
is about to be placed on the table
before rushing into the room with
a dutiful look
and saying,
"You must let me do something!"

A Lusty Rendition

Dustmen, postmen, newspaper boys:
like you, they hate to see
Christmas becoming too commercialised.
So this year make theirs a
Christmas to remember by
treating them to a
beaming smile, a joyful wave
and a lusty rendition of
"*Glor-or-or-or-or*
-or-or-or-or-or-or-
or-or-or-or-or-ia".

Expansive

Who wants
a Christmas card
which just says,

"Happy Christmas!"?
So delight your friends
by taking time to inform them
how well your entire family
has done this year, including
full GCSE and music grades,
sporting achievements,
new vehicles purchased
and holidays abroad,
before launching
into a full round-up of
excitingly different plans
for the coming year, all with
plenty of exclamation marks (!!!).

That Extra-Special Present
The delight on a child's face
as he opens that extra-special present
at Christmas
is a thing of magic.
So be sure to eschew
the electrical, the plastic, the gimmicky
and the overpriced
for something
you have created with your own hands
out of raffia, clay or
pipe-cleaners, or
a combination thereof.

The Child With Everything
What to give the child with
everything?
How about a sixth game of Cluedo?

When Helping Out
When helping out in the kitchen,
be sure to rummage vainly in drawers

slam cupboard doors, lift up lids, poke
about in the larder and sigh a lot:
on no account
be so vulgar as to
ask where anything is.

Their Inner Souls
Your friends are at one with
nature and in touch with
their inner souls.
They radiate peace, contentment.
Time, then, to let their son have a
set of drums, a whoopee cushion, a superball
a karaoke machine and a
Rolf Harris Stylophone.

Throwing Away the Vouchers
Children! Be sure to wait until your
father has picked up all your
discarded wrapping paper,
screwed it into bundles,
squashed it into the dustbin and
thrown the old chicken stock on top of it
before piping up,
"Anyone seen my book token?"

Peace on Earth
All is calm.
All is bright.
So how about a game
of Monopoly?

Anti-Social Behaviour

EastEnders update

Monday – All is still
Then –
"Shut it, you pill!"
Yells Phil to Jill
"Or I'll kill
Yer, I will!"

Tuesday – Enter Lil:
"Drop it guys! Chill!
Or blood will spill!"

Wednesday – Too late: Jill
Knows Phil
Thinks baby Cill
Is his until
Comparing her to Bill
(Never still,
Voice too shrill,
Hands in till,
No particular skill)
He screams, "I've 'ad my fill!
I get the drill:
Cill's the child of Bill!"

Thursday – Now Phil
Has it in for Bill
Who's givin' grief to Jill
Who's hasslin' Will

To leave Big Lil
Who moans, "That's bloody brill!"
And starts to feel ill.

Friday – Now Lil's prospects are nil
And Jill's
On the Pill
And Will's
Dahn the bill
And Cill's
Over the hill
And Phil's
Out on the sill
Sobbing, "It'd give you a thrill
To watch me spill!"

Moral – When the only agenda
Is to be put through the blender
Who'd be an EastEnder?

The Aura of Election Upon Her

MANY READERS MAY, like me, have been vaguely aware of the works
of the literary critic Harold Bloom and the feminist author Naomi
Wolf without ever having quite got around to reading them.

Every year or two, one or other of them writes a book with a
word such as "canon" or "myth" in its title. The work in question is
then reviewed, favourably or unfavourably, in the literary pages.
Those of us who try to keep abreast of such things (whither feminism? whither literature?) then skim-read the reviews (I tend to start
at the end and work backwards), before sitting back contentedly,
feeling that we have got the gist.

There is nothing commendable about such superficiality but,
these days, there are so many famous people, distinguished or
otherwise, vying for our attention that it is hard to know where to
begin, or, more importantly, where to stop. Occasionally, there will

be newspaper profiles of either Professor Bloom or Ms Wolf to coincide with publication, and we might also give these a go. Totting it up, I have probably devoted roughly an hour of my life to reading articles about Bloom, and another hour to reading articles about Wolf.

How much of it really sinks in? If you had asked me a week ago to tell you all I knew about the two of them, my answer would have gone like this: Bloom: large, old, critic, American, Olympian, bossy; Wolf: sexy, young, feminist, American, panicky, bossy. All in all, those two hours would probably have been better spent sucking on a boiled sweet.

But now, after years of exile in the literary pages, Bloom and Wolf have burst on to the news pages, protagonists in a tale of passion and fury. Ms Wolf claims that, twenty-odd years ago, she invited Professor Bloom to her student house for a candlelit dinner. "He was a vortex of power and intellectual charisma," she recalls, and she was consequently "sick with excitement" at the prospect of the professor reading her poetry.

After dinner, her student housemates made their excuses and departed, leaving Bloom and Wolf alone together. "Finally! I thought we could discuss our poetry manuscript. He did not look at it… He leaned towards me and put his face inches from mine. 'You have the aura of election upon you,' he breathed."

The scene already has a strong feel of Benny Hill about it, which leads me to think that Ms Wolf may have misheard the key word. Anyway, the tale now grows hot and steamy: "The next thing I knew, his heavy, boneless hand was hot on my thigh. The whole thing had suddenly taken on the quality of a bad horror film. The floor spun. By now my back was against the sink which was as far away as I could get. He came at me. I turned away from him toward the sink and found myself vomiting in shock. He disappeared. When he re-emerged – from the bedroom with his coat – a moment later, I was still frozen, my back against the sink. He said, 'You are a deeply troubled girl.' Then he went to the table, took the rest of his sherry, corked the bottle, and left."

As if this were not enough, the spiky, fast-talking iconoclast Camille Paglia – no Kofi Annan she – has popped up to lay into Ms

Wolf with her rat-a-tat-tat delivery. "Naomi Wolf, for her entire life, has been batting her eyes and bobbing her boobs, and made a profession out of courting male attention by flirting and offering her sexual allure," she says.

My own view, for what it's worth, is that Professor Bloom would have been wiser to cast an encouraging eye over Ms Wolf's poetry, jamming all the margins with as many ticks, stars, smiley-faces and A-pluses as he could muster, before making his move. It showed poor tactics to go straight from candlelit dinner to hand-on-thigh without stopping along the way to plough through the poetry. It also seems a little unsporting of him to have made off with the remaining sherry the moment he was given the thumbs-down.

But Ms Wolf is not without fault either. Her stomach seems peculiarly prone to upset at the best of times. Not only was she "sick with excitement" before his arrival but she also found herself "vomiting in shock" before his departure. Open the windows, someone! Small wonder, you may think, that her house-mates planned an early exit. I wonder if she has ever availed herself of well-known household brands such as Settlers or Alka-Seltzer?

The cockney crooner Tommy Steele was once quoted as saying he preferred to read the classics in comic-strip form. In a modern-day variation of this, most of us prefer to read the work of our leading feminists and English professors in tabloid sex-scandal form. Personally, I take up a position somewhere on the middle ground. I would like a serious, pull-out supplement devoted to the whole affair, with commentary from all the top experts, not to mention numerous artist's reconstructions of Ms Wolf's dining and kitchen areas. It would all be rounded off with diagrams full of arrows showing the likely route taken by Professor Bloom's hand, and more arrows showing all the various twists and turns performed by Ms Wolf beside her sink. Then, and only then, would I consider myself completely up to snuff on all the latest developments in feminism and literary criticism.

(February 28, 2004)

My Minnelli Wedding Diary

(I) STORING UP TROUBLE

Life may not have taught me much, but this I have learnt: the gift of an assortment of luxury glassware induces feelings of anxiety and guilt. It acts as a ticking timebomb: bit by bit, item by item, all those expensive glasses are sure to break. With each new bang and crash comes a fresh blossoming of guilt and anxiety.

Strange, then, that the veteran singer Liza Minnelli, who has already been through so much, should decide to place an assortment of expensive glassware on her various wedding lists at New York stores, including three hundred Lalique drinking glasses costing £92 each.

Any qualified psychoanalyst might have warned her that she was only storing up trouble ahead. Luxury is a euphemism for an expensive problem. With breakages running at an average rate of, say, one glass per week, by my calculation Miss Minnelli will not have smashed her final Lalique drinking glass until June 2008. This suggests six years and three months of anxiety and guilt, guilt and anxiety. If my experience of household breakages is anything to go by, as Miss Minnelli brushes the last shards of her final smashed glass into the dustpan, she will feel an overwhelming sense of relief. At this point, she should revert to inexpensive glassware (four leakproof glasses for under £3.20, if she shops around). She will find these do the job every bit as well, and are more resilient when dropped.

(March 21, 2002)

(II) AN ACCIDENT WAITING TO HAPPEN

It was only a few weeks ago that I tried to persuade Liza Minnelli to cut back on the expensive glassware on her wedding list, advising her that it could only lead to breakages, tears and mutual recrimination. Cheap tumblers (80p each, if she had only shopped around) do the job just as well, and no one worries too much when they break, as inevitably they must.

Alas, Miss Minnelli has a stubborn streak. She simply would not listen. Accordingly, she is now lumbered with cupboard upon cupboard jam-packed with three hundred easily breakable Lalique drinking glasses costing £92 each. The early days of any marriage are often fraught; she now has only herself to blame if she and her husband spend their first six months together pointing accusing fingers at one another over a steadily increasing mountain of broken Lalique glassware.

Now we hear that Mr Charles Kennedy, the leader of the Liberal Democrats, is travelling down the same perilous path. For his marriage in July, he and his bride-to-be have opened a wedding list at the House of Fraser store in Edinburgh. Though it comes to a commendably modest £3,533 (Minnelli's nudged £250,000), over a third of it – £1,244 in all – is devoted to "crystal stemware", including eight goblets at £19, eight sherry glasses at £15 and two decanters at £130.

Oddly enough, the model Claudia Schiffer, who married at the weekend, also went overboard on the glassware.. Her wedding list (total cost £26,333) included twenty-four crystal goblets from Thomas Goode at £38 each, a silver and crystal decanter in the shape of a golf ball at £295, and a crystal and silver Pimm's jug at £180, plus one "oil and vinegar set in silver-plated stand" at £688.

Few modern marriages could survive the unbearable tension of being surrounded by kitchen shelves stacked with fragile and expensive glassware. Why do couples choose to jeopardise their future in this way? As far as I know, no survey has yet offered conclusive evidence that the increase in expensive glassware on wedding lists is to blame for our spiralling divorce rate, but the two must surely be linked.

(May 28, 2002)

(III) I TOLD YOU SO

The four most satisfying words in the English language are "I told you so". Sadly, it is a phrase one rarely gets a chance to use. My most confident predictions in recent years have been that, on leaving Take That, the group's least talented member, Robbie Williams, would disappear without a trace, and that no one would go to see a three-and-a-half hour film in which the outcome was known and the hero died at the end (*Titanic*).

But, as with all those monkeys typing Shakespeare, every now and then a prediction comes true. When Miss Liza Minnelli married Mr David Gest in March last year, I warned of trouble to come.

Others noticed that her choice of bridesmaids – Joan Collins, Diana Ross, Carol Channing, Petula Clark, Elizabeth Taylor and so forth – did not augur well. But it was the wedding list that sent shivers down my spine.

Noticing that the list included three hundred Lalique drinking glasses costing £92 each, I worried that Miss Minnelli must – perhaps subconsciously – have already been allowing for multiple breakages ahead. I urged her – begged her – to switch her order to unbreakable plastic drinking glasses, available from leading garages at a very reasonable £3.20 for four. Alas, she chose to ignore my advice, and now look what's happened.

Eighteen months and goodness knows how many Lalique drinking glasses later, Liza-with-a-G-and-a-T has found that her marriage has come to an end. Her husband, David Gest, has filed a lawsuit for £7 million claiming to be a victim of domestic violence. His marriage to Ms Minnelli apparently left him taking eleven pain-killing medications a day to deal with "severe, unrelenting headaches, nausea, hypertension, scalp tenderness and insomnia".

After eighteen months of listening to "Come to the Cabaaaar-aaaaaay", Mr Gest also claims to be suffering from "phonophobia", a fear of voices. The doors are presumably now open for any member of the public with a *Cabaret* soundtrack album to sue Ms Minnelli for the same amount: in America, these things are always worth a punt.

We have not yet been told exactly how many of the original three hundred Lalique drinking glasses are still in one piece. At times like these, one begins to feel sorry for the celebrities who attended the Minnelli/Gest wedding, one or two of whom are believed to have known the couple personally. How they must be wishing they had taken heed of my fears for the future, and had saved a fortune by forking out on Breville Toasted Sandwich Makers, which are both more traditional and far more reasonable. On the other hand, they sometimes fail to disintegrate on impact, so perhaps Mr Gest should count himself lucky.

(October 25, 2003)

Meet and Greet

ALL THAT ANY OF US really want is praise, even if we have to pay for it. Whenever I attend a concert at the Regent Theatre in Ipswich, there is nothing I enjoy more than the performer kicking off the evening by saying: "It's great to be back in Ipswich!" And the evening ends on an even warmer note when, an hour or two later, he signs off by saying: "Thank you all dearly – you've been the most MARVELLOUS audience." Seasoned performers – Lesley Garrett, Clodagh Rodgers, Bryan Ferry, the lot – can always be relied upon to remember their manners. But sometimes in recent weeks it has seemed that the younger generation has left theirs at home.

At the start of the month, the sixteen-year-old Charlotte Church was in a bit of a mood when she took to the stage at the US Bank Arena in Cincinnati. Asked to say hello to some disabled fans backstage afterwards, the singer – whose most recent record was called "Voice of an Angel" – is said to have replied, "F— this. I didn't agree to no meet and greet. Hello?" before stomping off.

A week later, the group Oasis took to the stage of the Brighton Centre. Within seconds Mr Liam Gallagher, 30, began yelling abuse into his microphone at technicians. His two front teeth had been knocked out in a fracas in Germany a day or two before, and his new teeth were obviously playing up. Instead of singing the proper chorus to the group's new single, "Stop Crying Your Heart Out", he simply hissed, "*Sssss*" all the way through. He then took a leaf from Charlotte Church's book and stormed off the stage in a bate.

His older brother Noel, 35, is usually much less trouble, but when he attempted to fill the hiatus with an acoustic number, he became irritable with fans who insisted on singing along. "You've got to be quiet. If you don't, I won't play," he barked. As luck would have it, the fans joined in again, so he snapped back: "I hope you all die of hypothermia." Dame Vera Lynn he is not.

Brighton people tend to wrap up well, so it seems unlikely that Mr Gallagher's hope will come true. But I suspect today's fans are all masochists at heart, and one of the reasons they pay so much to go to concerts is so that they can be abused live by multi-millionaires. Whether it is Noel or Liam or Charlotte who delivers the abuse is purely a matter of personal preference. None of us are immune to this strange modern perversion. Personally, I would travel a long way to hear Miss Church sing the words "F— this. I didn't agree to no meet and greet. Hello?" to the tune of "There'll Be a Welcome in the Hillside."

(December 19, 2002)

Wallace Arnold: Tricky Times at the Garrick

IT WAS, if I recall, a delightful autumn evening in the late 1980s when the portals of the Garrick Club swung open and who should stride in but the American "pop" singer Mr Michael Jackson.

What on earth was he doing there, you may well ask! The Garrick enjoys reciprocal membership, if memory serves, with the Cosmetic Surgeons' Club of Los Angeles. (I well remember my old friend and quaffing partner Kingsley Amis paying a trip to Los Angeles, to promote one new novel or another, nipping into the wrong room by mistake and emerging looking like the late Princess Margaret in a trouser suit.) So I can only suppose that Jackson was saving money by making use of his club's reciprocal arrangements around the world. Certainly, he looked a mite ill at ease as he "moonwalked" his way up the stairs and through the upper bar with a young friend in tow. And he certainly raised eyebrows when he summoned the head barman by extending his right hand from his "crotch" (dread word!) to the ceiling and back again, in rapid succession. It is, as you probably know, a firm rule of the Garrick's that one's "private parts" are to be touched only in the gentlemen's lavatories, and then by oneself, except on Members' Nights.

Nevertheless, conviviality is the byword of the Garrick. One was determined to make Jackson and his young friend feel at home, so a small group of us from the Entertainments Committee went over and made the right noises. I was, needless to say, in charge of introductions. "And have you met my old friend, little Arthur Askey?" I asked, adding, by way of forging some sort of link. "Little Arthur's a performer like your own good self."

Jackson looked a little flummoxed by this information, but I finally persuaded the incorrigible Arthur to perform a rendition of his immortal classic "Buzz, Buzz, Buzz, Buzzy Bee, Buzzy Bee", along with a high-spirited tap-routine. Jackson and his friend were visibly moved by this performance, so much so that they did, indeed, visibly move. Within seconds they were in the next room, finding themselves buttonholed by Sir Donald Sinden with hilarious tales of the famously ill-fated Wolfit production of "The Scottish Play", with Anna Neagle as Lady Macbeth and the late Reg Varney in the title role.

As the anecdotes rolled out, Jackson looked a little nonplussed, but just as he was growing a little fidgety, the Black and White Minstrels all entered the room in strict formation, as they always did prior to treading the boards in the first of their twice-nightly shows at the St Martin's Theatre, just around the corner. Appearances can be deceptive. It is a little-known fact that the Black and White Minstrels were not naturally black. Quite the opposite. They were in fact all white men who, by ingenious use of make-up, had got themselves up to look exactly like African-American minstrels, the better to sing and dance their way through a glittering showcase of much-loved tunes.

Spotting Jackson and his young friend on the sofa, the minstrels burst into a spirited rendition of "Swanee" in his honour, complete with beautifully choreographed dance routine. Tickled pink by the tribute, Michael clapped his hands to the beat, and encouraged his friend to do the same.

A magical, magical evening, then, and attended by a very special performer. A motion to make Jackson an honorary member of the Garrick was later passed unanimously, and in the intervening years he has risen "through the ranks", as it were, until, just before Christmas, he was appointed vice-chairman of the Wine and Spirits Committee, his name lending much lustre to the club's image.

And so to now. *Quel horreur*! Deep breath, Wallace: deep breath. And big blow! All better! As one might imagine, the news of Michael Jackson's impending trial hit the Garrick like the proverbial bombshell. It must be years since one of our members found himself in the dock for an incident of this nature (though, now I come to think of it, I do remember a little unpleasantness last year involving one of our members, a prominent actor, being detained by the police for soliciting in Leicester Square, dressed as Mother Goose. And wasn't there a brouhaha yonks ago involving the late Gracie Fields warbling something about aspidistras at the top of her voice after lights out in the Gentlemen's Dormitory? Such things are best forgotten, methinks). But what of M Jackson, Esq? Innocent or, well, perhaps not quite so innocent, his continued presence on our List of Members – let alone upon the Wine Committee! – would bring the club into serious disrepute.

Some of the stuffier clubs would be able to get rid of him in an instant, being blessed with historic bylaws forbidding gentlemen and their guests from wearing excessive make-up in the public rooms. But if we were to enforce such a ruling, we would, I fear, lose half our membership, many of whom are distinguished female impersonators, or Cabinet ministers. One can only hope that Mr Jackson emerges scot-free from his ordeal, and, moreover, that throughout his time in the dock he resists the temptation to sport his Garrick Club tie.

I Can't Explain:
Pop Stars in Heaven

CONDUCTING THE FUNERAL of John Entwistle, the bass player with the Who, the Reverend Colin Wilson announced: "It is my firm belief that John is in heaven reunited with Keith Moon. Up there making great music."

This is no time to argue. Young and old, we are all in the same boat. Before too long, each of us will be able to judge for himself whether the clergyman's belief holds water. If, upon entering heaven, I am welcomed by the distinctive noise of Keith Moon's drums and John Entwistle's bass, I will take my hat off to the Rev Wilson.

On the other hand, others may be inclined to believe that vintage Who songs like "I Can't Explain" and "My Generation" do not lend themselves to renditions solely for percussion and bass guitar. It is, for those of a more classical bent, a bit like scoring the *1812 Overture* as a duet for flute and triangle.

A keen Who fan from an early age, I always used to dread Keith Moon's extended drum solos. Indeed, the other members of the band would often leave the stage while they went on, leaving the audience to bear them alone. If the Rev Colin Wilson is right, then at least heaven's other residents – a good proportion of them keener on classical music or "easy listening" – may now find that the past twenty-four years of incessant madcap drum solos – Moon died in 1978 – are supplemented by John Entwistle's rather more precise bass-playing.

A halfway-decent singer might make things bearable. The Who's original vocalist, Roger Daltrey, is not yet dead. He runs a fish farm in East Sussex, which is not the same thing. But heaven is choc-a-bloc with excellent rock singers. The matronly clairvoyant Doris Stokes used to boast of being in touch with various pop stars who had "passed over". "Although a lot of pop singers are very nice people they do seem to get themselves into awful messes, and end up passing over long before their time," she observed in her autobiography, *Voices of Love* (1986). In chapter eight, she claimed to have chatted to Elvis Presley, to whom she had been introduced by Marc Bolan, who had also "passed over".

Either Presley or Bolan would be only too happy to provide lead vocals on "Pinball Wizard" or "Substitute". Coincidentally, Mama Cass, of the Mamas and the Papas, died in the very same London flat as Keith Moon, just four years before. But this does not necessarily give her first refusal. Her voice was possibly too pure for the brash Who oeuvre. Conversely, I find it hard to believe Keith Moon would be prepared to take a backseat on her charming lullaby, "Dream a Little Dream of Me". He would ruin its gentle lilt with his incessant smashing of the cymbals.

Oh, dear. We seem to have reached an impasse. Now that Doris Stokes has herself "passed over", perhaps the Rev Colin Wilson should intervene. He seems to know more than most about these things.

(July 16, 2002)

Mood Conjugations

I am depressed
You are moody
He is in a sulk.

I am a one-off
You are an eccentric
He is a bit odd.

I find it a little noisy
You are hard of hearing
He is stone deaf.

I can talk to anyone
You are a chatterbox
He goes on and on.

I am shy
You are standoffish
He is anti-social.

I am laid-back
You take it easy
He is bone idle.

I am a connoisseur
You are picky
He is a fusspot.

I put my foot down
You stamp your feet
He goes all queeny.

I am a natural leader
You are bossy
He is a fascist.

I am a gourmet
You love your food
He is a greedy pig.

I enjoy a drop
You never say no
He is an alcoholic.

I am frank
You are outspoken
He is plain rude.

I can talk to anyone
You don't mind who you talk to
He is in public relations.

I've been to hell and back
You've taken a wrong turn
He is a loser.

I am the soul of discretion
You are reserved
He has nothing to say for
himself.

I am the life and soul
You are a show-off
He must be On Something.

I have learnt to love myself
You are in love with yourself
She is the Duchess of York.

I value tradition
You are set in your ways
He is a stick-in-the-mud.

I am social
You are socially ambitious
He is a social climber.

I invest
You dabble
He is a shark.

I advise
You are a consultant
He is a bullshitter.

I am a raconteur
You are a socialite
He is a gossip.

I am self-assertive
You are self-centred
He is self-obsessed.

I am energetic
You are hyperactive
He can't relax.

I am wealthy
You are well-off
He is filthy rich.

I have full and frank discussion
You kick up a fuss
He rants.

I build for the future
You put empty spaces to
good use
He is a property developer.

I am meticulous
You are anally retentive
He is a solicitor.

I am a risk-taker
You are a wide-boy
He is a crook.

I am a live wire
You are on edge
He is stressy.

I charm
You fib
He spins.

I have personality
You have a sense of humour
He has a bow tie.

I am easily moved
You are highly strung
Must he always make a scene?

I am an artist
You are a Bohemian
He forgot to shave this
morning.

My face has character
Yours has that lived-in look
He's aged terribly.

I am self-confident
You are self-satisfied
She is Anne Robinson.

I enthuse
You gush
He simpers.

I am young at heart
You are childlike
He's gaga.

I am loyal
You are a loyalist
He is a yes-man.

I am an independent
You are a maverick
He is a traitor.

I stand up for myself
You rub everyone up the
wrong way
He is Dr David Starkey.

I keep them on their toes
You crack the whip
He is a bully.

I value personal contact
You are touchy-feely
He is facing charges of sexual
harassment.

I am a people person
You like to know what's going on
He is a gossip.

I explore my sexuality
You confront your sexuality
He is a pervert.

I am a Romeo
You are a Lothario
He should be locked up.

I am a mine of information
You are a mine of useless
information
He is an anorak.

I stick to my guns
You are stubborn
He is intransigent.

I chat
You hold forth
He never draws breath.

I seem to know everyone
You are a name-dropper
He is a snob.

I am active
You are hyperactive
He is on drugs.

I am fashionable
You follow fashion
He is a fashion victim.

I am well-covered
You are fat
He is clinically obese.

I am a good listener
You are a man of few words
He has nothing to say.

I have an individual style
You don't mind making a fool of yourself
He is Laurence Llewelyn-Bowen.

Ordure! Ordure!

WHEN THREE-YEAR-OLD Harry Branch-Shaw was caught short while out for a walk in New York's Rockefeller Park, he had no alternative but to nip behind the nearest tree. "It was either that or wet his pants," confirms his mother, Gigi.

But just as his nanny was helping him pull up his shorts, a New York police officer appeared on the scene and slapped a $35 summons on the poor little chap for urinating in a public place.

Harry's father, Martin Branch-Shaw, is understandably upset by this turn of events. "He's a three-year-old and he just had to go," he protests.

Only the most cold-hearted or iron-bladdered will be able to read about this upsetting incident without feeling a good deal of sympathy for young Harry. It is hard enough for adults to go for a walk in a park without stopping to relieve themselves; harder still for young Harry, who had probably just enjoyed rather too much fizzy pop before jumping up and down and spinning round and round, as children are prone to do.

The United States has an odd obsession with people of all ages peeing in public. In Europe, you can't walk anywhere without bumping into someone-or-other relieving himself discreetly, or even not so discreetly, behind a bush. Yet in America, anyone found having a pee beyond the confines of a "rest room" – even miles from civilisation in, say, the great open plains of Kansas – faces a stringent fine, no doubt soon to be followed by a humane execution, if President George W Bush has anything to do with it.

How to avoid a fine? The case of Mrs Lorena Bobbitt and her husband Wayne shows that if you take care to leave the penis in question on the side of the highway, you will be found not guilty and let off with no fine at all. Those travelling to the United States this summer, particularly those with weak bladders, may care to consider this option, though most will probably find what commentators call "the cost in human terms" too steep a price to pay.

If we in Britain take a more lenient view of the call of nature, it ill-behoves us to feel too smug.

In Suffolk, new signs pop up every day warning of ever greater penalties – £250, £500, £1,000 – for dog-owners whose pets go where they shouldn't.

Obviously no one wants to have to trip about the place in galoshes, particularly during this hot spell, but am I alone in feeling an hysterical element has entered into this great dogs' mess purge?

The signs invariably portray a badly drawn dog standing above what can only be described as an Olympian mountain of ordure; the picture is then rounded off with three wavy lines emerging from the mess, suggesting some sort of grotesque steam.

Personally, I would be prepared to suffer the sight of three or four hundred real dogs' messes in exchange for each one of these hideous signs. While dogs' messes decompose within a day or two, the signs will go on for ever, or until they are replaced by bigger and ever more monstrous signs, depicting great Etna-like eruptions of fire and steam, doubtless with one or two badly drawn people trapped beneath.

Out for a walk on a path in Wiltshire last weekend, I was struck, not for the first time, by how very much larger horse messes are than dog messes. Yet I have never once come across a bossy sign saying "Horse Owners – Clean Up After You", alongside a badly drawn horse plus great waves of steam, etc, etc.

This seems unfair. Were the penalties for leaving horse-droppings commensurate with their size, horse-owners would be looking at fines of anything up to £14,000, plus VAT.

Of course, this would leave the question of what to do about owners of cats and pet rabbits. Cats would probably be fined at two-thirds of the rate of dogs, while rabbits' droppings would have to be measured in terms of quantity rather than acreage: I would suggest a standard fine of 75p per item.

But where does this leave pet mice, guinea pigs, parrots, hamsters, hens and so forth? My least favourite droppings are the long, stringy ones delivered by goldfish, who then insist on swimming around with them still attached, like skipping ropes. But only the most ostentatious goldfish owners take their goldfish for walks in public places, so the law could afford to turn a blind eye.

(August 2, 2001)

One Thing Leads To Another

SIR – In the mid-1970s, my twelve-year-old boy was offered a chocolate cigarette at a neighbour's birthday party. Aged seventeen, I caught him experimenting with a real cigarette. Aged twenty-two, he was smoking between ten and fifteen cigarettes a day. By twenty-five he had been offered cannabis. To my horror, he recently confessed to me that for three years in the 1980s he had been a full-time student. I trust this serves as a warning to those of your readers who persist in the belief that one thing does not lead to another.

~ Bea Hayve (Ms)

SIR – Aged just six years old, my parents gave me a so-called "Dinky Toy" for my birthday. Aged eight, I owned and drove my own pogo stick. There was no going back. By the time I was twelve, I was riding a bicycle. I am now aged forty-three. Last year, I lost control of my car and drove into a bus queue, causing distress and injury to seventeen innocent passers-by. How long will it be before this government realises that one thing leads to another?

~ Dan Hill-Slope (Mr)

SIR – As a youth, I found myself the victim of peer pressure. Against my better judgement, I wrote a letter to the school magazine. When it was published, I felt a moment's elation. I wrote another, then another: before long, I was forcing my increasingly mad opinions on local, then national newspapers. I trust you will print this letter as a dire warning that one thing really does lead to another.

~ Ed Ache (Mr)

The Flying Sausage

SOME NEWS STORIES come within a hair's breadth of poetry. On page five of the *Daily Telegraph* recently was the sublime headline, "Flying sausage breaks driver's nose". Beneath it was the following story, which, at just thirty-six words, came in at barely longer than a haiku: "A frozen sausage thrown through the open window of a car broke the driver's nose. It was hurled from a car travelling in the opposite direction in South Woodham Ferrers, Essex, on Monday. Police are investigating." As with all the best poetry, not a single word is wasted. If only the uncredited author of the piece had written it with parentheses in the title, an absence of capital letters, and foreshortened lines, he would now be up for a major poetry award, or, at very least, an Arts Council grant:

<blockquote>

flying sausage (breaks driver's nose)

(i)

a frozen sausage thrown through

the open window of a car broke

(ii)

the driver's nose.

it was hurled from a car travelling in the opposite

(iii)

direction in south woodham ferrers, essex, on monday.

police are investigating.

</blockquote>

Professor Christopher Ricks, author of *Dylan's Visions of Sin* (2004), might, even now, be drafting an appreciation of the poem. No doubt he would draw his students' attention to the way in which, by dividing stanza (i) from stanza (ii) at the exact point at which the nose itself is fractured ("a car broke/ the driver's nose") the poet was brilliantly echoing the damage – both physical and, no doubt, psychological – caused by the flying sausage, in a structural upheaval to the established form that is at once both resonantly chilling and chillingly resonant.

I suspect Professor Ricks might also wish to draw our attention to a similar fracture between stanzas (ii) and (iii), in which the bleak impossibility of any real form of human communication between two cars speeding past one another ("travelling in the opposite/direction in south woodham") is hauntingly captured.

But there are many other aspects of the news story to be tackled beyond the purely poetic. Was it, perhaps, a revenge sausage-hurling? Earlier in the day, had the victim thrown a frozen rasher of streaky bacon into his assailant's vehicle? If it was a planned attack, why was a frozen sausage the assailant's weapon of choice? And how many months or even years of practice did it take before he was sufficiently proficient in the art of sausage-hurling to hurl his sausage through the open window of a car travelling in the opposite direction, certain in the knowledge that he would break his victim's nose?

More than forty years after the assassination of President Kennedy in Dallas, the same sort of questions are still being asked about the ability of Lee Harvey Oswald to hit a moving target with pinpoint accuracy from a sixth-floor window with a mail-order Italian rifle. Yet far greater accuracy would be required by anyone plotting to break someone's nose with a frozen sausage hurled from a car driven in the opposite direction. If ever the South Woodham Ferrers sausage-hurler is brought to justice, questions of a conspiracy are bound to arise. Was just one sausage hurled – or were the three sausages hurled within a split second of one another, each from a different hand?

With all these tell-tale signs pointing to a conspiracy, it seems inevitable that there will be an attempt to hurl a sausage at the assailant when he is escorted by police into South Woodham Ferrers magistrates court following his arrest. On the other hand, those who subscribe to the cock-up theory of history may prefer to see the South Woodham Ferrers Sausage Mystery not as a conspiracy but as an accident. Struggling to find something on the floor of his car – a cassette of *Phil Collins's Greatest Hits*, or a packet of Wrigley's Spearmint Gum – without taking his eyes off the road, the unknown driver picks up a frozen sausage by mistake. Perhaps he doesn't realise what he has done until he tries to slot the frozen sausage into his cassette player and finds the sound that emerges overly experimental or – worse – he puts it in his mouth and attempts to chew it. Horrified, he winds down his window and hurls the sausage out of the car with great force. As luck would have it, at that very moment another car is passing with its window open, and by a million-to-one chance the sausage flies into the car and hits the driver slap-bang on the nose.

But, if this was indeed the case, what was the frozen sausage doing in his car in the first place? Was he trying to defrost the sausage by holding it out of the window, only to let it go in a moment of madness? And why only a single sausage? Sausages come in strings: where were all its little friends?

These are just some of the unanswered questions concerning the flying sausage. I look forward to the reconstruction on *Crimewatch*, followed by an appeal for witnesses. But one thing is for sure: this is a sausage that will not go away.

Postman Parp

UNDER THE POETIC headline "Postman Parp", the *Sun* newspaper reports that the fifteen postal workers in the delivery office at Yatton have received this letter:

> *Following my letter of 24th July 2001, I did not think that it would be necessary to have to write a further letter on this subject.*
>
> *I have now received further complaints of certain members of staff breaking wind in the delivery office.*
>
> *I know that last time I treated these complaints in a fairly lighthearted manner, but in view of this latest outburst I must remind you that I will use the full force of the Conduct Code where necessary to stop this disgusting habit.*
>
> *I also had cause to speak to you about the flicking of rubber bands. This is a dangerous breach of the Health and Safety regulations and should cease with immediate effect.*
>
> *Peter Floyd, Delivery Office*
> *Manager for Yatton and Clevedon"*

This letter raises all sorts of interesting questions. If, for instance, Mr Floyd's threat to use the full force of the Conduct Code proves fruitless, and wind continues to be broken, then how on earth will he identify the culprit or culprits?

Of course, many offices these days have CCTV cameras, but even the most sophisticated infra-red camera would be hard-pressed to catch an offender red-handed. Those who know about such matters inform me that a seasoned perpetrator is often able to repeat the offence to his heart's content without so much as batting an eyelid.

If Mr Floyd really wants to get his man I am afraid he will have to don a false specs-nose-and-whiskers mask (as used by Sir Roy Strong) and go undercover. Yet even at close quarters, it may be hard to collar the perpetrator. I worry that when Mr Floyd comes to make his first formal accusation, he will be met by the pithy rhyme, popular in my schooldays and, I'm sorry to say, still popular now: "He who smelt it, dealt it."

Let us hope the poor man arrives primed with the traditional counter-argument: "He who made the rhyme, did the crime."

In my experience, neither verse is particularly accurate. It seems most unlikely that any perpetrator would be the first to call attention to his offence, and almost as unlikely that such a coarse act would be committed by someone with a taste for poetry. On the other hand, many of our greatest poets – Dylan Thomas, John Clare, Christopher Smart, Alfred Lord Tennyson – have maintained a scant regard for personal hygiene, so perhaps there is something in it, after all.

Letter from Sir Roy Strong

SIR – Over the past week, I have read with increasing interest your series of items on the vexed subject of breaking wind, and the rhymes employed thereof for the detection of perpetrators.

I, too, share your grave concerns as to the accuracy of the phrase "He who made the rhyme did the crime", having once fallen victim to a false accusation based wholly upon this unscientific premise.

May I share the episode with your readers? It was on a Woden's Day evening in that deliciously hot summer of '69. Dressed entirely in purple crushed velvet with plumed lace neckerchief and matching moccasins, I was attending a dinner party for dearest darling Lady Diana Cooper. It was the fifth birthday celebration for her beloved pooch Archibald (a grand old thirty-five in doggy years!) and we had all brought our cats and dogs along with us, garlanded, needless to add, in the most splendid array of colourful ribbons and bows.

Suddenly, from down my end of *la table* there arose a most frightful pong. At first, one's innate sense of tact told one to ignore it, but within minutes the stench had become so overwhelming that my neighbour, the then Mr Norman St John-Stevas, was groping in his patent leather clutch bag for his smelling-salts, while to his left the rather more forthright Margaret, Duchess of Argyll, who had come prepared for such an eventuality, clipped a wooden clothes peg to her nose. Sensing a commotion, she immediately clipped one to the nose of her pet Pekinese Alphonse, too.

It was, as I recall, Sir Harold Acton, sitting with his ageing pooch, Venus de Fido, who first broke the ranks of civility to point an accusing finger at Bubbles, Lady Rothermere. Greatly distressed, Bubbles denied everything. I found myself forced to spring to her defence. "He who sniffed it, piffed it!" quoth I, pointing my own finger back at Sir Harold. Sir Harold looked simply livid, and his squat forefinger now swung forty-five degrees to point at me, as he spluttered: "He who m-m-made the rhyme, d-d-did the crime."

Never have I been so incensed. With alacrity, I placed my hands over the ears of my beloved moggy, the Rt Rev Wenceslas Muff, so as to protect his delicate sensibilities from this vicious slander to his lord and master.

A scuffle then broke out, the table divided evenly between what one might call the sniffing and rhyming factions. At the evening's end, Dame Edith Sitwell sported a classic "shiner", but not before landing a couple of very useful punches bang in the centre of Sir Harold Acton's (to my mind rather too prominent) nose.

But who, pray, was the real villain of the piece? The truth was to emerge, twenty years later, in *Never Again* (Weidenfeld, 1989), Brian Masters's wide-ranging investigative book of the subject. It seems that poor Cecil Beaton's divine red setter, Poppet, was to blame, having consumed one too many "doggy drops" before setting out for the evening, and recent DNA tests have borne this out.

Moral: don't trust to rhyme, at any time.

Yours all along,

Sir Roy Strong.

Clerihews

Countess Spencer
Makes me awfully tense, sir:
That almighty hair
Is intended to scare.

A L Rowse
Enjoyed a grouse:
He considered his mater
A simply ghastly second-rater.

Geoffrey Levy
Never grieves, he
Feels your pain –
Then kicks again.

Though Marmaduke Hussey
Never kicked up a fuss, he
Could be quite curt
To John Birt.

Field Marshal Lord Alanbrooke
Favoured a dull, moustachioed look,
Belying the speed with which he
Would mutter something bitchy.

Edward Wessex
Is a dab hand at ethics
But in his A–Z of Royalty
There's no D for disloyalty.

For Sir Christopher Bland
The applause is canned:
He's an unlikely solution
To the digital revolution.

Professor Gunther von Hagens,
On the look-out for bargains,
Returned from East Sheen
With three buttocks and a spleen.

I fear Marks and Spencer
Are a trifle dense, sir:
They still think beige
Is all the rage.

Jimmy Young
Goes from swinging to swung,
It's the way the wind blows:
Orft he jolly well goes.

For Vanessa Feltz
My tender heart melts.
I enjoyed her last trauma
Over a takeaway korma.

Liza Minnelli
Is seldom on telly:
There's no call today
To come to the Cabaret.

Please don't go,
P Y Gerbeau!
We're so rarely adored
By someone from abroad.

Menzies Campbell
Needs no preamble
(But he'll go into frenzies
If you pronounce it Menzies).

Mary Archer
Makes a speedy departure

When the door opens a crack
To the sound of "Honey, I'm back!"

Slobodan Milosevic
Gobbles down his sausage which
Makes him protest, "This is INSANITY!
It's a RHYME against HUMANITY!"

Osama bin Laden
Seldom says "Pardon".
Told to behave
He retires to his cave.

General Colin Powell
Favours the rounded vowel
For "Pow". But when it comes to "Col"
He lets it roll.

President Chirac
Enjoyed beaucoup de kickback
At least he'll be spared *une harangue*
From Giscard d'Estaing.

Laurens van der Post
Seldom got lost:
After driving through Epping in a car he
Penned *The Lost World of the Kalahari*.

Francis Fukuyama's
Retired to his pyjamas
To ponder this mystery:
Whither The End of History?

Stephen Byers
Has no time for liars
And he'll hit the roof
If you tell the truth.

The collection of Charles Saatchi
Is looking a little paatchi:
Without Damien Hirst
It goes from worse to worst.

Leonardo DiCaprio
Has a handicap, y'know:
He finds acting rough, tough
And ardour, harder.

Richard Dawkins thinks it odd,
So he's searching for the key:
"I do not believe in God
But does God believe in me?"

Ted Hughes
Cooked stews
Of rabbit, otter, beaver, frog,
Crow, weasel, rat and dog;
But he avoided stoat:
It tends to float.

Department of Culture

LITERATURE:
Don't Laugh: Comedians and Novelists

THE COVERS of Penguin Classics, and many other books, have established a connection in our minds between this novelist and that painter: somehow, Edith Wharton and John Singer Sargent go together, as do Conrad and Turner, or Oscar Wilde and Aubrey Beardsley, or Patrick White and Sidney Nolan. The pairings are endless. But for some reason, no such connections are ever made between novelists and comedians. This is a strange omission, as they are every bit as clear.

Graham Greene and Frankie Howerd have much in common. The art of both men was stimulated by spiritual decay and physical discomfort. "To me, comfort is like the wrong memory at the wrong place or time: if one is lonely, one prefers discomfort," writes Greene at the beginning of *The End of the Affair*. "Poor soul!" Howerd would say whenever a woman in the audience laughed too loud. "Loosen something! Loosen something! There's nothing worse than your knickers out of focus!"

Graham Greene was born into prosperity in Berkhamsted in 1904. Aged twenty-six, he wrote in a newspaper article that he hoped to find time in the future "to become thoroughly acquainted with such strange and slightly sinister suburbs as Brixton and Streatham Hill". Frankie Howerd, born thirteen years after Greene, was in many ways his real-life counterpart: he had no need to dream of suburbia, as he was brought up in Eltham, on the route out of London to Kent, his mother keeping the family going by working as a cleaner.

In the same way, Greene had to convert to Catholicism in his twenties in order to harness his artistic interest in God, while Howerd was brought up in the shadow of the Lord: his mother was a strict Scottish Presbyterian; as a teenager, he became an active Sunday School teacher and thought seriously of becoming a clergyman.

An air of contrivance surrounds Greene's determination to spot God beneath the banalities of everyday life. "Those who marry God can become domesticated too," he writes in *A Burnt-Out Case*, "– it's just as humdrum a marriage as all the others." But for Howerd, God's omnipotence was all too real, and he didn't have to invent whisky-sodden old priests to enact his own loss of faith. Jeanne Mockfort, who played the crazed soothsayer Senna in *Up Pompeii!*, told his biographer, Graham McCann, "Over the years, something was gnawing at him. When I first met Frankie, he had a Bible by his bedside. But not at the end. The Bible had gone. He just turned away from it."

Instead, he read Plato and Aristotle. Friends remember Frankie growing drunk and maudlin over brandy, struggling to reconcile the question of a loving God in a cruel world. Like Greene, he managed to find an avenging force in the most unlikely places ("He's a strange man, isn't he?" he once said of Robin Day. "Funny man. Ye-ess. And hasn't he got cruel glasses!") but, for my taste, Howerd is the artist who locates his religious fears less self-consciously, and therefore more successfully, within the humdrum artefacts of real life.

Both men created art out of the sense of dislocation that had been with them since childhood, but Greene expressed it in a more solemn yet cackhanded way, once famously boasting that his first memory was of a dead dog lying at the bottom of his pram. To me, there is something smug about Greene's worries, a certain pomp and swagger to his professions of dread ("He trailed the clouds of his own glory after him; hell lay about him in his infancy").

Howerd, on the other hand, always appeared genuinely restless and fearful. His symbol of this fear was funnier than Greene's dead dog, and, in a strange way, it rings more true: in his autobiography, he recalled falling down the stairs as an infant and landing on his head. "To this day, I get vertigo when the heels of my shoes are repaired," he confessed.

Howerd was a shy, tormented man (friends estimate he had as many as twenty-four different psychoanalysts over the course of his life), who tortured himself with fear every time he walked out on stage. He once said that the great paradox of showbusiness is that the most insecure people are drawn to one of the most insecure professions in the world. "In my case," he added, "I was a nervous wreck with tremendous determination." He was homosexual, and wished he wasn't. Terrified lest his secret be made public and turn him into an object of scorn, he managed to sublimate these fears and transform them into the stuff of comedy.

This put him in the odd position of being able to produce uproarious laughter from his audiences by imploring them to take him more seriously. ("No. Don't laugh. No. Don't, please. You'll make trouble. I beg of you. Don't laugh.")

Using double entendres, Howerd would, at one and the same time, disclose his homosexuality to his audience while chiding them ("No, missus, ooh, aah, I mean, the very idea. No! Control yourselves!") for being so very dirty-minded as to get the wrong end of the stick. In his art and in his life, Graham Greene also liked to place the idea of sexual guilt centre-stage, but it was just play and titillation: he had to engineer peril for himself by making love to his mistress in forbidden places, such as churches. He, too, dealt in double entendres ("onion" was his code-word for sex – "I like onion sandwiches" he once wrote on a postcard from Amsterdam to Catharine Walston) but there was little imagination to them, and no art.

Graham Greene died in 1991, Frankie Howerd in 1992. "One ought to write funny books," Greene had once observed. "Life is really too horribly funny." But it was Frankie for whom life was all the more horrible, and therefore all the more funny: Graham Greene had less to build on, so was forced to camp it up.

* * *

The novelist Anthony Burgess and the comedian Benny Hill were both hugely successful, yet went to their graves thinking of themselves as neglected outsiders. Both delighted to an almost obsessive extent in wordplay. Both liked to explore sex in their work, while, by all accounts, shying away from it in real life.

Watching old Benny Hill shows in Monaco (long after they had been condemned in Britain), Burgess became an unabashed admirer. Reviewing a new biography of Hill, *Saucy Boy*, in the *Guardian* in 1990, Burgess declared him not only "a comic genius steeped in the British music-hall tradition" but also "one of the great artists of our age".

The two men met for the first time shortly after the review appeared. I was lucky enough to be present at this bizarre meeting. Both of them behaved remarkably like they did on television. Hill arrived first, as perky as can be, apparently over the moon at having been driven by a female taxi driver ("Oooh, I said, you can take me anywhere, my love!"). Burgess – histrionic, loquacious, with deep voice and furrowed brow, often putting the emphasis on unexpected words – behaved just like a slightly hammy actor playing the part of Anthony Burgess.

The two of them were full of mutual admiration, but never quite found common ground. All in all, it followed a similar pattern to T S Eliot's meeting with Groucho Marx: the author wanted to show off his knowledge of comedians, while the comedian wanted to show off his knowledge of authors. By the end of the dinner it seemed to me unlikely they would ever meet again, and, as far as I know, they did not. But then neither man had long to live. Hill died in 1992; Burgess in 1993. Reading their biographies, I now realise that they had rather more in common than either would have suspected, or would have been prepared to admit.

For a start, they had each changed their names: Anthony Burgess was born John Wilson and Benny Hill was born Alfie Hill. Both had early experiences which made them scared of sex. Burgess claimed to have been seduced, aged seven, by an Irish parlour maid. He later told Anthony Clare that it "confirmed everything the Church had said about sex being a dirty business ... it frightened me out of my wits". Hill's father had worked for a company that manufactured condoms and sex manuals, among them one called *What Every Woman Should Know*. The young Alfie was remorselessly teased about this at school. "Alfie's dad sells Frenchies!" they would chant.

Both men used their art to turn timidity into bravado, mining their early lives for material. Burgess wrote *The Malayan Trilogy* about his life of "uncontrollable lust" as an English teacher in Malaya. Hill based his number one single "Ernie (The Fastest

Milkman in the West)" on his days as a shy young milkman driving a horse and cart through the outskirts of Southampton, all the while fantasising that he was a cowboy riding through Dodge City. In his youth, Hill had fallen in love with a girl he saw on a merry-go-round. Each day he would walk six miles there and six miles back, just to see her go in and out of a shop at lunchtime. He never discovered her name.

Burgess's best-known line is probably the opening sentence of *Earthly Powers*: "It was in the afternoon of my eighty-first birthday, and I was in bed with my catamite when Ali announced that the archbishop had come to see me." Hill's comes in "Ernie": "*He said you wanted pasteurised, 'cos pasteurised is best. She says, Ernie, I'll be happy if it comes up to me chest.*"

The two men adopt a nudge-nudge approach to sex, depicting it as alluring and forbidding at one and the same time. And for both of them, the sound of words often proves more powerful than their meaning, often to the point of subverting it. Burgess wrote a whole book, *A Clockwork Orange*, in an invented dialect; one of the reasons he loved Kipling was for his sound: on the voyage out to Malaya he stood on deck reciting "Mandalay", which he knew by heart.

Similarly, Hill wrote and performed numerous sketches in which he would twist double meanings from foreign accents. "Rye you no risten? You shtoopid iriot!" was the constant refrain of his impatient Chinaman, Chow-Mein. Like Burgess, Hill delighted in Kipling, though in a slightly different way. "Do you like Kipling?" he asks of a busty woman in an early sketch. "I don't know, you naughty boy, I've never kippled," she replies, suggestively.

It is a common misconception that his television shows always ended with Hill chasing scantily clad women around the place. In fact, it went the other way around: it was Hill who did the running away. It chimed with his fears offstage: he preferred his love unrequited, only ever proposing marriage to women who could be guaranteed to turn him down. Though he liked to be seen as the neighbourhood Lothario, leaving his home with a bevy of beauties, Hill once confessed to a close friend that he last had full intercourse in 1954. Burgess, too, liked to be thought of as a Casanova. His first volume of autobiography is full of his conquests, but it now appears that these boasts were largely fantasies. Interviewing him once in a bar in Venice, I remember him telling me that he had always found the smell of garlic powerfully erotic. "You never told me that!" his wife chipped in. Like Hill, he preferred to channel the "dirty business" of sex into comedy. "He said it was artificial respiration," reports a woman in *Inside Mr Enderby*, "but now I find that I am to have his child."

Small wonder that Anthony Burgess was so drawn to Benny Hill: his ogling, leering, bashful persona was surely the comic embodiment of Burgess's secret self. Small wonder, too, that Hill so coveted the respect of Burgess: traditionally, intellectuals tend to think of end-of-the-pier comedians as shallow, and often overlook the heartfelt depths from which springs their curious art.

* * *

D H Lawrence (1885–1930) and Les Dawson (1934–1993) are, for some reason, seldom compared. Though Lawrence's great champion, F R Leavis, lived until 1978, allowing him plenty of time to catch the *Sez Les* television shows ('69–'76), he never, as far as I know, brought Les Dawson into his lectures on D H Lawrence.

Yet Dawson and Lawrence had a good deal in common. Both came from poor working-class backgrounds (Dawson from Manchester, Lawrence from Eastwood in Nottinghamshire), both left school early (Dawson at fourteen, Lawrence at fifteen) and both went to work in jobs that held no interest for them (Dawson in the drapery department of his local co-operative society, Lawrence in a surgical goods factory in Nottingham).

Of the two, Dawson probably experienced the harder struggle. While Lawrence soon managed to find work as a teacher, and from there gained a scholarship to Nottingham University, Dawson found himself sacked just two weeks after his big break, going to work as a journalist on his local paper. His writing was, they said, too flowery; having penned a 150-word obituary of an ex-deputy mayor, he found it cut down to just five words: "Councillor X was buried yesterday."

Dawson then made his way to Paris, where he intended to write a great novel. Instead, he found work as a pianist in a brothel near the Rue de la Goutte d'Or. Returning to Manchester, he got a job as a salesman for Hoover. He used his first-hand knowledge of this world in his novel *The Amy Pluckett Letters*, in which one of the central characters is placed in a mental asylum, believing herself to be a Hoover. "She seems to be picking up well," reports her doctor.

Brought up in a Collyhurst slum, Dawson had a tougher upbringing than Lawrence. This may have given him a less romantic view of poverty. In his youth, his jaw was smashed in a fight in Manchester; he later transformed the fracture into art, by pulling his chin over his nose. "I used to sell furniture for a living," he once said, with his perpetual air of despondency. "The trouble was, it was my own."

Lawrence had contempt for the bourgeoisie, but praised the working classes for managing to keep "the natural glow of life". Dawson's grimmer experience – not for him a cosy teaching job – made his vision less sunny. "I'm not saying the place is dirty," he said of his home at the time, "but you have to spray the kitchen with DDT before the flies will come in." He once recalled meeting a working-class girl walking across the Pennines with a sack of wheat on her back. "Excuse me, do you know where there's an all-night windmill?" she asked him.

Lawrence's mother was highly possessive of her son, and passed on to him her contempt for his father. Lawrence was unable to escape her influence, and hated her for it, though (or perhaps because) she had managed to keep him from following his father down the mines. His dislike of her social aspirations contributed to his lifelong contempt for the middle classes. "How beastly the bourgeois is" was the title of one of his poems. "Curse the blasted, jelly-boned swines, the slimy, the belly-wriggling invertebrates, the miserable sodding rotters ..." he wrote to Edward Garnett in 1912.

Dawson was much more easy-going in his attitude to the bourgeoisie, and, later in life, was unembarrassed about having moved to Lytham St Annes "where it is so posh that when we eat cod and chips we wear a yachting cap".

It is undoubtedly the subject of women that most excites the two artists. Personally, I always find Dawson's portrait of the two gossiping Lancashire women Cissie and Ada far more observant than any of the creations of D H Lawrence, especially when the two women start mouthing silently to each other about such unmentionable matters as sex or illness.

Though Lawrence was once famous for his frankness, his sexual descriptions now seem sentimental and even slightly silly. "John Thomas says good night to Lady Jane, a little droopingly, but with a hopeful heart": can anyone still read *Lady Chatterley's Lover* with a straight face? Les Dawson, on the other hand, is much more down-to-earth. "I met my wife in the tunnel of love," he once revealed. "She was digging it."

Many of Mellors's graver pronouncements on sexual relations now read like the bland truisms of A Doctor in *Private Eye*. "Some things can't be ravished. You can't ravish a tin of sardines," intones Mellors to Lady Chatterley. Dawson is infinitely more imaginative with his food imagery: "When she lightly kissed my cheek," he recalled, " it felt as though I had been savaged by a frankfurter."

Lawrence's mother was the great inescapable presence in his life. Towards the end of her life, he remembered placing the very first copy of his book *The White Peacock* in her dying hands. "She looked at the outside, and then at the title page, and then at me, with darkening eyes ... I think she doubted whether it could be much of a book, since no one more important than I had written it ... This David would never get a stone across Goliath. And why try? Let Goliath alone!"

For Dawson, as for so many Northern comedians, it was his mother-in-law, real or imagined, who filled this all-powerful role, filling him with the requisite amounts of fear and trepidation, but with none of Lawrence's self-pity, or, indeed, self-glorification. "There was a knock on the door. I knew it was the mother-in-law because the mice were throwing themselves on the traps ... I'm not saying she's ugly, but every time she puts make-up on, the lipstick backs into the tube ... For all that, she does possess things that men admire; like muscles and a duelling scar."

It used to be de rigueur to scorn the early critics of DH Lawrence for their philistinism, but, reading them again, you have to admit that they were on to something. "The thud, thud, thud of his hectic phrases is intolerably wearisome," wrote one reviewer of *The*

Rainbow. Prissy, maybe – but also true. Send for Les! "Lazy? He used to ride his bike over cobblestones to knock the ash off his ciggie." If ever there's a thud, thud, thud in the Dawson oeuvre, it is always there for a purpose.

Miss Goody and Mr Darcy

"YOUR EXAMINATION of Mr Darcy is over, I presume," says Miss Bingley to Elizabeth Bennett early in Jane Austen's *Pride and Prejudice*, "and pray what is the result?"

"I am perfectly convinced by it that Mr Darcy has no defect. He owns it himself without disguise," replies Miss Bennett.

"No," interrupts Mr Darcy, "I have made no such pretension. I have faults enough, but they are not, I hope, of understanding. My temper I dare not vouch for. It is I believe too little yielding – certainly too little for the convenience of the world."

And so the tale of their romance starts to take shape.

Compare and contrast this with the romance, two hundred years later, between Miss Jade Goody, from Bermondsey, and Mr "P J", from Birmingham, as enacted before our eyes in the Big Brother house.

On Day 34, Miss Goody attempts to break the ice by jumping naked into bed with P J – who, paradoxically, is not wearing PJs – and kissing his back. She then asks: "Do you find me f—able?"

"One thousand per cent, yes," he replies.

"Would you like to?" adds Miss Goody.

"One thousand per cent yes."

But on further questioning, Miss Goody discovers that Mr P J's deepest desires lie elsewhere. "In the outside world I probably wouldn't go for you," he admits. "You are good-looking, have nice lips, a nice face and you are a good laugh. But there is one other person in here who fits the bill better. Adele is gorgeous, she's got looks, brains and a wicked personality. If it was just for sex, I'd pick you, but Adele is great."

At this, Miss Goody goes back to her own bed in a huff.

"Oh, I've put my foot right in it there, haven't I?" says P J.

Sharp-eyed students of the romantic genre may well observe that, across the span of two centuries, a certain measure of reticence in matters romantic may be seen to have evaporated. But in many other respects, the two romances are strikingly similar.

Agreed, incidents and events now happen with far greater alacrity – it takes Mr Darcy more than three hundred pages before he comes round to admitting that he admires Miss Bennett (primarily, it would seem, for the liveliness of her mind). At no point in the entire novel does Miss Bennett go so far as to ask of Mr Darcy: "Do you find me f—able?" But who is to say that this question, however differently expressed, was not on her mind?

Human nature does not change. If anything is to blame for this century's faster, coarser approach to romance, I suspect it is the clothes. Mr Darcy and Miss Bennett would have had to struggle with any number of buttons and bows before anything untoward could possibly take place. By contrast, Miss Goody and Mr P J wander around in their underclothes. On Wednesday, Miss Goody's breasts sprang out of her bikini top as she was splashing in the pool. Small wonder, then, that in today's overheated world things come to a head in the first few pages. Global warming has much to answer for.

(June 29, 2002)

Wallace Arnold: A Grievous Blow

DEEP BREATH, Wallace, deep breath. And blow! Once more! And wipe! All better. All better. There's a good boy!

The words of dear old Nanny flood back across the decades, and I feel strangely consoled. Were Nanny still alive today, she would be 133 years young. Needless to say, I shall still be celebrating her birthday, as I do each year, with the requisite number of candles and a single festive cracker, which I pull with myself.

As I extract the party hat and rootle around for the novelty whistle and amusing riddle-me-ree, I feel as though in some strange way Nanny is still in the room with me. I sometimes even feel her warm bristles against my cheek, and fancy I can see her firm but affectionate hand raised in preparation for discipline.

But I digress!

I have been in sore need of Nanny's comfort recently, for I have suffered a grievous upset. Let me, perforce, explain. I have long been regarded as the foremost authority on HM Queen Elizabeth the Queen Mother. And rightly so. Perusing my bookshelves, I see that I have, o'er the years, penned upwards of a dozen books in her honour, including *Sunshine on a Rainy Day: A Right Royal Celebration* (1963), *God Bless You, Ma'am* (1971), *The Queen Mother: A Salute in Verse* (1981), *Leave It To Chef: The Queen Mother Cookbook* (1985), *The Lady Who Stood Up to Hitler* (1989) and *The Nation's Favourite Nan: The Woman's Own Book of the Queen Mother* (with Roy Strong, 1992). Thus, I had every reason to believe that, when the time came, Buckingham Palace would have the common decency to honour me with the title of Authorised Biographer.

Small wonder that, on receiving the summons to the Palace last week, I considered my appointment a mere formality. So I was a little surprised, when ushered into a junior waiting room by Her Majesty's Chief Press Officer, Sir Max Clifford, to find half a dozen scriveners staring back at me, namely Mr Hugo Vickers, the Hon William Shawcross, Mr Kenneth Rose, Dr David Starkey, Lord St John of Fawsley and Lady Antonia Fraser.

"I suppose you are all applying for the job of my trusty researcher!" I remarked, jovially. "But regrettably I have already entrusted the post to little Simon Schama. It could be the leg-up the poor fellow so desperately needs!"

Imagine my horror, then, when it emerged that, far from being prospective researchers, the six of them were competing for the job I had earmarked as my own! We were, it transpired, to be subjected to a series of in-depth interviews and psychological tests by the Duke of Edinburgh. At the close of the day, the winner would be formally announced, and the losers sent packing, presumably to grub around for the job of official ghost-writer to the Princess Beatrice.

Frankly, the merest glimpse at the opposition was sufficient to assure me of victory, particularly after I had tied Mr Hugo Vickers's shoelaces together, causing him to rocket headlong into a potted plant as the rest of us stood up to greet the arrival of the Duke. Alas, it was a potted plant of which the Duke was particularly fond, and Mr Vickers found himself booted on to the street without further ado.

One down, and five to go! As it happened, Starkey proved no trouble at all. Within seconds of being ushered in to the Duke's sitting room, he was out on his ear. "B-b-but I only said she possessed the dress sense of a barmaid," whimpered Starkey, fighting back the tears.

Next to enter was Lord St John. "A handy tip, if I may, Norman," I whispered as he rose from his chair. "The Duke loves people who stand up to him. When he says, 'How are you?' all you have to do is reply, 'None of your beeswax' – and he'll be all over you." A minute later, Norman, too, was being shown the door. The wind was behind me now: before very long I would be splashing past that finishing line, sails a-billow!

But first I had to deal with Lady Antonia. As luck would have it, she was being troubled by a slight tickle in her throat. I seized the opportunity to dip into my pocket. "Help yourself to a throat lozenge, Antonia!" I purred, holding out a packet. Fortunately, her eyesight is not what it was, and she failed to notice the telltale words "Extra strength bubblegum" on the packaging. Alas, when the Duke asked her to expound on her qualifications for the task ahead, her reply was upstaged by an ever-expanding bubble emerging from her lips – a bubble which burst, seconds later, all o'er the Duke's face.

We were now down to the final two. I was confident that young Shawcross would offer no serious challenge – for all its modish egalitarianism, the Palace would never choose a bellboy as a biographer – so I marched into the Duke's room with a spring in my step. "Ah, Arnold," said the Duke. "Take a seat!"

As I did so, a loud trumpeting noise emerged from my behind. Too late, I realised that someone had hastily secreted a whoopee cushion beneath my seat! As I was frogmarched from the room, I could not help but notice a knowing smirk playing upon young Shawcross's lips.

Oh, Nanny, Nanny, Nanny! Tell me, Nanny, why is the world so very unfair?

The Perfect Danish: Hamlet, Prince of Denmark by Joanna Trollope

"To be," said Hamlet, spearing a Danish pastry with his fork and calling for another cappuccino from the slim, red-headed thirty-four-year-old waitress, whose boyfriend Rick had left her the night before after a row that had been simmering for some time, "or not to be. That is the question."

"Sorry?" said Ophelia, distractedly.

"I was saying," repeated Hamlet, irritably chewing on his Danish pastry, freshly baked that morning, "that the basic question is to be – or not to be."

"Come again?" said Ophelia. What was Hamlet on about? Ophelia's mind was on other things. As Hamlet rambled on – typical! – she picked up her Filofax – dark leather with gilt trim – and her Mont Blanc pen – bought at a sale in Asprey's on her last visit to New Bond Street – and began to flick through it, hoping to squeeze in a time to herself. She owed it to herself, she thought: it was high time she went mad and floated on her back down a stream.

"To die, to sleep," continued Hamlet. "To sleep: perchance to dream."

"Refill?" said the red-headed waitress, who had been working at the café for six months, and had enjoyed it, but was now thinking she might be better off taking an adult education course, and continuing her interest in Japanese ceramics, which she'd given up when Rick – cruel, heartbreaking, Rick – had encouraged her to come with him to Denmark.

"Ay, there's the rub."

Ophelia thought it best to let him ramble on. Hamlet simply hadn't been himself since his dad had died. "The death of a parent," reflected Ophelia, thoughtfully, "can affect us all in different ways. But time's a great healer." She decided to let Hamlet get it off his chest: at times like these, it was good to talk.

Hamlet took another bite of his Danish. Very tasty, too. The Danish, he reflected, are famous for their pastries. That, and their bacon. Perhaps this afternoon he would catch up on a bit of retail therapy in the colourful main street of Denmark's capital of Copenhagen, situated on the islands of Zealand and Amager (population 1.3 million, including suburbs).

"For in that sleep of death what dreams may come," he continued half-heartedly, while Ophelia rummaged in her Louis Vuitton bag – a present from Laertes, bless him – "when we have shuffled off this mortal coil."

Ophelia could bear it no more. It was high time he got over it. "Shall we get the bill, Hammy?" she sighed, demonstratively. "Some of us have work to do." That was the trouble these days, she reflected, sucking on a top-of-the range Danish peppermint: there's simply too much time for thinking.

The Memoirs of Tom Maschler

GEORGE ORWELL

I was born in 1933, the year that the highly regarded author George Orwell published *In and Out of Paris and London*, a highly original and extremely entertaining book.

The two of us never met. Orwell had misfortunately died before I had become the man most sane people hailed as the world's most brilliant publisher.

If only he had taken the trouble to live another few decades, I would have published Orwell brilliantly and his reputation would now be assured. We would have enjoyed many scintillating lunches together, and he would have been envious of my selection of beautiful girlfriends!

But it was not to be.

Incidentally, mutual friends have told me that his real name was Eric Blair. I never played tennis with him. This was lucky for him. Close friends regularly compliment me on my tremendous volleys.

JOHN LENNON

Another person I remember vividly is John Lennon. I published his verse and so put him on the map. Thanks in no small part to myself, his name still means something today.

My view of his verse was that it was highly original and extremely entertaining.

And what of the man himself? Once, when I was going into a room with him, I stood aside and said, "You first," I don't recall whether he replied or not, but I remember he went first, thanks to me, and I followed him in. It was a memorable meeting.

Some years later, John died, I forget how.

THE TRIUMVIRATE

I published Martin Amis, Julian Barnes and Ian McEwan. They all wrote highly original and extremely entertaining books. It is interesting to comparison them.

Of the three, Julian Barnes was the tallest. Martin Amis was the smallest. And Ian McEwan was somewhere in between.

On the other hand, in strictly alphabetical order, Amis came first. Then came Barnes. And McEwan came last. Unless one was going by their first names. In that case, McEwan (Ian) would be first, Barnes (Julian) second and Amis (Martin) last.

Whose hair was the darkest? Julian's was certainly the lightest. I now find it hard to recall whether Martin's hair was lighter than Ian's. Or if, on the other hand, Ian's hair was lighter than Martin's. My personal guess would be that there was not much in it.

I had many scintillating lunches with each of them (for which, I may add, they pointedly let me pick up the bills, a not inconsiderable expense in those days).

Over lunch, each of them told me time and time again how exceptionally flattered he was to be published by me. They had a high regard for my flair, and for my flares. It would not be true to say that I wrote their books for them. Far from it. I made it clear from the start that that was their job. Nevertheless, when they won prizes for the books I had published, I was good enough to let them go up onstage to collect them.

As a child, I regularly won prizes for my precocious ability with the ping-pong bat.

ALEXANDER SOLZHENITSYN

When he met me, Alexander Solzhenitsyn was a Russian novelist with a beard. This he continues to be. I found his novels highly original and extremely entertaining, in their typically Russian way.

We met in a restaurant somewhere. I asked him if he knew Edna O'Brien. Apparently, he did not. So I told him my story of the time I had, after considerable thoughting, decided against publishing her second novel. I then ordered the Poached Quenelles in a Lobster Sauce followed by Hot Shellfish with Olive Oil, Garlic and Lemon Juice. My meal was accompanied by an excellent Pouilly Fumé.

Over lunch, I told Alexander of my plans for bringing some highly regarded names to our non-fiction list and expanding our children's list to include some of the top illustrators in the country. I then confided in him that my good friend Joe Heller had apparently told George Weidenfeld I was the greatest young publisher in the world. "Little does he know," I concluded, "that I am also a wizard at badminton!"

I finished our lunch together by asking Alexander if he would care to join me in a Baked Egg Custard Tart with Nutmeg Ice Cream and Blackcurrant Sauce. "Would you care to join me in a Baked Egg Custard Tart with Nutmeg Ice Cream and Blackcurrant Sauce?" I said.

He declined. I think the word he used was "No". But he was content to watch as I ate mine. I was saddened that he left me to pay the bill.

WILLIAM SHAKESPEARE

Another bearded author was William Shakespeare. Close friends who greatly admired me (and who also knew Arthur Miller) took me to see a play of his, I forget which. I found it highly original and extremely entertaining.

I felt he had the raw talent I could do something with. I set about arranging lunch only to be curtly informed that he was dead. But I had the lunch anyway: Terrine of Ham and Foie Gras, Roast Turbot with Onion Confit, Tartlet of Soft Fruits with a decent Muscadet.

William's absence inevitably meant that, once again, it was me who was forced to pay the bill.

BRIGITTE BARDOT

I cannot say I got to know Brigitte Bardot as well as she might have liked.

At that stage, I was only recently married. In view of this, I would certainly not have allowed her to take our acquaintance any further, even if she had begged me.

Nevertheless, I found her highly original and extremely entertaining. I retain a vivid memory of her. She was a French actress.

I will never forget our lunch together. It was Zucchini and Saffron Risotto, followed by a Millefeuille of Red Mullet, then a Passion Fruit Terrine. I ate it brilliantly, or so I am informed.

Literary Conjugations

I am prolific
You are busy
He churns them out.

I am consistent
You are predictable
He is formulaic.

I am neglected
You are forgotten
Isn't he dead?

I am a dirty realist
You are a realist
He is dirty.

I have my finger on the pulse
You need the money
He is ghost-writing the Posh 'n' Becks Christmas Pop-Up Book.

I am a satirist
You are a humorist
He writes toilet books.

I write bestsellers
You pen crowd-pleasers
He is Jeffrey Archer.

I am an iconoclast
You are a trouble-maker
He is an infernal nuisance.

I am an international author
You are available in translation
He is well known in Uruguay.

I am a cult
You are obscure
He is unknown.

I make history accessible
You make history sell
He compares Anne Boleyn to Britney Spears.

I look deep into the human heart
You look deep into your own soul
He is an alcoholic.

I am Trollopean
You are a trollop
He is a troll.

I am a communicator
You'd crawl 500 miles over nails to appear on Radio Chippenham
Drivetime
She is Edwina Currie.

I am a poet
You write the odd poem
He is unemployed.

My prose is sinuous
Your prose is sensuous
He writes hard-core porn.

I celebrate working-class life
You have a sharp ear for human foibles
He pokes fun at Northerners.

How to Judge a Novel

A HEADLINE IN the *Observer* ran, "Too many long and dreary reads, says Booker judge". This would be in with a good chance for scooping the top prize in an All-Time Dullest Headlines competition, but a separate story about the Booker Prize in the same newspaper struck me as genuinely odd. It seems that when the Booker jury was debating this year's shortlist, an argument broke out concerning the plausibility of the ending of *Who's Sorry Now?*, a comic novel by Howard Jacobson.

This ending apparently involves a reconciliation between a husband and wife while riding on the London Eye. Most of the panel were convinced that, though the scene might carry punch in a Hollywood movie, it was far too implausible for a Booker shortlisted novel.

At this point, one of the novel's champions, Salley Vickers, asked the others how they could be so sure that such a scene wouldn't take place on the London Eye. The head of the judges, Lisa Jardine, turned to her and said: "Salley, have you ever been on the London Eye?" Vickers admitted she hadn't.

"Then let's go!" exclaimed the eager Jardine. And so the entire Booker Prize panel upped sticks and took taxis to the South Bank to check out for themselves the likelihood of Jacobson's final scene.

This story then takes a bizarre twist. Standing in a capsule above London, Salley Vickers turned to her fellow jurors and conceded that, yes, they were right: Jacobson's reconciliation scene between husband and wife couldn't possibly have happened on the London Eye. And with this, *Who's Sorry Now?* was struck off the Booker shortlist.

Was the Booker panel right or wrong? Should a novel be judged in terms of probability? To reach a conclusion on this matter, one must first weigh these two separate scenarios to see which is the more probable:

a) You have just stepped aboard the London Eye when a warring couple enters your capsule. Over the course of your ride, they effect a reconciliation.

b) You have just stepped aboard the London Eye when Prof Jardine and her Booker Prize jury barge their way into your capsule. Over the course of your ride, one juror admits she was wrong; before the ride is over, they have all voted to throw out the book under discussion.

On the face of it, I would say that scenario (b) is a good deal less likely than scenario (a). Yet we are now reliably informed that scenario (b) actually happened, while scenario (a) could not possibly have happened. Strangely enough, one of the favourites to win tonight's prize is *Life of Pi* by Yann Martel. It features a sixteen-year-old boy all alone on a lifeboat in the middle of the ocean with a hyena, a Bengal tiger, a seasick orang-utan and a zebra (which the hyena is eating alive). It pains me to think of the ordeal Prof Jardine and her jury must have endured before giving it the go-ahead for the shortlist.

And how would this year's hands-on Booker Prize jury have fared in previous years? In 1999, when J M Coetzee won with *Disgrace*, would they have felt obliged to hang about in a bleak South African farm so as to test the percentage possibility of being raped by their next-door neighbour? In 1981, would they have hot-footed it to India to peruse hospital records, just to check that exactly 581 children had been born on the stroke of midnight on August 15, 1947?

A good many books would have faced earlier Booker Prize juries with almost insuperable fact-checking difficulties, not least John Milton's *Paradise Lost*. One can only imagine the difficulties that faced the jury in 1886, for instance, when Robert Louis Stevenson's *The Strange Case of Dr Jekyll and Mr Hyde* was published ("more potion, anyone?"), and they would have had to do a considerable amount of packing before mounting their fact-checking expedition for Jules Verne's *Journey to the Centre of the Earth*.

Exactly one hundred years ago, the jury for the Booker Prize 1902 would have had to wrestle with Joseph Conrad's *Heart of Darkness*. After much debate, Prof Jardine would chime in with: "Salley, have you ever been to the heart of darkness?" Before they knew where they were, the whole panel would be floating on a raft down the Congo in search of anyone who looked even remotely like poor old Mr Kurtz.

Speaking for myself, I have always found Snow White and the Seven Dwarves a little far-fetched. Was that her real name? Were all seven of them on the short side, or were one or two blessed with average height? Send for Booker!

MUSIC:
Jonathan Ross meets Madonna

JONATHAN ROSS: Fand-asdic! You look fablus! Cwoor! You look gwate! Just gwate! Darn she look fablus, lazen gennulmun? Fant-astic! Wooh! I twuly can't bleev you're here with me today! Unbleevbul! Fancy a quickie? Fand-asdic! And you've also done all of us in this little countwy of ours the gwate honour of atchly coming to live amongst us!

MADONNA: Yes.

JONATHAN ROSS: Unbleevbaw. We all thank you fwom the bottom of our hearts for coming to live here. Just think of that lazen gennulmun – Madonna atchly living in England! Canyer bleev it? So er I guess you um must like it here?

MADONNA: Yes. Quite.

JONATHAN ROSS: Fand-asdic! Gwate! Thank you so much for answerwing that question! Hilawious! So now Madonna's gonna tweat us to a toadly genius new song! Let's hear it for Madonna, lazen gennulmun!

MADONNA:
Ah trahda stayur head, trahda stayon tarp
Trahda playapart, but somehow ahfugart
Ahdlark to spress my stream parnda view

Ahm not chrisjun nodda jew
Ooohweeoooweeoooh
This is American Lahf

JONATHAN ROSS: FABLUS! GWATE! FAND-ASDIC! Now, lez facey, you are the singaw biggest star in the histwy of the whirl of wall time ever. Thas quite an achievemun!

MADONNA: Wodever.

JONATHAN ROSS: Gwate! It must be litwully amazing being you! Tell us what you do on a normal day?!

MADONNA: This and that.

JONATHAN ROSS: Fand-asdic! Gwate weply! Tellyawha, if I was Madonna, I'd get out of bed, stwip naked and just look at myself in the miwwor for hours on end!!! I mean, you've got the most FAND-ASTIC physique, you weally have! Gwate bweasts! Cwooor! If I were you, I'd just go STARKERS and look at them in the miwwor all day long – then I'd turn wownd and take a gander at that incwed-ibull bum! Is that what you do on a normal day, then? Is it?

MADONNA: No.

JONATHAN ROSS: Gwate! Um. So, Madonna, tell us about a day when you do somethin you weally want to do. Like, what would you do on a day when you do somethin you weally want to do – like, a day when you could do anything, so you decide to do not just anything but, like, somethin you weally want to do, f'rinstance?

MADONNA: Hmmm. A day when I do something I really wanna do. Hmmm.

JONATHAN ROSS: Yeah. I mean, like a day when you just wake up and you think, hey, I'm Madonna, I can do wodever I wanna do and what I wanna do today is to do, like, wodever I wanna do. Like, if I were you, I'd fondaw my bweasts all day, thas what I'd do! I mean, lez face it, you got twuly gwate tits, you weally have!

MADONNA: My husband and I might go do the movies. We read books. Go to a pub.

JONATHAN ROSS: Amazin! Lazen gennulmun, Madonna goes into our English pubs! Thank you so much, Madonna – you're a world superstar, but you are happy to go into an English pub! Thaz fand-asdic!

MADONNA: My husband and I go down to the Old Bull and Bush

with Burlington Bertie to spend our bobs and quids on a pint of ale and eat fish and chips with brown sauce served by Pearly Kings and Queens. Chim chiminee, chim chiminee, chim-chim-cherooo. And then my husband and I jump aboard a double-decker bus and rabbit in cockney rhyming slang with Mrs Tiggywinkle and the cheery local bobbies.

JONATHAN ROSS: Fand-asdic! And do you let them feel your bweasts at all?

MADONNA: No.

JONATHAN ROSS: Shame! Ha ha ha! Let's have another bwilliand classic song. Les hearwifaw Madonna, lazen gennulmun!

MADONNA:

> Doan tellmedur staaarp
> Tell the rain nodder draaarp
> Tell the win nodder blow
> Cos you said so
> Tell meeee larvissun drew
> Is jist somethin thad we do-oo-oo.

JONATHAN ROSS: Fan-dasdic! Fab-lus! We are so deeply honoured to have you among us! Now, not only do you have the most fand-asdic physique – wiwya just look at that arse, lazen gennulmun – but you are a positive GENIUS at we-invention. Like, one moment you are, like wolling naked on the sand in just a wimple, then you toadly we-invent yourself and for the next album you've toadly we-invented yourself and this time you're wolling naked on the sand – in a cowboy hat! Bwilliand!

MADONNA: I don't stick to the programme. I re-invent myself. I, like, play with the whole concept of adopting different personas as a means of, like, playing with the whole concept of different personas. By, like, reinventing myself. As a whole concept.

JONATHAN ROSS: Wight! I tell you when you looked slo49ply fablus – when you we-invented yourself for the vidjo for the whole sex concept – and you were wolling naked in the sand in that littaw pill-box hat. Wowa fan-tastic body! Then before the waw in Iwaq you toadly we-invented yourself with a whole new concept in an anti-waw vidjo – wolling awound naked in the sand in a gas-mask.

MADONNA: I wanted to wake people up to the whole notion that people get hurt in wars. By appearing naked in a gas mask I wanted to say, like, people wake up, war is such a negative concept.

JONATHAN ROSS: But then you withdwew the vidjo.

MADONNA: Sure. I withdrew the video because by then the war had started, and I wanted people to, like, get behind the whole concept of war, and wake them up to the more positive notion that war could actually stop more people getting hurt.

JONATHAN ROSS: Smashin'! Fand-astic! Tellyawhat, that Guy Witchie's a lucky bloke! Fwankly, I wouldn't mind givin' you one in my dwessing woom later! Less heary for Madonna, lazen gennul-mun – and the gwatest tits in the histwy of poplar music!

A-Z of Rock Biopics

✱ **Abraham, Father:** The tragic story of the last days of Father Abraham and the Smurfs is recounted in *Smurfed Out* (1981) by cult director Gus van Sant. After twenty-four hours bingeing on drink and drugs, Father Abraham (Oliver Reed) wakes up in a deserted multi-storey car park on the outskirts of Amsterdam to find three little pink helmets beside him. It dawns on him that during the night he has unwittingly consumed three of his favourite Smurfs. Abraham is visited in prison by Sister Mary Benedict (Susan Sarandon) and walks to his execution begging forgiveness from the Smurf families foregathered in the viewing room. Bleakly shot in black and white, the movie acts as a twentieth-century urban morality tale, a dire warning to men wearing artificial beards never to eat glove puppets.

✱ **Beatles, The:** Stephen Woolley's powerful movie, *Ringo: Birth of a Genius* (2003) tells the story of the first five years in the life of Ringo Starr. We witness the two-year-old Ringo's first, tentative tappings with a spoon and fork on his plate, and his family's unbridled excitement when, unprompted, he sings his own "Octopus's Garden" around the tree one Christmas. "Few people realise that Ringo was the major creative talent in the Beatles – and this movie sets out to put the record straight," says director Woolley. The film ends with John, Paul and George arriving at

Ringo's house to audition for places in his backing band. The older Ringo is played by Russell Crowe.

* **Choking on one's own vomit:** The current wave of rock biopics has made one British company, Vom of Norwich, a world leader in the production of artificial vomit. "In the old days, producers of rock biopics found it impossible to find a product with the right texture and consistency, but since 1999 we've changed all that," says chief executive Brian Spanner. "We make it to our own unique recipe, and are now producing 10,000 gallons a month. It's a great British success story."

* **Cobain, Kurt:** Scripted by Dan Brown, Oliver Stone's powerful new biopic of the fated lead singer with American rock group Nirvana suggests that Kurt Cobain (Matt Lucas) was in fact murdered by direct descendants of Pontius Pilate (Alan Rickman) to stop him blowing the whistle on who killed President Kennedy. Dame Judi Dench plays Cobain's live-in lover Courtney Love, with her customary dignity and restraint.

* **Death:** Every rock biopic must end in a solitary death, preferably in an unfurnished flat, with gold records strewn higgledy-piggledy over the bare floorboards. This can present an obstacle in biopics about groups rather than individuals. Michael Winner's seminal biopic, *The Black and White Minstrels: Slaughterhouse* (2004) solved the problem by having all twenty-two Black and White Minstrels herded into an abattoir outside Swindon and gunned down by the Mafia. "People often ask me why we never see the Black and White Minstrels on our television sets any more," explained Winner. "Well, this is the only plausible solution, dear." Winner is now filming *Blood Everywhere*, the true story of the unsolved murder of Lord Rockingham's XI.

* **Dylan, Bob:** Some critics maintain that the great English classical actor Sir John Gielgud was miscast as Bob Dylan in the 1975 biopic *A Tiresome Rain Is Expected Shortly*.

* **"Edelweiss":** Perhaps the most catchy and popular of all the tunes in *The Sound of Music* (1966). This is often seen as the very first rock biopic, telling the story of the Von Trapp family singers and their flight from Nazi Austria. The original director, Alfred Hitchcock, had planned to make it a much darker, more disturbing

film, with the ageing Joan Crawford as the drink-addled Maria, Edward G Robinson as her sadistic employer and the Von Trapp children played entirely by surviving extras from Tod Browning's classic 1932 movie *Freaks*. In the original screenplay, Maria attempts to get rid of the first Countess Von Trapp by cutting up a clump of poisonous edelweiss and baking it in a chicken pie.

✻ Forsyth, Bruce: Popular British entertainer, compere of *The Generation Game*. As a straight actor, Forsyth is probably best remembered for playing the title role in the low-budget British movie *Elvis!* (1977), though some Presley fans continue to complain that Elvis Presley never said, "Nice to see you – to see you nice!" before performing "Hound Dog".

✻ *Gorillas in the Mist*: This 1988 movie stars Sigourney Weaver in the true story of a glamorous young zoologist who lives for over a year as a member of Status Quo. At first shunned by them, over the next few months she learns to imitate their lolloping walk and strange grunting noises; after six months, she has them eating nuts out of her outstretched hand. In the film's moving climax, they permit her to join them in a rousing chorus of "Rocking All Over the World".

✻ Hendrix, Jimi: In the forthcoming movie *Legend: The Life and Death of Jimi Hendrix*, the famous guitarist is played by noted classical actor Ralph Fiennes. "The refined, reticent, slightly buttoned-up quality of Jimi has been overlooked for too long," comments cult director Michael Priest. "So the focus of our film is on his all-important school years." Priest remains fiercely opposed to the all-too-literal interpretations offered by so many rock biopics; for this reason, he has relocated Hendrix's schooldays from Seattle High to Rugby, the English public school perhaps best known as the setting for *Tom Brown's Schooldays*.

"Jimi very much enjoys his time at Rugby, where he becomes a House Captain," explains Priest. "He emerges with an expertise in the flute." Still in his teens, Hendrix becomes a world-renowned flautist, invited to play before the court of Queen Victoria. It seems to his fans that he can do anything with a flute – at one point in the film, he is even seen taking off his shoes and socks and playing it with his toes.

In *Legend*, Hendrix dies tragically young, saving a young girl from a house-fire. "I know some people claim he died choking on his own vomit," says Priest, "but I am aiming for a truth deeper than reality."

✱ **Inspiration**: Directors of rock biopics are always seeking to depict the dramatic moment behind the inspiration of their hero's best-known song. In Ken Russell's acclaimed *Cliff* (1973), for instance, the key point in the film comes when the hero, Cliff Richard (played by Kenneth Williams), comes back from his triumphant world tour, only to be welcomed by his mother, stark naked but for a crow's mask and a bloodied dagger, surrounded by medieval monks equipped with instruments of torture. Mrs Richard tells Cliff it is her birthday.

"We cut straight away to a close-up of Cliff looking frightened and perplexed," says Ken Russell, "and at that exact moment he is inspired to sing what will become his best-selling song of all time – "Congratulations". It's a truly electrifying moment."

✱ **Jones, Brian:** Stephen Woolley is soon to release his new movie, *Stoned*, about the life and death of Brian Jones (powerfully played by Ray Winstone). The film's likely success has prompted other producers to look around for other dead Rolling Stones whose tragic stories could be fashioned into rock biopics. "Sadly, all the other Stones appear to be alive," confesses veteran biopic director Howard V Krass, "but of course I've asked the doctors for a second opinion." It is rumoured that *Coronation Street* veteran William Roache has bought the rights to *The Bill Wyman Story* and is anxious to play the title role, opposite Joan Collins as Mandy Smith.

✱ **Joplin, Janis:** There have been many movies based on the life of the hard-living Texas-born singer who died at the tragically early age of twenty-seven. The most successful is probably *Beautiful* (2001), starring Barbra Streisand as Janet Jopling, a beautiful young Jewish woman with a crystal-clear voice who successfully battles with her childhood demons to become a world star. In the final scene, she marries a handsome American senator of outstanding integrity, played by George Clooney, and they vow to rid the world of war and poverty, winning a prolonged standing ovation from the congregation.

❋ **Knightley, Keira:** The young English star of *Pride and Prejudice* is set to play the title role in the movie *Cass!* "It will be quite a challenge to put on fifteen stone before we start shooting in November," says Keira, "but I have already started doubling my helpings of Special K." In January, she takes on a very different role when she starts shooting *The Karen Carpenter Story*.

❋ **Lavatory:** With more than twenty-five rock biopics a year featuring scenes with syringes and/or groupies and/or corpses set in public lavatories, Granada Films have recently built a permanent public lavatory set complete with mould available to international producers for a modest fee of $25,000 a day. "Our conveniences have got the lot," says location manager Doug Deep, "but if you want fully trained cockroaches, they're extra."

❋ **Marley, Bob:** The legendary Rastafarian reggae artiste has been celebrated in many rock biopics, among them *Trenchtown Frock*, in which he is portrayed as a cutting-edge fashion designer, and *Frenchtown Truck*, in which he is a lorry driver from Marseilles. In the new Stephen Woolley movie, *The Life of Bob Marley*, he is played by the twenty-stone English actor Richard Griffiths.

"Richard's casting is perfect," explains Woolley. "I had originally intended to film the life of Robert Morley, but then the backers pulled out."

❋ **Nudity:** Nudity is a standard feature in many rock films, though curiously enough not in *Cass!*, about the life of Mama Cass, nor *Forever and Ever*, about the life of the legendary Greek singer Demis Roussos, nor, indeed, the forthcoming biopic *Noddy: The True Story of Noddy Holder*.

❋ **Peel, John:** *Young Peel* stars Orlando Bloom as the teenage John Peel who is spotted by a big-time radio producer spinning plates in a touring circus. "Hey, the way that guy spins plates makes me think he'd make a truly great disc jockey!" cries a visiting producer – and the rest is history. Also shooting is the low-budget *Peel's Shirt*. Filmed entirely in black and white on location, it follows a single morning in Peel's life, when he is deciding whether to wear the same T-shirt he wore yesterday or if it's time to put a new one on. The ending leaves things ambiguous.

❋ *Queen:* Some critics continue to argue that the English classical actor Sir John Gielgud was miscast as Freddy Mercury in the rock biopic about the lead singer of Queen. But the director argues that the ninety-two-year-old thespian brought out the more contemplative, lyrical side to the famous entertainer, particularly in the scene where the rest of the group sing "We Will, We Will Rock You" while Freddy sits back in his rocking chair.

✱ **Rice, Tim:** The celebrated English lyricist is currently putting the finishing touches to *Vicious!*, a musical based on the life of Sid Vicious. "We aim to bring out the very loving, very sensitive, very emotional side of a great guy who was too often misunderstood," explains master of rhyme Sir Tim. The opening number, "They Call me Vicious", has the following chorus: "*If I had three wishes/They wouldn't call me Vicious/Cos I love my Missus/The other thing I can't abide/Is being called Sid.*"

✱ **Russell, Ken:** The noted British film director Ken Russell has made many rock biopics, among them *The Jive Bunny Story* (1991), in which the young Jive Bunny witnesses his mother having sex with any number of strangers. She then succumbs to a bout of myxomatosis. On her deathbed, Jive Bunny slices off her head and tail, skins her and cooks her in a pot with carrots and onions. "It was the great traumatic experience of Bunny's youth," observes Russell, "but without it, he would never have given the world 'Let's Party'."

✱ **Syringes:** Quik-Fix is a British company with a $50 million turnover which is exclusively concerned with manufacturing all the syringes for the harrowing scenes that take place in dingy toilets three-quarters of the way through all rock biopics. Industry insiders predict that profits of Quik-Fix are set to rise still further with next year's remake of *The Sound of Music* by Quentin Tarantino.

✱ *Thorogood, Frank*: A new film about Brian Jones sets out to show how the Rolling Stone gradually comes under the increasingly domestic influence of his local builder, Frank Thorogood. First, Jones starts playing the odd game of cribbage, then he gets a taste for Birdseye Fish Fingers, and finally he becomes an addict of *The Black and White Minstrel Show* on Saturday nights. The film ends with Jones leaving the Rolling Stones to pursue a career as a kitchen designer in Cheam and surrounding areas.

✱ **Van:** Every rock biopic features an early scene in which a groupie is enticed by the group into a rickety van, much to the horror of the priggish gay manager. The only exception to this rule is *The True Story of Pinky and Perky* (Norman Jewison, 1987).

✱ Wyman, Bill: *Droned* is a new rock biopic based on the life of Rolling Stone Bill Wyman, played by former BBC newsreader Kenneth Kendall. "We have tried to bring out the duller, rather more dreary side of this, the least memorable of the Rolling Stones," says director Jeff Budge. The film centres on Wyman spending a quiet night in, watching television, and is said to capture perfectly the era in which it is set (2004).

My Song: "Tantum Ergo"

If you were 20 in the summer of 1967, San Francisco was the only place to be. Scott Mackenzie told us to wear flowers in our hair, and to be sure to wear some flowers in our hair, as we were going to meet some gentle people there.

But I was 10 in the summer of 1967, and boarding two miles from Basingstoke, in a Roman Catholic prep school. My friend Miller tried wearing a flower in his hair, only to be told by Major Watt to take it out at once. Major Watt was rumoured to be a Nazi spy. Someone had seen him in the school grounds late at night flashing secret messages to the Germans with a torch.

Gentle people were few and far between. Our new history master, Mr Wall, who wore pink socks, had a slapdash, bohemian air to him, but he left under a cloud, after dropping his trousers when someone inquired what colour his pants were. Gentleness, flowers, and even hair were in short supply.

I was studying hard for my Confirmation. Why did God make me? God made me to know him, love him and serve him in this world, and be happy with him forever in the next.

In our Confirmation classes, we took a peculiar delight in cross-questioning Mr Callaghan on the finer points of Roman Catholic theology. It always came back to the same old desert island. Sir, sir, sir! But what if you were stuck on a desert island, and there was a baby who was dying, and the baby hadn't been christened, sir, and there was no water about, sir. Would you be allowed to use your spit, sir? Would you be allowed to use your PEE, sir?

We had two Masses a week, on Wednesdays and Sundays, and two Benedictions, on Tuesdays and Fridays. Every Benediction, we would sing a hymn called "Tantum Ergo". "Tantum ergo/ Sacramentum/ Veneremur cernui/ Et antiquo/ Documentum..." We sang it twice a week for five years. We never asked what it meant, and I still don't know. Sacraments, venerate, antique, documents ... but its meaning didn't matter. Its sound was its meaning; its absence of meaning was its meaning. Latin was God's first language, its meaning floating direct to heaven on a cloud of incense pouring out of a thurible swung with such vigour by the seniors that the new boys in the front row would often disappear, coughing and spluttering, in an unholy fog.

"Lady Madonna" came out halfway through the next spring term. I have a vivid memory of hearing it coming from a radio belonging to builders who were patching up the school swimming pool. Its title represented the perfect amalgam of the two essentials of a private Catholic education, suggesting that the Virgin herself was an aristocrat.

But what did it all mean? "Lady Madonna" was followed by "Hey Jude" and "Instant Karma". Pop music was moving away from meaning, and closer to the language of "Tantum Ergo", forcing sense to make way for something more mysterious.

At Scout camp we sang "Gin Gan Gooly-Gooly Watch-a, gin gan goo, gin gan goo". In maths, we drew Venn diagrams. The Beatles sang "I am the Walrus Goo-Goo-Ga Joo". On Ash Wednesday, we heard the priest repeat "Remember man that thou art dust and unto dust thou shalt return" over and over again as he rubbed ash onto our foreheads. On Holy Days of Obligation, we all went to visit priests' hidey-holes in Catholic stately homes. I often wondered whether groups with Latin names like Procul Harum and Status Quo were Catholics too. And, behind it all, "Tantum Ergo" was our soundtrack.

My reverence for the far-away heaven of San Francisco was never at odds with my reverence for what in another hymn we called the "Faith of Our Fathers". I remember feeling a sharp sense of shock on first glimpsing the heading at the top of the music master's sheet music for "While Shepherds Watched". It simply said "Sox".

Thirty or more years on, I make my living from parody, nudging sense into nonsense, translating the words of others back into their original gibberish. I find "Tantum Ergo" has lodged in my head, a dissident group of my brain cells forming a chapel choir, singing it at full blast in impromptu moments. And my imagination keeps returning to Farleigh House, Farleigh Wallop, Basingstoke, Hants. Or perhaps it has always been stranded there, the boarder that never came home.

With Her Tongue Down His Throat

THE NAME Pamela Anderson has always seemed better suited to the spinster headmistress of a leading Scottish girls' school than to a busty Hollywood sex kitten. The former *Baywatch* star's near-namesake, the dour newsreader Pamela Armstrong, seems much closer in character to what her name leads one to expect.

This dichotomy between name and character means that every time I read of Pamela Anderson's raunchy exploits – generally illustrated with a close-up shot of what Sir Peregrine Worsthorne would call her embonpoint – I find myself doubly fascinated.

Miss Anderson's publicist, the more aptly named Marleah Leslie, recently announced that her client is engaged to a rapper called Kid Rock. Mr Rock's proposal took place somewhere in the Nevada desert. "Pamela is elated," exclaimed Miss Leslie. "I'm not sure if he got down on bended knee or not but he definitely asked her to marry him and she said yes. I'm sure it was romantic, as it was just the two of them."

This is neither the time nor the place to bring up the circumstances of her previous engagement, to the unreliable Motley Crue drummer Tommy Lee. Nevertheless, in his account of their first meeting, published in the band's official autobiography, *The Dirt*, Mr Lee described how Pamela Anderson sent a glass of vodka over to his table in a nightclub called the Sanctuary.

He then went over to her, said, "Hey, Pamela, I'm Tommy," sat down next to her and, in his own words, "grabbed her face and just licked the side of it, from chin to temple".

Oddly enough, it did the trick. After a brief courtship, Lee proposed to Anderson in a discotheque called La Boom. "She said yes, hugged me, and stuck her tongue down my throat." The two of them obtained a marriage licence the very next morning. "We were on the beach in our swim trunks getting married before the day was over. Instead of wedding bands, we went for something more permanent: tattoos of each other's names around our fingers."

A fairytale marriage then – but a fairytale told, alas, by the Brothers Grimm. The marriage was brief and rocky, ending under something of a cloud when Lee was sent to prison for six months for attacking Miss Anderson. Mutual recrimination remains at a pitch: only last month Miss Anderson claimed she had caught hepatitis C from sharing Mr Lee's tattoo needle.

Had any of us come across the engagement between Mr Thomas Lee and Miss Pamela Anderson in the Forthcoming Marriages column of the *Daily Telegraph*, we would no doubt have wished them well, our only slight worry being that they sounded a little on the dull side. The moral of this story is thus never to judge people on their names alone.

Incidentally, Kid Rock was born Robert Ritchie, which sends out a mixed message as to whether he will prove worthy of Miss Anderson's hand.

Coldplay or Crazy Frog?
The Experts Take Sides

✻ Maya Angelou: There is an old African saying of many years, handed down from sage to sage, from parsley to parsley. This saying is as true as an old stone washed by the flow of a fast-running stream, but less wet. Heed it well, my children, but do not re-heed it, as it is frozen in time. "The Crazy Frog which basks upon the uppermost pinnacle of the charts must needs be destined to fear being trodden underfoot."

How true. Mine is the broadest, the softest of human hearts. For no wish have I to hear the Crazy Frog croak his last. So I urge you, good-hearted citizens of Coldplay, to ascend that charted mountain with due care, and to stop at number two, and let Crazy Frog remain unsquelched.

✳ **Lord Tebbit:** It frankly gets my goat, the media attention that's been lavished upon the so-called Crazy Frog. If the gentleman in question is a frog, and if he is indeed crazy, then he should be locked up, though not at the taxpayers' expense. We should charge this self-confessedly lunatic frog to lock himself up. Ordinary, decent Britons have nothing to learn from a mentally disturbed Frenchman. Is Crazy Frog a family man? From the look of him, I very much doubt it. Coldplay are more my cup of tea: four normal English blokes. They may well make a fearful din, but at least they have the grace to look sorry about it – unlike certain frogs I could name.

✳ **Anita Roddick:** Coldplay, and the lovely, lovely Chris Martin, are desperate to join me in saving the planet. To this end, Chris and the lads are helping me promote my new Crazy Frog Ankle Scrub, made entirely from organic Crazy Frog, humanely cut up into little bits, lovingly descaled and then passed caringly through a tribal liquidiser. Together, we'll save the planet from more ruinous ringtones, and that must be a good thing.

✳ **Professor Christopher Ricks:** I am a Crazy Frog man, or, rather, Crazy Frog is all men, for there is surely a crazy frog in all of us. But what, one is obliged to ask, does Frog mean when he sings – so plaintively, yet in many ways with such assurance, even exuberance – "Ragga ding ding ding ding didda ding ding"?

"Ragga" is a word that instantly calls to mind rags – poverty both physical and spiritual, powerfully evoking the nursery legend of Cinderella and her Prince Charming (for did he not also turn into a frog when kissed?). But what of "ding"? For me, "ding" is a word of infinite meaning, incorporating not only "in" but "din" and "ing" too, "ing" being the final three letters – poignant, apocalyptic – of the word "ending". Is it a happy ending? That next word – "didda" – so eerily reminiscent of a toddler attempting to use just two syllables to pronounce its own father – dadda – dead – is perhaps the bleakest ever employed by a four-legged poet.

Was Frog born crazy, or was craziness forced upon him by a society that rejected his very frogginess? The next line, "binkhm daahm bahahm dehm babarambamba bohm bohm", with its resonant allusions to Ezekiel's furiously cursing Yahweh ("daahm ... dehm") calls on the listener to recognise that his craziness was imposed on Mr Frog, and, furthermore, that he now sees it as his mission, via the ringtone ("ding... ding"), to impose it on us.

✱ **David Davis:** Frankly, it's not case of either/or. Far from it. We as a party must learn to love both Coldplay and Crazy Frog. In the past, small tail-less amphibians with mental disorders may, for whatever reason, have felt excluded from the Conservative Party. That's something we've got to change. Under my leadership, we'll make sure far more frogs – and not only frogs, but toads and lizards too – come to us as their party of choice. But we must also continue to embrace melancholic public school millionaires, and that's why the Coldplay vote is so vital. And let me say this. Not until we have seen Crazy Frog on lead vocals, with Coldplay providing the backing, will we ever be re-elected.

✱ **Mohamed Fayed:** Crazy Frog, he no Crazy at all, no way, he Sensible Frog, he my good friend, he come to Mohamed and he saying, "Mohamed, you honest man, I want knowing this: everyone say you honestest most handsomer man in world – you tell me how I getting chart of tops?" So I tell Frog how British Establishment homos – the pervert Tone Blair and his nancy boyfriends Duke of Edinburgh and Michael Howard – they fixing Pop of the Tops so Coldplay make number one slot, is plot. And Crazy Frog, he say, "But I ringtone" and I say, "You crazy, Frog! You no ring Tone! He send MI5 and MI6 and M25 to kill you, I telling you, is Establishment cover-up."

32,000 Pop Stars

GEORGE MELLY once wrote a prescient book about popular music called *Revolt Into Style*. Its title encapsulated the book's central theme: what starts life as revolution will transform, as the years go by, into an adjunct of style.

In the history of pop, this format has been repeated time and time again, from Thin Elvis causing outrage with each thrust of his pelvis to Fat Elvis delighting the blue-rinse matrons in Las Vegas, from the twenty-one-year-old Johnny Rotten shocking the middle-aged at the Silver Jubilee, to Johnny Rotten, the forty-six-year-old property speculator flying in from Malibu to charge £32.50 a head for a nostalgia concert at the Golden Jubilee.

I wonder whether the time is ripe for Melly to bring out a second volume called *Style Into Anorak*, for pop music now seems destined to become a branch of list-making, satisfying the urges of those who, in an earlier era, would have channelled their energies into trainspotting or stamp collecting.

There are now so many pop stars and ex-pop stars that only the most obsessively nerdy can ever hope to keep track of them. Every year, the *Guinness Book of British Hit Singles* gets bigger and bigger, its pages filled with more and more pop stars. The new edition, the fifteenth, consists of 640 pages of very small type, listing all the 25,000 singles by the 8,000 different acts who have managed to get into the Top Seventy-Five.

Eight thousand different acts! As most acts are groups, and most groups consist of at least four people, this adds up to something in the region of 32,000 different pop stars. This means that the number of people who can claim to have been in the charts now amounts to the population of a town slightly larger than Windsor.

Pick any name, and you will find a pop star to go with it. Looking up "Brown", I found Bobby Brown, the singer who was once married to Whitney Houston; Arthur Brown, who sang *Fire* in 1968 and used to appear on *Top of the Pops* with his head on fire; James Brown, the priapic seventy-four-year-old soul singer; Joe Brown of Joe Brown and the Bruvvers, described as "chirpy Cockney singer-guitarist", Errol Brown, who was the shaven-headed singer in Hot Chocolate; Roy "Chubby" Brown, the comedian, who seems to have had a number three hit in 1995; and Sam Brown, who reached number four in February, 1989 with "Stop".

But these are only the Browns that ring a bell with me. There are dozens more, all of whom had hits, including Dennis Brown, Kathy Brown, Peter Brown, Polly Brown, Miquel Brown, Sharon Brown, Jocelyn Brown, Jennifer Brown, Ian Brown, Horace Brown, Gloria D Brown and Diana Brown, not to mention two

Brownes with "e"s, Duncan and Jackson, and an entire group called the Browns.

At first, I felt a bit sore at not recognising all these Browns (and there are quite as many pop star Smiths and Joneses and Robinsons) as I have always counted myself a bit of a pop buff. But then I realised that my ignorance comes not just through growing older and less in touch, but also from Guinness deciding to cover the whole Top Seventy-Five rather than just the Top Twenty. This means that virtually everyone who has ever opened their mouth and bawled "I Love You" into a microphone has managed to sneak into the book somewhere.

Peter Brown, for instance, got to number forty-three in February, 1978 with a song called "Do You Wanna Get Funky With Me" and Miquel Brown reached number sixty-eight in February, 1984 with "He's a Saint, He's a Sinner".

If all the other Browns are there, then why not me? I looked myself up in the list of Browns, just on the off-chance that my hesitant rendition of "A Spoonful of Sugar" in a Record-Your-Own-Disc booth on Victoria Station in 1967 had somehow sneaked in, but mine was obviously one of the very few songs recorded by a Brown not to have achieved some sort of chart position.

This dotty elongation of the charts also has the bizarre effect of making redundant pop stars look as though they are still going strong: judging by these lists, Sandie Shaw continued to have hits in the 1980s and the 1990s. It is only when you look a little closer that you realise her 1985 hit "Are You Ready to Be Heartbroken?" spent one week in the Top Seventy-Five, peaking at number sixty-eight, and her 1994 hit "Nothing Less Than Brilliant" enjoyed two weeks in the Top Seventy-Five, peaking at number sixty-six. By the same token, Ken Dodd has had more hits than Bob Dylan, and Adam Faith is twice as successful as Paul Simon.

There is, you might say, an EC Pop Star Mountain – and it is growing bigger every year, as the turnover is getting ever more rapid, and the average length of time a record stays in the Top Twenty is now just three weeks. In the beginning, there were pop fans, then there were pop experts, then pop historians, and now there are pop statisticians, all of them beadily working out exactly which acts spent longest in the charts without ever reaching number one, or who was the seventeenth most successful pop producer of all time.

Did you know that Sweet had just one number one, but no less than five number twos? Or that Chris de Burgh was the first act to enter the Swiss album chart at number one? If these are the sort of statistics you crave, you will enjoy nothing more than spending a year poring over this book, and by the time you have finished, the 2003 edition will be out, fuller and fatter than ever before.

It is, I suppose, a necessary part of the human life cycle that interest in pop music, like vulnerability to acne, peaks somewhere between the ages of thirteen to sixteen. From that point on, nostalgia begins to take over. This may be sad, but nothing like as sad as attempts by middle-aged men to pretend it isn't so. One despairs at the very thought of Sir Tim Rice-but-Dim, who has a permanent order to buy every pop single that makes the charts, and dutifully files them away in a barn especially constructed for the purpose.

Most of the *Guinness Book of British Hit Singles* is taken up with an alphabetical list of all the thousands and thousands of pop stars and the chart positions of their thousands and thousands of singles. As this is also the fiftieth anniversary of what is pompously called "The Official UK Singles Chart", there are also pen-portraits of the events of each year, most of them so moronic as to make one gasp in horror. Of 2001, we read that "In the year in which the world was overcome by the tragic events of September 11 and the resulting war in Afghanistan, and George Harrison lost his battle with cancer, a brighter note was struck by Hear'Say who sold 549,823 copies of "Pure and Simple" in its first week: a record for a debut act which earned them a Guinness World Records British Hit Singles Number One Award." Was a more crass and insensitive sentence ever written?

There is plenty here for old stick-in-the-muds to get steamed up about. For instance, it now seems obligatory for pop groups to misspell their names, the worst offender in this category being Sureal Ruff Dr verz, closely followed by Sho Nuff. But on the other hand, as spelling goes, the Beatles never set a very good example, and nor did the Monkees or Wizzard. Above all, one comes away from this vast acreage of fifty years of hit singles with the suspicion that the well of pop has run dry, and every musical and lyrical variation is now utterly exhausted. Under *Love Is...* the index offers no less than fifty-eight options. Love is a battlefield, a beautiful thing, a golden ring, a killer, a many splendoured thing, a stranger, a wonderful colour, a wonderful thing, all around, all right, all that matters, all we need, blue, contagious, everywhere, for ever ... and so on, and on, and on, and on.

A further 112 different titles offer variations on "*I Want...*" or "*I Wanna...*". No doubt they will be joined by twenty more next year, and another thirty the year after. At this rate, the 3001 annual edition of *British Hit Singles* will be the size of a double-decker bus, and everyone in Britain will be in it somewhere. As Diana Ross once put it, "*Stop! In the name of love!*"

Arockstocrats

IN *AKENFIELD*, Ronald Blythe's great oral history of rural Suffolk, originally published in 1969, a gardener called Christopher Falconer recalls going to work at the big house in 1942, aged fourteen.

"Ladyship drove about the grounds in a motorchair and would have run us over rather than have to say, 'get out the way'," recalled Falconer. "We must never look at her and she never looked at us. It was the same in the house. If a maid was in a passage and Lordship or Ladyship happened to come along, she would have to face the wall and stand perfectly still until they had passed. I wouldn't think that they felt anything about their servants. We were just there because we were necessary, like water from the tap."

I remember reading this passage for the first time some years ago and thinking to myself that, for all the faults of the present age, at least those days were past. But are they? Last week, I met a student who had taken temporary employment in the catering business. He had found himself booked to act as a waiter (no waitresses were to be hired) for a leading pop star's grand party. Before the evening commenced, all the waiters were given strict instructions that, when serving the meals, on no account should they look at the guests.

When an oral history of Britain in the twenty-first century comes to be written, I suspect there will be many similar anecdotes, all demonstrating how it was the multi-millionaire rock stars who maintained the ancient class barriers. Not long ago, Lorraine Kelly, the amiable GMTV presenter, told of a female singer who had a young woman in her entourage whose specific job was to receive the singer's chewed gum into her hand the moment she grew tired of it.

Each year the televised Brit Awards shows the increasing divide between the rock elite and the commoners. The grandees perform a song or two before being whisked away in their limousines. Up close to the stage, the common fans stand for hours on end, dodging hither and thither as the cameras plough their way through them. Behind them the rock middle classes – producers, agents, impresarios, record pluggers and so forth – all sit at candlelit tables, tucking into lavish dinners served by the lowest rung of all, the dutiful waiters.

These days, virtually every other section of British society does its best to play down its differences. Members of the Royal Family, for instance, now expend most of their energy showing how very like everyone else they all are. Only pop stars are permitted, even encouraged, to trumpet their wealth and status.

The more they spend on expensive jewellery, watches, flowers, clothes, stately homes, fancy dress balls, servants, the more respect they command: no one even seems to mind when they insist on stores opening after hours so they may shop without fear of brushing shoulders with the common people.

Who would have imagined that the class system would receive its greatest boost from the very same people who, only a few decades ago, seemed most likely to destroy it, and that, in the year 2003, a pauper could not look at a pop star?

Clerihews for Rock's Rich

Fifty rock millionaires made it on to the Sunday Times Rich List 2003

George Michael
Has no need to cycle.
If he wants to be seen he
Prefers the Lamborghini.

Charlie Watts
Earns pots and pots:
Thirty years of looking bored
Lets him live like a Lord.

Tom Jones
Has no need of loans
(Though few things sound viler
Than *Why Why Why Delilah*).

Jimmy Page
Earns a decent wage.
(He's been on a spree
Since Led Zeppelin Three.)

Van Morrison
Says, "Don't worry, son.
I made a lot of bread
From 'Jackie Wilson Said'."

Brian May
Is on reasonable pay
Though he still has to save
For his permanent wave.

Ringo Starr
Has gone very far
Since passing the test
Of not being Pete Best.

Roger Waters
Certainly taught us
How to make the tills chime
To *Money – it's a crime*.

Engelbert Humperdinck
Wears a fur jumper (mink).
I wish I had a share
In his facial hair.

Tim Rice
Is ever so nice
So I must fight the whim
To call him Tim Rice-But-Dim.

Madonna
Can outspend Des O'Connor
But I still prefer to hum
Dick-a-dum-dum.

Mark Knopfler
Says, "I'm 26th from the top, sir –
Even though my fate's
To be in Dire Straits."

Sir Mick Jagger
Likes to strut and swagger
But if dinner costs too much
He'll suggest you go Dutch.

Barry Gibb
Likes to ad lib.
"*I was born in the ghetto*,"
He'll sing in falsetto.

Sir Paul McCartney
Says, "I'm dead smart, me –

I'll let nothing I own go
To Ms Yoko Ono."

Sir Elton John
Won't be outshone:
He'd spend an arm and a leg
On the ultimate boiled egg.

The Black and White Minstrels: A Correspondence

From Mr Wallace Arnold, CH

SIR: Further to the obituary of George Mitchell, rightly described as the driving musical talent behind *The Black and White Minstrel Show*, might I add a few reminiscences of my own regarding this most evergreen of family entertainments?

I myself was one of the original Black and White Minstrels, appearing in their very first BBC show way back in 1958. The exact identities of my fellow Minstrels must remain a closely guarded secret, but I think most people now know that they included song-and-dance man Frankie Vaughan, the young John Osborne, Francis Bacon (shortly to become a hugely successful painter), and the late Enoch Powell, whose spirited solo rendition of "De Camptown Races" on the third show in the series remains fresh in all our minds.

Legend has it that George Mitchell instantly saw the magic that was Enoch Powell upon first spotting Enoch – then an out-of-work politician – working as a Redcoat at the Butlins holiday camp in Wolverhampton. To the casual observer, Enoch would have seemed hopelessly ill-suited to the task – he refused to remove his pinstriped suit for volleyball, and would call out the bingo numbers in an almost funereal monotone – but George spotted an underlying rhythm in him, a rhythm he was later to employ to such memorable effect in some of his most historic speeches.

In his authorised biography, Simon Heffer (who himself served a valuable apprenticeship as a junior Smurf under the watchful eye of Father Abraham) points out that, played at a speed just 10rpm faster than the original, an underlying reggae rhythm can be heard on recordings of Enoch's famous "Rivers of Blood" speech. This may well account for its popular appeal, particularly as Enoch originally delivered it wearing his trademark white gloves and sparkly lapels, prior to launching into his show-stopping rendition of "Ole Man River".

From The President of the Pedants' Society (formerly the Pedant's Society, originally the Pedants Society, soon to be re-named Pedants, Society of)

SIR: Let us not grow too nostalgic for *The Black and White Minstrel Show*. Broadcast at a time of the rapid disintegration of our society, it served only to accelerate the liberal ethos of the late 1950s and early 1960s with its total disregard for the apostrophe.

It was clear to me then, and remains clear to me now, that it should either have been named *The Black and White Minstrel's Show*, or more properly, *The Black and White Minstrels' Show*, as there was, or were, more than one of them. By cocking a snook at the tradition of the apostrophe, the performers in question no doubt sought to cock a snook at society. Needless to say, just a few short years later came The Rolling Stones, the Three-Day Week and the sinking of the *Torrey Canyon*.

From Sir Marmaduke Hussey

SIR: Further to Mr Wallace Arnold's delightful reminiscences of Enoch's pioneering appearances on *The Black and White Minstrel Show*, might I be permitted a trip down Memory Lane?

As a Tin Pan Alley talent scout in the mid-1960s, I would tune into the *Minstrels*, regular as clockwork, every Saturday evening at 6.15. One Saturday in October, 1966, I was witness to a unforgettable performance of "Would You Like To Ride (In My Beautiful Balloo-oo-oo-oon)" fronted by a Minstrel who was completely new to me. This, I knew at once, was a star.

Who was this mystery star? Leaping into a taxi, I arrived at BBC Television Centre just seconds before the show's grand finale (an up-tempo rendition of "The Yellow Rose of Texas" performed by full cast and chorus).

Brandishing my pass, I rushed backstage, elbowing my way past Billy Cotton, who was flat out rehearsing his inimitable shout of "Wakey! Waaaakey!" for the next programme but one.

As the fully blacked-up cast swept past me, I stared hard at each and every face, eager to identify which of them had sung that memorable solo. Alas, to the untutored eye, they all looked the same; I was about to give up hope when from the far end of the corridor I heard the words *"And we can fly-y-y! We can fly-y-y!"* sung in that magical tenor.

Barging my way past cast and crew, I came face to face with the mystery singer. Without a word, I took a freshly dampened cloth to his face and scrubbed as hard as I'd ever scrubbed in my life before. Hey presto! Who should it be but a young man called Norman Tebbit, filling in time as a Minstrel while training for his full pilot's licence. "Happy-go-lucky – that's me" was his catchphrase.

Sadly, I never heard of Tebbit again. Does anyone know what became of him?

Kylie Down Under: A Symposium

UNDER THE HEADLINE "What Happened to Kylie Down Under?" the Sun newspaper launched a special investigation into widespread claims that the pocket-sized Australian pop singer Kylie Minogue has entertained cosmetic surgery upon her bottom. Long-time observers suggested that it "appeared noticeably fleshier two years ago". They add that it now looks "more pert and less rounded". In pursuit of a definitive answer to this complex question, the great debate is thrown open to a forum of leading experts, commentators and academics:

✱ **Harold Pinter:** Don't talk to me about uplifting, buddy. We're talking about the end. And it is an end that will not go away, however much our American "friends" (please note those inverted commas – they indicate irony, chum) may wish to cover it up. Minogue's bum is staring at us straight in the face. But it's a question that is much, much broader than either her bum or my bum, chum. FACT: Fuhrer Bush and his evil sidekicks have brought up the Minogue rear in order to distract attention from their stated policy of award-winning international genocide on an unprecedented scale. FACT: before very long, they will start putting about rumours that the persecuted philosopher Osama bin Laden, too, has had his bottom lifted – regardless of whether in so doing they are hurting the guy's feelings. There's only one word for it. Cheek.

✳ **Frank McCourt:** Oh Jasus, oh Jasus, oh Jasus. The roof's fallen in with the rainwater, the soup's all over the barnyard floor and me mam is goin' to have her bottom lifted. Did you ever see the sense in that? She says to me she says, if Kylie can do it so can I, but Mam, says Malachy, t'would take a forklift truck to lift your behind and Mam says how could you say such a thing and the tears spring from her eyes like a thousand fountains and as she hits at Malachy with the newspaper and Malachy yelps there am I sittin' on the bucket in the corner thinkin', if ever I have my cheeks lifted I'll keep right quiet about it, so I will.

✳ **The Rt Rev George Carey, Archbishop of Canterbury:** It is good that we as a society are all uplifted. But what exactly is uplift – and how does one set about finding it in our hectic jungle? Do you know, I think we are all of us looking for some sort of uplift. Many vital questions arise out of Miss Minogue's behind, and I welcome them. But let us not forget her knees, her ankles and even her elbows: these are all important and equally valid parts of her body, and we should respect them as such.

✳ **Professor George Steiner:** Concomitantly, the bum, deriving derivatively from the Arabic *b'um* (*bahm* in Hindustani, *bwm* in Swahili) is, as it were, the globe, or circular three-dimensional world map, in microcosm, albeit attached to the human body, and without the upstanding appendage of a curved piece, or bit, or thing, of metal inserted at a 180 degree distance, from top or uppermost point, to, as it were, bottom. What exactly do we mean, or convey, when we say, exclaim, issue the statement, that a bottom or derrière has been "lifted" and is now "less rounded"? I understand that the bottom in question has been compared to a "peach", and the analogy is indeed fruitful, but the peach, or pêche, though it, too, can be lifted, remains without legs. This much is clear, obvious, self-evident.

✳ **The Rt Hon Stephen Byers:** At no time did I get involved with the decision as to whether to lift Miss Minogue's bottom. That remains entirely a matter for her and her personnel. Let me state that very clearly. I have, however, been kept informed of these matters at all times. Though I have certainly not met or spoken to Miss Minogue at any time since her bottom was lifted – or not, as the case may be – I was, I am now prepared to admit, personally involved throughout this tough decision, and though I had nothing to do with it, it was my decision, and mine alone, as to whether she should have her bottom lifted. Or not. As the case may be. I have clarified my position quite sufficiently. Now go away, will you?

✳ **Mohamed Fayed:** Is viciously rumour, spreading about by Prince so-called Philip of Scotland and his no-good MI5 henchermen. They jealous Kylie, they riddling with evil jealous, they say, "We no top charts no more, we yesterday peoples, we spreading dirty filthy lies about Kylie's preposterous region." You callin' me liar? You want proof? I got proof. Kylie good friend Mohamed, Kylie personal friend, Kylie phone Mohamed clockwork as regular, say, Mohamed, I no want my prosperity lifting, no way, but if I want posterity lifting I want it lifting only by you, Uncle Mohamed. You callin' me liar? I got proof, I got best proof money can buy.

✳ **Sir Edward Heath:** Let me make one thing absolutely clear. You can't expect me to be impressed by Kylie's bottom. Do let's try to keep it in perspective. Historians and other specialists in the field make no bones about it: there are far more impressive bottoms the length and breadth of Europe and it is high time this government faced up to the fact. In my day we would not have been so easily impressed. Far from it. Giscard had a far greater bottom, and so did Chancellor Kohl. These were statesmen with real bottom, world figures who would have looked askance at Kylie's bottom, and taken pains to keep it at arm's length.

✳ **Dr David Starkey:** I put it to you, Miss Minogue, that your derrière is quite grotesquely overrated. Frankly, it makes me want to vomit. How does that so-called song of yours go? "*La la la, can't get you outta my head.*" A typically fatuous comment, if I may say so. And nothing could be further from the truth.

I am perfectly capable of getting the female dwarf in question out of my head for exceptionally lengthy periods of every day. I don't want to say another word about Kylie's bottom. It is beneath contempt. And I will be expressing this opinion in no uncertain terms on Radio Five Live, *Richard and Judy* and an LBC phone-in later today, for a very great deal of money, may I add.

✳ **Martin Amis:** Kylie's bottom. The bottom. Of Kylie.

It was the bumcrack of a coming future, an implosive region curved like the lacquered finish of a nuclear warhead, pert yet reproachful, causing novelists and world leaders to tremble backwards – let's call it elbmert – with a non-specific anxiety that threatened to engulf the world in a tidal wave of overstatement.

It was, in the month of February in the year 2003, a quidditive experience, Kylie's sublunary bum, stretching taut and untouchable like the Grand Canyon over a vertiginous nation transfixed by the impact of futurewar. Kylie's bottom: it was a hubristic distraction from Iraq, and the coming worldwobble: a megawobble, a wobble to end all wobbles.

✳ **Tony Benn:** Let's never forget, shall we, that there's a very real problem lying deep in the heart of Kylie's bottom.

Let's not beat about the bush. This Blair so-called government controls our media, and is consequently running photographs of Kylie's bottom twenty-four hours a day so as to distract ordinary, decent people from the struggle of our firemen, lovely blokes, really super lads. Frankly, it's an open secret that Kylie is working under direct instructions from MI5, with her bottom personally overseen by our current wicked Home Secretary.

Incidentally, Jack sent me a letter the other day saying how much he had enjoyed my *Diaries*. What a lovely fellow he is.

ART:
Read

THE TATE GALLERY has paid £22,300 for a thirty-gram can of faeces created, or at least expelled, by the Italian artist Piero Manzoni. The can comes with a label announcing it as *Merde Artista*.

"The Manzoni was a very important purchase for an extremely small amount of money: nobody can deny that," announced a spokesman for the Tate, a touch optimistically. "He was an incredibly important international artist. What he was doing with this work was looking at a lot of issues that are pertinent to twentieth-century art, like authorship and the production of art. It was a seminal work."

Though brief, this statement exhibits a number of the hallmarks of contemporary art-flannel. Anything which happens to fall outside even the most generous definition of art is said to "look at issues ... pertinent to twentieth-century art". The catch-all word "seminal", with its suggestion of weighty historical thought, is then chucked in for good measure.

Why is the art world so much more absurdly gullible than, say, the world of books, or the world of music? It is impossible to imagine a public library, however wealthy, buying the equivalent book – say, a volume formed from stapling together the used loo paper of "an incredibly important international author". Similarly, no concert hall would think of forking out £22,300 for an "incredibly important international composer" to defecate live on stage.

What is particularly odd is that Piero Manzoni, who died in 1963, placed his excrement in fancy cans and proclaimed it art simply as a satirical joke against the idiotic pretensions of the art world. Forty years on, Sir Nicholas Serota is happy to prove that those self-same pretensions are still flourishing under his stewardship. He does this by purchasing the very object that was intended to show him up. He reminds me of nothing so much as a village idiot, maniacally sitting on a whoopee cushion over and over again, convinced in his own mind that people are laughing with him, and not at him.

For some reason, presumably commercial, the contemporary art world, with its chorus line of professional interpreters, has developed the notion that anything may be stamped as art, just so long as it can be said to be "about" death, or "about" the zeitgeist, or "about" anything sufficiently solemn to make brows furrow and heads nod.

Strangely enough, eighteen months ago, in December 2000, I wrote a spoof, "The Shock of the Poo", for *Private Eye*. In it, I imagined Sir Nicholas Serota enthusing over buying a work of art called *My Turd*: "*My Turd* has a lot to say about birth and death, a lot to say about the nature of self, a lot to say about the whole process of defecation and renewal in contemporary society, and it has a hell of a lot to say about art itself. It is almost as if, in some extraordinary way, the artist were asking us to confront the very nature of what we call 'shit'. What is it? Where is it? And who will buy it?"

One might have hoped that this squib would have served as some sort of early warning system to Serota, and that a small bell of embarrassment might have gone off in his head before he decided, a year or two later, to spend £22,300 of public money on a real-life *My Turd*. But no. Once again, satire – Manzoni's, mine, anyone's – proves itself utterly useless in the battle against stupidity. Manzoni had drunk himself to death by the age of 30. It is not hard to see why.

(July 2, 2002)

On

A YEAR OR TWO ago, I found myself talking to a Tate gallery bigwig about whether Damien Hirst should be awarded the Turner Prize. "Say what you like about Damien," he said, "he's brought a lot of publicity to the art world." This is a bit like saying, "Say what you like about Osama, he's brought a lot of publicity to tall buildings."

Publicity has become the benchmark by which art is judged, the worth of an artist measurable by the number of column inches he generates. It goes without saying that J W M Turner himself would have no hope of winning the Turner Prize nowadays, unless, of course, he consented to turn his paintings into "installations", generating storms at sea with hair dryers and paddling pools, and fiery sunsets with a couple of 150-watt light bulbs, a bit of corrugated iron and some brightly coloured tissue paper.

How fitting it is, then, that Madonna has been invited to present this year's Turner Prize. Her fame is universal and undeniable; no doubt the Tate and all its little conceptual artists are trusting some of it will rub off on them. Needless to say, the Tate emphasise that Madonna is not just a pop star, but a "serious collector". Apparently, she collects Frida Kahlo. But these days virtually every star from Rod Stewart to Sylvester Stallone is "a serious collector" of art. Is there a bass player who doesn't own a Braque?

I can't remember Lord Clark of *Civilisation* ever inviting Freddie and the Dreamers to give away the prizes when he was director of the National Gallery. Even Sir Anthony Blunt, for all his shortcomings, never asked Alvin Stardust to present the Essay Award at the Courtauld Institute. But times move on, and the pecking order changes. These days, the art world is only too happy to put up its paws and beg at the high table of pop, touchingly grateful for whatever crumbs of glamour may drop into its mouth.

Many

IT WAS ONLY last year that Sir Nicholas Serota was busy puffing the claims of Damien Hirst in his Dimbleby Lecture, "Who's Afraid of Modern Art?" "Hirst's work raises difficult questions about modern art," he said. This is par for the course. Whenever people in the art world are unsure what to say about an artist's work, they say it raises questions.

If they haven't got a clue, they say it raises difficult questions. And if they can't even tell which way up it should be they say it raises difficult questions about modern art.

"For me, the undoubted shock, even disgust provoked by the work," whimpered Serota, as a slide of Hirst's cow cut in half flashed on to the screen, "is all part of its appeal." He went on to coo that it was an "unforgettable image, at once raw and tender, brazen and subtle".

This automatic coupling of daffy adjectives has become part and parcel of art waffle. I imagine Sir Nicholas had been having a good dip in his curator's lexicon, stopping on the page where it lists all the recommended permutations of opposites (raw and tender, brazen and subtle, cool and tanned, rough and ready, naughty and nice, little and large, up and at 'em, Peters and Lee, over and out).

Anyway, the poor man was only doing his best. Sadly, Damien Hirst has now chosen to repay this brave stab at an explanation by calling Serota names. In a new book, he rounds on both his principal patrons, saying they are "failed artists". "Nick Serota's telling me I'm a genius; I've got Charles Saatchi kissing me on the lips ... What the f— do you do? ... I'm not Charles Saatchi's barrel-organ monkey, and I'm not Nick Serota's barrel-organ monkey. But when they see you, after you've been in the bowels of hell, when they see you surviving, they start touchy-feeling you, going, 'Gosh, you made it. Against all odds.' You just want them to f— rot in hell and die."

Damien was always a little highly strung. Those unversed in the ways of the modern art market may worry that this time he may have gone too far. But Hirst is not as thick as he seems. He knows full well that, like clients in a kinky house of correction, Saatchi and Serota will simply gurgle with delight at all this abuse, reaching for their chequebooks as they plead for more. What an odd, topsy-turvy world these deep-pocketed patrons of conceptual art inhabit, at once raw and tender, brazen and subtle, down and out, gin and tonic, Huntley & Palmers ...

(October 1, 2001)

Different

A NEW GALLERY at Tate Modern, measuring twenty-five metres by seven metres, opened last night. Its launch exhibition contains only one exhibit, which measures four inches by two inches. It is a lifesize sparrow, made out of feathers and latex, placed between the panes of a double-glazed window. Thanks to the wonders of electricity, it passes its days lying on its back, heaving and twitching, as though in its death throes.

There is nothing that excites the Serota school of art more than a dead animal. Sharks, sheep, cows, chickens, butterflies, rats and flies have all been done, so it was perhaps inevitable that the bird kingdom should be the next to be raided. Asked whether this toy bird was art, the curator of the exhibition, Susan May, replied, "Oh, it is art, absolutely." Asked why, she said: "Because it makes us look at something afresh. It can be read on many different levels."

I have noticed that when experts on conceptual art haven't got the foggiest idea what their latest exhibit is meant to mean, they say, "It can be read on many different levels." For example, Sarah Kent, the author of the official Saatchi catalogue, wrote of one artist's works: "They are seductive, silent and insistently shut; emblems of the comings and goings, our entrances and exits. On one level they are utterly banal, on another profound."

You simply can't go wrong by saying that this or that can be read on many different levels. In fact, it would be perfectly possible for any tongue-tied novice partygoer at any launch for a conceptual art exhibition to keep going a good two or three hours employing only this phrase. What do you think the artist is trying to say? "It can be read on many different levels." Have you met Sir Nicholas Serota? "He can be read on many different levels." Would you like to help yourself to the smoked salmon vol-au-vents? "They can be read on many different levels." How's your drink? "It can be read on many different levels." Where is the door marked exit? "It can be read on many different levels."

But even if Mr Dragset's preferred Cockney sparrow level of interpretation must now be thrown out of the window, there are still plenty of other different levels to choose from. Speaking for myself, I think the dying sparrow may well be an earthly symbol of Sir Nicholas Serota, trapped in a vacuum and gasping for breath.

Is it not high time this spooky, birdlike man brought a little clarity to the new gallery by taking the place of the electric sparrow for a day or two? He is quite skinny, so he could probably just about squeeze into the space between the two panes of double glazing. Messrs Dragset and Elmgreen could then wire Sir Nicholas up, and, at the push of a button, visitors to the exhibition could make him flap his wings. I think it would tell us an awful lot about the shock of the unexpected, an awful lot about the fear of death, and an awful lot about the horror of Iraq. Indeed, it could be read on many different levels.

Levels

THIS YEAR'S TURNER PRIZE selection confirms that nowadays the worth of a work of art lies in inverse proportion to the grandeur of its title. This means the winner will be *The Cosmic Legend of the Uroboros Serpent* by Mike Nelson, with Isaac Julien's *The Long Road to Mazatlan* the runner-up.

The Cosmic Legend of the Uroboros Serpent consists of service corridors that look like the service corridors at the Tate. Inevitably, it has been greeted with all the obligatory oohs and ahhs by the art critics. The *Guardian*'s critic, Adrian Searle, wrote that: "You forget where you are, becoming disoriented as you emerge through one last door and imagine yourself back where you began. It's an illusion; retracing your steps, you arrive at a dead end, and a mop in a dirty, galvanised bucket."

Ooh! Of course, the same effect can be achieved with less effort by shutting oneself in a broom cupboard and downing a bottle of Scotch, but it is hard to imagine the director of the Tate, Sir Nicholas Serota, has ever seen a broom cupboard, let alone a bottle of Scotch.

But a swanky title is all, as Damien Hirst discovered when he named a stuffed shark *The Physical Impossibility of Death in the Mind of Someone Living*, and a set of stuffed fish *Isolated Elements Swimming in the Same Direction for the Purpose of Understanding*. In this way, conceptual art in the 2000s is eerily comparable to rock music in the 1970s, when "concept albums" were all the rage and there was nothing critics liked more than a grandiose title containing floaty words such as "cosmic" and "legend".

Those hailed as geniuses at the time included the Moody Blues for *In Search of the Lost Chord*, Yes for *Tales from Topographic Oceans* and Pink Floyd for *The Piper at the Gates of Dawn*. For me, the overall winner will always be *My People Were Fair and Had Sky in Their Hair But Now They're Content to Wear Stars in Their Brows*, by Tyrannosaurus Rex, with Yoko Ono's first solo album, *Approximately Infinite Universe*, coming a close second. Twenty-five years on, these concept albums languish unplayed in dank garages, a source of shame to their owners.

But if history has a lesson to teach us, it is that history never teaches us a lesson. True to form, the Turner Prize judges will vote for the piece with the swankiest words in its title. Only after twenty-five years will they start to wriggle with embarrassment, the latest victims of man's eternal need to be taken seriously.

(November 8, 2001)

The Fame Thing

GORDON BURN is a highly original writer, probably best known for his macabre, compelling books about Peter Sutcliffe and Fred West. So it is a shame that he should have spent much of the past ten years chronicling the thoughts, if that is not too big a word for them, of Damien Hirst.

In mountaineering terms, it is as though Sir Edmund Hillary had donned all his ropes and clamping-irons and spent his days climbing up and down a molehill at the bottom of his garden. Or, to give it a more literary spin, as though James Boswell had decided that Dr Johnson was rather too wordy for the general reader, and that Daft Dave down the coffee-house had a much better story to tell.

But for some reason Gordon Burn has developed a fascination for Damien Hirst, so much so that he has been interviewing him on tape, on and off, since 1992. "You usually expect a lot of wastage with these kinds of tapes," he observes at the beginning of the assembled transcripts. "We've had to throw very little away."

Heaven knows what they threw away. Reading the published transcripts of Hirst's monotonous pub-bore dronings,* it is hard to imagine anything scoring a greater level of dreariness. For instance, you might have thought that the one question for which a famous artist might have an interesting or unusual answer is, "What is art?" Time and time again, Burn asks him this question or variations of it; time and time again, Hirst demonstrates, albeit very long-windedly, that he has absolutely nothing to say on the matter:

---

* *On The Way To Work* by Damien Hirst and Gordon Burn

Gordon Burn: "What is art?"

Damien Hirst: "It's a fucking poor excuse for life, innit, eh?! Art-schmart, God-schmod, Jesus-schmeesus. I have proved it to myself that art is about life and the art world's about money. And I'm the only one who fucking knows that."

Over the years, as the question pops up again in their conversations, Hirst doesn't have an awful lot to contribute to the discussion, though he certainly makes a little go a long way. "I tell you what: art is f***ing unusual. It's just f***ing unusual." "You can't believe in art if you don't believe in God. And I don't believe in God in those terms." "Art's magic. I'm an artist. Let's get one thing f***ing straight here: I'm an artist."

Eventually, perhaps intending to inject fresh life into this increasingly moribund debate, Burn alters his question from "What is art?" to "What is great art?" Hirst's reply seems unlikely to make it into any dictionary of quotations: "Great art is when you just walk round a corner and go, 'F***ing hell! What's that!'" Nor, I suspect, will his *aperçus* on his fellow painters ever enter into the mainstream. Picasso: "Can't be arsed with him." Warhol: "Honest f***ing geezer." Duchamp: "To put a f***ing toilet in a gallery is fantastic."

Damien Hirst, born in 1965, is probably still best known for his stuffed shark, or rather for employing someone to catch a shark, someone to stuff it, someone to design a container and someone else to place it in the container. But he himself can claim credit for giving it an arty title – *The Physical Impossibility of Death in the Mind of Someone Living* – which, it emerges, was borrowed from a school essay he'd written some years before ("it really stuck in my mind"). He had sold the whole installation in advance to the advertising mogul Charles Saatchi. Saatchi, you will remember, had first become famous in 1978 for his poster "Labour Isn't Working", in which he claimed – entirely bogusly, as it turned out – that a Conservative government would bring down unemployment.

This is the strange way in which reputations in the art world were made in the latter part of the twentieth century. There is a fascinating book to be written about how a handful of dealers, curators and entrepreneurs managed to turn contemporary art into a hard-nosed commercial enterprise, its products to be ordered-up and pre-sold willy-nilly, the tentacles of its spin-offs stretching into restaurants, videos, pop and fashion, its frontmen, or "artists", a Big Brother style collection of lippy, drunken thirty-somethings, selected by the powers-that-be on grounds of attitude rather than talent.

Happily, Damien Hirst, like Chauncey Gardiner in *Being There*, appears sublimely unaware of the randomness of his fame and fortune. Even though he is now a multi-millionaire who has a London office devoted to associated activities such as restaurants, TV commercials and litigation, he identifies himself with the mad, neglected artists of yesteryear, whose dark visions made them ostracised by society and left them poor and wretched. "There's something fundamentally wrong with the world. And unfortunately I've glimpsed it. And I don't like it," he says.

Ooh-er. As far as one can tell, the unfortunate design fault in the world that Hirst has glimpsed is that life ends in death, or "the death thing" as he prefers to call it. "It boils down to death. I mean, we're f***ing dying," he says, adding, "It's a shambles. Total f***ing shambles."

Well, even the thickest among us must have noticed, at one time or another, that death is the fly in the ointment. But at least for Damien, all is not lost. "I definitely already know that if I died tomorrow the contribution I've made is important ... What I do affects the course of art."

Hirst is, in any real sense, far closer to an entrepreneur than to an artist; little separates him from, say, Sir Bernard Matthews of Turkey Roasts (*"Mmm...they're boodivul"*), a man who has also, incidentally, glimpsed the profit to be found in corpses.

Yet it must be said for Damien Hirst that at least he has the integrity to believe his own publicity. As the book progresses, he becomes ever less backward in coming forward. "I'm a fantastic phenomenal f***ing colourist," he declares, more than once. "It's like I'm a Bonnard, a Turner, a Matisse." In fact, his spot-paintings, pleasant enough as wallpaper, put him more on a par with a Llewellyn-Bowen or a Carol Smillie.

At a point roughly halfway through this pricey book, padded out with bad, blurry photographs of Damien larking around naked with his famous mates, Damien with his hand in his mouth, Damien without his hand in his mouth, Damien pulling a face, Damien not pulling a face, Damien in the bath, Damien in bed, Damien in the garden, Damien's child, Damien's wife, and Damien's granny, the thought occured to me that perhaps Gordon Burn had performed a merciless double-bluff on his subject, and that his secret mission over all those years was to make Damien Hirst look silly.

The evidence mounts up. For instance, Burn encourages Hirst to believe not only that he is very, very famous but also that his fame ("the fame thing") represents the same sort of insufferable burden as other artists' – eg Van Gogh's – lack of fame. "I hate all this s**t ... It's the famous s**t. That's been a burden for ages. It knackers me out. You've got to BECOME a celebrity before you can undermine it, and take it apart, and show people that there's no difference between celebrities and real life."

There, there. If it's any comfort, I should inform him, quite candidly, that, on any reasonable scale of fame, he only merits about two or three out of ten. I was once in the same theatre as Damien, and apart from me, no one seemed to recognise him at all. He is far less famous than, Des O'Connor, say, or Lorraine Kelly, and infinitely less famous than Sporty Spice, yet they all seem to be able to cope with it. And if you feel duty-bound to proclaim your dislike of fame, surely there are better places to do so than in a book that is transparently designed to increase it?

Desert Island Drips

Sue Lawley: My castaway this week is an artist who is impossible to ignore. She has appeared on *The Frank Skinner Show*, the Brit Awards, *Stop the Week*, *Blankety Blank* and *Room 101*. She regularly adorns the pages of the *Sun* and the *Daily Mail*. She has been drunk to the point of incoherence on live television. As a result of these achievements, she now has a room at Tate Britain, and we welcome her to *Desert Island Discs*. She is, of course, Tracey Emin. And, if I'm right, Tracey, you're still only fourteen...
Tracey Emin: Forty-one...

Sue Lawley: Yes, fourteen! So young, and with such a precocious talent! I mean, when you draw a person, you know how many arms and legs they have, because you've gone to all the trouble of counting. Brilliant! Now, Tracey, you've been raped twice, and –

Tracey Emin: Yeah but no but. Like, not really raped as such, well, I s'pose you could call it rape but, like, well not really rape and that. More like heavy pettin'.

Sue Lawley: Well, let's call it rape. So, Tracey Emin, you've been raped three times, you've had two abortions, you've attempted suicide –

Tracey Emin: Well, I wouldn't call it suicide exactly.

Sue Lawley: Yes, definitely suicide. That's what you told Jonathan Ross, and that's what you told our researcher –

Tracey Emin: Yeah but no but. I just sorta jumped into the sea with my clothes on when I was, like, pissed. It was quite shallow, though. Only a foot deep, really. But – yeah – I did get my feet wet.

Sue Lawley: And if you'd fallen over face first into the sea, and stayed there for, say, five minutes, then it would have been suicide, wouldn't it?

Tracey Emin: Well, I s'pose...

Sue Lawley: Of course it would. So that's three abortions, four rapes, and five successful suicides. Marvellous! Your first record, please.

* * *

Sue Lawley: Tell me, Tracey, how much has your art, which is so autobiographical, so confessional, if you like, saved you from yourself?

Tracey Emin: What I like about my art is that it's like what I like about my art is what I like about my art. No one can take away from me the fact that when I make my art it's the art I make and no one can take that away from me. So what I mean is what I like about my art is it's all about communication and communicationing. What I am doing with my art is I'm communicationing to other people.

Sue Lawley: Four abortions, five rapes and six successful suicides! That's an awful lot of pain! Super! But there's enormous professionalism in your work, too. Hard work is very much part of you, isn't it?

Tracey Emin: Yeah but no but. I didn't get where I am today by being slack. My name's not Tracey Emin for nothing. I'm at the very top of my profession. I mean, your Rembrandts and your Picassos, I'm not saying they're crap but face it, they never had their beds exhibited in a gallery, did they? You see, with my bed and my tent I've changed the face of art twice. They're inseminal. Most artists don't manage it even once, but I've twice created an absolutely semolina work.

Sue Lawley: Your next record, Tracey.

* * *

Sue Lawley: Now, alongside your unmade bed –

Tracey Emin: Yeah but no but. You call it unmade, but I made it. Like, I made it unmade. And you can't take that away from me. It's not something you can unmake.

Sue Lawley: And alongside your unmade bed there were some lovely little watercolours. They were very beautiful, weren't they? Describe them for us.

Tracey Emin: While I was painting them, I was committing suicide. And making toast. But mainly committing suicide.

Sue Lawley: Remarkable. And for a long time, you were very, very promiscuous...

Tracey Emin: I haven't had any sex for seventeen months, can you believe it!

Sue Lawley: But until quite recently you were very, very VERY promiscuous!

Tracey Emin: Yeah but no bu–

Sue Lawley: Really EXTREMELY promiscuous for a fourteen-year-old! Well done, Tracey! Lucky you! Ha ha! Your next record, please.

* * *

Sue Lawley: All your work is autobiographical. Your bed, your tent. And your remarkable work, *My Chewing Gum*, is also intensely personal. Explain *My Chewing Gum* to me.

Tracey Emin: Basically, it's my chewing gum. I'd been chewing it for like an hour or more then I decided to turn it into a work of art.

Sue Lawley: As I say, an intensely personal work of art. And how did you go about it?

Tracey Emin: I scooped it out with my tongue, then I picked it off my tongue, and then, taking care not to alter its shape not one little bit, I placed it on a plinth.

Sue Lawley: And it still carries the exact indentations it had when you were chewing it. Remarkable! And since then, you've issued a limited edition of *My Chewing Gum*, Tracey, though some people say you now get other people to chew the gum for you...

Tracey Emin: Yeah but no but. Of course, other people chew it for me, but I buy the packets of gum, and I decide exactly where it should go on the plinth, and no one does nothing without my say-so. Also, I believe really really strongly in the redistribution of wealth, and if I can give employment to six people to like chew my gum for me, then to me that's a real advance for socialism.

Sue Lawley: And what about love? Are you looking for love, Tracey?

Tracey Emin: Y'know, money can't buy you love. Love's what makes the world go round. Love is all you need. Love changes everything. Love grows where my Rosemary goes. Love don't live here any more.

Sue Lawley: Wise words indeed, from one so young. Tracey Emin, thank you very much indeed for letting us hear your Desert Island Discs.

Wallace Arnold: My Life with Frida

IT WAS, I freely admit, at my insistence that our wedding reception should be held at the Garrick, but she could have made an effort to abide by the rules, dammit. Instead, she ignored the dress code and walked stark naked into the Members' Dining Room, but for a Mexican bonnet on her head, an arrow through her neck and a paper clip on her left knee. How could she? How could she?

Pull yourself together, man! Deep breath, Wallace, deep breath. And big blow! And again! All better, now. All better! May I begin at the beginning?

My marriage to Frida Kahlo was never going to be easy, of course it wasn't. But I never expected it to be half so tricky as it proved. I was very much the young man with his life ahead of him, a natural Conservative, eminently clubbable, much given to tweed, a passionate pipe-smoker, cutting quite a dash about town with a well-received biography, *Those Marvellous Mitfords*! And my own rib-tickling column about foreigners in the *Illustrated London News* called "Pardon My Swahili!". Frida, on the other hand, was a very different kettle of fish. She was, I would say, the artistic type, prone to bursting into tears in the middle of a dinner party and flying out of the room, only to reappear with a dead rat dangling from each ear-lobe and a picture of the Madonna tattooed any old how on her elbow.

What was it, you might wonder, that attracted me to her in the first place? I think I fell in love with her when first we touched. My parents had always taught me to trust a woman with a firm handshake, and Frida's was by far and away the firmest of anyone – man or woman – I have ever encountered, causing my knuckles to crack, and leaving me with a fractured wrist which still plays me up even now, nearly half a century later. One should also remember that, in those days, all the most distinguished personages – Rudyard Kipling, Neville Chamberlain, Field Marshal Montgomery, Mr Pastry – sported a moustache; in retrospect, it seems all too inevitable that I should have lost my heart to Frida.

When we were first introduced, the room had been dreadfully noisy and I had misheard, taking her to be one of the Yorkshire Barlows – decent, hard-working people of property, with their feet firmly on the ground. We both smoked a pipe, so it seemed we had much in common. Yes, my friends told me she might be a painter, but I had refused to heed their warnings; two weeks after our first meeting, Frida Kahlo and I were engaged.

By way of celebration, I treated her to a candlelit dinner for two at the Savoy Grill. After a brief contretemps at the door – they insisted she left her anaconda at the front desk – the first course went tolerably well, though she would insist upon smearing her Cream of Tomato soup all over the lace ruffles of her Tehuana national costume rather than sip it from the spoon provided.

Her performance during the main course should have sounded all the warning bells, but love (dread word!) must have inured me to the insistence of their jangle. I had just asked Frida if she had ever felt at all fondly towards a man before she met me, and she had, to my astonishment, started to reel off a list consisting of upwards of two hundred names, including Leon Trotsky, Diego Rivera, D H Lawrence, Lord Haw-Haw, Chan Canasta, Lord Rockingham's XI, Freddie "Parrot-Face" Davis, Old Uncle Tom Cobbley and all.

By the time she got to roughly number 151 (George Formby, if I remember right), silence had descended upon our fellow diners. Something told me the looks they cast in our direction were composed of one part horror to three parts pity, but once again I chose to ignore them, perhaps distracted by the manner in which Frida was simultaneously attempting to saw through her little finger with a butter knife.

The following week, we received a letter from the editor of *Country Life* curtly informing us that Frida had not been selected for their full-page engagement photograph, on account of the six-inch nails sticking out of her forehead. We soldiered on, but, alas, the marriage lasted only a matter of weeks, coming to an abrupt end upon my receipt of an official warning from the Secretary of the Garrick following a regrettable incident in the ladies room involving a crucifix, a pair of scissors and a spider monkey.

An exhibition of Frida's work opens at Tate Modern today, but I shall be giving it a miss. Women artists and the Garrick simply don't mix, no matter what the Lord Braggs of this world would have us believe.

The Opposition

A Brief History of the Bow Tie

IT WOULD BE WRONG to suggest that Neil Hamilton is his own worst enemy when there are so many people better qualified for the post. In fact, there is something about him – the self-satisfied little upturn to those thin, fidgety lips – that suggests he is more likely to be his own best friend.

But if I had to bet, my guess would be that he is telling the truth when he insists he did not take money in brown envelopes from Mohamed Fayed. My instinct is based on nothing better than a suspicion that, doing what comes naturally, Mr Fayed is capable of producing bigger and better stories, more beautifully packaged, than a Conservative backbencher new to the game. Match a professional against an amateur, and the professional usually wins.

So why does Mr Hamilton continue to let himself down? Why, just as one is beginning to believe him, does a shudder rush down one's spine? However much he protests his innocence before House of Commons committees, on *Newsnight*, outside his own front door, on chat shows and panel games, in the street and in parks, a little something always gets in the way. I think I have isolated what that little something might be. I blame the bow tie.

Bow ties wear their owners. However forceful its owner, the bow tie elbows itself into the driving seat. And like the string that is pulled from a dolly's back, the bow tie permits a very limited choice of phrases to emerge from its wearer's mouth. These five phrases are:
1) I am fat; 2) I am smug; 3) I am waggish; 4) I am a charlatan;
 – or, as often as not, the full monty:
5) I am a fat, smug, waggish charlatan.

The late Robert Maxwell was, I think, the archetypal bow tie man. Many of his bow ties seemed to have been manufactured from odd materials, as unreliable as their master; looking at photographs of Mr Maxwell, I can see one that looks as if it were made from Aertex, another sculpted from some sort of bendy rubber. If only people at the time had paid more attention to his dodgy bow ties and less attention to his *Who's Who* entry, just think of the calamities that might have been avoided.

When Mr Maxwell began wearing one, the bow tie must still have had overtones of Churchillian integrity: it was these associations with greatness that made them so appealing to so many post-war spivs. Other post-war Members of Parliament who sported bow ties include Lord Boothby, philanderer, "TV personality" and warm-hearted friend of the Kray brothers, and more recently the almost equally caddish Sir Nicholas Fairbairn, who is pictured in an oil painting on the dust jacket of his autobiography wearing what looks like a conjuror's cape, a wing collar and a red-and-green spotty bow tie that measures at least eight inches across. Sir Nicholas titled his autobiography *A Life Is Too Short*; he would have been well advised to subtitle it, *A Bow Tie Is Too Long*.

When the spy Guy Burgess died in Moscow, correspondents were allowed into his apartment to rummage around. One journalist pulled open the bottom drawer in a chest of drawers in Burgess's bedroom. It contained fourteen Old Etonian bow ties. There is something very poignant about this lonely old traitor, slowly dying of drink in Moscow, his only comfort an ample stock of a garment that symbolised all he had once conspired to eradicate. Yet there is a sharp difference between an Old Etonian tie and an Old Etonian bow tie, and it is a difference that would not have been lost on Burgess. It is still possible – just – to find an OE tie around the neck of someone who is not a fraud, but wearing an Old Etonian bow tie is as straightforward a confession of fraudulence as wearing a placard around one's neck bearing the legend "Fibs Galore".

With such a history of charlatanism behind it, the bow tie must hold some greater pull for those who find themselves so irresistibly drawn to it. Why did Mr Maxwell plump for the bow tie? "Plump" would seem to be the operative word: there is something about a bow tie that makes it uncommonly appealing to fatties. Yet it has no power to slim its wearer; on the contrary, as I learnt during a brief and lamentable period of experimentation more than a decade ago, it has the unique ability to make the chubby chubbier. Small wonder that the creators of the cartoon character Porky Pig gave him a bow tie to wear, and nothing else.

But fatties like to eat, and the bow tie is well suited to gluttony. Mr Maxwell was a particularly ravenous eater, and, like a greedy winner on *The Generation Game*, is reputed to have gobbled up whatever came into his line of fire – a roast chicken, a leg of lamb, a suet pudding – and generally with his bare hands, to guzzle it more speedily.

Such mammoth slobbering leads to a Technicolor spray of drips and stains; the bow tie, tucked under the chin or chins, is sheltered from the storm. Mr Maxwell's junior doppelganger, Billy Bunter, The Fat Owl of the Fifth, also wore bow ties, though they do not seem to have been a mainstay of the Greyfriars uniform. The bow tie signals its owner's separation from his fellow men: both Mr Hamilton and Mr Maxwell must have wished to single themselves out from the common herd. But in poor old Billy Bunter's case, one senses that his choice was not conscious, that he would have liked, more than anything, to be one of the gang, and that his bow tie, acknowledged by all but himself as a beacon for ridicule, acted as a great barrier to his acceptance by his classmates.

The bow tie has now become such a staple of comedy that it is hard to understand why anyone not wishing to become a figure of fun would ever contemplate wearing one. Circus clowns sport bow ties that light up and go round and round, like Catherine wheels. In the *Beezer*, the desperately myopic Colonel Blink ("The Short-Sighted Gink") was an inveterate bow tie wearer, as was the similarly short-sighted Mr Magoo. Oliver Hardy, Kenneth Widmerpool, Lord Wyatt, Sir Roy Strong: these seminal comic creations would never have achieved half the laughs without the benefit of their bow ties.

For this reason, Hollywood sex symbols and pop stars tend to eschew them. It's hard to think of any pop star worth his salt who has been spotted in a bow tie. Bill Haley used to wear one, but he was hardly a pin-up, and is so far the only pop star to have died of old age. I imagine Ginger Spice could pull it off, but bow ties on women are another matter, signalling either a vampy lesbian, or, as in Ginger's case, a buxom bunny-girl willing to please.

So why does Neil Hamilton persist in his folly? Any trained media adviser would tell him that he would be more likely to win public confidence with a dead ferret tied round his neck. His only hope is that Mr Fayed will continue to sport a plain white collar with a stripy coloured shirt, two garments which, when combined, exceed even the bow tie in their dodginess.

(November 22, 1997)

Two Conservative Diarists and an Addendum

I) EDWINA CURRIE

It still has the imaginary air of a childhood game of Consequences.

John Major

met

Edwina Currie

in

the bath.

He said:

"Do you believe in God?"

She said:

"Yes, but not in all that ritual."

And the consequence was:

He became Prime Minister, and fourteen years later she blabbed and made £1 million.

Perhaps the most important thing to make clear about Edwina Currie's *Diaries** is that they are, for the most part, very, very, boring. They begin at the end of August, 1987, when her affair with John Major was all but over. This means that most of her references to it are retrospective: it soon becomes clear to the reader that Edwina Currie is struggling to remember anything her lover ever

---

* *Diaries 1987–1992* by Edwina Currie

said or did, for she has a poor memory for detail, particularly when it concerns people other than herself.

So most of the book is taken up with her excessively dull views on issues that no longer matter ("if you switch from taxation to insurance, and take into account that in the UK the bulk of demand is uninsurable, what progress have you made?") and tedious descriptions of long-forgotten government initiatives that took place in the late 1980s. The text is then peppered with catty remarks ("he can be VERY boring and pedestrian") about former bigwigs such as John Moore, who no one can remember any more. Her insults, even those directed towards people who are still just about in the public eye, are singularly inept, with none of the vituperative skill of a Chips Channon or an Alan Clark. Norman Lamont is "not a nice man", Redwood and Lilley "not my kind of people", Gerald Kaufman "a Jew with no soul" and as for David Mellor, "I don't trust him an inch".

Even in her hate figures, she seems to have backed all the wrong horses. Indeed, there are nearly twice as many references to John Moore in the index as there are to "B", her code name for what a footnote coyly calls "EC's highly placed lover". The newspapers have already skilfully filleted the book for anything remotely saucy: what remains is weary, badly written, conceited, pedestrian, solipsistic and crass.

Nasty, too, in its blinkered, self-centred little way: not only has Currie sold her old lover down the river, but she has bunged in her ex-husband and both her daughters for good measure. On page one, she is complaining that poor old Ray Currie is looking fat and tired, and the abuse (snoring, moaning, sullen, lethargic, morose, etc, etc) rattles on throughout the book, culminating in a hateful and revealing passage in which she says that if only he'd lived up to his early promise "we'd be a lot wealthier and we'd have a circle of influential friends and acquaintances. Instead, his pals are local builders, retired policemen, an electrician at Rolls-Royce..."

Her two daughters fare scarcely any better. Susie is "hard as nails", while Debbie is "still so shallow and trivial in many of her attitudes". She celebrates Debbie's sixteenth birthday by outing her for having illegal underage sex, "which left me sad, that she should be so casual about sex – that's missing a lot. She has to take a low dosage pill to regulate her periods so I have no worries for her, but I doubt if she'll ever quite enjoy it as I do; the fire is missing."

Thanks, Mum! As in all areas, Currie's hypocrisy is quite breath-taking. As a junior health minister, she is happy, for instance, to give an interview advising people "Don't screw around" ("got plenty of headlines"), while happily screwing around herself. At another point, she criticises Geoffrey Howe's wife for spending a night in a cardboard box with the homeless, calling it "a distasteful publicity stunt" – yet her diaries can be read as a veritable inventory of personal publicity stunts, initially to boost her political profile, later simply for cash ("I launched *She* magazine's assertiveness course (a handy £2,000) complete with red stetson hat").

As a politician Edwina Currie (or "Edwina Currie Jones" as she styles herself in her introduction) made the early mistake of confus-ing publicity with popularity. In her diaries she constantly labours under the illusion that every new publicity stunt is an extra rung up the ladder to Number Ten. "I will have a crack at the leadership as soon as I can," she writes in October 1988, when she was nothing more than a parliamentary Under-Secretary, "partly because I am in touch with real people, partly because I can offer some leadership and view the future." In fact, the only ladder she was on was the ladder down to political oblivion: unbeknown to her, her country and her party were increasingly coming to see her as a figure of fun, a daft blabbermouth who could, in a dull week, lend a little spice to *Spitting Image*.

In competent hands, this could have been a fascinating study of two politicians on the path to power, one of them becoming Prime Minister, the other having to be content to pocket £500 for a fleet-ing appearance on the *Noel Edmonds TV Show*.

Greed and resentment are the dark threads that bind this raggedy book together. Every twenty pages or so, she thinks that her big chance for high office is about to come, and it never does. On page seventeen, when Mrs Thatcher makes Peter Brooke party chair-man, she says, "I'm mostly relieved, and not surprised, that I wasn't asked." A few pages later, she hears "rumours that I might go to the Treasury". And so it goes on. "I WOULD like a place in Cabinet please, asap," she writes after her ex-lover becomes Prime Minister.

But still she is left outside, pressing her nose against the glass, frantically signalling to be let in. "I feel so resentful that Gill Shephard was made deputy chairman and not me," she writes, just before the diary ends. And slowly it has dawned on her just who is to blame.

John Major, dull old dependable John Major, won the race, and now he won't even share the prize. It's the old story of the tortoise and the hare, and the writer is the hare. "He didn't keep his promise to me, as I understood it, that I would be offered a worthwhile post," she writes in one of those rare moments when anger overtakes self-delusion. "That hurt so terribly – and I would have been useful to this lacklustre government. I think I'd like the man to know exactly what he did last winter, and how I felt. Preferably not when the knowledge could do any damage; but he won't always be Prime Minister, and it won't always matter."

Edwina Currie has made endless attempts to claim that the publication of these diaries was motivated by high ideals – by feminism, by the demands of historical accuracy, by the public's right to know, by righteous indignation at Back to Basics – but her lofty pretences shrivel to nothing when set alongside the passage quoted above. The tortoise won the race; the hare thirsts for revenge.

The moment she is forced to resign over the salmonella crisis, Edwina Currie starts looking around for ways of making money ("Willie Whitelaw's memoirs just out. £300,000 advance!") and hits on the idea of putting pen to paper. She starts thinking of books, one of which would be about "the unequal way men and women move up, so that the marginally less able chap gets on and the lass doesn't". In such off-hand moments the shafts of bitterness arrive, more often than not masquerading as high-minded ideals.

The diary ends in mid-air, just before the 1992 election, which she seems to think the Tories will lose. Is there more to come? Even though she maintains it was she who broke off the affair with Major, there are plenty of signs that she then tried to revive it. "Saw B several times recently. Will try to get it going again this week," she writes in November, 1988. The following February, she sends him a Valentine. Presumably goaded on by this, a month later "he started to touch". She explains to him that if the affair is still on, "he must come and find time to come".

On such foundations is the £1million political diary created. But without John Major, how on earth will she sustain a follow-up? If I were the present Tory leader, I would put a padlock on my flies.

II) ALAN CLARK

Alan Clark had sensed the imminence of death for many years before it actually came. In earlier diaries, in the very pink of health, he couldn't stop estimating the days he had left ("Two thousand? Three thousand at most"). But when death finally approached, he seemed to know. His entry for July 12, 1999, less than two months before he died, reads, "The stage hands are now fiddling about with the curtains."

What a beautiful, sad and funny sentence that is! It shows that, even facing death, he is still able to separate himself from himself: looking down on our bleak human comedy, he offers us a last wry look at his own final exit. It is the thought of the stage hands "fiddling about" with the curtains – suggesting a kind of irritable indifference to the performance they are about to close – that makes this entry so masterful, so witty, so essentially Alan Clark.

Those who have yet to read the two previous volumes of Alan Clark's diaries sometimes make the mistake of thinking him nothing but a vain and catty right-wing philanderer. Read with one eye shut, this last volume of his diaries* could certainly help fuel that impression. At a Christmas carol service, he is delighted that there is "not one mention, from start to finish, of the Third World or the need to 'combat' racism or homelessness or poverty or any of that crap". As in the previous diaries, he makes a number of passing references to Hitler, who he always calls by the affectionate nickname "Wolf", culminating in his celebrating his likely return to Parliament by removing the signed portrait of Wolf he had kept in his safe and putting it back in its rightful place on the wall.

He is as catty as ever, even if he puts less energy than before into the hand-picking of his insults. William Hague is now the principal object of his scorn: "shifty little bureaucrat" "jarringly ghastly" "awful little git", and so on; but others, too, get it in the back – not

---

* *The Last Diaries – In and Out of the Wilderness* by Alan Clark

only his regular *bête noir* Michael Heseltine ("hair coiffed (I mean Teasy-Weasy coiffed) from behind – loathsome") but also HM the Queen for her "frumpish and ill-natured features".

Those who suspect Alan Clark of vanity will find that, once again, he is his own best witness for the prosecution. Early in this volume of diaries, the original volume, covering the Thatcher years, is published; as a result, Clark is elevated to a household name. Consequently, strangers are always coming up to him bearing compliments, each one of which, however banal, however absurd, he dutifully records. "I am always delighted when I impress," he purrs. And whenever he is rebuffed, he rounds on the rebuffer. When his heroine Margaret Thatcher decides that she doesn't want him to employ him as the ghostwriter of her autobiography, he snaps "she's got no sense of art or scholarship".

His philandering, too, continues pretty well unabated. This volume opens with Clark besotted with a woman known as "X" (his editor has removed her real name). She is, he says, "in my thoughts the entire time" and his wife Jane is "devastated by what is happening". A little later, Jane is upset to discover that the girlfriend has been dealing with builders about putting an extra bathroom into the Clarks' London flat. "Jane had a bad night and this morning at breakfast staged a duet of wailing and recrimination in the course of which she threw and smashed a coffee cup," he writes.

This entry strongly reminds me of the passage with which Claire Tomalin began her recent biography of Samuel Pepys, a diary entry in which Pepys and his wife Elizabeth were having a blazing row over his treachery, full of pulling and tearing and crying and raging. It is Pepys's refusal to paint himself in fine colours, says Tomalin, that makes him a diarist of genius. "He struggles into his breeches, he behaves unjustly and cruelly, he offers no justification of any kind for his behaviour except his anger and fear of being blamed. This is what he had seen and what he had felt, transmuted into words ... It is life, but as he writes it down it becomes art..."

And so it is with Alan Clark. The skill in the diaries and memoirs of most politicians lies in the delicate – or, more often, clumsy – airbrushing out of their faults and weaknesses. Alan Clark's self-portrait, on the other hand, is defiantly warts-and-all. On the one hand, he is a fantasist, dreaming right up to the last minute that the Tory party will be "smashed to pieces" and the country will turn to him for leadership. After a London cabbie tells him he should take over from John Major, "I went for a walk and my fantasy developed, even down to choosing the government." But another side of him is able to see the comic absurdity of these fantasies, and to record them for all to see. In a funny entry in 1996, written at a time when he is not even a backbench MP, he admits to telling a journalist that he is travelling to Mexico "on behalf of the Prime Minister". He then simultanaeously records the deception, scolds himself for it, and regards it with the detached curiosity of an observer: "Extraordinary, this weakness of mine – and just as I thought I had it under control."

This last volume covers the years 1991 to 1999, years in which he resigns as an MP, immediately regrets it ("the biggest mistake I ever made"), finds a new seat ("I don't honestly think I have been so utterly happy in my entire life") and is triumphantly re-elected in 1997. It must be said that Clark's wilderness years from 1992–97 are not best suited to his skills as a diarist. However bizarre it may seem to the rest of us, it was being on the inner loop of politics that fuelled his pen. This is why the original of his three volumes of diaries (now the second in the sequence) remains by far the best, detailing in marvellously comic style the plottings and manoeuvrings of the Thatcher high command.

Out of the political loop, Clark feels cast adrift, no longer privy to top-notch gossip. Stuck in the audience at a Conservative Party conference, he admits to feelings of hopelessness. "I get depressed (more depressed that I should say) watching the Cabinet moving around congratulating each other on the platform." For other writers, the sense of being an outsider would have provided material every bit as rich, but beyond the world of politics, one senses Clark's curiosity waning. As his editor points out, key moments in his life – his sons' weddings, the Matrix Churchill trial and Scott inquiry, the Harkness scandal – are barely touched upon, if at all. Sometimes, he gives the bare outline of an event without then bothering to join the dots. Thus on July 13, 1994, he mentions visiting Highgrove for some sort of small party. Aside from saying that Highgrove is "terribly nice", that Prince Charles is "very magnetic – greatly to my surprise", John Selwyn Gummer "notably unfriendly" and that he "took a liking to Paul McCartney" he offers no further information. In earlier years, such a scene would surely have inspired some of his most alert and humorous flourishes, but here it comes across as a day like any other.

Much of his diary is filled with gloom and introspection, neither of which was, one feels, his true muse. However, as the prospect of his own death moves from possibility through likelihood to certainty, his diary becomes almost unbearably poignant, the diarist's voice once again finding its subject. As the cancer sets in, he is filled with sorrow, fear, regret and remorse ("how horribly I treated her … salutary that I should be punished for my callousness in former times", thankfully softened by a deep and enduring faith in God. He prays regularly. "God; I am frightened," he prays at the end of May, 1999, days before a massive tumour is removed from his brain. "You have given me so much, everything really; and particularly my little love, whom I betrayed. How I wish I hadn't done so! The thing I fear most is leaving her. She is so good, so important. Please, please will you care for her also."

The book ends with Jane Clark's simple and desperately moving account of his last days. "I cried tears for a future that Al was not to share." Anyone who reads this volume will understand that theirs was a love story far more intense than many more conventional marriages.

His family buried Alan Clark in a shroud in the grounds of his castle, together with lots of keepsakes, including his racing goggles, biscuits for his dogs, some heather from Scotland, and his House of Commons pass. His three volumes of diaries will ensure his immortality.

(III) An Addendum

In her diaries, Edwina Currie suspects fellow Conservatives of keeping diaries. On February 11, 1988, she sees Virginia Bottomley taking notes at a dinner for Margaret Thatcher in the Cholmondeley Room in the House of Commons. "I'll bet she is keeping a diary!" she comments. She is fond of the exclamation mark.

Later, on October 7, 1988, she discovers that Douglas Hurd keeps a diary: "so we have something to look forward to there as well". Someone has told her that Hurd writes his diary every night, whereas her own is much more sporadic, often with two- or three-month gaps. "It suggests a more ambitious person," she writes of Hurd, adding, "he thinks he is going to be worth writing about in future! Perhaps that is in my mind too as I write this." Five lines on, she is prompted to reflect: "I have slowly come to realise, and somewhat unwillingly, that I will have a crack at the leadership as soon as I can. I look at rivals like David Mellor and I like me better."

Oddly enough, the one person she doesn't suspect of keeping a diary is her Conservative colleague Alan Clark. She is working in the Department of Health and Social Security and he is the Minister for Trade, so probably they seldom meet. It is also often forgotten that, while Mrs Currie was a celebrity MP from the word go, having first attracted headlines by waving a pair of handcuffs at a Tory party conference, Alan Clark remained largely unknown outside the House of Commons until the publication of his diaries in 1993. I would imagine that whenever their paths crossed each diarist would have considered the other too much of a no-hoper to merit inclusion. But on one occasion they crossed not only paths but swords; happily, each considered the encounter worth a mention.

It was Wednesday, November 21, 1990, the evening before Margaret Thatcher resigned. Currie had voted for Heseltine, Clark for Thatcher. Currie records that "Wednesday ended in tears for me, though no one saw them". She had, she writes, been walking past a group sitting behind the Speaker's chair. The group, she writes, consisted of Tristan Garel-Jones, Alan Clark and Richard Ryder. "Everything all right?" Ryder asks her, as she walks past.

"Prat, I thought, vacuous unctuous prat," she writes. Edwina turns on him. "No, it isn't," she snaps. "The party is falling apart and you're just sitting there grinning." After a little more banter, she records Alan Clark saying, angrily: "Why don't you apply for the Chiltern Hundreds right now? Then you can have a different career."

"Snob, I thought, and turd with it," she writes. She then turns on Clark. "I have other things I do now, Alan, and you don't need to be insulting to me: I'm not going to insult you. But we cannot win the election on the basis of safe seats in the south alone. We have to win my seat, and many others like it in the Midlands and the north." She then exits: "I will not be faced down by these men, I thought, and walked off to the car park, where I cried in my car for ten minutes."

Oddly enough, not a single word of dialogue in Clark's account of their meeting coincides with Currie's. In Clark's version, he makes no reference to the presence of Richard Ryder, but he does mention sitting with Tristan Garel-Jones, who "had little to say".

"Then along came Edwina. 'Hullo, aren't you Edwina Currie?'"

"Now then, Alan, there's no need to be objectionable."

"If that is who you are, I must congratulate you on the combination of loyalty and restraint that you have shown in going on television to announce your intention to vote against the Prime Minister in the leadership election."

"Alan, I'm perfectly prepared to argue this with you, if you'll listen."

"Piss off."

Which she did.

Tristan said: "She's not a bad girl really."

Which of the two diary entries comes closest to the truth? Clark wrote up his diary only a few hours later, in an Indian restaurant around the corner from the House of Commons. Clark's account was thus hot off the press. Currie waited until the following Sunday to write up hers, while sitting in a hotel in Bangladesh. In the same entry, she included the whole of the rest of the week, including attending an aerobics class and then dancing round her flat at the news of Mrs Thatcher's resignation.

The accuracy of recorded speech is often best judged by reading it aloud. In Clark's dialogue one can hear his authentic camp acidity and the pert, flouncy tone of Currie, though both could be said to carry a hint of caricature. But I would defy even the most skilled actor to speak the line Currie gives herself – "But we cannot win the election on the basis of safe seats in the south alone. We have to win my seat, and many like it in the Midlands and the north" – and make it sound natural.

In the end, even if Virginia Bottomley and Douglas Hurd turn out to have been eavesdropping, we will never know which of the two diarists to trust. It may well be, of course, that both accounts are partial, and neither can be relied upon. But posterity will favour Alan Clark, for posterity has no need of truth, opting for the good writer over the bad.

In the Wilderness

THE HAGUE YEARS: THE CONSERVATIVE MANIFESTO 2001

It's time for common sense.

The sort of common sense that says there's a fundamental difference between town and country.

Town has lots of buildings.

Country doesn't.

Unless you count farm buildings.

Yes, it's time for common sense.

The sort of common sense that tells you the earth is certainly not round – no matter what Labour's politically correct spin-doctors may try to tell us.

Otherwise, how on earth would we stand up without falling down into the sky?

Knowing who we are.

Common sense means valuing what makes us distinctive as a nation.

The bright red pillar-box. The Hillman Hunter. Heinz Spaghetti Hoops on Mother's Pride. Fishpaste. Sir Stanley Matthews on our cigarette cards. A high-spirited youngster receiving a clip round the ear from his local bobby – and so growing up to become a leading Captain of Industry.

With Labour, our heritage is under threat as never before.

The bogus asylum seeker rampages down our village streets, vandalising married couples and covering our elderly in graffiti.

Bogus schoolchildren play truant, taunting up to 73 per cent of ordinary, decent passers-by and torching up to 67 per cent of our motor vehicles – before scurrying back to school to pick up cash handouts from the Arts Council.

Senior Labour ministers skulk around the country persistently punching decent working people on the nose.

It's time for common sense.

Conservatives will target bogus asylum seekers as never before. First, we will sift the bogus asylum seekers from the genuine bogus asylum seekers. And then we'll place both sets on the fast boat back to Brussels.

We must build on Britain's strengths.

Some married couples aren't getting enough.

We will remove the red tape from married couples.

It's time for common sense.

* * *

Knowing what we mean – in Europe and beyond.

For too long, we have not known what we mean. What do we as Conservatives mean by "not knowing what we mean"?

This meddling Labour government will never tell us.

So it is our job to find out.

As Conservatives, we trust the British people to know what we mean. They know we want to be in Europe but not from Europe. On Europe but not on top of Europe. Over Europe but not under Europe. Out of Europe but not in Europe. In Europe but not out of Europe.

It's time for common sense.

The deepest instincts of the British people grow ever deeper every day.

When they voted at the last election, they made their message clear: they wanted a Conservative government. A Conservative government on the edge of Europe but not under Europe.

We will bring back the Home Guard. Ordinary, decent men and women will give up their hard-won time to patrol Britain's coastline day and night on the look-out for any invading Euro infected with politically correct New Labour Foot and Mouth disease.

It's time for common sense.

* * *

A world leader

Britain continues to lead the world in its claims to world leadership. We want to see good new schools springing up – at no extra cost to the taxpayer. We want to see every citizen prosperous and healthy – at no extra cost to the taxpayer.

To ensure fast-track cures for more and more people, we plan to abolish Labour's failed waiting list initiative. Instead, we will introduce a bold new list (waiting) initiative – at no extra cost to the taxpayer.

We will prosecute criminals, not their victims.

We will take persistent young people off the streets.

We will lock up more bogus non-offenders for longer than ever before.

We will direct an extra £2 billion into stopping money being thrown at problems.

Yes – it's time for common sense.

(www.mon.sense.dot.com.)

THE DUNCAN SMITH YEARS: LEADER'S SPEECH TO THE CONSERVATIVE CONFERENCE 2003

Two years ago, we'd lost a second general election. Labour were twenty points ahead in the polls. The critics said it couldn't get worse. But we proved them wrong!

To the Prime Minister, I say this. This is what I say. And what I am saying is this: the quiet man is here to stay. And he's turning up the volume.

Government – never there when you need it. Always there when you don't.

Think about everyday life. You struggle to get to work because the traffic's jammed. You look at the petrol gauge. You're clean out. Where did all that petrol go?

Government – never there when you need it. Always there when you don't.

The car stalls. You have to ring the AA. Your membership's expired. Two hours fifty minutes later, you make it to the office. You've missed that crucial meeting. The client's gone home in a strop. Your boss is furious. And your colleagues are sniggering behind your back.

Government – never there when you need it. Always there when you don't.

So you work longer to make up for it. You get home late – to find your daughter's been bullied at school, your son's had his mobile pinched, your dog's chewed your favourite slippers, your cat's up a tree and your wife's run off with the milkman.

Government – never there when you need it. Always there when you don't.

And then Gran's on the phone. Never there when you need her. Always there when you don't. She's full of the usual moans. She can't find the remote, she's clean out of Fairy Liquid, there's a spider in the bathroom, her toaster's on the blink and there's nothing but repeats on the telly.

You don't expect the earth. Just a fair deal. And a new toaster for Gran. Tony Blair's in your face when you just don't need the hassle. And when you want him in your face, he's just not there. So where the hell is he? He's in the hassle. And where's the hassle? It's in your face!

And now we come to Tony Blair's darkest act. This government used Lorraine Kelly as a pawn in its battle with the BBC. That delightful breakfast television presenter with the cheery smile. And the happy-go-lucky manner. And Tony Blair put his hands around her throat. And proceeded to throttle her. And if he didn't do it, well, it's just the kind of thing he would have done if he had wanted to.

Make no mistake. I stand before you today and I tell you this: I stand before you today and I tell you this. Make no mistake.

I will fight with all my strength to defend the British people's right to be governed by me. Make no mistake. I put this government on notice. From tomorrow, Michael Ancram and I will be travelling up and down the country, introducing ourselves to ordinary decent people at home and in the high street.

And Michael will say, loud and clear: Hello, I'm Michael Ancram. And I will say this: And I'm Iain Duncan Smith; please don't run away.

And I promise you this, Mr Blair. I will fight, fight and fight again with all my strength to save the country that I love from not doing what I think it should do.

Blimey! Did you see Tony Blair's performance in Bournemouth last week? Did you? Did you hear that speech? You know, I sometimes wonder if that guy lives in the same world as the rest of us ordinary geezers! Lor-luv-a-duck, me old pork pie! Know what I mean, guv? Chim-chim-inee, Chim-chim-inee, Chim-Chim-Cheroo. Good luck will rub orf. When I shakes hands with you.

I know what I believe. I know what I value. I value my beliefs. And – yes – I believe in my values.

We must project fresh ideas for the twentieth century. A thoroughly up-to-date set of stocks for every village green. Fully digitalised deportation to Van Diemen's Land for the theft of one or more vegetables. A ration book and designer gas masks for all the family. A complete set of Gracie Fields recordings on compact disc for every household in the land. Uncle Mac on the Light Programme, and low-fat cocoa before bedtime, any nonsense and it'll be six of the best when your father or common-law parent gets home.

Society is changing. Whatever happened to the bubble car and the goitre, the cross-your-heart girdle and the Lyons Corner House, the Peppermint Cream, the bowler hat and the Black and White Minstrels?

To be a Conservative is not about turning back the clock. No one can do that. But it is perfectly possible to stop the clock. You open up the little compartment in the back and remove the batteries.

Is there anyone out there?

Is there a Conservative out there? Hello? Hello?

I am getting a Margaret. Does anyone here know a Margaret – a Margaret from the Eighties?

Hello? Hello?

THE HOWARD YEARS: LEADER'S SPEECH TO THE CONSERVATIVE PARTY CONFERENCE 2004

Let me start with a little joke.

Iain Duncan Smith. (laughter, applause).

Without him, we would not be where we are today.

But seriously.

Let's talk about the real world for a change. In the real world, if you say you're going to do something, you do it. And if you screw up, you lose your job.

So we all wish Iain the very best.

It's all down to one thing. Accountability. Remember that word – Ac-count-a-bil-it-y.

It means being ac-count-a-bil.

And let's remember another word. Patronising.

Pat-ro-ni-sing.

What does "patronising" mean, I hear the brighter among you asking?

I'll tell you what it means.

It means talking to people as though they are very, very stupid. Do you think you'll be able to remember that, do you? Well done you!

You know, politicians don't have all the solutions. People are sick and tired of their promises. So I make you no promises today. And that is a promise.

From now on, we will promise what we can deliver. What we promise, we will start. What we start, we will follow through. What we follow through, we will deliver. And what we deliver, we promise to start.

Today we unveil our Timetable for Action. What we'll do. When we'll do it. You will be able to hold us to account. We will have no place to hide.

People are fed up with talk. They want us to live in the real world. They want a Timetable for Action. So. Day One after the next general election – I will offer my resignation.

Week One – I'll see that my shadow cabinet go too.

This way, we can make Britain the envy of the world.

Where there is cynicism, we can bring hope.

Month One – you will all have the chance to elect another man of proven inability to lead this great party of ours to defeat at the next election.

As Conservatives, we instinctively trust the generosity, the common sense and the compassion of the British people.

And that is why we promise to put more of them behind bars.

Day One – we'll recruit lots more police officers a year.

Week One – they'll start arresting lots more British people.

Month One – we'll build lots more British prisons to put them in.

Billions of pounds of taxpayers' money has been spent on the National Health Service. And what have we got to show for it?

Hospitals full of sick people. People with all manner of maladies. Some of them very seriously ill indeed.

It's simply not good enough.

More people die every year in hospital than are killed on Britain's roads.

Week One – we will insert speed bumps in all our hospitals.

Week Two – we will set up a ten-point Action Plan to allow us to patronise all our marvellous little doctors and nurses, and to make it absolutely clear to them what a splendid job they're doing. They deserve a pat on the back – and that is what they will get.

Nothing more, nothing less.

Schools, too. Parents know what is best for their children. A jolly good slap. Some more Pot Noodles. Or perhaps a new Gameboy. That is for the parents to decide. And what about our marvellous old pensioners, bless?

I want to live in a country where we honour our older generations, cherish their wisdom, care for their needs and – if that is what they really want – give them a crack at being Prime Minister. That is why in our first month David Willetts will take steps to restore a grip on plans to respond to the steps necessary to restore a grip on our plans to respond to the steps we need to take.

It's as simple as that.

* * *

Everyone's been let down by Labour
The family with a new baby who's up all night.

The couple who both work during the day but can't stop bickering when they get home in the evening.

The pensioner living next door to the selfish young hooligan who likes his music loud.

The hard-working young man living next door to the selfish pensioner who is moaning at him to turn his music down.

It's all wrong. It's all unfair. So on Day One, we will put them all in prison.

And that's accountability.

THE CAMERON YEARS: TEACH YOURSELF CAMEROON

Adults: Let's treat adults like adults.

Amazing things: We've done them in the past. We can do them again in the future. But what are they? That's for us to find out.

Articulate a central theme: We must articulate a central theme. And that theme must be absolutely central to the way we articulate it. Only by centralising the articulation of that theme can we ever truly call ourselves, whatever.

Attractive: To be attractive, our programme must be balanced.

Balanced: To be balanced, our programme must be compassionate.

Compassionate: To be compassionate, our programme must be attractive.

Debate: Always broader and/or wider, and worth contributing to. SEE ALSO: Great debate.

Define, Important to: (SEE Our Shared Values)

Determination: Only by undertaking to renew our sense of determination can we ever gain a renewed sense of determination.

Dream: Let's dream a new generation of Conservative dreams. "Stars shining bright above you. Night breezes seem to whisper I love you. Birds singing in the sycamore tree. Dream a little dream of me" (from a speech to the Exeter Conservative Association, June 2005).

Drugs: What can be done? Frankly, they get up my nose.

Dynamism: Optimism. A sense of purpose: These are all incredible things. Slobbishness. Pessimism. And an overwhelming sense of the pointlessness of it all: these all have a vital part to play too.

Eggcups: Let's treat eggcups like eggcups. Only if the egg fits in the cup can we truly call it an eggcup under the rule of law. But if an egg does not fit in the cup, then we should set out to see whether we cannot find a larger cup. Or indeed a smaller egg.

Engage: Vital to engage, particularly if we are to win the great debate (SEE Great Debate)

Family: The building block of our society. Come in all shapes and sizes. The foundation for a civilised society.

Finger-pointing: It's time to stop the finger-pointing. Yes, it's time to point the finger at the finger-pointers, and to say, "Finger pointing has got to go." But on the other hand, a certain amount of finger-pointing is vital for an attractive, balanced, and compassionate society.

Flexibility: The best and indeed only way to retain flexibility is by remaining flexible.

Focus: Always both a need for, and a question of. Let's focus on the things that really matter, whilst never forgetting that for the good of our society it is also vital to keep an eye on those things that don't really matter. It's all a question of focus.

Foundation of a civilised society: Building blocks are the foundation of a civilised society.

Freedom: Let me say this. I value our freedom.

Fundamental change: Vital if we are to win the great debate.

Great Debate: Vital if we are to secure fundamental change. But first we must win the great debate. And the only way to win the great debate is to secure fundamental change.

Harness: Let's harness what needs to be harnessed. That's why I came into politics.

Hat: Everyone should be allowed to wear a hat under the rule of law. But equally nobody should be forced to wear a hat, unless it is absolutely necessary.

Incredible: This is an incredible country. That's why I came into politics.

In tune: We must be in tune with modern Britain because only by being in tune with modern Britain can we remain in tune with modern Britain.

Kiss: "Stars fading, but I linger on, dear. Still craving your kiss. I'm longing to linger til dawn, dear. Just saying this" (from a speech to the International Trade Association, October 2005).

Legs: Let's treat legs like legs. Legs are amazing things for walking and running, as well as standing still. You can put them in trousers, or in something less confining. That is your fundamental right. But at the same time those who, through no fault of their own, have only one leg, or even fewer, also have their part to play, very much so.

Life: Changing fast. The building block of our society. Vital to engage with. You don't get anywhere in life unless you are honest with yourself. On the one hand, you only get out of life what you put into it. But on the other, many people, through no fault of their own, find life an uphill struggle. At its best, life is not only a bowl of cherries but also a bed of roses. We must engage in the wider debate.

Matter most: Children. They're the adults of tomorrow.

Modernise: What exactly do we mean when we say that we have to modernise our culture and our attitudes and our identity? That is for us to find out. It is a voyage of discovery I am inviting each and every one of you to join me in. But let's start by wearing a cravat at weekends and perhaps a nice tweed jacket with well-pressed jeans rather than a stuffy old suit!

Must change: We must change to win. Smart/casual, no need for a tie!

Night: Night follows day. Day follows night. That's central to our philosophy.

Nighty-night: "Say nighty-night and kiss me. Just hold me tight and tell me you'll miss me. When I'm alone and blue as can be, dream a little dream of me" (from a speech to the Centre for Policy Studies, September 2005).

Our shared values: (see also Define, important to): Our shared values are the values we share. It is only by sharing these values that we will create a set of shared values.

Optimism: Your glass may be half empty – but mine is half full. In the interests of a sound economy, if you would be frightfully kind and let me have your half-empty glass, then I'll pour it into mine, and then I'll end up with one that's completely full. Much better not only for you and me, but more importantly for the country as a whole!

Priorities: There are always three priorities – the first priority, the second priority and the third priority. But for pity's sake let's not get bogged down in detail.

Quality of life concerns: My quality of life concerns reflect my concerns for the quality of life. And will always do so, because that is the sort of person I am.

Reach out: We as a party must reach out and touch those millions of people who may look like us, and speak like us, and perhaps even know people we know, but who, for one reason or another, have never voted Conservative. I have an address book full of them.

Recasting our values: By recasting our values, we do not seek to change them. Far from it. We simply want them played by a different cast.

Reconnecting with the young: As a young man myself, I enjoy the rich, vibrant melodies of Chris de Burgh and Coldplay.

Relevant to people's lives: Only by making ourselves relevant to people's lives can we make ourselves relevant to people's lives.

Rhetoric: "Do we want to lose again? Or do we want to win? Do we want to repeat the mistakes of the past and consign our party to permanent opposition? Or do we want to establish ourselves as the party of government?"

Saying: "Stars fading but I linger on dear. Still craving your kiss. I'm longing to linger till dawn, dear. Just saying this" (from a speech to the CBI, July 2005).

Sense of direction: Without a sense of direction, we will lose our way. We need a map, and luckily I have one handy.

Sense that our best days lie ahead, we need a: The day after tomorrow will be better than tomorrow, which, in turn, will be better than today. Because today's often a Monday, worse luck!

Stand up, we must have the courage to: It's all too easy to sit down, but sometimes we must have the courage to stand up. On the other hand, there will always be those who, for whatever reason, have to stay seated, and they too have a part to play.

Strategy: Always "bold".

Strong: We want strong universities, though weak universities also have their part to play.

Tackle: Challenges must be tackled. And tackles must be challenged.

Time: What time is it? It's time to stop point-scoring.

Twentieth-century party, a truly: That's what I want this party to be. A party of buttons, not cufflinks. Of bicycles, not penny-farthings. A party of hoodies, not foodies.

Up to date, we in the Conservative Party must always be: That's why I always find a watch invaluable.

Wee: "There is a we in politics. And a wee. But not a week, because that is a long time" (from a speech to the Conservative Party conference, September 2005).

Windows: Only by putting windows in our house will we ever be able to see out. But equally it is essential that the window pane fits exactly into the space for which it was designed, or it will fall out.

Worries: "Sweet dreams till sunbeams find you. Sweet dreams that leave all your worries behind you. But in your dreams, whatever they be, dream a little dream of me" (from a speech to the Association of Conservative Councillors, September 2005).

Young people: I know this is how young people feel because this is how I feel. I want every young person in this country with ideas and talent and energy to say: "Yes, I want to make a difference. Yes, I've got something to offer. Yes, I'll get involved. But definitely not in drugs."

The Two John Majors

THE VILLAGERS of Lugànga in Uganda are celebrating the capture of a killer crocodile that has feasted on at least eighty-three people in its sixty years. The man-eater is sixteen foot long and weighs a ton. In his gourmand career, he developed his own special fast-food technique. Rather than simply skulking around in the water on the off-chance that something would turn up, he would take a more proactive role, leaping out of the water into fishing boats and gobbling people up.

He was eventually caught in a trap laid by the Uganda Wildlife Authority, who had draped a pair of cow's lungs over a copper snare, and dangled the whole thing over a tree. He will now be taken to a crocodile farm, where he will spend his remaining days breeding with lady crocodiles. Obviously, the Uganda Wildlife Authority are not believers in the deterrent principle. Once news of the benefits leaks out, they will have only themselves to blame if hundreds more crocodiles start going round eating people.

But the most fascinating thing about this killer crocodile is his name. After the al-Qaeda attacks on the American embassies in Kenya and Tanzania, the villagers of Luganga renamed the killer crocodile Osama, and that is the name by which he is now known. But from 1991 to the late 1990s, he was called John Major, "in recognition" reports the *Sunday Telegraph*, "of his size and his namesake's global prominence at the time".

Some may find it hard to credit that Mr Major was ever so globally prominent as to have a crocodile named after him in Uganda. In Britain, we didn't even bother to name a shopping centre or a roundabout after him. If we had ever got round to naming an animal after him, it would probably have been a frog. He always had the wistful, hard-done-by look of Kermit.

On the other hand, a close reading of Edwina Currie's *1987–1992 Diaries* suggests the villagers of Luganga may have had a point. Compare these two accounts of grappling with the two different John Majors, one by a Luganga villager, the other by Mrs Currie.

a) "He just emerged from the water vertically and flopped into the boat... The crocodile latched on to Peter's leg and began to pull. Peter was clutching the side screaming. They fought for about five minutes until I heard a tearing sound... Then he let go and was dragged into the lake."

b) "I met and talked to him at his request, sitting in his room drinking tomato juice. Why? He said he liked talking to me; I was amusing and nice, and underneath I was as soft as butter. He started to touch, but I couldn't cope with it and got a bit upset and tried rather tearfully to explain that he must not mess me about."

Can you tell which is which?

(March 15, 2005)

The Way Ahead

(I) WALLACE ARNOLD: HOW TO REVITALISE OUR PARTY

✱ **Step One.** It was on Monday – or was it Tuesday? – that a small but substantial group of Tory MPs came knocking on my door around teatime and, over hot-buttered crumpets and port, called on me to help "revitalise" (dread word!) the Conservative Party.

"We really have got to reach out!" urged my old friend and quaffing partner Nicholas Soames. "What was it Diana Dors used to sing? That's it – '*Reach out and touch somebody's hand! Make this world a better place, if you can*'." Nicholas then stretched out both his arms in a most moving and plaintive gesture. At that very moment, to the undisguised horror of the assembled company, an almighty ripping sound erupted from Nicholas's beautifully cut City suit as it tore in three different places.

"Oh, well. You can't make an omelette without breaking eggs," I observed, sagely. "Or so cook tells me."

As Nicholas bustled out to change into a pair of fawn leggings, the remaining wise owls gathered around my desk, all ears.

"I am," I announced, "more than happy to take on the formidable task of 'revitalising' the party. But first let's sleep on it." So saying, I poured us all another generous finger of port, kicked off my shoes, placed my head well back in my seat, and bought myself a first-class ticket to the Land of Nod.

✳ **Step Two.** Upon awakening from my zizz, I found myself surrounded by the very same eager beavers in shirtsleeves, clipboards at the ready.

"Where were we?" I said.

"We were revitalising the party!" said Francis Maude, punching the air.

"We were reaching out and reconnecting with the ordinary man!"

"And woman!" piped up little Tim Yeo. "Let's not forget the ordinary woman!"

"Vital not to forget the bows and frills brigade!" I agreed, encouragingly.

"The ladies love a bit of pink, bless their pretty little heads!!"

"On the one hand, we mustn't alienate our core voters," fizzed Michael Ancram. "But on the other hand, we – um – deary me, I've clean forgotten what was on the other hand."

"On the other hand, we mustn't alienate our core voters – was that it?" suggested Malcolm Rifkind.

"No – that was on the first hand, Malcolm," said Ancram. "There was something else on the other hand. Now what was it?"

"Some sort of … glove, maybe?" I said, helpfully. "Or a wristwatch? Digital wristwatches are all the rage these days – or so I'm told."

"That's it! We've got it!" said young David Cameron, absolutely cock-a-hoop. "We will insist that all our candidates wear digital wristwatches whenever they're on radio or television! That's the only way to drag the party kicking and screaming into the twentieth century!"

✻ **Step Three.** "Might I put in a word, Wallace?" asked Maude. "My spies tell me that shirtsleeves are all the rage. Ordinary people respond well to shirtsleeves. Shirtsleeves prove beyond doubt that a man is prepared to take off his jacket. Yes, poor old Howard employed his shirtsleeves to reasonably good effect in the election, but an awful lot of people are saying he didn't go far enough."

"The feeling at grassroots," said Cameron, employing the modish jargon of the young, "is that frankly he should have gone a step further, and removed his shirtsleeves, too. These days, it's all about vests. Coloured vests, cotton vests, nylon vests, string vests. In future, elections are going to be won or lost in vests."

"And pants," chipped in Yeo, ever-anxious to prove himself young at heart. "A lot of ordinary, decent people are saying that Michael should have spent far more time in his underpants. Virtually everyone wears some form of underpant these days, and by showing loud and clear that he was a committed underpant-wearer, Michael really could have wiped up."

✻ **Step Four.** It had been a most fruitful first meeting, with plenty of ideas batted about; it was left to me to pull all the various bats together and place them face up on the table.

"Point one," I summed up. "We need more candidates in position in their underwear, made from any fabric, but preferably grassroots, and with their digital wristwatches clearly visible. Point two, we must reconnect – dread word! – with our core voters, or at least those who are still alive. Point three, we must extend our appeal to the fairer sex – or should that be the UNfairer sex???!!! Johnny Redwood certainly knows how to win 'em round – something tells me he'd make an excellent Secretary of State for the birds of the unfeathered variety!"

"First class!" said Ancram. "But to revitalise the party by broadening our appeal with the ladies while reconnecting with our core vote, what we really need is a gutsy woman with a proven track record!"

Then it struck me.

"Anyone have a number for Margaret?" I asked.

(May 12, 2005)

(II) Look to the Future: A Symposium

Andrew Neil (Chairman): Good to see you! We're here to discuss the Conservative Party. Remember them?!!! Back in the Eighties, you could walk down the King's Road in your finest cravat, braces and flares, a lovely young lady on each arm, swinging to something with a bit of a beat to it by the Bee Gees, and still find plenty of time to edit THE leading Sunday newspaper. So what went wrong? Charles?

Charles Moore: One reason that people used to vote Tory was that Tory MPs always wore lovely tweed suits. And they respected them for it. But nowadays they see them in off-the-peg grey or black suits, many of them two-piece and without watch chains, and consequently they have no one to look up to. And we wonder why so many unmarried teenagers have triplets and nose rings!

Michael Heseltine: We've got to look to the future, Charles. It all comes back to Westland. Thatcherism was a disaster for this country. I mean, backing the Sikorsky bid! Really! Talk about cloud cuckoo land. Ordinary people knew that Sikorsky was wholly unsuited to the task. But did she listen? Of course she didn't. And that's why we're in the mess in which we find ourselves today. Cloud cuckoo land!

Liam Fox: There is a crying need for framing a wide-ranging debate within the party on the whole issue of the need for framing a wide-ranging debate. We must generate debate with the country at large. Only the other day, I was talking to a gentleman in Solihull. And later in the week, I went abseiling. And after that I spoke to a gentleman from Birmingham. We've got to learn lessons.

Iain Duncan Smith: I agree with Liam. I spoke to the same gentleman from Solihull. Or if not exactly the same gentleman, jolly nearly. And he agreed with me. And I agree with Liam. And so did he. Over the past two years, I've been going up and down the country, and I've found a very strong measure of agreement. What people in the country are saying is there's a crying need for a firm measure of agreement.

Liam Fox: And we mustn't be afraid to tackle problems either. Or raise serious issues. That's at the root of it. Incidentally, did anyone see that photo of me abseiling? It attracted a lot of comment, which must be good for the party. I'm hoping to go down a mine soon, and they're letting me wear a miner's helmet with a little torch on it. As a party, we really mustn't be afraid to wear different hats.

Charles Moore: I couldn't disagree more. People don't want us to wear different hats, they want us to wear our traditional hat. The reason we lost the last election is because none of our candidates wore a trilby. If the Conservative Party fails to pick a leader who promises to wear tweeds and a trilby, it'll be out of power for a generation.

Michael Heseltine: Thatcherism was a disaster. There was a crying need for a leader with a proven record of supporting the European consortium over the narrow Sikorsky bid. Believe me, Charles, the people out there – ordinary people doing ordinary little jobs, candlestick makers and so forth – never trusted Thatcher, not one little bit. I know, because I've spoken to them and I told them so.

Iain Duncan Smith: How are we going to win poor people back, Michael? I've set up my very own foundation to tackle the whole problem of poor people. I go up and down the country shaking their hands, asking them what it's like to be poor. From what they tell me, it's very much like being rich, but without the money. But for goodness sake, let's not throw money at them, that's the last thing they want.

Charles Moore: The only way to get poor people to vote Conservative is to promise them major cuts in their state handouts. At the moment, they absolutely hate all that free money coming in, hand over fist, jamming up their postboxes and making their cleaning ladies' lives a misery. It makes them feel dependent and they simply don't know what to do with it, so they spend it all on binge drinking and having teenage babies when what they really yearn for is the days of real poverty, when people would go from house to house offering one another nutritious scraps and the friendly old barrow-man would call on them with a cheery nod and a wink, asking them to bring out their dead.

Liam Fox: There's a strong argument for cutting tax. And there's an equally strong argument for raising tax. Personally, I favour both. And we've got to debate the whole issue of Britain's position in the world. Yes, we're to the west of Europe. But we're also to the east of America. Unless you go the other way round the globe, in which case we're west of America but a long way east of Europe. There's a strong argument for both. And next week I'm going on a Fun Run in a baseball cap to draw attention to it.

Theresa May: The Conservatives are seen as negative and out of touch and indifferent.

Iain Duncan Smith: No, we're not. And who cares if we are, anyway?

Andrew Neil: The younger generation are naturally Eurosceptic. They'd much rather go to Los Angeles than Paris. They like to go clubbing at Tramp till the early hours, and to swing to the very latest from Andy Williams, preferably with a delicious young lady in their arms, wearing something that leaves precious little to the imagination and with a cooling glass of ice-cold Dubonnet to hand. But you don't see this reflected anywhere in your party's foreign policy. I mean, get a life, you guys!

Michael Heseltine: It all boils down to leadership, Andrew. The party desperately needs someone who can cut a dash on the international stage, someone with a proven track record as a party leader, someone who's prepared to embrace private enterprise while continuing to safeguard the public sector, someone who can bridge the divide: someone like Tony Blair, in fact, but perhaps a bit younger. For my money, a Conservative Party led by Euan Blair would be a tremendously exciting prospect.

Theresa May: But he's not black, Michael. We don't want to send out the wrong message.

Michael Heseltine: But Teresa, we live in a technological age. Skin colour isn't a problem. A simple course of injections, and you wouldn't know him from Bob Marley.

Charles Moore: Robert Morley! Excellent! Just the sort of larger-than-life figure who'd make the perfect leader of the Conservative Party.

Liam Fox: But isn't he dead?

Charles Moore: Exactly!

Department of Trade and Industry

"You're Fired!": Sir Alan Sugar's Diary

When I started out, I didn't go out to posh restaurants to eat their fancy nosh. D'you think I had time for all that toffee-nosed crap? I left that to the schmoozers and the bullshitters – and look where it bloody got them. Today, I'm sitting with my arse on top of a global empire worth £700 million. And they can't even afford a pair of second-hand knickers from Ox-bloody-fam.

So much for schmoozers and bullshitters.

No. I wanted to get on in life. Even if it meant missing my bloody nosebag.

But I believe in rewarding loyalty. That's the bottom line.

✱ **Rule One: A dog does well, you throw him a bone. That way, he'll come when you whistle.**

So yesterday I took three of my colleagues out for a slap-up meal at the Savoy, and, take it from me, that costs.

"OK," I said. "Have whatever you want from the menu, and I'll pick up the tab. Generous offer, and I never go back on my word. You got forty minutes from ... NOW! – so you better eat your bollocks off, do I make myself clear? I said, do I make myself clear?"

The waitress comes, and they was ordering like there's no tomorrow – starter, main course, the whole bloody bollocks. But from the outset they made some serious mistakes.

Gareth goes first. Orders the Prawn Cocktail. "The Prawn Cocktail!" I says. "What you want to go and do that for, Gareth? You must be out of your tiny mind!"

"Oh Sir Alan," says Gareth, "I've always liked the pink sauce what they comes with."

"Don't you Oh Sir Bloody Alan me, my son," I says. "You bloody what? You bloody what? You always liked the pink – don't give me that! You're sending me a suicide message, my friend. Pink sauce costs nothing. You know what sort of mark-up they're asking on that pink sauce? Eight hundred, nine hundred per cent. And he says he's always liked pink sauce! What kind of bloody fool is that? You order a Prawn Cocktail, you're going to get dished, my friend."

"Actually, Sir Alan," says Gareth, "I just changed my mind. I'll have the pâté."

✳ Rule Two: Never chop and change. It sends out all the wrong messages, and you'll get your head sliced off.

"That's your second mistake, my friend," I says. "Place like this, you don't just say, 'I'll have the pâté.' You say, 'Look, mate, what's the best price you can do me for the pâté?' Or else the waitress will never respect you."

"Ow d'you know the waitress's name was Else, then, Sir Alan?" says Gareth.

"Gareth – you're fired!" I says.

✳ Rule Three: In the dining-out game, keep your eye on the ball, or you'll be kicked to death by your own team.

So we're all settling in nicely, having a bit of a chat – remember, teamleaders, always encourage your team members to have a bit of a chat but IN THEIR OWN TIME – when a waiter comes up with this bloody great basket and asks us if we want some.

"What's the product?" I says.

"Bread, sir," he says.

"How much, my friend?" I says.

"It's free, sir," he says.

"I'll take the lot," I says. "Then fill your basket up again, bring it back here, and I'll take that load too."

And that's precisely what he did. Be under no illusion: if you're offered something, and the deal's to your advantage, buy up the stock before they up the price. I didn't get where I am today by settling for a single bread roll when I could have had dozens. When I get behind a project, I give it 200 per cent.

"Henry," I says to my number three. "We got here, what? Twenty, twenty-five bread rolls? But they're not buttered, are they? Big mistake! Listen here. What I want you to do is butter them, then go round the tables and pitch directly to them, offering them READY-BUTTERED bread on a decent mark-up. These are big businessmen, men of the world, captains of bloody industry, leaders of the business comunity – they're not the sort of clientele who wants to waste valuable trading time buttering their own bread!"

✳ Rule Four: Focus on the bottom line. In the world of restaurants, it's dog eat dog.

So Henry's finished his buttering and he's off round the restaurant with his breadbasket, Gareth's out on his arse, and I'm left looking at this piece of fancy white cloth in front of me.

"Whatya call this, then, Denise?" I say to my secretary.

"It's a napkin, Sir Alan," she says.

"That's as maybe. And what would you use this 'napkin' for, Denise?"

"Wiping your mouth and hands, Sir Alan."

"What they charge for 'em, you reckon?"

"Nothing, Sir Alan."

"Nothing! I got this right? They're handing out good clean linen, asking the punters to cover it with muck, then spending time washing it and ironing it and whatever – AND ALL FOR NO CASH BLOODY RETURN? They must be stark staring bloody mad! Off you go, Denise!"

And with that, Denise is off to negotiate with the management vis-a-vis taking a hundredweight of paper serviettes off our hands, which we pick up wholesale for a tenth of the price. The bottom line is there's no downside to waste matter: there's always cash in getting rid of it.

✳ Rule Five: Never underestimate me, my friend, because you'll be making a fatal mistake and I'll sue the bloody pants off you.

My dining companions might have been otherwise employed, but my solo meal's the pig's bloody bollocks. OK, so I don't like cabbage, never have, but in the eating-out game you got to roll with the punches.

Exactly forty minutes on, I tot up the bill on my Amstrad calculator, but the battery must've gone. So I settle the bill through a subsidiary company based in the Caymans, and I'm being transported back to my boardroom in my personalised Bentley, registered in Hong Kong. From my vehicle, I ring through to the office on my Amstrad mobile phone. Then I ring again, and again, but I still can't get a bloody peep out of it. 'What a pile of bloody toot!' I say to my chauffeur, throwing the piece of crap out the window.

✳ **Rule Six: Never be content with second best.**

Mnemonic Corner

M&M is a sweet, too small to suck
M&S is a chainstore, down on its luck
M&P is a Ministry, back to the wall
Eminem is a rock star (no manners at all)
MSP takes to the podium to brew debate
MSG stands for Monosodium Glutamate
F&M is a disease caught by cattle and sheep
S&M involves whips and bleep bleep bleep
EMU is destined to divide the nation
MTV is a sure way to stop conversation
FM is on the wireless, replacing MW
Who knows what they stand for? (Sorry to trouble you)

The Swiss Family Fayed

AFTER A FAILED *attempt to overturn the Inland Revenue's decision to end his special tax status, Mohamed Fayed has issued a statement saying that, because "the Establishment attacks on me have intensified" he will henceforth live in Switzerland.*

MONDAY: dong-ding, dong-ding, dong-ding. Is morning in Swiz

Land. Dong-ding, dong-ding. OK, OK, I get the painting, you shaddup, drat clock can go get lost for all I caring. Dong-ding, dong-ding – and then, I tell you this, a little bird, size my thumb, it leaps out of hidey-hole in clock and beginning to chirrup.

OK, so I call guards. "Who that bird, eh? Who letting that bird in?" I say.

"What bird, we no see no bird, guvnor," they say.

"In dratting clock!" I explaining. "Little bird in drat clock!"

So I pointing at clock, but little bird he has vanishinged into fat air. "Was there, I spotting it with own eyes – are you call me LIAR?" I yelling.

The guards they leave room. Fifteen minutes later and bird spring out, making noise. I scream for guards and they run coming. "Was bird again!" I explaining to them.

"This bird – what this bird saying, boss?"

"Cook who? Cook who?" I telling them, "The bird saying 'Cook who?' is threat. Is some sort blackmail threat from government hit man Robin Cook. I tell you, cloud and lear: that bird is out to getting me.

TUESDAY: personal guardsman, real shart-shoopers, top-notch, they with me all night, training shotguns on bloody clock, ready for blackmail bird to popping out, is deal. What you know – eight o'clock on dot, little doors to hidey-hole swinging open, and out comes blackmail bird, repeating threat – "Cook who?"

"Letting him having it, boys!" I scream – and the shoop-sharters fire fifty rounds at bird, hitting he through heart, shattering clock and sending wires and wheels flying through air.

"So much for Establishment clock! Mohamed outwit filthy stooge bird! I telling you, boys, we hear no more from that little bird in long, long time," I have chuckleding.

WEDNESDAY: William Tell, William Tell, William Tell. All I hearing all days long is William Tell. So I asking, who this William? And what he bloody Tell?

THURSDAY: OK, so William Tell, my security, they information me that William Tell he Swiz man who putting apple on son's head and shooting it with arrow. Very bad thing be doing. He grown man and he shoot through apple on son's head! Very waste of money. Fresh fruit very, very costly in Swiz Land, and William Tell go wrecking good perfectly apple just to be showy-off. Swiz Establishment, they no care for fresh fruit, they shoot it to bittings just to show they stig and brong.

FRIDAY: Swiz Land all up and down, mountains, valleys – so you tell me where's the bloody lifts and escalators? I tell you, my friend – is nowhere. You want going up hill, you have to walk all the way. Is no way to run top-quality leisure business.

So Mohamed he go to famous Matterhorn mountain with big idea to turn into top-tip high-class commercial business for upmarket tourist, no riff-raff, you take bloody jeans off or you no come here, OK.

Matterhorn very famous mountain – but no lifts, no escalators, believe me, my friend, I telling you truth, NOT ONE. And even tourists who reaching top Matterhorn after many hour climb, all way to top without elevator – and they no find luxury retail outlet, can you believing! They very dispoint, very dispoint indeed. You know what they find, my friend, on top world's most famous Matterhorn mountain? I tell you what they find. No postcard, no high-class top store Harrods franchise, no restaurant – nothing. All they find is VIEW. And is FREE! That no way to run a country, my friend!

SATURDAY: I surveying Matterhorn, hear tinkle, like bell. "Who bloody hell that tinkle?" I get to asking bodyguard.

"Is cow," he saying.

"What you mean – 'is cow'?" I say.

Bodyguard tell Mohamed how in Swiz Land cows, they all have bells round necks.

"Bells round necks?" I say. "They no fool Mohamed – they have telephones inside! No way they cows – no way! They spies for MI5, sent by Duke Philip, dressed to look like bloody cows!"

I am saying exactly what happen, OK? I turn corner of meadow, and what I see? I see whole field full of bloody MI5 snooper cows, all with bells round necks, bunch of snoopy gangsters, tell-tale-titties, want very much start Establishment smear campaign against Mohamed, is true.

I go up to group cows, I asking them straight, "Who you cows buggin? Who you bloody want plot revenge on?" And I tell you, my friend, you know what they all replies?

"Mo," they all replying, "moooooo!"

My name! Is true! I hearding it with my own ears. And now you say I paranoid – but I only paranoiding because every cow in Swiz Land is against me, is true!

The BT History of England in Verse

The Charge of the Light Brigade*
Half a league, half a league,
Half a league onward
All in the valley of Death
Phoned the six hundred.
"Forward the Light Brigade!
Charge for the guns!" they said.
Across the valley the touchphone blew:
"Welcome to the Crimea
You are being held in a queue."
"Forward, the Light Brigade!"
"Thanks for calling – we're afraid
Our lines are busy, but for a cannon or gun
Please press star button, then One."
Theirs not to reason why,
Theirs but to curse and sigh.
Across the valley the touchphone blew:
"For all other queries, please press Two."
"Forward the Light Brigade!"
Was there a man dismayed?
Not though the soldiers knew

---

* 80p a minute at peak rate

For Customer Care, you just press Two.
Theirs not to make reply
Theirs but to chirrup: "Hi!
Welcome to Information Hotline!
For further queries, please press Nine!"
Touchphone to the right of them
Touchphone to the left of them
Touchphone in front of them
All playing Stevie Nicks.
"Our service team is currently engaged
But should you wish to be further enraged
Please press Star then Hash then Six."
When can their patience fade?
O the vast bill they paid!
All the world wondered
At the charges they made!
"If you wish to be held in a queue
Please now press button Two!"
Into the valley of debt they blundered,
The nobbled six hundred!

Department of Sport

Back of the Net!: The Professor and the Footballer

IT MIGHT SEEM like only yesterday, but it is a full thirteen years since Prof Karl Miller wrote his essay in praise of the footballer Paul Gascoigne in the *London Review of Books*. At the time, many of us felt that such writing would never be surpassed. "He was," explained Miller, "a highly charged spectacle on the field of play: fierce and comic, formidable and vulnerable, urchin-like and waif-like, a strong head and torso with comparatively frail-looking breakable legs, strange-eyed, pink-faced, fair-haired, tense and upright, a priapic monolith in the Mediterranean sun – a marvellous equivocal sight."

For thirteen long years, we waited and waited, but no one came near it. Then, a few days ago, Peter Conrad, Fellow of the Royal Society of Literature, lecturer in English at Christ Church, Oxford and Fellow of All Souls, finally took up the challenge.

Conrad's chosen footballer was, unsurprisingly, David Beckham. He started by wondering what Nelson Mandela thought of Beckham's hair when the two men met last week. "Perhaps it looked to him like a blond version of the barbed wire that once stretched around his prison," he surmised. At this point, I began to realise that Prof Miller had a serious challenger on his hands. "He has become a planetary phenomenon. It's his world, he has it at his feet and we wait to see which way he will kick our imploded, aerated globe. Like his own guardian angel, Beckham extends sheltering wings over the world."

Already, in a few short sentences, Conrad was showing he meant business – and it soon became apparent that this was merely a little light dribbling before kick-off.

"Beckham is our collective brainchild," he continued, before posing the key question, so beloved of deconstructionists. "So what does the status we have wished on him tell us about ourselves?"

And with that, he was away: "Well, we get the gods we deserve, and this one has been expressly fabricated to embody all we hold dear. Mystics regard him as a Zen master, the possessor of a divine grace. Structural linguists would call him a floating signifier. He's significant without being much interested in the specific signals he sends out. Silence intensifies Beckham's Garboesque mystery: the impenetrability of that bland, blank surface recalls Roland Barthes's claim that the face of Garbo is an Idea, that of Hepburn, an Event. He is available for interactive fantasising, like your other half during phone sex: that is the deal the celebrity makes with us, and Beckham solemnises the transaction with that shy, dazed, long-suffering smile of his – a promise of surrender, compliance, infinite availability. He bends the ball, and we bend him like the ball."

Back of the net, as Alan Partridge would say. Conrad is King! It will surely be a good thirteen years before Conrad is forced to concede his crown. Until that moment comes, we must content ourselves with re-reading all the old masterpieces: George Steiner on Nobby Stiles, W G Sebald on Kevin Keegan, Salman Rushdie on Steve Hodge, A S Byatt on Vinnie Jones.

Party Conjugations

Our party is lively
Your party is deafening
Their party is out of control.

I believe in human contact
You are tactile
He is a groper.

I make worthwhile points
You hold forth
He just won't shut up.

I've made an effort
You are dressed up to the nines
What does she think she looks like?

I charm
You simper
She gushes.

I am the life and soul
You are letting your hair down
He is rat-arsed.

I am Fred Astaire
You are Mick Jagger
He is David Brent.

I am Ginger Rogers
You are Geri Halliwell
She's just fallen over.

I am waspish
You are caustic
She is a bitch.

I say what I think
You get steamed up
She makes a scene.

I am drot nunk
You are a mit berry
He is nissed as a pewt.

I am artistic
You are a Bohemian
He wears an old jersey and
smells.

I bare my soul
You bear a grudge
He bares his bottom.

My top is décolleté
Your top is risqué
Her top is tarty.

We asked a cross-section
You asked all types
They didn't mind who they
asked.

I'm a bit of a joker
You're a bit of a laugh
He can make farty noises with
his armpits.

I shed a tear or two
You were in floods
She made a fool of herself.

My speech was off-the-cuff
Your speech was unprepared
His speech went on and on.

I've come as Nell Gwynne
You've come as Fergie
She's come as Jade Goody.

I am a character
You are larger than life
He wears a bow tie.

I favour a natural look
You could do with a bit more
make-up
She is looking her age.

My shirt is fun
Your shirt is loud
What's he trying to prove?

My dancing is minimalist
Your dancing is cautious
He taps his toe now and then.

I am self-assured
You are self-centred
He is self-obsessed.

I have a natural empathy
You try to look interested
She nods her head now and
then.

I can't hear what you're
saying
You can't hear what I'm
saying
He's as deaf as a post.

I am depressed
You are down in the dumps
He is in a sulk.

I charm
You flirt
He can't keep his hands to
himself.

I am grappling with the
meaning of life
You are coming over all
philosophical
He's lost it.

I am a raconteur
You are an anecdotalist
He is a crashing bore.

We invite old friends
You invite familiar faces
They invite the same old bores.

I am shy
You are a loner
He is paranoid.

I am friendly
You are forward
She is pushy.

Whisting the Night Away

HOW YOU REACT to the suggestion "Let's dance!" is a handy barom-
eter of your age. At fifteen, it produces excitement; at forty-five,
embarrassment; at sixty, a suspected hernia.

Last weekend, I went to a party at the National Liberal Club.
There, under portraits of Gladstone, David Steel (dressed up, for no
good reason, as a bell-hop) and a rather severe-looking Jeremy
Thorpe, a Queen tribute band (Freddie Mercury looking the spitting image of Peter Mandelson: surely he can't be moonlighting?)
played its way through a selection of all those ghastly old numbers,
such as "I Want to Break Free" and "Killer Queen".

While the less inhibited were busy dancing, I was happy to
huddle in the next room with my fellow wallflowers, chewing the

cud over the issues of the day. For a good twenty minutes, I imagined I had got away with it, but then my wife came over and said "Let's dance!" Ten minutes later, she said it again. Before I knew where I was, I was on the dance floor.

"*Scaramouche! Scaramouche! Will you do the fandango? Beelzebub duh duh duh duh duh for me, FOR ME, FOR ME, FOR MEEEEEEEE!*" How on earth do you dance to this impossibly jerky song? Nowadays, when called upon to dance, my tactic is to head for the very centre of the dance floor, letting the other dancers form a sort of praetorian guard, protecting me from the pitiless gaze of onlookers.

But with each new year, my self-consciousness increases, and I become more aware of sudden vistas opening up on the dance floor. Just as I have grown sufficiently confident to try a modest twiddle of my forefinger, a gap opens and I find myself exposed to a stern jury of onlookers, their eyebrows raised in Paxman-style rictuses of quizzical contempt.

Sometimes, I become so paranoid on the dance floor that I even begin to feel that these bystanders are about to produce large scorecards from behind their backs, holding them high in the air – ZERO! ZERO! ZERO! – at the end of the song. "*I will not let you go! Let me go! I will not let you go! Let me go!*" sang Mandelson, while the Brian May lookalike, his head enveloped in a vast ink-blot of a wig, closed his eyes and placed his upper teeth over his lower lip, in the way guitarists do in moments of high seriousness.

Up to that point, I had been performing what I believe is known as the "dog-mess" dance step. It entails being entirely stationary but for your right toe, which you twist purposefully on the floor this way and that. But then, in another flash of acute self-consciousness, I realised to my horror that I had been mouthing along with the words ("*I will not let you go! Let me go!*"), which, as everyone knows, is the naffest action (short of playing dummy guitar, or knocking your partner flat in the course of punching the air to "Hi Ho Silver Lining") that anyone can possibly do on a dance floor.

Is there a magic age for men beyond which they can't dance without feeling awkward? I am often haunted by that image, frequently repeated on television, of Peter Mandelson, Neil Kinnock and John Prescott on the night of New Labour's election victory in

1997, all of them squeezed behind a metal barrier outside the Royal Festival Hall, awkwardly jigging and moving their hands up and down to the rhythm – or almost to the rhythm – of "Things Can Only Get Better". Even at that moment of jubilation, the three of them look excruciatingly embarrassed, yet they seem to find no solidarity in their mutual embarrassment, their eyes darting about the place, nervously avoiding one another's glance.

I suspect that the acute sense of embarrassment that embraces middle-aged men when they attempt to dance is not wholly physical. Of course, most of us are not in such good shape as we were when we used to buzz about the dance floor like whirling dervishes (and there would surely be something off-putting about John Prescott dancing with all the lissome self-confidence of Christina Aguilera), but the reasons behind our loss of nerve are probably less physical than psychological.

By the time most men hit forty, there is far too much stuff clogging up their brains for them to be able to lose themselves in a pop song. Mick Jagger manages it, of course, but even with him you feel that, like the rest of us, he is really just someone pretending to be Mick Jagger. His biographer tells us that, in his youth, Tony Blair used to dance like Mick Jagger. His group's drummer, James Moon, now an investment banker, describes the young Blair as "hip-wriggler in chief", while their guitarist, Mark Ellen, creates this word-picture of Blair at full-throttle on stage: "He comes on stage in purple loons and cut-off T-shirt, giving it a bit of serious Mick Jagger, a bit of finger wagging and punching the air... 'Are you having a good time? I can't hear you at the back!'" But these days it is hard to imagine that Blair could wag his finger in the air with much abandon before the National Health Service and Iraq and Gordon Brown started wagging their collective fingers back in his direction.

Most middle-aged men either stop dancing altogether, or else they opt for (i) the ironic or (ii) the minimalist solution. Non-participation is obviously the most dignified option, but it always strikes me as cowardly, unless one can produce a valid doctor's certificate.

Other men prefer to act the giddy-goat, performing loosely parodic dance routines involving running on the spot with a bit of daft window-cleaning thrown in. Instead, I tend to go for the minimalist approach, though even performing the dog-mess or the Queen Mother (a faraway smile accompanied by the odd distant wave) for more than three or four songs can leave me out of breath. What can be done? I suspect the only real solution to dance parties for the middle-aged is to blindfold all participants. Either that, or confine us all to whist drives.

Charles Moore's Gamebook

I went toad-hunting last weekend. The most obviously useful of all forms of hunting – no one likes a toad – it also has a strange beauty about it. Is there a sound closer to the deep, mystic spirit of the English countryside than the sudden squelch of toad beneath Wellington boot?

We gathered at dawn, each of us wearing boots several sizes too big, for maximum impact. Never has the English countryside looked more peculiarly beautiful. In the distance, the early sun bounced off the warty, dappled backs of a squadron of basking toads. It was as if, in some mysterious way, these toads were beckoning us over, yearning for the firm squash of reinforced boot upon their enticingly rubbery bodies.

My host, the Earl of Crowborough, represents the fifteenth generation of his family to have squashed toads in their corner of East Sussex. Toad-squashing is close to the heart of an aristocratic approach to life because it is communal, ceremonial, democratic (in the true meaning of the word – "demo" meaning "toad" and "cratic" meaning "let's stamp on a") and makes a beautiful sound – like an explosion from a whoopee cushion, but less vulgar.

Spadefoot toads feed on mosquitoes, so as we approached them, Johnny Crowborough instructed us to make high-pitched buzzing noises, and flap our arms around. Then we moved in for the kill, putting on our bowler hats and rushing at the toads with great, purposeful strides. I had a toad cornered, and he knew it. Is it too fanciful to suggest that, in the split-second before the firm smack of my heel met the groaning bulk of his body, a look of gratitude shone from his toady eyes? And I think he smiled. Nothing but a humble toad, he was able to relish the privilege of being permitted to partake in this great tradition. This is something New Labour would never be able to understand. Today, the fox-hunt. Tomorrow, the toad-hunt. Who knows what will be banned next week?

This week I was talking to a local GP. He is hard-working and decent, and everything else the Labour legislators dislike. He told me that Labour is developing secret plans to further curtail the freedom of doctors. If Labour wins the next election, Blair plans to "crack down" (to employ the fashionable jargon) on doctors – however skilled or diligent they may be – who wish to do away with their patients.

For centuries, tradition let doctors knock off the odd patient. There will, of course, always be the odd bad apple who takes it too far. Dr Shipman certainly deserved some sort of dressing down, even if the actual punishment measured out to him by Labour was typically draconian and humourless. But if all doctors are to be denied the right to put down any patient who irritates or provokes them, the number of bright youngsters wishing to sign up for medical school will plummet accordingly. Is this really what Blair wants? On second thoughts, I suspect it is. From Labour's point of view, too many doctors support fox-hunting, so the sooner the entire profession is abolished, the better.

The liquid runs out of our Fairy Liquid just as we are about to embark on the washing-up. I have noticed the strange fact that this occurs with disarming regularity. Is this a fluke, or is it part of an unspoken policy by Labour? And why should Blair and his busy-body cohorts so hate to see dishes clean? Could it be because they wish to spread MRSA? At the moment it is confined to hospitals, but if they can spread it beyond, to dish-washing, Conservative-voting households, the General Election will be theirs for the asking.

In the evening, Johnny Crowborough led us into his delightful neo-classical barn for the Toad Dinner. A piper gave us a fine rendering of *Nearer My God To Thee* on the Natterjacks, a more plangent version of the bagpipes, sewn from the matured bellies of twenty natterjack toads.

The main course consisted of a magnificent toad stew, cooked from the morning's bag. When we had finished our feasting, we were led by Vince, the friendly lower-class Head Toadier, down a long corridor to a centuries-old marble basin. At a given signal from Vince, we proceeded to "vomit up" the entire feast in the traditional manner.

As the evening sun shone through the fine neo-Gothic tracery, spreading its warm dappled rays o'er the lively yellows, greens and browns of the gloriously regurgitated toads, I couldn't help but feel that this was one part of England that Blair must wish to see abolished for ever, along with fresh air, the Royal Family, and white people.

BBC announcers insist on using the expression, "This is the news." One hears it every night, without fail. Yet news is plural. They should say, "These are the news" and, half an hour later, "Those were the news." They never will, of course, because the BBC is a socialist institution, within which correct English is regarded as the enemy of the state. Have we ever had a more horrid public culture?

Some annoying things encountered too often at present: bicyclists who insist on pedalling slowly uphill and then sue the poor drivers who attempt to run them over; innocent people who refuse to admit they are rightfully imprisoned; politicians who puff themselves up by declaring that there is something intrinsically "wrong" about poor people starving but who never stop to worry about wealthy people who are inflicted with indigestion quite as often; discrimination in our so-called "public" services against those educated at public school (when was the last time you bumped into a railway ticket collector with a public school education?); men and women who work in the city but who nevertheless modishly refuse to wear bowler hats and wing collars; bus drivers who refuse to go just a little out of their way to deliver you to your front door, preferring to suit themselves by dropping you at a Maoist "bus stop"; characters in soap operas who forget to say "good morning" or "good afternoon" before addressing one another; Gordon Brown's churlish refusal to wear a kilt and sporran while simultanaeously affecting a Scottish accent; the conspiracy by BBC Radio to limit the airtime given to Lord Rockingham's XI. Where will it end?

Fun with Figures: Nasty's Women

IN HIS RECENT autobiography, *Mr Nastase*, the Romanian tennis player Ilie Nastase devotes a paragraph to totting up his sexual conquests, most of them from his heyday in the 1970s.

"I think I've slept with about 2,500 women," he writes, adding, "sex in those days was like taking a daily shower – you take one, it feels nice, then you forget it." Many people who enjoy a daily shower will wish to take issue with Mr Nastase's analogy. After all, most people who take a daily shower do so in the same shower each day, rather than nipping from one strange shower to another. Pocket calculators at the ready! If Nastase's figure of 2,500 is to be believed, he slept with a new woman every day for seven years, or every other day for fourteen years, or, if you would prefer, every third day for twenty-one years.

His boast knocks spots off the records set by our two English Casanovas. Last year, the waspish television personality Simon Cowell claimed in the *Mail on Sunday*, "I've had between seventy and 100 women, if I were to hazard a guess." In the autobiography of Tony Blackburn, the chirpy Millfield-educated disc jockey more than doubles this figure. "Sex is very important to me; I adore making love," he confesses, adding, "I've made love to about 250 women."

This means that for every lady our own Mr Blackburn has been to bed with, Mr Nastase has been to bed with nine more. It is all very damaging to our sense of national pride. But is Blackburn really the best competitor we can come up with? Sadly, I suspect our national problem lies not in abstinence but in reticence. There must be many Britons who have done better than Blackburn, but they have been brought up to believe that it is rude to boast.

Not so the Continentals. In 1977, the great Belgian detective writer Georges Simenon, then aged seventy-four, boasted to Federico Fellini that he could easily beat him: "I did the sum a year or two ago, and, since the age of thirteen and a half, I have had 10,000 women."

This makes a different woman every other day for sixty years. Surely this must be a fib? It is high time we Britons followed suit and began tacking on a few extra noughts when no one is looking.

As it is, we are too easily impressed. The redoubtable Jordan, Brighton born and bred, confesses to just nine affairs (Jeff, Kieran, Gary, Dane, Dwight, Dwayne, Gareth, Scott, Peter) in her autobiography. Here in Britain, this modest amount has earned Jordan a reputation as a sex-bomb, and has sent her book rocketing to the top of the bestseller lists. But on the Continent it would mean that she was officially classified a virgin, and might well be eligible for a senior position in a reputable convent.

My Everest

Tony Blair: I – that's my colleagues and myself – are both proud and, yes, truly humbled, to have reached the summit of Everest.

Yes, we did it in record time. And, yes, we managed to do it without any climbing gear. And for this we give thanks.

Of course, there will always be those who scoff at the sidelines and say it's somehow "not true". That we never reached that historic summit.

And to them, I say this.

Look, this is what I honestly believe. I honestly believe we climbed Everest. And, look, I'm not making it up. I'm not that sort of guy.

Y'know, I've got to say it. I couldn't have climbed Everest without the help of you, the British people. You're the best. And – yes – it's only fair you should take pride in the fact that you picked the right guy to be your Prime Minister. And that is a wonderful, wonderful achievement.

Dr David Starkey: Mount Everest? I can think of nothing more painful! Everest may be on the tall side, but it's hardly very handsome! How dare it – how DARE it – take up all that space, just sitting there like a peaked blancmange, completely blocking out the view of the other side! Doesn't it genuinely make you want to vomit?

Everest has always been disgracefully overrated. It's not even all that big, not compared with me. Let me ask you this, though I would hardly expect an honest answer. Has Everest ever hosted the most popular history series on television? Has it? Of course it hasn't! Yet it sits there in the Himalayas, all shining white and peaky, looking so desperately, desperately pleased with itself!

Why on earth do people still persist in going up Everest? "Because it's there" – a typically fatuous comment, if I may say so! Away with you!

Tony Benn: In truth, it's not a mountain at all, now, is it? I don't think any of us are going to fall for that one any more! It's the multinationals up to their old tricks again! Of course, we're always being told by Whitehall and Downing Street and their chums in the Armed Forces that Everest is some sort of mountain, some sort of high peak, but I'm a great believer in the facts, and if you take a long hard look at the available facts you discover that Everest is not a mountain at all. Not a bit of it. It's a valley. Let's for goodness' sake keep personalities out of it, but those photographs of members of the Establishment standing on the so-called summit really do take the biscuit, don't they? Are they honestly expecting us to believe that they were snapped at the top of a mountain? Yes – that's what the powers-that-be would have us think! But I'm reliably informed that if you look very closely, you'll see curtains and a window in the left-hand corner – it was taken in someone's living room, would y'believe! Of course, I'd've climbed the mountain m'self, but Harold and Jim and their pals in MI5 made absolutely certain I was at my desk. No hard feelings though!

Sir Tim Rice: Though I almost hurt my shin
I've taken quite a shine
So I'll go out on a limb
And say "It's really quite a climb
(chorus) Up lovely, lovely Everest!
No, you must hardly ever rest
But it's better than second best
So try not to hurt your wrist
(chorus) Up lovely, lovely Everest!

John Prescott: Our thoughts are with Sherpa Tenzing and his lady wife Hillary. It was a remarkablising achievement-style achievement. Could I do it myself? No question about it! All it takes is a decent mode rap. But for me, it's the attitude sickness that's a bedful draw. Let's bake no moans about it: who wants to go uphill mad in a clask? There's also the snow-type situation to be contendivated with. Make it from tee, you don't want to get catched in a stowsnorm, with flow-snakes blowing all over the place, and that's a factual. If you're planning on an ascendation to the heak of the pill, you're best off packing a very jot humper in your suckrack.

Jilly Cooper: "So here we are on the top of Everest," sighed Cassandra, peeling off her tremendously tight, wet-look Gucci T-shirt to reveal a pair of marvellously bouncing bosoms beneath.

"Gosh, Cassie!" gasped tall, devastatingly handsome but secretly desperately sad though soon to be made much happier Jasper, whose third wife had just run back to her second husband after the incident with the fourth child. "Thanks awfully for letting me take a 'PEAK'. After all, 'Snowman is an island'!"

The pair of them hooted with laughter. Below them stretched literally yards of snow, with blissful glaciers whooshing down into the meadows below at a rate of absolute knots. "Just time for a quick sunbathe," exclaimed Jasper, ripping off his Calvin Klein shorts to reveal the Matterhorn beneath.

The Game of Christmas Squabble

CHRISTMAS SQUABBLE is the classic game of family domination for all ages. It may be played at any time during December, with combat continuing well into the New Year.

OBJECTIVE
Each player struggles for world domination while obstructing his fellow competitors ("The Family") from achieving their objectives at every turn.

Play takes place in the FUGGY HOUSE. This is divided into

LIVING ROOM, KITCHEN and BEDROOMS (where contestants are permitted to play their SOB CARDS).

The defence of these territories must be planned carefully, or victory may soon turn to defeat. Heavy casualties may result in the loss of CHRISTMAS SQUABBLE.

EQUIPMENT

Each player starts the game with the following: Two Chips, Six Petty Grievances, Three Sour Grapes, Four Major Resentments, Two Annoying Habits.

IMPORTANT: All MAJOR RESENTMENTS must remain unspoken until the final round, just when things seem to be settling down. The first player to produce them from his sleeve at this crucial juncture will thus gain TEMPORARY SUPREMACY.

TIP FOR PLAY: Take care to NURSE your SIX PETTY GRIEVANCES throughout CHRISTMAS SQUABBLE, so that they are fighting fit when you find yourself in a position to reveal them.

DICE

Before the commencement of CHRISTMAS SQUABBLE, all dice should be declared lost. The third player then repeats the following phrase: "Why is it always me who has to look for everything?" four times before play commences.

Six months after close of play, the dice may be found EITHER under the sofa OR in that drawer that's full of old keys, used batteries, elastic bands and bits of Blu-Tack.

PREPARING TO PLAY

Before the game commences, each player elects himself or herself the General.

The General is in charge of everyone else, and must control the other contestants at all times. WARNING: Having elected yourself the General, be careful not to inform anyone else too soon, or they may immediately bring into play one of their MAJOR RESENTMENTS.

Remove all jokers. Now shuffle all the queens and make sure any pairs are separated.

SETTING UP FORCES

Each player of CHRISTMAS SQUABBLE enters the game having first formed a SECRET ALLIANCE. A Secret Alliance is formed by whispering EITHER "Well, someone had to tell her" OR "Frankly, I don't blame you one little bit" OR "He told me not to tell anyone else, but ...". These alliances may be broken at any time during the course of the game by repeating the words, "That's the last time I tell you a secret."

CLAIMING THE HIGHER GROUND

KITCHEN: Any player found in the kitchen may be tackled by the General with the words "You couldn't be a dear and ..." He or she will then suffer the forfeit of being given EITHER a bag of Brussels sprouts and a blunt knife OR five dirty pans and the scrappy remains of a Brillo pad.

LIVING ROOM: Players taking refuge in the living room must repeat the phrase: "You'll have to turn over – it's the *EastEnders Christmas Omnibus*." This allows other players to FLOUNCE OUT and claim one new PETTY GRIEVANCE per player.

BEDROOM: Any player FLOUNCING OUT must immediately retreat to their bedroom and slam the door. On hearing an upstairs door slammed, any player remaining in the KITCHEN must sigh: "I turn my back for five minutes and ..." thereby CLAIMING THE HIGHER GROUND.

COMBAT

Combat commences at the stroke of eleven on Christmas morning. Player One passes the first present to Player Two on his left. Player Two opens it, finds that it is a GARISH JUMPER, and attempts to STIFLE HIS DISAPPOINTMENT.

Player One says: "You can always change it if you don't like it."

Player Two replies, "I didn't say I didn't like it."

Player Three can now step in and say: "Well, you don't sound very grateful!" To beat Player Two, Player Three must give Player Two a box of chocolate-covered sultanas filled with Drambuie and something slightly lavendery. Player Three now awaits his response.

If Player Two is unable to smile and say thank you, he must retire from the game of CHRISTMAS SQUABBLE.

MANOEUVRE

Once he has completed all his attacks, a player may conduct ONE manoeuvre.

Each player may move from room to room, but only: a) to avoid another player or players; b) to exchange PETTY GRIEVANCES; or c) to take it out on the cat.

WINNING

The winner is the player left behind in the LIVING ROOM with the TV remote control. He declares his victory by shouting "AND ANOTHER THING!" before slumping into a prolonged doze.

ADVANCED CHRISTMAS SQUABBLE

CHRISTMAS SQUABBLE is also available in an EXECUTIVE EDITION, including disappointing Christmas crackers, pre-squashed satsumas, a whoopee cushion and five torn paper crowns. Or why not splash out on the LUXURY DELUXE EDITION, which includes all the above, plus an oven-roasted turkey, still frozen towards the centre?

Department of Heritage

Three Seventies Keepsakes:

(1) A QUIZ BOOK

Where would you find the most accurate account of the way we lived twenty-five years ago? Some would advise you to go to a work of sociology, full of statistics about the number of washing machines per thousand households. Some would opt for a pacier overview by a fashionable historian, packed with relevant quotes from Margaret Thatcher and Sid Vicious. Others might put their faith in fiction, picking state-of-the-nation 1979 novels written by Martin Amis or Margaret Drabble or Melvyn Bragg.

Of course, it's always interesting to know about the washing arrangements of other people, modern historians are supremely skilled at tying even the most banal pop lyrics in with the winter of discontent, and Margaret Drabble is a past master at conveying the various states of depression and restlessness within north London fondue parties in the mid to late 1970s.

But I myself would reach for a little book long since out of print and widely overlooked in its day. The work in question is *Mr and Mrs* by Derek Batey, published in 1979 and subtitled *The Quiz Book from the Programme Watched by Millions*.

"Derek Batey, popular host of the long-running TV series, has personally compiled the questions in the *Mr and Mrs Quiz Book*," explains the blurb. "Here's your chance to play the *Mr and Mrs* quiz at home with your partner and friends!"

Anyone as glued to the television as I was throughout the 1970s will hold fond memories of *Mr and Mrs*. It had a winning formula. A married couple are led on to the somewhat cardboardy set by a sparkly dolly-bird called Susan. The immaculately coiffed host, Derek Batey, invariably sporting a matching-shirt-tie-and-hankie combination, warms them up with some perky chat ("So, it says here you're from Manchester? Is it true it always rains in Manchester! Not at all! Smashing!"). Then either the husband or the wife ("So who's first in the hot seat?") is led into a special soundproof booth. Susan places headphones over their ears.

Batey (who was in fact notably calm) then asks the remaining spouse three questions about their partner's habits and foibles, generally with a choice of tick-in-the-box-style answers. A typical question would be: "When she's putting on her lipstick, does your wife generally apply it to her top lip first, her bottom lip first – or does it vary?" He then makes a careful note of each choice before calling the other spouse back from the booth to see if their answers coincide. If the couple get all the answers right, they go away with a silver tray, a loving cup, or a special *Mr and Mrs* carriage clock.

The *Mr and Mrs* book comes as a shock to those of us who like to think that life has trotted on, pretty much the same, for the past twenty-five years. Reading it, one is transported to a world as distant as the moon. Take this question, on page fourteen, for instance: "On your wedding night, who decided on which sides of the bed you would both sleep? Did you let your wife have first choice, did she ask you which side you wanted – or did it just sort of happen by accident?"

The question assumes that no couple would have been to bed together before their wedding night. And this was only twenty-five years ago! Today, the equivalent TV quiz, full of Jade Goodyish contestants, would require couples to give a blow-by-blow account of their first night in bed together, and possibly even to re-enact it to hoots and cheers from the studio audience.

Some might yearn for those far-off days of marital shyness, but for me this embarrassed bedside debate conjures up a singularly bleak short story by William Trevor. And if sexual liberation has made the world less awkward, the past twenty-five years have also witnessed a marked decline in problems with sniffing. A striking number of Derek Batey's questions concern dos and don'ts with hankies. "You are going out for the night and your wife and you get about two hundred yards from your house when she discovers she hasn't got a handkerchief with her – what happens?" he asks. "Would you tell her you'd lend her yours, would she insist on going back for it – or would she say she'd just chance it and sniff?" Or "When he's in bed at night, does he normally have a handkerchief in his pyjama jacket pocket, does he only have one if he has a cold – or does he never have one?" Or again: "Imagine your husband has a very bad cold and needs to blow his nose. Does he generally blow it with his handkerchief in his left hand only, his right hand only, or does he hold the handkerchief in both hands?"

So much sniffing and sneezing and blowing makes one wonder whether far more people had colds in 1979, or whether – as this evidence suggests – everyone's reliance on handkerchiefs simply encouraged them to blow their noses regardless. Gloves are rarely seen these days, but they, too, played a dominant role in 1979. "When she's going out shopping in summertime," Batey asks the husband, "does your wife wear gloves with her dress – sometimes, always, or never?" If a contemporary television host were to ask the same question, he would be greeted with either a mystified silence or ribald laughter, for the audience would presume that "glove" is code for some form of sex aid.

Though it is something rarely mentioned by historians or diarists, and imperceptible in film or photos, this book suggests we were all much smellier back then. "On the subject of feet," begins Batey, "if your husband takes his shoes off at the end of the day, do you never really notice, move back a yard or two – or leave the room quickly?" Apart from the technical advances that once seemed to offer such dizzying choice ("If your wife is watching a programme on a colour television set, how does she like the colours? Turned up fairly strong, as natural as possible – or turned down to a pale shade?"), the forgotten world of *Mr and Mrs* suggests that life today is less drab, less dogged, and less burdened with drudgery, particularly for women.

"Does your husband accept without comment whatever meals you serve to him," runs a typical question, "does he grumble or complain occasionally about your meals – or does he grumble a lot about them?"

Much as we may blanch at the world of Jade Goody, which of us would wish to return to the world of Derek Batey?

(II) A WEDDING CATALOGUE

As luck would have it, a bookdealer friend of mine has just chanced upon the catalogue that was issued to coincide with an exhibition at St James's Palace of all the wedding presents given to Princess Anne and Mark Phillips. It passed unmentioned at the time, but it seems to me a work of bottomless fascination. More than a hundred pages long, it lists the 1,529 items given to the happy couple by people ranging from Queen Elizabeth the Queen Mother ("an aquamarine and diamond tiara") to Miss Doris Betts ("souvenir spoon from Weston-super-Mare").

Thirty-one years on, the catalogue is remarkable in many ways, not least as a period piece. These were the days when fondue parties were at the very height of chic: among the presents are three fondue sets. "Music systems", too, were all the rage, and Mr Phillips's best man, Captain Eric Grounds, is listed at number 812, giving the royal couple "a Sony stereo music system". There is no present from Auberon Waugh, alas, but might he have disguised himself as Mr John A Waugh, listed at number 1,325 for his present of a "Souvenir tablecloth from Tasmania"?

The catalogue is unexpectedly democratic, grandees and commoners bundled together in no particular order. The first twenty gifts listed include an embroidered tray cloth from Miss Ruby Tutt, an embroidered handkerchief from Miss Claire Meaney and, most meagre of all, a duster, a joint present from Mr and Mrs Nicholas Kendal. It is only when you have ploughed your way through a parade of handkerchiefs, good luck charms and corn dollys that you get to something with any sort of resell value (number seventy: "Small statue from Ecuador of the Esmeraldas-Tolita culture 500 BC" from Major and Mrs H S Strouth).

One or two presents – a Russell Hobbs automatic kettle, a Ronson electric carving knife, a three-tier spice rack given by Mr and Mrs Shotts Hedderwick, an array of crystal paperweights (one of them from Mr and Mrs Jeremy Thorpe) – would be of equal use to both bride and groom. But most have only Princess Anne in mind. Apart from an Old Marlburian tie, there is nothing that would appeal to Captain Phillips alone. But for the Princess, there is more than enough, including "pair of pink gloves", "pair of white tights", "blue nylon dressing table set", the car number plate "I ANN" (donated by Nottinghamshire County Council), an endless amount of crochet-work, handmade silk scarf with "PRINCESS ANNE" embroidered in sequins, a book *I Married a Soldier* written by the donor, Mrs D V M Cook and a poem, "Anne", by the donor, Signor Mario Binda.

The books presented are a mixed bunch, to say the least. Characteristically, Lord Longford gives his own biography of Eamon de Valera. Others include *The Splendid Art of Decorating Eggs*, three copies of *The Encyclopedia of Horses*, and, from a Miss Angela Kilmartin, a volume with the notably unfancy title *Understanding Cystitis*.

I was just sixteen years old at the time, and had not yet got into the habit of reading newspapers. Instead, I received all my news from *Private Eye*, in particular the irresistible fortnightly Diary of Auberon Waugh. Six months before the big day, Waugh had recorded how, "to make myself known", he had invited himself to tea with Mark Phillips's parents in Wiltshire.

Phillips's father was, you may remember, a director of Walls, and it is this that Waugh homes in on. "The meal may not have been up to the best," he recalled, "and I would have been happier if the pork pies had been served unwrapped. I also noticed that the wooden spoon was missing from the Walls Family Pack, but tea was plentiful and service was prompt."

This happy encounter was, I now realise, the product of Waugh's imagination. But, looking through the real list of wedding presents thirty-one years later, I am struck by how acutely his satirist's eye caught the edge of tawdriness that now seems so representative of the 1970s.

The majority of the 1,529 presents listed were from members of the public, most of them ardent Royalists, though there is a possibility of republicanism in some of the more skinflint gifts, such as Miss Alexandra Griffin's "1p in plastic case" and Mrs E E Gott's "nine 2½p stamps", not to mention Miss M E A Colman's "sachet of shampoo". Talking of stingy, the chairman, governors and staff of the BBC obviously had a whip-round and raised only enough cash to buy the couple a "record of wedding music and a Philips radio recorder".

But more wholehearted gifts abound, including a multitude of knitted tea cosies, crocheted napkin holders and good luck charms, plus numerous portraits in oils of this or that member of the Royal Family, generally painted by the donors themselves. One of them is "picture of HRH Duke of Windsor as Prince of Wales", which must have gone down well. Other paintings on the list sound rather more whimsical, with titles such as "A Penny for Your Thoughts" and "Tranquil Moments". One donor sends in "four ornamental dolls depicting HRH the Princess Anne, Captain Mark Phillips, HRH the Prince Edward and the Lady Sarah Armstrong-Jones in wedding clothes"; another "two dolls – a boy and a girl in native costume of Czechoslovakia".

When it came to the thank-you letters, Princess Anne, like many a young bride before her, must have faced an uphill struggle thinking of suitably enthusiastic expressions of delight. What to say in praise of the "two *Love Is* pillow cases" from Miss Angela Horsford, for instance, or the "crayon futuristic pictures" from Mrs Gerald Snow Noyes, or the "wind chimes and Leo charm on a chain" from Gypsy Rose Lee?

By far the most riveting gifts in this marvellous time capsule of a catalogue are those from the great and the good. Between them, the Hon Lady Bowes-Lyon, Col the Earl and Countess of Stair and Mr and Mrs Simon Bowes-Lyon bought the appropriately titled "Ekco Hostess Royale warming trolley", an appliance that these days is seen as very *Abigail's Party*, but was then, presumably, at the very height of chic. Lord and Lady Byers are catalogued as having given "four long-lasting Black Diamond non-stick saucepans". It is that boastful "long-lasting" which catches the eye. It's hard not to wonder how long they actually lasted. In those pioneering days of non-stick, no plate of scrambled eggs was complete without a windfall of black flakes and other scrapings from each Apollo-tested pan.

It must be said that quite a few of the presents sound very well-chosen, among them the "19th-century English painting of a saddled cob in landscape with a dismounted huntsman and hounds in the background", from Major and Mrs Andrew Parker-Bowles, no less. Others send something pleasantly predictable, such as the "video cassette recorder and ten tapes" from Sir Lew and Lady

Grade and Family, or the "Sodastream" from Sodastream, Ltd. But the "eight dozen coat hangers" presented by HRH Princess Margaretha is surely overdoing it.

One or two friends push the boat out a little too far, among them Mr and Mrs Jackie Stewart, who send "two dozen crystal wine glasses, twelve magnums of champagne, and a backgammon table". But grandest of all must surely be the showy Conservative MP Sir Gerald Nabarro, whose gift to the royal couple is listed simply as "cheque", the exact amount unspecified. Oddly enough, Sir Gerald died just a few days after the royal wedding. His passing was duly noted by Auberon Waugh. "He once confided to me that if anything should happen to him, all he asked was for Parliament Square and New Palace Yard to be made into a Nabarro Memorial Roundabout, with a largish statue of himself in the middle," he wrote, adding: "It does not seem too much to ask."

(III) A TELEVISION BROADCAST

We now have a television that has all sorts of odd channels worth avoiding. On Sunday night, I was scooting through all the various news channels when, by mistake, I pressed one called BBC Parliament.

To my surprise, up popped Robin Day, interviewing Edward du Cann.

"And do you agree with me, Mr du Cann," asked Day, "that there's no question of Mr Heath giving up the leadership of the Conservative Party?"

Du Cann did agree, at least in principle, but said that it was really a matter for Mr Heath and his colleagues in the party to decide. Robin Day then apologised for interrupting du Cann, but said that he'd just got word that Mr Wilson was leaving his home in Lord North Street to join the victory celebrations around the corner, in Transport House.

It turned out that BBC Parliament was devoting the entire evening to an uninterrupted repeat of the BBC election broadcast for October 10, 1974. Heaven knows how many viewers had bothered to tune in – barely a handful, I imagine – but it was utterly mesmerising. Of course, it was hard to get very excited when messages like

"Maurice Macmillan holds Farnham" popped up on the screen. But what it lacked in urgency it more than made up for in poignancy. Every politician, trade unionist, television pundit or captain of industry who turned up on the screen bristling with authority and grandeur was now thirty years older, or, more often, dead and buried. As Robert Louis Stevenson once wrote: "Old and young, we are all on our last cruise." Looking at old telly programmes makes this truth all too painfully clear.

"And your comments, please, Mr Whitelaw, on the news just in that Captain Robert Maxwell has once again failed to win Buckingham for Labour?" "As you know, Robin, I never care to comment on individual personalities, but this is certainly good news."

Television is the medium of the eternal present: watching television news thirty years on, you find yourself wanting to shout warnings ("Don't do it!") back through time to those politicians, so robust and self-confident, whose careers are doomed to end in tears – du Cann, Maxwell, Stonehouse, Archer, Thorpe.

After Mr Whitelaw had had his say, Captain Maxwell came on, live from the town hall, saying that, yes, he was slightly disappointed but he was also delighted that the country had given Labour a mandate to implement its economic policies in these difficult times, and, no, he did not think he himself would be standing at Buckingham again – it was time to give someone else a chance.

And so, a few minutes later, to the leader of the Liberal Party, Mr Jeremy Thorpe, speaking live from his North Devon constituency. The Liberals had failed to achieve the historic breakthrough for which they had been hoping, so Mr Thorpe looked very down in the mouth. And did he not also look a mite sinister, with his long dark face and pantomime-devil eyebrows, or was one overlaying his image with the knowledge of hindsight?

Other, less gloomy, observations struck me as I sat watching the October 1974 election results coming through. One was that 1974 must surely have been the low water mark for long hair in this country. Even otherwise very square and starchy figures wore their hair at pop-star length. Geoffrey Howe's ears, for instance, were only just visible through his locks (surprisingly, he also seemed very slightly camp in those days, his fey hand-gestures giving him the air of Larry Grayson's duller brother).

Also, every panel assembled in front of Robin Day to talk about important issues such as the Social Contract or the Wealth Tax had a prominent trade unionist sitting on it, to whom the others, Labour or Tory, would automatically defer. These days, the very phrase "prominent trade unionist" reads like an oxymoron – in fact, I can't name a single one – but in 1974 Joe Gormley and Hugh Scanlon were never off the television.

And how much posher people's accents were back then! I had a vague feeling that in the 1970s we were all aiming towards classless accents, and that only recently, under a public school Prime Minister, has poshness reasserted itself. But when the youthful Sue Lawley came on screen and said: "Mrs Thatcher, who has been mentioned in some of the papers today as a possible successor to Mr Heath, is back in Finchley," she pronounced the key words "Thetcher" and "mairntioned" and "parsible" and "beck".

I was struck, too, by how much less panicky we all were then. Minutes after Harold Wilson had arrived at Transport House for the victory celebrations, there was a bomb alert and everyone was told to leave the building. Even though five people had died in the Guildford pub bombings just five days before (and three further bombs were set to explode in London before the month was out), everyone in Transport House sauntered out very casually, many of them stopping for a quick refill of drinks and sandwiches on the way out.

How strange to think that tonight's television news will look just as quaint, and just as pre-ordained, when I watch it again in October, 2034, as an old man.

Ancient History: The Diaries of Bernard Donoughue

WHO CAN REMEMBER them now, those forgotten rogues and charlatans? Yet not so very long ago, Joseph Kagan and Eric Miller were part of the Downing Street circle, basking in the friendship of the Prime Minister. Joe Haines, Marcia Williams, Bernard Donoughue: these were the so-called "kitchen cabinet", as famous in their day as Alastair Campbell is now.

It was thirty years ago, but, reading this diary,* it seems more like sixty. Even the chapter titles – Tony Benn and Industry Policy, Who Governs Britain? Public Expenditure Crisis – have the half-remembered quality of old hymns in a dusty missal. Elwyn Jones, Fred Peart, Eric Varley, Roy Mason – these were once on the A-list for Radio 4's *Today* programme. Nowadays, their names would crop up only in a specialist round of *Mastermind*.

Bernard Donoughue had lectured at the LSE for many years on the post-war General Elections when he was called in by the then Leader of the Opposition Harold Wilson to help win the first of the two 1974 General Elections. It is now perhaps necessary to add that Harold Wilson had been Labour Prime Minister from 1964–70, when he lost to the Conservative Edward Heath, and was to be Prime Minister again, from 1974–76, when he retired from public life, exhausted and bored and perhaps already aware that his remarkable brain was beginning to disintegrate.

"You could not imagine, seeing him now, what a brilliant Rolls-Royce mind he once had," Wilson's tough Press Secretary, Joe Haines, mutters to the young Donoughue, when Wilson is still Prime Minister, "...this is just the fag-end of a very great politician."

By the mid-1970s Wilson is drinking an awful lot – five brandies before pitting himself against Margaret Thatcher in Prime Minister's Questions – and feeling the strain of being in charge of a feuding party, and a country on the skids, for quite so long. At one point, Donoughue meets him coming out of the lavatory. "The PM stopped and put his head in his hands. 'I am so exhausted,' he said."

One reason for Wilson's weariness must surely have been the people with whom he chose to surround himself, chief among them Marcia Williams (the soon-to-be Lady Falkender) who had been his personal and political secretary since 1956. By Donoughue's account, she was a tyrant and harridan, screaming abuse at one and all, not least the Prime Minister himself, who regularly emerges from meetings with Marcia a gibbering wreck.

What was the source of Marcia's peculiar hold over Harold? At the time, it was always rumoured that sex was at the heart of it, but

---

Downing Street Diary: With Harold Wilson in No. 10 by Bernard Donoughue

Donoughue seems to think her grip was psychological. "I feel that everything he does in politics is to please her," he observes. Looking back, he says that Wilson "often indulged her wildest whims almost like a daughter ... and equally feared her like a fierce mother ... she was adept at mobilising his demons, stimulating nightmares and evoking his alleged enemies".

In case anyone at this point should imagine that they are in for an exciting Gothic horror along the lines of *Whatever Happened to Baby Jane?*, I should perhaps make it clear that most of the 785 pages of Donoughue's two years of diaries are quite exceptionally boring, and will prove a hard slog for all but the closest relatives of the principal figures.

The first page sets the tone, recalling the drab, grey, broken-down mood of the era. "HW asked me to boil down James Callaghan's statement on incomes policy. The typing was slow. Nearly every photocopier in Transport House was not working. Our office was out of paper." On and on he goes – ("Roy Jenkins read his statement on the balance of payments. Immensely impressive.") – chronicling ups and downs that may well have had one on the edge of one's seat had they emerged hot off the press the following day, or even the following week, but thirty years on are so dull as to be meaningless. There is plenty of gossip – Joe Haines having secret talks with the IRA, a civil servant in Number Ten caught working as a call girl, the gruesome old lefty MPs Ian Mikardo and Renee Short having an affair – but gossip is a dish best served hot, not left to mould.

By and large, Donoughue is not a natural diarist. The great political diarists like Chips Channon and Alan Clark look for the needle in the haystack of events. But Donoughue shoves it all in, the needle, the haystack and most of the surrounding field too. "My drip-dry shirt was nice and dry," he kicks off his entry for July 31, 1974, "but my socks still wet from overnight washing."

This is political history written by Chauncey Gardiner. He meets famous people, but takes nothing in. The Queen is "very bright and interesting". He fails to recognise Raquel Welch until he is introduced to her, and then notes that "her bosom was much smaller than I had been led to believe". He often goes to the theatre, but his reactions wouldn't even scrape a poor fail in GCSE ("Quite enjoyed *Equus*").

But something happens to his pen whenever Marcia Williams flounces on to the page, snarling and spitting: it quivers into life, fuelled by rage and resentment. Much as Donoughue may still loathe her, with her "eyes like a hawk and teeth like a hare", she is his Hannibal Lecter, his Dracula, his Jaws. Whenever she enters, it is as though a window has been opened and a blast of ice-cold air is whooshing through a fuggy old office. Had I been Donoghue's editor, I would have forced him to reduce his diary to a hundred-odd pages of pure Harold and Marcia. After all, that classic chiller *Dr Jekyll and Mr Hyde* is barely any longer.

How strange, that the Prime Minister of Great Britain and all those around him should have had to dance to the whims and sudden furies of his unprepossessing secretary. Her paranoia is all-embracing – over lunch, she gets upset that the whitebait on her plate are all looking at her – and her wrath is unstoppable. She sacks the Downing Street cook for being too pretty: she even sacks her own brother, because he wants to marry the wrong girl.

Joe Haines – who was later to blot his copybook for all time by writing a fawning hagiography of – ahem – Robert Maxwell – gives the young Donoughue all the juiciest gossip on Marcia.

"Joe told me a story of how three years ago on Mary Wilson's birthday Marcia was angry because HW had taken Mary out for a birthday lunch instead of having lunch with her, and so in revenge she told Mary some hurtful sexual information about herself and HW long ago. It produced a terrible crisis, and HW – who told Joe the allegation was totally untrue – broke with her for a while. Joe also said Marcia claimed that Mrs Wilson had a Polish friend in Rome – which Marcia was threatening to tell the press last Friday evening ..."

The oddest of the many odd details about Marcia Williams is that she believed her mother had had an affair with King Edward VII, and that she was thus his great-grand-daughter. This, she thought, was why the Queen never invited her to Buckingham Palace.

Haines also tells Donoughue that Wilson stored his private papers in Marcia's garage, and during their falling-out she refused to let him have them. So one night Wilson and Marcia's brother Tony broke into the garage and stole them back. Throughout the diary,

Marcia is forever threatening Wilson. "She said she would bring us all down. She would destroy Harold Wilson, who she said was up to his neck in the land deals ... She said she would earn her living writing books about us."

Was Marcia Williams really that ghastly? There is another side to every coin. In Tony Benn's diaries for the same period, Marcia tells Benn that it is Bernard Donoughue who is "just feeding Harold's insecurities". Benn seems to sympathise with her ("I like Marcia ... if she went it would be awful") and to mistrust Donoughue ("he is power mad and he just wants to establish a dominant position for himself in Whitehall"). There is, you are forced to conclude, only one thing worse than a can of worms, and that is a can of worms in which each worm is busy keeping a diary about the others.

Dark Days at *Crossroads*

VIEWING FIGURES for the new *Crossroads* have, alas, nearly halved since its relaunch. Its future is now said to be in jeopardy.

When it returned to our screens at the beginning of March, five million viewers sat glued to their sets, myself among them. I am ashamed to say I was also one of the first to jump ship, put off by far too many exciting new characters and needlessly gripping story lines.

The joy of the old *Crossroads* was that things happened even more slowly than they do in real life. A new guest to the motel would appear in the reception area on the Monday, but it would not be until Friday that he would be shown to his room, and only on the following Tuesday would he begin to unpack.

By contrast, in the new *Crossroads* everything is speeded up to a terrifying extent. Within five minutes of checking in, a new guest will be having an affair with a chambermaid, who will be announcing her pregnancy ("I don't know how to put this, but") by lunchtime the next day; before the week is over, the chambermaid will have been knocked down and killed by a shadowy hit-and-run driver, who, on the following Monday, will turn out to be her baby, now a grown man of twenty-one.

Many will blame the failure of the new *Crossroads* on the continued refusal by the powers-that-be to implement my proposal that Meg Mortimer be brought back as the proprietor of the motel. The character of Meg was, of course, originally created by Noele Gordon, who sadly died some years ago. Some would say that her death is no reason to disbar her from reviving the role. A skeleton behind the reception desk might give the series a Bergmanesque quality rare in daytime television, as well as acting as a sharp warning to any new characters who might have been thinking of behaving in too hasty or lustful a manner.

Failing that, I still hold out the hope, even at this late stage, that Margaret Jay could be persuaded to take over. Not only does she have time on her hands, but she also has something of Noele Gordon's brusque, haughty quality; and what more suitable place could there be for Baroness Jay than behind the reception desk of a three-star motel on a ring road on the outskirts of Birmingham?

Oddly enough, with his sharp suits and spruce hairdo, Peter Mandelson bears an uncanny resemblance to Meg's dapper deputy, David Hunter. Faced with the possibility of a challenge in Hartlepool, Mandelson might welcome the chance to take on the crown vacated by the late Ronald Allen. But one nagging question remains. Who will play Benny, the benevolent odd-job boy? At first sight, Nicholas Soames would appear too grand for the role, but there is no telling the miracles a bobble hat can work.

(May 8, 2001)

Wallace Arnold: A Brief History of the Garrick Club

AS ENTERTAINMENTS SECRETARY (Ladies' Clothing) of the Garrick, I am thrilled that my old friend and quaffing partner Geoffrey Wansell has managed to find a publisher for his new history of that most eminently civilised of all gentlemen's clubs.

It is a wonderfully far-ranging tome, rich in detail of all the ups and downs in our club's proud history; after burrowing away in the archives for a good few days, Wansell has managed to unearth some fascinating details.

Who would have guessed, for instance, that the club was founded (a full 173 years ago, forsooth!) by seven out-of-work actors? These colourful thespians had been booked to perform in the celebrated pantomime *Snow White and the Seven Dwarfs* at the Adelphi, with Sir David Garrick in the title role, but at the eleventh hour, Sir David had been tempted by the chance to play the title role in *Dick Whittington* at the Haymarket, and the show had been called off. Undaunted, the Seven Dwarfs decided to become the founding members of their own club, and immediately ordered club furniture specially sized down to suit their own diminutive statures. This tiny furniture is still used to this very day, and that is why first-time visitors to the Garrick often come away with the impression that its members are all clinically obese.

The seven of them took little more than a week to come up with a set of Garrick Club Rules, and those rules are, I am delighted to say, still enforced to this very day, from Rule One ("All gentlemen are required to repeat the same comical anecdote in a loud voice on the hour, every hour") right through to Rule Twenty-Three ("Only those members who are closet homosexuals are permitted to wear the Club Tie"). Nearly two hundred years on, our theatrical tradition is going strong. At present, we number seventy-five thespians in our membership, among them Reg Varney of *On the Buses* fame, veteran quizmaster Dale Winton, and the celebrated television actor Leslie Grantham, who in recent years has honoured the club by creating "home videos" on our premises, and sending them to a select circle via the "internet".

In keeping with the club's roots, on the second Thursday of each January, there is a select luncheon for those members currently starring in pantomime. Last year, the meal was attended by four Baron Hardups, three Widow Twankeys, two pantomime horses, and a Mother Goose. Sadly, three Prince Charmings had to be sent packing, having failed their random sex tests, conducted under strict medical supervision by the Club Chairman in a specially erected booth to the right of the main entrance.

And the evictions, I regret to say, did not end there: when one of the pantomime horses was opened, it was found to contain Mr and Mrs Neil Hamilton. After a hastily convened meeting between myself and the Chairman, it was formally agreed that Mr Neil Hamilton could remain at the luncheon, but that his wife would be obliged to eat a chicken sandwich in an alleyway across the road.

But those who imagine the Garrick Club to be made up entirely of theatricals could not be more wrong. We also have a fair number of sports commentators (twelve), television arts presenters (fifteen), weather forecasters (seven) and personalities (eight) on our books, though they are outnumbered by raconteurs (ninety-seven), professional bores (forty-nine) and complete arseholes (two hundred and twelve). There are also a dozen or so members who are fully qualified ventriloquists, though this can lead to confusion. One member who, mistaking former newscaster Martyn Lewis for a ventriloquist's dummy, tried to put his hand up his backside, has, I regret to say, found himself subject to a formal caution.

Leafing through Wansell's hugely agreeable tome, one is struck by how many illustrious murderers have been members of the club. Dr Crippen was for fifteen years Club Treasurer. Crippen was eventually asked to hand in his resignation, not on account of his disposal of Mrs Crippen, however botched, but for the far more beastly crime of sharing a cabin on a cruise liner with a young lady. Legend has it that poor Crippen went to the scaffold wearing his Garrick Club blazer. Granted one last wish, he asked permission to relate an amusing anecdote, but, alas, his request was denied.

The stuffier clubs of Pall Mall may turn up their noses at even the most discreet attempt at manslaughter, but at the Garrick Club murder has never been a resigning issue, just so long as the dread act is performed with aplomb. Wansell's excellent book reminds us that the late Fred West was a life member of the Garrick (and a very efficient Secretary of the Maintenance Committee: his excellence as a plumber is too often overlooked), and so too was the redoubtable Dr Shipman. They are both fondly remembered as convivial and energetic clubmen, though I believe there were, from time to time, complaints about Shipman's beard.

I now reach the hardest part of this history, in which I am obliged to "name and shame" those members who, for reasons best known to themselves, have attempted to "gatecrash" private parties within the building. In March, I was obliged to stop Dr David

Starkey, resplendent in his club tie, when he tried to lose himself amidst the crowd of ventriloquists' dummies as they poured into the upper dining room, led by Lord Charles. It was a delicate matter, and I approached him, as you might imagine, with the utmost courtesy.

"Excuse me, Dr David," I intoned, "but may I see your certificate of accreditation from the Worshipful Company of Ventriloquists' Dummies?"

Sadly, Starkey chose to ascend his high horse. "How DARE you?" he hissed. "Do you know who I am? I am TV's Mr Rude – and you, sir, have absolutely NO RIGHT to bar my way! Make way, you DOLT!"

Since 1907, the word "dolt" has not been permitted in the club before 7.30pm on weekdays; but rather than issue Starkey with a formal warning, I attempted to calm matters down by asking him to step into the vestibule for a medical examination. Despite a certain amount of huffing and puffing ("I have never IN MY LIFE been treated so disgracefully!"), Dr Starkey acceded to my request, and, amidst much raising of the eyebrows and sideways glances from the ventriloquists' dummies foregathered in the hallway, together we withdrew.

"May I now ask you, Dr Starkey, to remove your dinner jacket and shirt?" I said.

"And may one ask WHY?" he retorted, indignantly.

I explained that those among our members who were, indeed, ventriloquists' dummies could be identified by the large hole in their backs, a hole affording ample space for a human hand to "dip into" for the purpose of operating the various levers for winking, talking, lip-curling, head-twisting, and so forth. Anyone without a cavity in his back, was, it went without saying, a charlatan.

Starkey seemed to take all this on board, proceeding to remove his jacket and shirt with a gusto that belied his initial reluctance. "There!" he exclaimed as he turned his bare back towards me. Placing my pince-nez firmly on my nose, I peered hard: but no luck.

"I'm sorry to say this, doctor," I sighed, "but there is no cavity in your back. So I cannot permit you to enter any meeting exclusive to dummies."

"The RING, man! Look at the RING!"

There on his back hung a small brass ring, at the end of a short line of string. Over the years, I had observed many such rings on club members, the late Lord Wyatt among them. "Well, GIVE IT A TUG, man! Go on – GIVE IT A TUG!"

Reluctantly, I pulled it. As I pulled, the string grew longer and longer. When it had reached its furthest limit, I let go.

"My name is Starkey. I am TV's Dr Rude. My name is Starkey. I am TV's Dr Rude. My name is –"

I pulled it again, just to make sure.

"Don't mess with me, you blithering nincompoop! Don't mess with me, you blithering nincompoop! Don't mess wi –" I had had enough. "You may well be a talking doll, Dr Starkey," I said. "But that is not the same thing as a ventriloquist's dummy. I cannot allow you to enter."

"Don't mess with me, you blither –" he replied. But by now I had reached the end of my proverbial tether. "That's enough from you, my man!" I exclaimed. So saying, I gathered him into my arms, carried him post-haste to the trunk below the stairs, and locked him in there with all the other talking dolls, to be released only when he had added common courtesy to his repertoire.

History Will Forgive Us

"IF WE ARE WRONG, we will have destroyed a threat that, at its least, is responsible for inhuman carnage and suffering," said Mr Blair in his address to Congress, adding: "That is something I am confident history will forgive.'

There is an increasing reliance on history's ability to judge everything. "History will judge New Labour more harshly than their fans at Wapping have done so far," said George Galloway at the beginning of April.

"History will judge the passing of the Human Rights Act as one of the greatest progressives of the Labour government," said Yvette Cooper in May. "I believe history will judge that we made the right choice," said the Prime Minister last month.

This confidence in history's judgement is not confined to those in power. Every Tom, Dick and Harry seems to believe history will set aside time to judge them. "History will judge whether Tom Jones is remembered as a kitsch artefact or a new lease of musical life," wrote a journalist in the *Guardian* in October 2002. And in the same newspaper this week, Noel Edmonds, the former personality, wrote an article containing the immortal sentence: "I always felt that history would be kind to *House Party*, even though the critics weren't."

Is Mr Edmonds being a little over-optimistic? It is hard to imagine historians devoting a very great deal of time to deciding on *House Party*'s place in history, or to puzzling out whether Tom Jones was a kitsch artefact or a new lease of musical life. It is not as though A J P Taylor ever wrote *The Origins of the Generation Game*, or as though A L Rowse, for all his prodigious output, ever tackled *The Question of Crossroads*.

But it is equally curious that serious politicians such as Tony Blair still make so free with the phrase "history will judge". In his book on President Clinton, Dick Morris painted a portrait of a man obsessed by the judgement of history. Yet history is only the product of historians, and historians never agree on anything. What, for instance, is "history's judgement" on Harold Wilson? Until recently, it seemed to judge him a pragmatist with neither ideology nor purpose. But ever since Mr Blair took Britain to war with Iraq, it turns out that Wilson was brilliantly clever to keep us out of Vietnam.

History is just as fickle in its judgements on American presidents. One minute, Richard Nixon is a scoundrel, the next, a master of diplomacy. With every fresh history book, Kennedy leaps from hero to fraud and back again. The same is bound to be true of Clinton. Napoleon, Henry V, George III, Edward VII, Florence Nightingale, General Custer, Scott of the Antarctic, Abraham Lincoln: historians delight in bouncing them back and forth, from good to bad.

If history really were a judge, it would surely be a judge of the most unsatisfactory kind, one moment setting the defendant free, the next moment donning his black cap and calling him back, saying he's just changed his mind.

(July 19, 2003)

A Brief History of Eyesores

March 30, 3000BC

SIR – Over the past few days, a significant number of large and ungainly stones have appeared on Salisbury Plain, destroying the outstanding natural beauty of the surrounding area. One need only imagine the disastrous effect on property prices in the neighbourhood. Repeated enquiries as to what on earth they are doing there have met with a blank. Rumour – happily still unconfirmed – has it that these hideous structures are designed to encourage the great unwashed to indulge in all manner of crude chants, outlandish behaviour and physical depravity on Midsummer Eve.

Now we are told that a marketing boffin has named this eyesore "Stonehenge". This ugly modern name makes it, if anything, even more unattractive. No doubt he was paid a handsome sum for his inspiration!

Needless to say, I am reliably informed by a leading expert in such matters that these ghastly stones are ill-equipped to withstand the ravages of time. Stonehenge will thus be very much a case of "here today, gone tomorrow". But in the meantime, we local residents must, as per usual, suffer in silence. Is Stonehenge, sir, the thin end of the wedge?

~ Dan Hill-Slope, 3, Salisbury Plain

January 19, 570BC

SIR – Like most long-term residents of Babylon, I have long relished this city for its quiet, unshowy appeal. As is widely acknowledged, we true Babylonians pride ourselves on our discreet good taste.

So imagine my horror when I read today of Nebuchadnezzar's vulgar – some might even say *nouveau riche* – plans to erect so-called "Hanging Gardens", no less than four acres of terraced gardens built on tiers of arches to a height of three hundred foot. As if this were not enough, he is also planning arbours and banqueting halls, and a profusion of flowers, many of them not native to this country.

The rest of us Babylonians are perfectly happy with a window-box, or at most a small patch of lawn with modest borders of seasonal flowers such as daffodils and/or primulas. But Nebuchadnezzar is obviously determined to show that he is a "cut above" the rest of us. No doubt he used his wealth and influence to get his gardens past the planners – but that is another matter.

Not only would his plan be hopelessly out of keeping with the surrounding area, which is well known for its flatness. It would also send out the wrong sort of message to outsiders, leading them to conclude that Babylon was some sort of permissive society, where anything goes.

For myself, I shall be planting a fresh crop of leylandii, in order to block out the sight of this unsightly new development. In time to come, it will be seen as one of the great blunders of the ancient world.

~ Jessica Wheatcroft (Mrs), Seymour Close, West Babylon

May 23, 1070

SIR – So, after all the advance hype, the so-called "Bayeux Tapestry" has finally been unveiled. To my mind, it is less a tapestry than a travesty.

To those of us who were actively involved in the invasion of England, the tapestry comes nowhere near to depicting the horror of the true events. It is quite simply not good enough to embroider a few poorly sewn figures prancing around on horses, as though it were all some sort of game. To my mind, it does a tremendous disservice to all those who fought and lost their lives in this terrible skirmish.

It may well bring in viewers in the short term, but like other reasonable people, I believe we have had quite enough of these "real life" docu-broideries. The makers of the Bayeux Tapestry claim it allows the viewer to enter imaginatively into the real events of those days. Nothing could be further from the truth.

Could we not now create something of more lasting value to commemorate this great event?

~ Simone Huffer, 3, Rue Barmi, Bayeux

September 4, 1710

SIR – Like many householders in my area, I used to have a clear view over the rooftops to the River Thames. Now that view is disfigured by the monstrous "modern" cathedral of St Paul's, dwarfing every

decent old-fashioned building in sight. Is there no end to the atrocities of modern architects in search of knighthoods?
~ **Anna Trossity, London EC4**

HM Queen Elizabeth the Queen Mother by Hugo Vickers

The moment war broke out, the King and Queen threw themselves into hard work on behalf of a grateful nation. The King learnt how to break into his own boiled egg with a spoon; for the duration of the war he insisted upon doing the job himself, brushing aside all offers of assistance. Seeing him hard at work at the breakfast table, the Queen would clap her hands together in an expression of delight. "So clever!" she would presently exclaim.

Her own war work was regarded by many as a crucial factor in the Allied victory. "Herr Hitler will not have defeated this great country of ours," she could often be heard saying, "as long as the Royal Family eats up its cream buns." And with a defiant laugh she would stuff another cream bun graciously into her mouth.

She had an especial talent for friendship. She took everyone on their own terms, and was as happy to be entertained by a duke as by a dustman; in fact much happier.

She introduced an element of fun wherever possible. For her, there was satisfaction in knowing that by her mere presence she could bring intense pleasure to a room.* To those she encountered, she gave much. It always greatly amused her to watch as her old friend Ruth, Lady Fermoy, would lie on the floor in front of her, her hands in the air and her tongue out. "I rather think Fido is in need of a reward!" she would exclaim with an infectious giggle – she was suffering from a bout of catarrh at the time – before popping a Good Boy doggie biscuit into Lady Fermoy's wide-open mouth.

---

* In 1973, 1974, 1981 and twice in 1992 I myself experienced violent orgasms as she walked into the room. I was not alone. Her Private Secretary, Sir Martin Gilliat, would make a point of always being at hand with a box of luxury paper tissues as she entered any roomful of admirers. Sir Roy Strong was once heard gasping, "Yes, yes, YES!" before collapsing in an exhausted heap as the Queen Mother arrived at the National Portrait Gallery to view a newly acquired miniature by Holbein in June, 1972.

She had the unique ability to say the right thing at the right time. On one memorable occasion, Osbert Sitwell asked her if she would care for another glass of champagne. In an instant, she held out her champagne flute and exclaimed, "Fill it up!" Her fellow guests remain convinced that this was not a 'prepared' remark, but a genuine 'ad lib'.

"With just three short words, she managed to transform that room!" recalled Norman Hartnell. "It was the most perfect display of wit and grace any of us had ever witnessed." Barely fifteen minutes later, possibly aided by the champagne, the Queen Mother broke wind. "The most wonderful thing about it was that she 'blew off' to the tune of "Land of Hope and Glory", which of course set us all at our ease," recalled the Duchess of Albermarle.

Others present recall an intense perfume of lavender and hibiscus filling the room at that moment. "It was the most perfect display of breaking wind any of us had ever witnessed," Ruth, Lady Fermoy, wrote in a letter to the author.*

The Queen Mother had a keen appreciation of art. "Had she ever lifted a brush, I have not the faintest scintilla of doubt she would have proved more than a match for Constable or Gainsborough," wrote Sir Roy Strong in his memoir, *Dearest Darling Mumsie* (John Murray, 2004). "But instead we, her people, were her true palette. She loved to mix us all up, then slap us all onto her canvas before getting someone to clear it away."

She displayed, too, a deep love of literature,** often getting through two or three books a year. "She was surely the most sensitive reader the world has ever known," recalls Lord St John of

---

* Perhaps influenced by a seventieth birthday fly-past by the Red Arrows earlier in the year, the Queen Mother entertained her guests at Glamis Castle to a similar display after dinner, employing a dye composed of her trademark pastels – a winning mix of lilac, violet and nectarine.

** On one memorable occasion, she summoned the authors and poets of the day to Clarence House, bidding them take part in a Christmas pantomime to delight an audience composed of her and her old friend Ruth, Lady Fermoy. The poet T S Eliot took the role of Buttons, with W Somerset Maugham and Osbert Sitwell as the Ugly Sisters and Edith Sitwell as Cinderella, while the noted art historians Sir Kenneth Clark and Bernard Berenson played respectively the front and back halves of Dobbin, the faithful horse.

Fawsley. "She always insisted on starting at the top left-hand corner of a page, and working her way down to the bottom right-hand corner, and going through exactly the same process with each page." Sometimes she would tear out and eat the page she had just finished reading, but only if she was feeling peckish, and always with the most consummate grace.

It has been erroneously suggested that the Queen Mother held the Duchess of Windsor in low regard. Nothing could be further from the truth. She always took a Christian view of the Duchess, regarding her as the woman taken in adultery. In a characteristic gesture, she even went so far as to send her a small packet of super-market own-brand digestive biscuits* as a token of her good wishes in the December following the Duke's death. "A joint Christmas and birthday present" read the inscription, written personally by an aide. "Invoice enclosed."

"It was the most perfect display of generosity I ever witnessed," recalls a close friend of the Queen Mother. She could have given her chocolates, but she knew how the Duchess kept a close eye on her figure, so she ate them all herself. "Always such a treat!" she exclaimed delightedly, tearing away the crinkly dividing paper to reveal the layer beneath.

Since the death of HM Queen Elizabeth the Queen Mother, there have been many moves afoot for the Vatican to recognise her as a saint. There have been a number of reports of miracles to support the growing call for canonisation. One senior member of her staff recalls seeing her right hand continuing to wave to passers-by a full three days after her death. Another remembers spotting tears fall from a box of Bendicks Bittermints that sat disconsolately by her

---

* Aged 93, the Queen Mother choked on a chocolate Bath Oliver, purchased specially for the occasion, at the author's own home, also purchased specially for the occasion. The author cupped his hands and bade the Queen Mother cough up the Bath Oliver into them. Happily, a major crisis was averted, and the evening's entertainment – the author – was allowed to go ahead as planned. To this day, the author maintains the coughed-up remnants of the Bath Oliver at a fixed temperature on a pedestal in his hallway. "It was the most perfect display of regurgitation I ever witnessed," recalls a fellow guest.

deathbed. Ordinary members of the public maintain that, viewed through a telescope, her familiar face can be seen beaming from the sun, leading to increased pressure on the Prime Minister to rename the sun, "Elizabeth, the Queen Mother", in her honour.

Clerihews for the Royal Wedding Guests

The Rt Rev the Lord Carey
Is a teensy bit scary:
His sermons lack pith
And he looks like Mel Smith.

Sandra Paul
Is the Belle of the Ball;
To me, she's always towered
Over her husband, Michael Howard.

Michael Howard
Is awfully high-powered
Though he'll barely cause a rippul
Among all those grand pippul.

Cherie Blair
Adopts a crazy stare
As if she's burnt the toast
Or just seen a ghost.

Andrew Parker Bowles
Is the most benevolent of souls
He was even overjoyed
To be done by Lucian Freud.

Richard E Grant
Drinks like a maiden aunt
Which does rather belie
His role in *Withnail and I*.

Stephen Fry?
Don't ask why:
You couldn't request a
Better Court Jester.

William Rees-Mogg
Peers through the fog:
"No marriage to the Prince of Wales,
In my view, ever fails."

Andrew Motion
Employs the perfect lotion
For mixing with a royal:
I rather think it's oil.

The Duke of York
Knows how to hold a fork
But there's one thing he can't hide:
His neck is fearfully wide.

Charles Kennedy
Sings a desperate threnody:
"Sir, I'm getting my coat
Unless you promise me your vote."

Jilly Cooper
Is no party-pooper:
She'll have them all in fits
Reciting the dirty bits.

Prince Harry
Says: "When I marry,
It'll be in fancy dress –
And I'll come as Rudolf Hess."

Joanna Lumley
Is ever so comely.

How I wish all mums
Had such perfect gums!

Tony Blair
Says: "Fair's fair –
After a spot of fawning
I'll issue a forty-five-minute warning."

Joan Rivers
Sends shivers
Down the spine.
(I'd never invite her to mine.)

Top of the Pops: The Heritage

AS A RESULT of falling ratings, Top of the Pops *is being dropped from BBC1. Six distinguished commentators pick their most memorable* Top of the Pops *moments from the past forty years:*

✱ **Fergal Keane:** My dear son, it was a hazy summer evening and the sun sat golden on the all-too-distant horizon when Gary Glitter arose to perform "Do You Wanna Touch Me?" clad entirely in skintight silver foil. Poised o'er my typewriter, I listen again to the distant beat of years gone by, and I see once more the reflection of my own face – mournful, yes, yet still poignantly optimistic – in Glitter's shiny suiting. And I think of the changes time has wrought, and as I listen to the music of my tears as they plip-plop on the page, I hear Gary Glitter asking once more that most plaintive of questions, "Do You Wanna Touch Me"?, and I now know, with a heavy heart, that the answer must surely be No.

✱ **Sir Edward Heath:** Without the shadow of a doubt, the single greatest moment on *Top of the Pops* was when Miss Gloria Gaynor sang "I Will Survive" live in the studio in February, 1979. It almost made one forget the ghastly spectre of Margaret Thatcher! Gloria has since become a personal friend. I know there are some who argue for Leo Sayer singing "The Show Must Go On" in his clown costume, but they are wrong. Frankly, I've never heard such nonsense. They honestly don't know what they're talking about.

* Lady Antonia Fraser: It is, I think, far too easily forgotten that the golden age of *Top of the Pops* came at around the time I became principal dancer with Pan's People in the spring of 1967. With one's background as an historian, one obviously preferred dancing to what one might call the more highbrow songs, and I'm thinking now of classics like "The Legend of Xanadu" by Dave Dee, Dozy, Beaky, Mick and Titch and Queen's perfectly thrilling "Bohemian Rhapsody".

But I performed my most memorable dance routine to Boney M's "Ra-Ra-Rasputin (Russia's Greatest Love Machine)". In the mind of my public, I was at that time very much more associated with Tudor England than with Tsarist Russia, but my performance in a Cossack shirt and hot-pants making extravagant billowy gestures was set to change all that. Golden days indeed! But, sadly, since Mr Blair turned his back on those who elected him, *Top of the Pops* has tragically lost its way.

* Professor Christopher Ricks: Who were the Archies? Or, to put it another way, Were Archies the Who? Their identity – concealed yet at the same time peculiarly unconcealed – is essentially inessential, or, to put it another way, inessentially essential. On one level, they were a manufactured cartoon pop group who reached number one with the meaningless ditty "Sugar Sugar". But on another, more profound, level, they represented an outpouring of considerable force with urban post-modern angst coupled with Old Testament echoes of judgement and retribution:

"Sugar, ooh Sugar, Sugar!"

In this line, the triple repetition of the word "sugar", carries undoubted echoes of the slave trade, and the way it is pronounced – "su" as a "sh" – suggests that the grim message of slavery must be hushed up for and on behalf of forces unknown. And so to the Candy Girl in the second line: what do the Archies mean by "Candy"? A "Can" in this context is both a vessel for holding liquids, the modern name given to a set of headphones and – most importantly – American slang for a prison. But might it not also be a Canaanite, an inhabitant of the biblical land of Canaan?

✱ **Jeffrey Archer:** A tough choice. Was my most memorable moment on *Top of the Pops* the time I performed my chart-topping version of "Why, Why, Why Delilah" with the Beatles as my backing group? Or was it my legendary duet with Frank Sinatra on an up-tempo version of "Blue Moon"? On balance, I suspect it was neither of these, but standing in on a hush-hush basis for Judy Collins when she couldn't make the recording of "Amazing Grace". Happily, my voice was just right for that particular song, Judy's blushes were spared – and at the very last minute the day was saved!

✱ **Tony Benn:** Quite terrifying, really, isn't it? The way that the Blair junta has pretty well succeeded in stifling all dissent? And now they've decided to forcibly transport the dissident voices on that admirable programme *Top of the Pops* away from BBC1 to the no-go area of BBC2, where they won't be able to cause so much harm.

What an untrustworthy man Blair really is. No doubt his friends in the White House put him up to it. So now we're told that lovely, decent, up-to-date acts like my own firm favourites, Gerry and the Pacemakers, aren't going to be allowed to sing their smashing songs on BBC1. It makes me absolutely sick, it really does. Next, they'll be telling us that top pop acts like Gracie Fields are going to have to go into retirement, and then there'll be no stopping them. Y'see, it's not only a war against *Top of the Pops*. It's a war against socialism.

(December 2, 2004)

Department of Health and Safety

Patricia Hewitt's Diary

HELLO everyone! Hello! **Hello!**
Hello may be a little word – **but it means a lot**. I employ it regularly.

Some of my Cabinet colleagues add a "How do you do?" or a "How are you?" That is entirely **up to them**. I salute them for it. I understand their concerns. But, with the greatest respect, they are **laying themselves open to abuse**. There will always be time wasters who wish to take advantage of a lengthy reply option.

It is up to our highly trained doctors and nurses to ask people how they are. That is their job. That is their challenge. That is what we pay them to do. **And they do it superbly.**

I just say Hello, to which a reply is not only unnecessary but also **frankly unhelpful**. A simple Hello to ordinary men, women and children encourages feelings of inclusivity while simultanaeously reducing verbal wastage. **And that must be a good thing.**

In the past, we saw far too many ill people occupying far too many beds in far too many hospitals.

We remain committed to changing all that.

Fewer invalids in fewer hospitals. **That is our aim.**

And we believe it is an aim worth striving for.

Let me explain. When I go round our hospitals, which I do, the one thing that strikes me time and time again is that they are **full of sick people**.

Now, that can't be a good thing. Not by any stretch of the imagination.

For too long, we as a caring, decent society have been faced with hospital wards cluttered up with the under-the-weather, the poorly, the ill, and the frankly terminal.

We want to challenge those people to get better of their own accord. We want to empower them. We want to put those patients in the driving seat. We want to say to them, "Hello! Here is the steering wheel! Here is the accelerator! Now drive yourself away from here. Goodbye!"

And that's why we also plan to bring in a **basic health threshold** for those who – for whatever reason – wish to become patients in our hospitals. We ask them to answer these four simple questions:

+ Are you too ill to walk for yourself?

+ Are you suffering from a disease which might well prove contagious?

+ Are you becoming a burden not only to yourself but also to your loved ones?

+ Is there frankly not much hope for you?

If they answer a positive "Yes" to any of the above, we take them to one side, where it's nice and warm, and we put a caring arm around them, and we tell them, in a very positive way, that they would be **much better off at home**. We call it our Rise and Shine Initiative.

Our hard-working teams of doctors and nurses already have quite enough to do without busying themselves over the indiscriminately infirm.

I don't know if you've visited a hospital recently, but I **most certainly** have. I visited over fifty-three yesterday, via closed-circuit television, and I was frankly shocked to find ill people everywhere.

Taking up valuable bed-space.

Clogging up our operating tables.

Occupying our corridors.

Wearing out our hard-pressed doctors and nurses.

If we are to achieve much-needed improvements in our hospital services, we must rid ourselves of the **frankly patronising** idea that ill people in some way need "keeping an eye on". That attitude is sadly typical of the willingness in some sectors to denigrate invalids as second-class citizens who can't look after themselves. Much better – not only for them but also for the rest of us – if they wrap up well and stay at home.

The NHS – **Putting Healthy People First**.

Inevitably, some people have their own axes to grind. They grumble about things like MRSA. They complain that people catch it in our hospitals. And they refuse to acknowledge the enormous benefits that have accrued from MRSA.

I understand their concerns. Of course I do. I wouldn't be human if I didn't. But first they must get their facts right. I've lost count of the leading medical experts who have told me that, when all is said and done, MRSA is a truly marvellous thing, a tremendous boon to hard-working men and women. We now have a waiting list of people who are queuing up to enjoy the benefits MRSA.

That's not just my belief. Far from it. It's the belief of hundreds of thousands of senior hospital administrators up and down the country who keep telling me how much they appreciate MRSA, even compared to all of our other **splendid new diseases**.

And another thing they tell me, time and time again, is that they wish more hospitals were in the open air. Let's not waste more and more taxpayers' money on hard-to-maintain roofs and pricy walls and expensive flooring, they beg me: let's concentrate our vital resources on accessing all that **wonderful fresh air**.

I've listened to them. And I'm determined to implement their intiatives. So next month, I'm proud to be opening our very first NHS Fresh Air Hospital, conveniently situated for easy access on the grassy area of a major roundabout just off the Chipping Norton ring road.

Our streets are full of people tripping over on their own and others' shoelaces. For far too long, undone shoelaces have been a **major cause** of accidents, and a **needless burden** on the NHS. That is why I have asked for CCTV to be installed with immediate effect in over 40,000 ground-level locations around the British Isles. In future, anyone with a loose or undone shoelace may expect to face a heavy fine or custodial sentence. Which just leaves me space to remind you that the Clean Underpants Act will soon become law: from the fifteenth of this month, highly trained teams of Pant Inspectors, working closely with the police, will be able to stop and search anyone suspected of wearing dirty underpants. Repeat offenders will be fitted with twenty-four-hour Trouser CCTV, an initiative that has been welcomed throughout Britain, and particularly, **if you'll just let me finish**, in the more disadvantaged areas.

Who Gave You Permission to Read This? The Association of Paranoid Insomniacs

I WAS LATE for the Association meeting. It's usually scheduled to begin at precisely 3.44am, which is just about right for me. But I had forgotten that at the last meeting a majority of our members had voted to bring it forward fifteen minutes, arguing that they would already be wide awake at 3.29am.

A small group of us had argued forcefully against the change, but we had been viciously shouted down, and accused of trying to wreck other people's lives. We in turn accused them of persecuting minorities, and only arguing for the change because everyone else was, but it didn't make any difference.

Personally, I blame the chairman, and the chairman blames the rest of the committee, and of course the rest of the committee blames me, but then they would, wouldn't they?

The Association of Paranoid Insomniacs is celebrating its twentieth anniversary this year. Well, celebrating isn't quite the word. I mean, what's there to celebrate? No one's told me about any party or anything. Mind you, that doesn't mean to say they aren't all planning to throw a party behind my back. It's just the sort of thing they would do. In fact, now I think of it, I noticed one or two of them glancing oddly at one another when they didn't think I was looking. It's obvious now that they wanted to keep the party a secret from me. What have I ever done to deserve this kind of treatment?

Anyway, they were all there at the Association meeting when I arrived quarter of an hour late. I noticed when I put my head around the door that a dreadful hush descended on the room. They had obviously all been talking about me, thanks very much.

"Sorry I'm late," I said. I then thought I'd pre-empt the inevitable hostility by adding, "Bloody hell, I said I'm sorry. Isn't that good enough for you? What do you want – blood?"

I took a seat at the back alongside Mrs Small, who immediately moved seats, ending up next to Mr Hascombe, who took one look at her before moving three seats along. Soon everyone in the hall was moving this way and that, and the chairman had to call for order. "I can't help it if everyone's moving away from me!" screamed Mr Pincher. "That's their business, not mine!"

The chairman banged his gavel. "Thanks a bunch," said the treasurer. "You nearly hit me, Mr Chairman. In future, if you really must aim your gavel at my hand, could you at least give me prior warning? It's not as though your position on the board is any more secure than mine."

"Stop going at me, everyone!" replied the chairman. He then looked down at his desk to see what item we were to discuss next. But the desk was empty.

"Typical!" said Mr Trimble. "Someone's hidden his agenda!"

Eventually, we agreed to discuss the sorts of problems faced by paranoid insomniacs. "After all, a problem aired," said the chairman, "is a problem viciously gossiped about behind your back."

The first speaker, Mrs Hartington, took to the podium. She kicked off her speech by asking if the microphone was bugged, and saying it reminded her of a gun pointed at her head. She then described her own experience of waking up in the early hours rigid with anxiety.

"I worry nothing's going to happen. And then it doesn't," she said. "And I worry something's going to happen, and then it doesn't. And I worry nothing's going to happen, and then it does. And I worry something's going to happen, and then it does. And I worry I won't be able to stop worrying, and then I worry I won't be able to stop worrying about worrying about how to stop worrying. And then I blame myself, and then I blame everyone I know, and then I blame everyone I don't know, and then I think everyone I know is talking about me with everyone I don't know, and then I think no one is talking about me. And sometimes I think everyone is bored by me and ..."

"Are you droning on like this just to ruin my life?" sighed the chairman, banging his gavel and taking another sleeping pill. "Next speaker please!"

The next speaker was the chief medical officer of the Association of Paranoid Insomniacs. "But I'm pretty sure they only call me chief medical officer to poke fun at me," he explained. He had kindly – though some said unkindly – agreed to discuss possible cures for our neuroses.

"If I can't get to sleep, I count sheep," he said. "But as time goes by, the sheep start staring back at me, and they begin to gather together, and it's then that I realise they're all muttering instructions to one another, and preparing to charge.

"Sometimes, I find just listening to the sound of the clock an enormous help. Tick-tock, ticked-off, tick-tock, ripped-off, tick-tock, tricked-mocked, tick-tock, lips-blocked, tick-tock, bricks-dropped, tick-tock, picked-pocks, tick-tock, sick-dog, tick-tock, thick-fog, tick-tock, dick-docked ... Aaargh! Sadly, it always ends with me sitting bolt upright, screaming."

"Any other business?" asked the secretary. Every arm in the room shot up.

"Why are you all pointing at me?" she shrieked, rushing out of the room in tears. It only goes to show that she's always had it in for me, I thought, vowing not to lose any sleep over it.

Five Go Morbidly Obese

"OH! BLOW!" said Dick. "I've clean forgotten the chocolate bars! And just as we were about to set off!"

Julian glanced into his own satchel. "You could always share my marshmallows, Dick!" he said, cheerfully.

But then he looked again. How would he be able to last without his full supply?

"On the other hand, Dick," he added pensively, "that wouldn't leave many for me! Once I run out of my cake, my biscuits and my family-sized Coco Pops, I'll only be left with my family pack of Cheese and Onion and my bumper Toblerone."

The Famous Five were preparing for a marvellous adventure. For some time, they had been planning a great big walk. If all went well, they would set out from the couch at one end of the sitting room, past the coffee-table, across the blue carpet and all the way to the armchair at the other end of the sitting room.

They had just stocked up on provisions for the journey when Dick had delivered his dreadful news.

"Honestly, Dick!" sighed George, chewing on a toffee and putting on her best scowl. "You'll just have to leave without your precious chocolate bars!"

She hated it when things didn't go according to plan – and her feet were killing her.

Timmy the dog barked sharply. Timmy obviously agreed! Timmy had eaten an extra helping of Doggie Biscuits and a couple of tins of Pedigree Chum in preparation for the trip, and had just managed to get to his feet. But after a couple of wags of his tail, he slumped back. Phew, that was hot work! He was out of breath from the strain of it all!

The four cousins and Timmy the dog were now all on their feet and ready for offs. "Roasted chocolate peanut before we go, anyone?" said Anne, good-naturedly.

"Oh, rather!" exclaimed Dick, holding out both hands. "Ten, please!"

The four gathered around Anne as she dealt out the roasted chocolate peanuts.

"Now I'm completely exhausted!" wheezed Anne, wiping some sweat off her brow, and pulling her light blue blouse to and fro, to create a bit of a draught.

"Me too!" agreed Julian, licking his fingers one by one. "I know! Let's all have a bit of a sit-down!"

"Good idea, Julian!" chorused the others, flopping back onto the couch.

"Woof!" said Timmy the dog. He had been intending to say "Woof! Woof!" but, what with one thing and another, he couldn't be arsed.

The five of them spent half an hour getting their breath back.

"Goodness!" said Anne, pointing to the clock. "Is that the time?!"

It was five past eleven in the morning.

"Oh no!" exclaimed Julian. "We were getting so excited about our big adventure that we jolly nearly forgot our elevenses!"

The four cousins chuckled, their necks all wobbling in agreement. They all valued their elevenses. A late morning snack formed that vital bridge between a mid to late morning snack and an early afternoon pre-luncheon snack.

* * *

"What have you got us to eat, George?" asked Dick.

"Cheesy Wotsits!" exclaimed George, delightedly. They all clapped their hands in excitement. After four claps each, they flopped back, exhausted.

"After all that exercise," wheezed George, good-humouredly, "we jolly well deserve a fizzy drink with artificial colouring and a high sugar content!"

"Rather!!" piped up Julian. "And, since we're almost into the lead-up to pre-lunch snacks, why don't we round it off with lashings of the tastiest Pot Noodles in the world?"

The Famous Five all leapt to their feet in delight, the sudden transfer of bodily mass causing long-term damage to their ankles, knees and spines.

Eventually they set off on their great expedition between lunch and afternoon tea. The friends had gone over two yards, and were just in sight of the coffee-table, when Dick collapsed in a heap.

"I can't take much more of this!" he moaned, clutching at his stomach. "We've gone over ten minutes without so much as a double cheeseburger with fries!"

"Look!" spluttered George, suddenly pointing at the coffee-table. "Do you see what I see? Look!"

The five of them stared ahead. "Golly!" whimpered Julian.

There in a box on the far corner of the coffee-table was a selection of family-sized bars of dairy milk chocolate – and five ready-buttered baguettes to eat them in. With one last heave, the five heroes managed to claw their way to the coffee-table. They were about to dive into the chocolate when a great shadow loomed over them.

"I don't think you kids should be eating these," boomed the intruder.

"Oh no!" gasped Julian. "It's the Health Visitor!"

* * *

"I DON'T think you kids ought to be eating all that chocolate," boomed the Health Visitor, bad-temperedly. She was a thin woman with a stern expression beneath her horn-rimmed glasses.

"B-b-but," retorted Julian, nervously. "We're awfully p-p-peck-ish, Miss!"

"Nowadays, there is a wide selection of healthy and nutritious cereal bars available to fill the gap between meals," claimed the Health Visitor, reaching to remove the chocolate bars from the coffee-table.

"She's going to take them away from us!" exclaimed Dick, his chins wobbling in anxiety. "Quick, George! Grab them and run!"

George trudged towards the chocolates on the coffee-table, but she ran out of breath halfway and had to have a breather.

"You kids could do with more fresh air and exercise!" barked the Health Visitor.

This made Julian curious. "Fresh air and exercise?" he said. "Remind me?"

"I know!" gasped George. "It's what they do on the ads! You know – between sweeties!"

Julian thought of the lady running along the sand before tuck-ing into her Curly Wurly. Why go to all that trouble?

Dick couldn't last another minute without a bite of chocolate. That second, he came up with a terrific wheeze. And then another. And another.

"You've forgotten your inhaler," observed George. But between wheezes, Dick told Julian he had brought a length of strong rope with him.

"Come on," whispered Dick eagerly into Julian's ear. "You keep her talking while I tie her up."

"I say! Stop this immediately, you tiresome little wretches!"

exclaimed the Health Visitor, imperiously. But with her feet tied up, she couldn't move an inch.

* * *

LEAVING the Health Visitor tied to the spot, the cousins chomped their way through the chocolate bars.

"I feel completely full up!" smiled Anne, wiping the last smears of chocolate off her chins.

"Have another Mars Bar, Anne!" suggested George, helpfully. "It'll make you feel better!"

"You've already consumed over five times your recommended daily intake – and it's still not lunchtime," moaned the Health Visitor, struggling desperately.

"Shut it!" exclaimed Julian, coarsely.

Once they had all eaten enough, and then some more, and then just a tiny bit more, the Famous Five decided to press on with their expedition. If they really tried, they could reach the far end of the room in time for a well-deserved lunch of something sugary.

"Best foot forward, gang!" said Julian, bossily.

"Woowoof! Woowoof," wheezed Timmy the dog.

"We really should have brought Timmy's inhaler along too," observed Anne, opening a packet of salt and vinegar to keep her going through the long trip ahead.

After half an hour spent moving one leg in front of the other, then vice versa, the Famous Five had almost reached the halfway mark.

"I'm so hungry I could positively murder a Strawberry Mivvi," said Dick, rolling his banana fingers around his outstretched tummy, "or any other ice-lolly product with a high sucrose content filled with a cream-style substance containing ninety-eight per cent animal fat."

"I know what," said Anne, gloomily surveying the distance they had to travel to the far end of the room. "Let's call off our big adventure and send out for bumper-sized pizzas instead!"

"Champion idea, Anne!" flumped George.

Dear Esther (i)

MY EYE KEEPS getting caught by little advertisements in the bottom left-hand corner of newspapers. "DEAR ESTHER" reads the heading, next to a photograph of Esther Rantzen struggling to look sympathetic, "SHOULD I CLAIM FOR MY INJURY?"

The question is asked by someone called Colin from Shenley. "While I was out shopping last year," he continues, "I slipped and damaged my shoulder, which still causes me pain. I know it's been a long time, but could I still claim compensation?"

Esther is all for it. "I'm sorry to hear about your accident. If the accident wasn't your fault then you should claim. It is very easy to do". She then gives the phone number of "an expert panel of solicitors" who will "work on your behalf on a NO WIN NO FEE basis".

Alongside Esther's advice is a box headed "Thank you!" from a Susan Bailey of Croydon, who says, "I picked up the phone and within minutes I discovered I could win substantial damages," adding: "I'd advise anyone who's suffered a personal injury to make that call right now." Beneath Susan's photograph is the enthusiastic message, "Claimed £9,560!"

On the advertiser's website, Susan goes into greater detail about her personal injury. It seems that, much like Colin from Shenley, she was walking along the street "when I tripped on an uneven pavement, causing me to fall forward. I landed very awkwardly, damaging both my right knee and ankle."

Colin from Shenley and Susan from Croydon were obviously never taught to look where they were going when they were children. If they can't manage to walk along a pavement without falling over, one dreads to think how they would fare in the countryside. Catching their toes on tufts of deliberately unpaved grass, Colin and Susan could well be pitched head first into cowpats, leaving them only a few minutes to struggle home, like Joe Simpson in *Touching the Void*, to compose their smudgy "Dear Esther" letters in time for the last post.

Esther Rantzen prefaced her autobiography, *Esther* (2001), with the well-known quote from Edmund Burke: "For the triumph of evil, it is only necessary that good men do nothing".

Some may have found the way she sought to ride piggyback on this noble sentiment a little self-regarding. Nonetheless, her autobiography demonstrates that there was no shortage of good men in Ms Rantzen's life. "I was seduced by the tour guide," she reveals, on page seventy-six, of a student holiday in the Greek islands. "He said he was a doctor. I think his name was Chris. He taught me to say 'I love you' in Greek, and invited me into his bed. He enjoyed the experience more than I did. He was indefatigable. No sooner had it ended than he started all over again, and again, and again.

"It was a tiring night, but it had two effects. It finally cost me my virginity, and it gave me a lasting love of Greece which stays with me today."

Just over thirty pages later, on page 109, she recalls a similar liaison with the late Nicholas Fairbairn MP. If I have quoted this extract before, I make no apology. For me, it is one of the most haunting passages in post-war literature, and I will go on quoting it until a leading contemporary composer like Thomas Ades finally agrees to set it to music, ideally with Ian Bostridge as Sir Nicholas and Dame Kiri te Kanawa as Esther. To demonstrate the ease with which it could be adapted to grand opera, I have arranged Esther's original words into the shape of a libretto and inserted a few exclamation marks for added emphasis:

....How did he seduce me?
He took me to lunch at the Ritz!
He gave me a long-stemmed rose,
And, when the menu arrived,
Barely glanced at it!
"I think Beluga caviare
And Krug champagne," he said.
The Beluga consisted of
Huge succulent globes
That exploded on the tongue!
If ever there was an aphrodisiac meal,
This was it!
Nicholas took me to some
Lord's house where he was staying

And the rest was
Inevitable!
I didn't realise he was married until it was
Far, far too late!

Some might think it an awful shame that a woman whose glorious career took off in such a flurry of passion should now be reduced to urging the feather-brained, the flat-footed and the butter-fingered to go cap in hand to their local councils. On the other hand, it could well be that if she herself were to ring the Accident Advice Helpline, the "expert panel of solicitors" may be able to redefine her downfalls on, respectively, the Greek Islands and the Ritz as personal injuries, paving her way to compensation galore.

Dear Esther (ii)

IN AN ARTICLE celebrating the joys of being sixty-one, Esther Rantzen wrote, "On my fiftieth birthday I threw off my clothes and danced naked round my garden in celebration. Life is there to be enjoyed." This is odd, because on page 159 of her autobiography, *Esther*, published last year, she claimed that it was on her fifty-eighth birthday that she found herself "running naked through the garden".

Of course, it is perfectly possible that Miss Rantzen indulged in both performances, dancing naked round her garden on her fiftieth birthday, then, eight years later, running naked through her garden on her fifty-eighth birthday. This suggests that some form of nude activity in the Rantzen garden on June 22 every year is pretty much de rigueur.

Alas, she fails to give an exact time for these events, but those who live in or around the New Forest might do well to circle the date in their diaries now, in the hope that a more specific schedule will be issued nearer the time.

I don't know the New Forest, so I am not in a position to know whether Miss Rantzen has erected some sort of grandstand over-looking her garden. Nor do I know how many acres the garden is, but she must be fairly wealthy so I don't imagine it would be less than a couple of acres. At a modest jog, a complete circumnavigation of such a garden would take anywhere between five and ten minutes, possibly more if her nudity means that she forsakes shoes, and is thus forced to tiptoe through patches of nettles, brambles, comically shaped vegetables and so forth.

On the other hand, this may be one of those years, like 1991, in which she chooses to dance rather than run. A Chubby Checker-style twist or a more up-to-the-minute *macarena* could add up to twenty minutes to the proceedings. It would be handy if the *Daily Telegraph* were to print a cut-out-and-keep pullout to the event.

Perhaps I am becoming over-excited. There are still two months to go, and she may choose to re-route this year's parade, in order to make crowd-control more manageable. However, those of a more priggish bent may find the words of the late Bill Shankly strangely comforting. "If Everton were playing down at the bottom of my garden," he once said, "I'd draw the curtains."

(April 13, 2002)

John Prescott's Step-by-Step Guide to Putting Out a Fire

STEP ONE: HOW TO IDENTIFICATE A FIRE

As for the question as to whether and if not how to identificate a fire let me say this, cloud and lear. A fire is easily recognisabubble to the all-too-human eye as it is very, very tot to the hutch.

Let's get down to the overall consequences of a fire once it is ignitified.

If you or similar personages set fire to a newspaper or any other meading-ratter, then first and foremostable it will start to smoke and as a consequence thereof it may well in due course go up in flames. This is what we call, and will continue to call for the unforeseeable future if and when it occurs and there is no reason to believe it either will or, on the other hand, will not, a fire-type situation.

STEP TWO: HOW TO RING FOR HELP

On noticing a fire-type situation, it is important to dress ourselves to what is the white ray to haul for kelp. The west bay of all is simply to open your mouth and/or mouths and following on from this immediate-style action to scream for assistance, or, as it is more generally known, sound the lamb.

To do thus, lean out of an upstairs widow and yell: "My house or domicile or flat-style arrangement is on fire and by my reckoning give or take a few degrees it's head-rot. I am now calling for your agreement and the agreement of all related parties in the provisioning of assistance-style help."

STEP THREE: COW TO HAUL THE FIRE BRIGADE

The most important inaction to take is first and foremost to locate the telephone. To do this, look for a hand-held object that can be placed over the ear and mouth. Once you have locationised it, be sure to rial the night dumber, which is simpleton to rememberise, namely and I quote "Nine, nine", and so on – for seven's hake let's not get bogged down in the detail at this stage in the procedurations.

The operator will ask whether you require police, firings or ambulations.

The correct answer to this question-type question-style question is to say, cloud and seer: "Not police or ambulatories, please, love, but firings, as the particularised problematic with which I am at pheasant fraced and will in all due courses have to deal with is of the flaming variety." The operator will then enquire as to details purtaining to the neat strumber of your flouse or hat, and also request to provide a coast pode if and when possible.

STEP FOUR: HOW TO FLOUSE THE DAMES

What you will necessitate to have need of is b) a bucket and a) water. First you must fill the water with a bucket. Water is readily available from the household tap, often locationised above the kitchen sink. The tap may be turned on by motioning it in a forwardly direction, clockwise or antiwokclise, depending on as to wherefore it is revolving vis-a-vis the particularised direction at the time.

A sucket of band should also be kept availabubble at all times for the likely preventuality of and to a flazing inburno. So you have your sucket of band licely nined up. Now what, to soot it pimply, should you be doings? Second, pick up the sucket of band. Then first, throw it – that's the band, not the sucket – over the flames. And fourth, if you have a harden goes hidden away somewhere, who knows, perhaps in your old shool ted, then it would be advisable in the circumstations to hoint the pose at the fire and spray it bull-flask.

STEP FIVE: HOW TO INVENT A FIRE IN FUTURE
There previously follows a series of helpful tints and hips for future fire invention in the home.

Question Three: How do fires beginning?

Answer: Fires are often begin by people or persons unknown letting site to a mousehold hatch. It only makes a tatter of a sew fecunds for a mit latch to set an entirety house on fire. So please keep that mox of batches well out of the reachables of kittle lids, who might not bow any netter.

Question Two: Is it safe to fight a liar on the floor of my kitchen – or should I restrictify myself to the cooker?

Answer: It is the policy of this government that liars should never be fit on the fiddle of any moor. But let me make things perfectly all for once and for clear. Hang on, hang on. Just let me answer the question, because I'm not going to question the answer until or before I've answered the question because the whole answer is very questionable, and I'm the one who's answerable. I'm sorry, I've had my say, now let me have mine. So what I was saying before I was saying what I was going to say and before I said what I was going to be saying was that when all is dead and sun what we as a governmentable should be doing in this or any other direction is first and foremost to make every allowance for the issues under consideration. You've asked me what the facts are, and I'll give you the facts if you'll just let me get a word in hedgeways. Put it this way: there's no folk without a smear.

Twelve Things You Didn't Know About Binge Drinking

1 BINGE drinking is named after the Hon Christopher Binge, the eighteenth-century aristocrat and noted bon viveur. Despite wrestling with a drink problem, Binge remained a well-respected Member of Parliament, responsible for introducing some of the most remarkable legislation of the time, including the On All Fours Act, which made it obligatory for those leaving drinking establishments after midnight to return to their place of domicile without using their feet.

2 Binge went on to become Admiral of the Fleet. He was forced to resign in 1756 after leading a bombardment of the port of Lisbon. In his defence, Binge claimed he had been intending to bombard Dieppe as ordered, but the two places looked much the same on the map and Dieppe was a lot closer and, anyway, what difference did it make?

3 In retirement, Binge devoted his energies to landscape and portrait painting. His most distinguished works include Salisbury Cathedral: The Twin Spires and Mr and Mrs and Mr and Mrs Joseph Andrews.

4 The game of bingo began life as binge. It was originally designed as a diverting pastime for those whom alcohol had rendered incapable of sustained thought.

5 The Surrey village of Abinger Hammer was originally called Binge Hammered, and was notorious in the late eighteenth century as a centre for extreme alcohol abuse. But after a crackdown in 1807, the parish council voted unanimously to change the name of the village to something more in keeping with a wholesome image. Since that time, the village has become home to many distinguished celebrities, among them Liam Gallagher, Oliver Reed, Tracey Emin, Chris Evans, Elizabeth Taylor and George Best.

6 In June 2003, binge drinkers formed their own union, the NUBD, or National Union of Binge Drinkers. A recent press release from the NUBD announced that its annual conference is to be held this year at "somewhere or other, like, I mean, who really cares?". The press release goes on to say that "delegates will then make their way to wherever". The main debate of the evening will commence at 3.07am. The motion before the house is: "This House believes that, look, you're my best friend, d'y'know that, do you, I mean, like, you and me, right, like, who you lookin' at, I said, who you lookin' at, you want your faced knocked in, do yer? Well, do yer?"

7 The National Union of Binge Drinkers yesterday launched its campaign for more handrails in city centres, particularly across busy roads. "At the moment, there is absolutely no way our members can get home without falling over," declared a spokesman, adding: "Furthermore, there is absolutely no way our members can get home without falling over. Or did I just say that?"

8 In the late 1960s, senior Cabinet minister George Brown vowed at a press conference "to cut out dinge brinking boot and ranch". It was high time, he said, "to shake more that our safes are street for bore-eliding citizens".

9 The New Labour government plans to crack down on binge drinking by increasing the hours available for binge drinking. "Only by allowing binge drinkers more time in which to pursue their irresponsible behaviour can we bring home to them how very irresponsible it is," said Home Secretary Charles Clarke last night, adding: "Are you looking at me?"

10 In a new book, *Tony Blair – Out of His Head*, leading political journalist Andy Anorak argues that, far from his goody-two-shoes public image, Tony Blair is in fact a relentless binge drinker who spends his Saturday nights picking fights in city centres before reeling home, yelling "Do you know who I am?" at his staff.

Former associates reveal that the Prime Minister has had the dispatch box converted into an executive drink cabinet, complete with a full range of cocktail umbrellas. The book is rumoured to have been written with the help of sources close to the Chancellor of the Exchequer.

11 The minister behind the proposed new twenty-four-hour drinking initiative is Culture Secretary Tessa Jowell, or Jessa Towell as she is known by her allies in the drink industry after 11.30pm.

Her previous initiatives include building more casinos in order to reduce the number of compulsive gamblers. In future, she hopes to cut down on armed robbery by making firearms more freely available and to reduce the number of glue-sniffers by sending pots of Gripfix free to all teenagers.

12 Tabloid journalists leading the campaign against the "wicked and pernicious" new twenty-four-hour drinking Bill plan to gather today in the King's Head to work out their plan of attack. Then it's on to the Crown to fix the finer details, and then to the Cricketers for a quick one. After an hour or two at the Cricketers, the group plans to reassemble at that pub by the river – what's it called? – you know the one. And by that time, they should have got something down on paper. Now where did we put it, has anyone seen that piece of paper, I never even saw it so don't blame me.

Hypochondriac Conjugations

I have a chronic spinal disorder
You have a bad back
He won't lift anything.

I suffer from insomnia
You had a bad night
Someone got out the wrong side of their bed.

I have flu
You have a cold
Will he never stop sniffing?

I am well covered
You are overweight
He is clinically obese.

I have post-traumatic stress disorder
You are stressy
He is a bag of nerves.

I am hyper-sensitive
You are touchy
He is paranoid.

I am well toned
You are thin
She should see a doctor.

I take sleeping pills
You are on sleeping pills
He is addicted to sleeping pills.

I am active
You are hyperactive
What's he on?

I have appendicitis
You have indigestion
He has tummy ache.

I have tonsillitis
You have a sore throat
He has a bit of a tickle.

I have a rash
You have spots
He has acne.

I have an abscess
You have toothache
He should lay off the sweets.

I have indigestion
You wolf it down
He can't stop burping.

I suffer a gastric disorder
You are a martyr to wind
What's that awful smell?

Put a Sock In It!
Ann Widdecombe's Problem Page

*Agony aunt Ann Widdecombe offers no-nonsense
solutions to readers' problems:*

DEAR ANN – When I was a child, my father developed an irrational fear that when I grew up, I would kill him. So he attempted to have me murdered, but I had a lucky escape when I was rescued by a passer-by. As luck would have it, when I grew up I did manage to murder my father, without having a clue who he was.

To cut a long story short, I then ended up married to my mother, again without guessing who she was. When I found out that I'd killed my dad and married my mum, I became so stressed that I put out my eyes. In the meantime, my mum hanged herself. Now not only am I an orphan, I can't see a thing. In my experience, one thing leads to another.

They say it never rains but it pours, Ann. What would you have done in my shoes?
~ **Oedipus, son of Laius and Jocasta, Thebes**

Ann Widdecombe writes: What a silly mess you've got yourself into, Oedipus! Your dad sounds a wholly irresponsible individual. Trying to have your son murdered is frankly what I call irresponsible parenthood. Why have a child if all you're going to do is attempt to have him murdered? You're well shot of him, dear. But in this day and age there really is no excuse for marrying your own mum. I've heard of keeping it in the family, but this is ridiculous. Just because you love your mother, it doesn't mean you have to marry her. Where would we be if every young man decided to marry his mother?

That said, putting your eyes out is a silly over-reaction to an awkward situation. I suppose you were after the attention. But where's it got you? Much better to have taken your mum to one side and told her, frankly and firmly, that it would be better if the two of you were to call it a day. As it is, Oedipus, it sounds as though you're getting a bit of a complex.

DEAR ANN – To be or not to be: that is the question: whether 'tis nobler in the mind to suffer the slings and arrows of outrageous fortune, or to take arms against a sea of troubles, and by opposing end them?
~ **Hamlet, Prince of Denmark**

Ann Widdecombe writes: Frankly, deary, you're making a lot of fuss about nothing. You pays your money and you takes your choice.

DEAR ANN – I recently went up a hill with my partner, Jill, to fetch a pail of water. Jill fell down and broke her crown, and I came tumbling after. I am pretty sure the local authorities were at fault. How do we go about gaining compensation?
~ **(name and address withheld)**

Ann Widdecombe writes: To my mind, you're both as daft as each other. What's wrong, may I ask, with water from the tap? If you will go slogging up a dangerous hill in order to get your snooty "designer" water, then you deserve everything you get. To my mind, Jill sounds a total pain in the neck. And frankly you don't sound an awful lot better.

If you'd seen the recent film Touching the Void, *you'd have known that the first thing you do in these situations is to cut the rope, so that you don't come tumbling after. As things stand, you've only got yourself to blame.*

DEAR ANN – When I'm driving in my car and that man comes on the radio and he's telling me more and more about some useless information, supposed to fire my imagination, I can't get no satisfaction, I can't get no satisfaction. Because I try and I try and I try and I try. I can't get no, I can't get no.

~ **M Jagger and K Richards**

Ann Widdecombe writes: What on earth are you two on about? I've heard a lot of stuff and nonsense in my life, but this really does take the biscuit. I've never read such complete and utter twaddle in all my born days.

Let's stick to facts, shall we? You claim you "can't get no" satisfaction. What the devil does that mean? You might like to know that it's a double negative, so it really means that you jolly well can get satisfaction. In which case, what on earth are the two of you whining about? But I presume you mean you can't get any satisfaction. Well, more fool you, frankly. You've only got yourselves to blame.

You claim to be trying, but I don't believe a word of it. If I were you, I'd turn off that wretched radio, park your car, and make my way to an evening class of some sort. What are you interested in? You obviously like your car, so perhaps you should think of applying your minds to becoming car mechanics and doing something worthwhile for a change.

Believe me, it would be a lot more use than just sitting around moaning all day long.

The Trouble with Parties

"I FIND more and more," I said to the man in the bow tie to whom I had just been introduced, "that the trouble with parties."

"Sorry?" he said.

"What I was saying," I repeated, raising my voice, "is that the trouble with parties is I can't hear a word that's being said."

"Shed? Where? In the garden?"

"No – said!"

"Sorry!" he shouted back. "I can't hear a word you're saying! I find the trouble with parties is that …"

I didn't catch exactly how his sentence ended – something about not being able to hear, I think. But I wanted to express my agreement.

"Quite right!" I shouted.

"Trite?" he said, tetchily. Then he turned to someone passing and shouted: "This chap's just said I'm trite."

"Well, you're certainly not SOBER!" said his friend.

He looked at his watch and replied: "Over? Not for an hour or more!"

"More? No thanks, I'm driving."

A few minutes later, I came across a group of partygoers discussing the very same problem.

"Can't hear anything above the clamour!" said one.

"Hammer – where?" said another, looking around in alarm.

"Wear what you want – you still won't be able to hear yourself think!"

"Ink? Some in the drawer!"

"More? No thanks – I'm full."

"On the pull? Same here!"

"Mere."

"What?"

"You told me to say 'mere'."

"Couldn't agree more! They get samier and samier!"

By chance, the next weekend I was invited to a reception for a new pressure group, SORRY?. It has been formed by those who find it impossible to hear what other people are saying at parties.

"Welc !" said the chairman, as he bustled me into the large hall, thronging with campaigners of all ages. "I'm so glad got on time! A lot of peop . But at least ."

I smiled and nodded in agreement.

"Wine?"

"Why not?"

"No – it's lukewarm."

"How about a ? prefer red or ," he continued.

"Red would be fine," I said.

"Eh?" he said.

"Red's FINE!" I said, rather louder.

"Wine? That's right!" he replied. "Red or whi-"

I was then delighted to be approached by a senior member of the board.

" introduce myself?" he said, "The name's erton. We've all got to about noise at ," he said. "It's increasingly hard to at all. And as for . Well, the only thing to do about is . Wouldn't you agree?"

I had been nodding away in an attempt to disguise the fact that I couldn't catch everything he was saying, so I felt that the only appropriate answer was "Yes".

"Excellent," said Mr erton, excitedly gesturing at a friend to join us.

"Geoffrey! This Brown! He agrees me we should STRING 'EM UP!"

Geoffrey looked excited. "Ring 'em up?" he said. "But who'd pay the BILL?"

"Bill? Bill?" said Mr erton. "He couldn't make it, but his wife's here instead!"

"In bed? Oh, I am SORRY!"

"More HAMPSHIRE, actually – somewhere on the border."

"Don't do yourself down, old man – I'm sure you FASCI-NATED her!"

There seemed to have been some misunderstanding. Matters became more confused when, at the far end of the room, the director of SORRY? wanted to begin his speech and started calling for quiet. He tried tinkling his glass with a spoon, but it had no effect. "QUIE EVERY ! QUIE EASE!"

When he finally started to speak, at least a quarter of those present stopped chatting and paid attention. Positioned towards the back, I brought out my notebook. This, as best as I could manage, is a verbatim transcript of his remarks:

"Good ladies and I'm del to elcome today. For too long, arties have been far too so that are times it is possible to self ink. This led form pressure grou. Our aim is to. And we will achieve by. And finally. Thank you and goo ni."

When he had finished speaking, I turned to my neighbour and said: "Here, here!"

"No, not a word," he replied. "But that's the **uble** with **arties**."

Jordan's Surgical Diary

I'd been working my arse off. Me being me, I felt like a nice change, so I booked into the clinic for a nice change of boobs.

Same clinic that fat bitch Victoria so-called Beckham used, but her boobs still don't have any life of their own, do they? I don't know what David sees in them (not much, considering he's always on the pull!).

Hits on the Jordan website was down 20 per cent last year, which well pissed me off, so I had to get my boobs modernised ASAP. Big, bigger or biggerer? Or maybe I should go for littler, for a change? Basically, after nearly two years with the same old boobs, I was after something well different.

The doctor – phwoar, phwoar and fucking phwoar, talk about a well-fit body but he must of been gay because he never even tried it on – showed me the brochure with its full-colour selection of brand new boobs for me to choose from.

"We could do you a pair of the Beckhams for fifteen per cent off," he said, "and we'd throw in an arse-lift." But I wasn't having no bargain basement, for all his sweet talking. What with the sponsorship, I get all my new boobs for free anyway – and that's before the magazine and DVD rights, so who's fretting?

"No disrespect, doctor," I said, flicking through the brochure, well bored, "but I've had all these sizes before. Ain't you got nothing more exciting?"

That's when I had the great idea. It came like a flash from heaven.

"I'll have a third," I said. "Just think! Jordan with an extra boob! That's 33 per cent extra – the TV companies will go well nuts for it, then we can revise the contract with *OK!* and the world rights will go for a fortune."

I told my manager about my plan for Boob Three. She didn't think it was such a great idea, she said – she thought two boobs was more normal.

"Thanks a lot for the vote of confidence," I replied. I thought, I don't need this aggro, I'm not going to be treated like shit, what's she ever done for me, she's history.

"Your fans might prefer the more natural two-boob look, Katie," she said. "And anyway where would you put a third boob?"

Talk about negative. The natural look is all very well if all you want to end up on is *University* Fucking *Challenge*. No one disses my ideas and gets away with it. I was burning with anger.

"I'm Jordan," I said, "I'll put it where I fucking want." There's a load of body-areas with fuck all going on in them, they're each crying out for a third boob. Top of the head, small of the back, forehead, shoulder, just below the bum, behind the knee, wherever. The guys would go well mad for it – and just think of the publicity, we're talking quarter of a million minimum from the *Sun* per extra boob.

I decided to consult my husband Pete. He loves my boobs something rotten, and I knew he'd be all hands at the prospect of another. "Sounds great, babe," he said. "You put it where you want it. Hey, babe, d'ya wanna hear my latest song?"

"Thanks a lot, Pete," I screamed. "You just ruined my fucking day! I tell you I'm gonna have an extra boob and you can't even be arsed to tell me where I should fucking put it. And no, I don't want to hear your latest fucking song, not now, not ever! And you can put that away while you're about it – I'm so not in the mood!"

I was fucking fuming, I can tell you. Not for the first time, I was going to have to go it alone. Recently, I've been going for a more sophisticated market, not just lad mags, so I definitely wanted my new boob somewhere tasteful. The doctor told me he thought it would look really in keeping if we put it in between the other two. "The bad news is it'll be a bit of a squeeze," he said, "but the good news is that it'll give you two cleavages."

"That'll potentially double her earnings, doctor," said my personal business manager, bringing out his pocket calculator. I always have him to hand before any of my major operations. "And with another bosom in the middle, we can launch a whole new Jordan Swimwear range, and let's face it, Katie, with all the extra press and TV coverage, they'll never be able to deny you that school-girl ambition of yours!"

"You mean I can at last become Principal Ballerina with the Royal Ballet?"

"With a third boob popping up through your tutu, how could they possibly refuse you?"

Yesterday, I got my extra boob. It looks fantastic. No peeping, fellas – or at least not 'til the deal with Sky TV and *Nuts* magazine is all signed and sealed (pictures including the kids, bless 'em, 50 per cent extra per kid, please note: I'm a very private person, so anything extra's got to be paid for, fair dos).

Royal Ballet here I come! Next week, I'll be squeezing into my new tutu and going up to claim my new job from whoever the bloke is who's in charge. Let's hope he's not one of them! I'll tell him I'll be Juliet in *Romeo and Juliet* or I'm not being nothing, thanks very much. Never underestimate Katie Price. I know what sells, and if you've got Jordan with her 33 per cent extra bosom at the Royal Ballet, well, you've got a fucking sell-out on your hands (and that's not all, lads!).

What next for Jordan? My corporate adviser has long-term plans for me to go for the complete transplant, so that I emerge from the clinic just as one gi-normous bosom. I certainly think that'll help me with my long-term ambition to become a senior member of the Royal Family, because they need something like that to keep them in the headlines, don't they. Meanwhile, by the time you read this, I'll have signed the deal with Endemol to put their TV cameras in our luxury gold-plated bathroom for their new reality TV show *Peter and Jordan Go Toilet*. We've already got Andrex to sponsor the luxury quilted toilet paper and Aqualoo of Swindon to sponsor each flush. I want it to show the fans that I'm not just the super-glamorous Jordan but also the very real, very human Katie Price. What I always say is, for fuck's sake let's keep it natural.

Dr Frank Harbinger's A-Z Guide to Your Health Fears Today

Aardvarks, bites from: More and more people are coming to my clinic complaining that they have been bitten by this termite-eating nocturnal mammal with a tubular snout and long, extensible tongue. It is indeed a matter of growing concern. Many now estimate that the number of aardvarks in British homes may be as high as six million, though conservative estimates put the exact number in single figures. My advice to those who think they may be suffering from extensive aardvark bites is to avoid all aardvarks in future, and to make sure your cat-flap is fitted with an anti-aardvark radar device, available from all good hardware stores.

Advent calendar: Every December, at least a dozen patients – many of them children as young as three or four years of age – come to my clinic complaining of ACWSI, or Advent Calendar Wrist Strain Injury. This is a common complaint caused by the repetitive opening of the small cardboard doors or "gates" on advent calendars. My advice is to avoid the constant pressure on the wrist, thumb and forefinger of opening a door or "gate" every twenty-four hours; instead, open only one door or "gate" each December. This will give you the additional benefit of needing a new advent calendar just once every twenty-five years: any money saved may be spent on vitamin supplements.

Aspidistra: *A plant of the genus Aspidistra, with broad tapering leaves, native to the Far East and often grown as a house plant.*

Consumed in quantity, the aspidistra may cause stomach upsets and/or loss of appetite, but as part of a balanced diet its consumption should result in nothing more than odd sideways glances from friends and acquaintances.

Backache: More man-hours a year are lost to backache than to the common cold. But this may be due to misdiagnosis. Many of my patients come to me telling me of backache in their throat, knee, index finger or upper thigh. I inform them that the symptoms suggest that backache is not the complaint.

Incidentally, backache is, more often than not, incorrectly pronounced as "bak-ayk". In fact, its correct pronunciation is "bak-ark-ay". Its name is derived from a Dr Backache, from Nigeria, who discovered it – and kept discovering it – while repeatedly lifting a heavy weight without bending his knees.

Bedsock: Ensure that the bedsock is worn only on the foot. Placing the bedsock over the head may cause temporary blindness and/or a fugged-up feeling. Bedsocks should be worn to the proportion of one per foot. If one bedsock is worn over two or more feet, no attempt should be made to walk or run.

Botox: Caution must be taken at all times with the Botox facial treatment. Incorrectly applied, it can result in a hundred-fold increase in lines and wrinkles. Early casualties of misapplied Botox include distinguished poet W H Auden, 1980s movie star ET, and Ayesha, formerly youthful heroine of Rider Haggard's *She*.

Caber: More and more people are coming to my clinic with severe back problems caused by caber-tossing. Cabers should be tossed only under the strictest medical supervision. At present, the caber is nineteen foot long and weighs 119lb; this makes it wholly unsuitable for the very young and the very old, those who find it hard to lift heavy weights, and anyone suffering from a heart problem. But moves are at last under way to bring caber-tossing into line with government health and safety guidelines. By autumn 2007, the maximum permitted size for a caber will be three foot two inches long, with an upper weight limit of six pounds. "This can only be good news for the Highland Games," says the Under-Secretary of Health for Scotland. "At last the competition will be wide open to the weak, the infirm and the bed-ridden."

Cactus: *Plant with thick fleshy stem and spikes.* Should not be swallowed whole. If swallowed whole, consult your doctor. Following the success of *CactusWatch* on BBC Radio's *You and Yours*, from 2008 garden centres selling cacti will be obliged to erect encircling fences and paint all cactus spikes bright red to ensure the protection of the general public. "We welcome this long-overdue move," explains Sandra Askew, chief medical officer for the Victims of Cacti support group. "Every year, up to five people attempt to swallow a whole cactus. If the number increases, we will be faced with a nationwide epidemic of sore throats."

Cardigan: *Casual knitted jacket fastening down the front, usually with long sleeves.* Though putting on a cardigan can be useful as part of a controlled weight-loss programme, it does not provide all the exercise necessary for a normal healthy human being. Injuries from cardigans have risen dramatically in recent years, according to figures released by the official cardigan health watchdog, CARDI (Cardigan and Anorak-Related Deaths and Injuries).

Carving: When carving a joint of meat, be careful not to place a finger or fingers immediately beneath the knife before cutting vigorously as severe injury may result.

Castanets: *Two small concave pieces of hardwood held in the hands and clicked together as a rhythmic accompaniment, especially by Spanish dancers.* Used without due care, castanets may cause CWSI, or Castanet Wrist Sprain Injury. Castanets should never be inserted into the ears, or placed over the eyes when driving.

Daddy-long-legs: One in every eight adults in the UK has some experience of what we know as the daddy-long-legs syndrome. This is a technical term for the eerie feeling one experiences that one's leg has inadvertently fallen off and is lying just a few yards away on the floor, wall or ceiling. This feeling should pass within a matter or hours, unless, of course, you are indeed a daddy-long-legs, or crane fly, and your leg really has fallen off, in which case, don't worry: this is perfectly normal.

Dalmatian: The Dalmatian is known for its white coat with black spots, often mistaken for a black coat with white spots. These spots are perfectly normal in this breed of dog. However, if they begin to appear on you or your family, consult your doctor at once.

Earlobe: *Soft pendulous external part of the ear.* The earlobe is purely decorative. It should not be used for heavy lifting.

Echo: *The repetition of a sound by the reflection of sound waves.* If you sense you are hearing the same thing over again, you should consult your doctor. If you sense you are hearing the same thing over again, you should consult your doctor.

Emphasis: *Stress laid on a word or words to indicate special meaning or importance.* In recent years, the IE (Incorrect Emphasis) bug has infected many radio and television news organisations. The victims may well have no idea they are suffering from IE. A patient who has been suffering from this condition on a long-term basis, Sir Trevor Macdonald, came to me the other day and said, "Good NEWS, Doctor: I think I have BEEN cured. I am PRETTY sure I now no LONGER emphasise THE wrong word IN each sentence. I AM so grateful TO you."

Ermine: *White winter fur of the stoat, used as trimming for the robes of judges, peers, etc.* Every year, up to a dozen judges and peers complain that their robes of office have been biting them. Many of the new firms charged with creating these robes have not yet mastered the age-old techniques: many leave the stoats only partially sedated before stitching them to the velvet. In a major speech to the House of Lords last September, Baroness Jay was heard to squeal and holler for between five and ten minutes; it later emerged that she was suffering severe bites to the shin from her ermine trimming. But luckily none of her colleagues noticed, and many congratulated her afterwards on what they described as her most impassioned speech in ages.

Escalator: Every year, up to 73 people worldwide find themselves distracted by advertisements for lingerie on the underground and forget to jump off their escalators in time. One survivor now tours the world, offering trauma counselling to fellow survivors. He is 29-foot-long computer analyst Simon Arkwright.

Gazpacho: *Spanish soup with tomatoes, peppers, cucumbers, garlic, etc, invariably served cold.* Place whatever you wish in your gazpacho, but to be on the safe side avoid non-liquidised plastics and metals. Live fish are becoming increasingly fashionable in gazpacho, but their excessive splashing can lead to stains, so napkins should be placed across those areas of the body likely to be affected.

Golf: When people come to me and ask how they can reduce the amount of stress and tension in their lives, and how they can cut down on negative emotions such as irritability and exasperation, I advise them to give up golf at the earliest possible opportunity.

H: *Eighth letter of the alphabet.* Whenever a patient enters my surgery expressing fears for his own health, I ask him to stand in one corner and to try forming the letter H, with both arms up in the air and legs wide apart. If he succeeds in looking like the letter H, his health fears are, alas, confirmed, for his torso has now become no more than a short, thin horizontal line linking his outer limbs together, and there is no sign of a head anywhere.

Human shield: Every year or so, a patient comes to me and says, "Doctor, I have been invited to join a select group of people placed in the line of fire by an enemy power so as to fend off an attack on a military or industrial installation. Should I accept?" I direct them to the official government health guidelines on human shields, which suggest that there is no evidence that taking part in one is in any way injurious to the health of the individual, just so long as he or she doesn't inhale cigarette smoke, or drink more than two units of alcohol a day.

Iceberg: *A huge mass of ice floating in the sea with the greater part under water.* If you come across an iceberg in your bath, you should immediately consult an expert: it may be a metaphor, a simile, or at worst a symbol.

Introvert: *Person primarily concerned with his or her own thoughts.* Whenever a patient comes to me complaining about an attack of introversion, I make them snap out of it. "Well, what about me?" I ask.

Jar: When replacing the lid on a jar, be sure not to shut your fingers inside.

Jitterbug: *Fast dance, performed to swing music.* Never attempt to perform the jitterbug in the dentist's chair, even though the soft music in the headphones may demand it.

Kettle: *A vessel with a lid, spout and handle, for boiling water in.* Recently, a German patient of mine came to me complaining of being attacked by a kettle while out walking his dog in a field. At first, I doubted his story. "In this country, we keep the kettle in the kitchen. We never let it outdoors to roam around by itself, spouting hot water over one and all," I assured him. On closer enquiry, I discovered that the patient had in fact been attacked by a herd of cows.

Knitwear: A recent edition of *You and Yours*, Radio 4's daily danger alert, featured a panel of experts calling for tighter government controls on knitwear in the home and workplace. "As recently as 1986," said the presenter, Liz Barclay, "a housewife in Kidderminster found that a stray loop in her knitwear cardigan happened to catch on a doorlatch. Luckily, this particular housewife managed to free herself in a couple of seconds, thus avoiding starving to death. But in future, others in the same position might not be so lucky. Yet the government refuses to act."

Lang Syne, Auld: Many of my patients tell me that they often experience a queasy sensation while linking arms and singing "Auld Lang Syne" with neighbours and distant relatives on New Year's Eve. Others complain of nausea, stomach cramp and even projectile vomiting. This is a perfectly normal reaction to nostalgic get-togethers. It can easily be cured by entering a darkened room and watching a late-night horror film on satellite television.

Larry, as happy as: In fact, the Larry in question is a regular patient of mine, and in recent weeks he has been suffering from nervous exhaustion and mild depression. "Everyone expects me to be so happy all the time, doctor," he tells me. "The pressure is unbearable."

Macabre: *Grim, gruesome.* This useful adjective derives from the eighteenth-century Scottish health expert Dr Hamish MacAbre, whose pioneering diet book, *Dieting the MacAbre Way*, advocated eating nothing but celery for the rest of your life. After nearly 1,500 MacAbre dieters had met with untimely ends, it emerged that the MacAbre family owned the only celery farm north of the border, as well as the second largest chain of undertakers on the west coast.

Mangetout: *A variety of pea eaten whole, including the pod.* In the mid-1980s, it became fashionable in many leading London restaurants and country house hotels to eat mangetout. Until then, plates of mangetout had been employed primarily to scare birds, or, singly, as draught-excluders in dolls houses.

Many of my patients asked me whether mangetout was good for you. "In the absence of dental floss, a string from the mangetout can prove invaluable," I informed them. A surprise survey in late 1988 revealed that not a single restaurant-goer had ever enjoyed eating a mangetout.

Manipulation: Many contemporary alternative therapies call for some form of manipulation, often involving loud cracking noises. My own Harbinger Homoeopathic Health Clinic (est. 1999) is specifically targeted at those who prefer to walk with their torso at right-angles to the rest of the body, and their head bent backwards and to the side.

Mascarpone: *A soft mild Italian cream cheese.* Not to be confused with Nivea.

Medusa: *Chief of the Gorgons.* Health experts now believe that Medusa would have been better off employing a non-biological shampoo, plus a conditioner for problem hair.

Nectar: *(In Greek mythology) the drink of the gods.* In a health scare in 2000 BC, major fears were expressed that all nectar was contaminated, so all supplies were recalled by manufacturers. For two months, the gods had to make do with hot chocolate, mineral water or orange squash.

Non-committal: More and more people come into my surgery asking me whether I have a cure for their lack of commitment. I tell them that I may have, but on the other hand I may not, I'll get back to them.

Non sequitur: *A conclusion that does not follow from the evidence given.* Many patients who come into my surgery complain of suffering from mild attacks of non sequitur. I remind them that it is a Thursday, and that anyway Canberra is the capital of Australia.

Nostalgia: *Yearning for things of the past.* In the old days, your GP would have thought nothing of bicycling twelve miles to your house, dabbing a little ointment on that spot on your chin, taking a quick look at the cat's boil, and popping out to check the oil level on your motor-car before cycling twelve miles back again through a seasonal blizzard. But nowadays we ask patients with life-threatening ailments to stay at home and follow the step-by-step guidelines provided by our excellent health-care leaflet ("Health in the Community:

Performing Your Own Heart Surgery With Kitchen Utensils") available for £2.99 from the Department of Health.

Organic: I always recommend my patients buy organic vegetables. If they say there are few organic outlets in the area, I advise them to make their own organic vegetables by taking these three simple steps: (i) buy a non-organic vegetable but give the greengrocer twice as much money for it; (ii) carve it into a peculiar shape; (iii) coat it in mud; (iv) with a small knife, gouge out a tunnel-like hole and place a creepy-crawly inside it; (v) boil and serve.

Quake: *Colloq. for earthquake. Convulsion of the earth's crust.* A major earthquake on the fault-line between Berkshire and Hampshire is long overdue. My book *The Basingstoke Survivors Manual* is to be published next month, the follow-up to my two previous bestsellers in the series, *Among the Ruins of Andover* (2005) and *Staying Alive in Hartley Wintney* (2004).

Quilt complex: *The mental obsession with feeling culpable for having created a folksy bedspread.*

Red carpet: The red carpet has often proved a safety hazard. Only last week, a red carpet specially unfurled for a Royal visit to the Arndale Centre in Doncaster refurled itself without warning. The emergency services are still working three hours a day trying to extract HRH Princess Michael of Kent, who was last seen bearing a posy and a faltering smile. ARC (Action on Red Carpets) continues to call for an outright ban.

Right-handed: A shock survey published this week by the IBO (Institute of the Bleeding Obvious) warns that right-handed people are dying in far greater numbers than left-handed people. The IBA further warns that the elderly are more likely to die than the young, and that people who repeatedly look over the top of high buildings are far more prone to vertigo than those who spend all their time at ground level.

Safety pin: *Brooch-shaped pin with protected point.* There are increasing concerns about the safety of safety pins. A Nevada-based research centre recently issued figures suggesting that eight out of ten volunteers who were forced to swallow a handful of safety pins felt either "ill" or "very ill" after the experience. Many experts are now calling for new safety guidelines on safety pins, and Esther

Rantzen has lent her voice to the campaign for safer safety pins. "Children can easily open a safety pin and hurt themselves," says one leading campaigner. "It is absurd that safety pins can still be opened. There is an urgent need for legislation to force manufacturers to seal them closed. Meanwhile, top film director Michael Winner is calling for a national monument in Hyde Park to commemorate all victims of safety pins. "I am delighted to say that it will be officially opened by my very good friend Her Majesty the Queen, weather permitting," he says.

Soup: Recent Health and Safety Guidelines on the Serving of Soup issued by the Department of Health recommend that soup is unsuitable for serving in a sandwich. The report further warns that pouring soup into a toaster can result in electrical malfunction. "I am delighted to say, John, that I welcome these new guidelines," Health Secretary Patricia Hewitt said on the *Today* programme. "For far too many years under the Conservatives, soup continued to be swept under the carpet."

Stick: *Thin shoot of wood.* A recent survey suggests that, contrary to earlier fears, playing with sticks may well be safe for children of all ages. "All the new evidence points to the fact that playing with sticks is risk-free," confirms the report, commissioned by the Stick Marketing Board.

Tank top: *Sleeveless close-fitting upper garment, often in bright colours, with a scoop neck.* Results of a poll of over 2,000 patients conducted by the *British Medical Journal* showed that 98 per cent of those interviewed felt either "secure" or "very secure" when examined by a doctor in a suit and tie, or in a white surgical uniform. Only 2 per cent said they preferred it if their doctor opted for the "Gilbert O'Sullivan" look of a brightly coloured tank top and shorts and a schoolboy cap.

Thing: *Shortened form of thingy, which is itself an abbreviation for thingummyjig.* When patients come to me for psychoanalysis, I always ask them to describe their most recent dream to me. "Well, there was this sort of great big ...THING," they begin. I then encouage them to go on about it at length; meanwhile, I retire to an adjoining room with a paperback book or motoring magazine.

Victorian novel: In the Victorian novel, a minor character with a slight sniff in chapter two will have developed flu by chapter five, double pneumonia by chapter six and will be dead by chapter seven.

WXYZ: Many of my patients come to me complaining of headaches, fuzzy vision and prolonged feelings of inertia. Asked whether they have recently been playing Scrabble they invariably confirm that they have. To help them with their addiction, I ask them to take a course of a high-scoring seven-letter word, first letter Z third letter X, sixth letter Y, last letter W.

Department of Education and Skills

The Historian's Life:
The Lost Diaries of A L Rowse

December 10, 1970

Typical! The third-rate nincompoops who compose the judging panel have once again turned down my application for the Nobel Prize for Literature. I hate the guts of the modern world, with its oafish ignorance of true value. Instead, they have awarded the prize to, of all things, a bald Russian with a beard.

He has, it seems, spent two decades in the Gulag. So jolly what? He can spend another two decades there, for all I care. The only book of his I have managed to plough through – *A Day in the Life of Ivan Hoodjamaflip* – is dreary, dreary, dreary, though I suppose one must be thankful the Day did not extend to the full Weekend.

What must one do to have one's worth recognised in this shift-less, tasteless, trivial modern age? It seems that nowadays, all one has to do to win a prize is clip a beard on, book into the Gulag for a few days and scowl for the cameras. Not only is Solzhenitsyn worthless but one couldn't help notice he has fat legs too. He now takes his place among a gallery of overrated Russians including Pasternak (wholly lacks that great Cornish quality of sympathy), Count Tolstoy (wordy! wordy! wordy!), and Dostoevsky (oh, do stop all that snivelling, Fyodor!).

July 9, 1973

After snubbing that dreadful skunk A J P Taylor in the street – a third-rater if ever there was one – I pay a call on Gary Glitter, a popular chanteur. I find him lying beside a kidney-shaped swimming pool (vulgar! vulgar! vulgar!) clad from top to toe in a one-piece silver suit.

He has a strong look of Rebecca West – always much over-estimated as second-rate by the third-raters who decide these matters. For want of anything better, I ask him whether he has considered putting pen to paper. He looks askance. "I Didn't Know I Loved You (Till I Saw You Rock 'n' Roll)," he says.

I am flummoxed. No one has ever said this to me before.

"Do You Wanna Touch Me?" he adds.

Something snaps. "Most certainly not," I reply. "Never have, never will."

I make a furious exit, once again boldly defying the moronic idiocy of this detestable age.

June 8, 1975

It is not often I visit the moving pictures. The only one I ever watched all the way through featured that fifth-rate vulgarian John Wayne togged up in cowboy hat, check blouson and baggy trousers. How one loathes such sissies.

But today I make an exception. As I pass the Odeon in Leicester Square, I notice a moving picture with the commendably straight-forward title of *The Bitch* is about to commence. Imagining it will be about my former colleague A J P Taylor, I queue up and purchase a ticket from the kiosk.

"Popcorn?" says the lady.

"How dare you!" I reply.

I sit among the Idiot People munching themselves into well-deserved oblivion. The curtain rises on a most unedifying spectacle. A woman of uncertain years (a Miss Joan Collins, I am later to discover) is in a lift with a well-built, impressively bronzed young man with the most beautiful blue eyes. Before one can say Jack Robinson, the lady has removed every last stitch of clothing and has thrown herself, bosoms and all, at the poor defenceless fellow. It is the purest demonstration of everything one has grown to loathe about womankind. Now I know what the third-raters mean when they talk about a "horror movie".

November 19, 1976

To dinner with Her Majesty and Prince Philip. Buckingham Palace v bourgeois. No furniture worth noticing. Paintings very second-rate, some third- or even fourth-rate. With all their money, I would have made it a real treasure house. But they simply can't be bothered. I sit at the over-polished table with mounting impatience.

It is one of the great unfairnesses of my life that I was not born into a senior position in the Royal Family. Queen Victoria remains a vastly overrated figure. I would undoubtedly have brought much more zest to the role, and I would have made infinitely more of myself than that little dumpling of a woman ever managed. Yet she continues to get rapturous reviews and worldwide fame, while all my work is dismissed with a supercilious sneer by jealous rivals.

I toy with proposing marriage to Princess Anne, and plotting my advancement from there. I tentatively suggest such a plan to HM. She curtly informs me that her daughter is already spoken for. I curse this feeble, peremptory age!

April 27, 1981

Poor, dear Hughie Trevor-Roper. I really couldn't feel more desperately sorry for him. Along with so many other first-rate minds, one always held his scholarship in such high regard. But now his reputation has been smashed to smithereens by his over-hasty authentication of the so-called *Hitler Diaries*. Oh, deary, deary me! It makes one want to weep!

On the other hand, what good would weeping do for poor, absurd, fallen Hughie? None whatsoever. Far better for him that we should all laugh out loud, and join in all the fun at witnessing a once-revered colleague falling flat on his silly face. It's what he would have wanted.

When the mirth has begun to subside, I pick up my pen and write a letter to poor old ruined Hughie, offering him whatever help I can give. "I see that my local 'branch' of Victoria Wine is advertising for a junior sales assistant, no experience necessary," I venture. "Do let me know whether this might be up your street – a friend in need, etc, etc."

And with this, I help myself to another consoling glass of first-rate champagne. Most agreeable.

January 22, 1983

I have never seen a reason to trust the Swedes. A plague on the smorgasbord! No surprise, then, that Bjorn Borg should announce his retirement from professional tennis after only winning Wimbledon a paltry five times.

Borg is bitterly jealous of me, of course. Always has been, always will be. HE never discovered the true identity of Shakespeare's Dark Lady – and he'll never forgive me for it.

Surveying the ruins of Borg's career offers one cause to be thankful that one was never tempted to become an international tennis star oneself. Of course, had one gone that erroneous path, one's prizes, cups, awards, and so forth would most certainly have exceeded his. That is not in question. But all those wretched forehands and backhands and "serves", etc, etc, would inevitably have distracted one from one's historical researches. Needless to say, the world of scholarship, already teeming with the petty jealousies of third-rate minds, would have leapt up and down with delight if only one had frittered away one's energy on winning Wimbledon umpteen times. But posterity? Ah, posterity would never have forgiven one.

January 28, 1986

I learn from the wireless that the American space "shuttle" (horrid word) Challenger has exploded seconds after lift-off. Serves them jolly well right. When will these tenth-raters learn to place me in charge of their operations? Instead, they leave it to nincompoops and incompetents. Of course, these sissies at Mission Control are interested only in themselves. Their instinct is to engineer matters in such a way that their achievements catch up – surpass, perchance! – my own. What nonsense! Do they not realise that I am widely regarded as the foremost expert in the world on the vast majority of subjects? In a huff, they conceitedly disregard me and "blast off" without so much as a by your leave. And look what happens! When will they ever learn?

June 22, 1987

The newspapers let it be known that Fred Astaire, self-appointed "King of the Hoofers", has died. To my mind, he was always desperately overrated. He would simply never keep still, and was always jigging about, even in the most inopportune moments. That is no way to behave. Had he performed like that in any halfway-decent library he would have been formally disciplined and asked to leave.

"I'm putting on my top hat, white tie and tails," he would warble. Very clever, I don't think! It didn't seem to occur to the poor ninny that this attire was vulgarly inappropriate for most of the tiresome, third-rate social occasions – "Tupperware parties" and whatnot – to which he ever had a hope of being invited.

I was always a better dancer than Astaire, but of course they would never admit it, would they, because they prefer to elevate the flat-footed over the truly majestic. How I detest and hate everything about the modern world, a world in which the one or two dancers really worth noticing are left to sit alone with their diaries while the fifth-raters with two left feet are exalted beyond measure!

Crash, Bang, Splat: The Duchess of York's Learning Difficulties

THE DUCHESS OF YORK wrote her children's book *Budgie the Little Helicopter* some years ago. Sadly, it does not stand the test of time, as I discovered when I re-read it yesterday. Though it is short (shorter than this piece) it is quite remarkably repetitive. Even the very first sentence – "It was a hot, hot day" – contains the same adjective twice. Much of the rest of the work is given over to noises. "Pippa soared. She looped the loop. Whee. Flew on her side. Brrr. Then swooped. Eoww," reads the whole of page nine. "Aaargh! Crash! Bang! Splat!" reads page twenty-five.

So it is with mixed emotions that one greets the news that the Duchess is staging a return to the world of literature. She is writing four new children's books based on a red-headed doll she designed last year called "Little Red". Apparently, one of these dolls was discovered intact amid the wreckage of the World Trade Center. "In emotional scenes" the doll was returned to the Duchess, who now carries it around everywhere with her.

It may be unseemly to mention this, but in past decades rag dolls have miraculously appeared in ruins the world over. To be brutally frank, this is because for many years a rag doll has been a standard item in the photojournalist's knapsack, ready for placing in front of any scene of devastation as a poignant symbol of loss, hope, innocence and so forth.

The Duchess of York's American spokesman, Mr Gerry Casanova, seems uncertain if all, or, indeed, any of the proceeds from *The Adventures of Little Red* will be given to charity. "It may not really earn very much. I don't know whether they have worked out what the charity portion will be – if there is one," he says.

Will Little Red be Little Read? There are already mumblings that the Duchess may have overstepped the mark. The Rev David Smith of Clevedon, near Bristol, who lost his cousin in the Twin Towers attack, says: "If she is seen to be making any money by association with the tragic events of September 11 then, particularly in the US, all hell will break loose."

My guess is that the world has more than enough children's stories about lovable little dolls. If making a doll a redhead made it more cuddly, then Mr Roger Scruton, Mr Simon Heffer and Mr Paul Johnson would already have been turned into a full range of nursery products.

(May 23, 2002)

Family Conjugations

Our child is gifted
Your child is precocious
Their child is a know-all.

Our child is shy
Your child is socially rather awkward
Their child is offhand.

Our child plays the violin
Your child learns the violin
They make their child do the violin.

Our child is friendly
Your child is a chatterbox
Their child is always answering back.

We encourage our child
You expect the most from your child
They are pushy parents.

Our child is self-motivated
Your child doesn't need other children
Their child is a loner.

Our child is not academic
Your child has learning difficulties
Their child is backward.

Our child is a keen sportsman
Your child loves to win
Their child is a bad loser.

My child is sensitive
Your child is over-sensitive
Their child is a cry-baby.

Our child is a natural performer
Your child loves to be the centre of attention
Their child is a little madam.

Our child wants to be a barrister
Your child likes arguing the toss
Their child never stops that awful whining.

Our child is a perfectionist
Your child has to have everything just so
Their child is anally retentive.

Our child has a lively imagination
Your child indulges in fantasy play
Their child is a compulsive liar.

My daughter keeps up with fashion
Your daughter knows how to attract the boys
Their daughter will end up pregnant.

Our teenager is at that interesting age
Your teenager is going through a phase
Their teenager has spots.

Our son has an inquiring mind
Your son can't stop asking questions
Their child is John Humphrys.

Our son finishes what's on his plate
Your son will eat anything
Their son has an eating disorder.

Our son is affectionate
Your son is clingy
Their son is a mummy's boy.

Our child is an all-rounder
Your child is always round
Their child is all round.

Our child needed a change
Your child didn't fit in
Their child was expelled.

Our daughter is advanced
Your daughter is precocious
Their daughter is too clever by half.

Our boy is computer literate
Your boy is computer mad
Their boy never comes out of his room.

Our son is a good sport
Your son is a good loser
Their son is a loser.

Our daughter is an avid reader
Your daughter always has her head in a book
Their daughter has no social skills.

Our child is full of beans
Your child is full of surprises
Their child is full of drugs.

Our boy is good at delegating
Your boy is self-assertive
Their boy is a bully.

Our son is a lateral thinker
Your son finds it hard to concentrate
Their son has attention deficit disorder.

Our child has a healthy appetite
Your child is well covered
Their child is clinically obese.

Our son fits in well
Your son is easily led
Their son has a weak character.

Our son questions authority
Your son is a bit of a rebel
Their son could be out within three years.

Our daughter is honest
Your daughter is brutally honest
Their daughter is brutal.

Our daughter stands up for herself
Your daughter won't take no for an answer
Did you hear what their daughter said to them?

Our son likes his own company
Your son keeps himself to himself
Their son is a loner.

Our child is bright
Your child is precocious
Their child answers back.

We are caring parents
You are concerned parents
They are neurotic parents.

Our teenager is going through a phase
Your teenager is going through my purse
Their teenager is going through the magistrates' courts.

Teach Yourself Jordan

Future Study Notes: Jordan: A Whole New World
Set text for A-Level English, June 2057

HISTORICAL BACKGROUND: Now aged 80, Lady Jordan of Titchfield is the distinguished recipient of many honours. Recently appointed Chancellor of Oxford Starbucks University (formerly Oxford University), she also chairs the Government Advisory

Committee on Public Morality. She recently received the Orange Prize Lifetime Achievement Award for her 40-volume list of autobiographies, which are all now available in Everyman Classics. They span her first, groundbreaking, *Being Jordan* (2004) to her mature reflections on a life spent in public service, *Who You Bloody Staring At?* (2054).

From pioneering appearances on the classic prestige landmark television series, *I'm a Celebrity – Get Me Out Of Here!* (2004) through to her recent award-winning survey of life-drawing since the Renaissance, *Tits in Art* (2055), Lady Jordan has become a well-loved institution. Three years ago, she was invited to deliver the prestigious Reith Lectures, for which she took as her topic "Confronting the Global Dilemma: Enlargement or Reduction?"

ADDITIONAL READING: Further to her autobiographical works (see above), *The Oxford Murdoch Guide to English Literature* lists another ten books by Lady Jordan, among them her collected love poems, *Fancy a Shag* (2039), and a collection of pensees, aphorisms and reflections, *Me, I'm Well Pissed Off* (2042).

Scholarly works on Jordan are now numbered in their many hundreds, but few have surpassed Professor Christopher Ricks's pioneering analysis *Jordan's XXXL Visions of Sin* (p 732, Faber, 2012), in which he argues the case of her Miltonic proportions. Other works of note include Naomi Wolf's *All Hands: The Portrayal of Men in the Works of Jordan* (Harvard, 2022), which offers a striking new feminist perspective.

COURSES: Several of Britain's leading universities offer Jordan Studies, among them Max Clifford University (formerly Durham), The Piers Morgan Institute (formerly University of East Anglia) and The London School of Fayed (formerly London School of Economics). Bristol University also offers The Lady Jordan Creative Writing course specifically for former glamour models, further details obtainable from the Vice Chancellor, Dame Jodie Marsh OM.

KEY AREAS FOR GENERAL REVISION

The examiner will want to assess your knowledge of the character and general history of Jordan, as well as how complete your command of her language is. Key Jordan phrases you may be tested on include: "*free zin m'titsov; nwan duz thatun gezzaway wiv it; dressder frill; kinder gross.*"

The examiner will also be anxious to test your knowledge of the other principal characters in Jordan's life. A sample question would be: "*Dwight; Dane; Dwayne. Compare and contrast these three former boyfriends of Jordan, citing dates.*"

There is also likely to be a question involving statistics. These may even involve mathematics and/or geometry. A sample question would be: "*Go from 32C to 34HH in three simple operations. Reduce from 34HH to 32F before changing your mind.*"

HISTORICAL CONTEXT AND COMPREHENSION
– SPECIMEN EXAMINATION PAPER

"*Posh has never admitted to having surgery, but I promise you she's had a boob job. One night in the ladies toilets I showed her mine and she showed me hers. She knows that I know that she's had it done, so I don't know why she denies it. You only have to look at her – skinny all over except her boobs. I know that she's faking it. I can spot a boob job a mile off.*" (extract from *Being Jordan* (2004))

Read and inwardly digest the above passage, then answer the following questions:

a) Who or what is Posh? Why? How? Whatever? (5 points)
b) What does the author mean by the phrase "boob job"?
c) What is the difference between "boob job" and "bob-a-job", if any?
d) How does the author bring out the theme of rivalry between herself and Posh?
e) With the aid of diagrams showing distance in kilometres, explain how you would "spot a boob job a mile off", using the binoculars provided.

Department of Environment, Food and Rural Affairs

Voices of the Countryside

Frederick Forsyth: It is a well-known fact that the Blair junta has commandeered army bases the length and breadth of this beleaguered isle in order to insert ultra-high frequency listening devices beneath the fur of a crack-squadron of a quarter of a million highly trained foxes.

Make no mistake. These foxes – full colonels in Blair's Secret Army, with the medals to prove it – are then sent out to spy on the civilian population – that's you and me, chum – reporting direct to Comrade Blunkett.

Cunning creature, the fox. I had one come to my door the other day asking to read my meter. Cap, uniform, identity badge, the lot. But I was alerted to his true identity when I heard the tell-tale swish of his tail.

"What's your name?" I demanded.

"Weynard," he replied.

The game was up! For all their mastery of disguise, foxes still can't pronounce their "Rs".

I let him have it with both barrels.

Quentin Tarantino: I ain't gonna take no f—in' insults from dumbass fox, man, like you know what I'm sayin', I'm sayin' if that dumbass fox comes up to me, right and like, says somethin' foxy, like, uhuh, Tony Blair says, like, you can't hunt me no more you dumbass motherf—er, then I'll baadass his brains till the blood spurts over the f—in' walls, you know what I'm sayin'? You gotta problem with that?

Sir Tim Rice:
"If I had the finance
I'd support Countryside Alliance!
So let's all blow the horn
For the folks who came to town!
Oh, there's nothing of which I'm such a fan as
Marching with banners!"

Sir Edward Heath: Over the course of a long and, may I add, distinguished career, I have had the pleasure of meeting Monsieur Reynard on a number of occasions. We have not always seen eye to eye. Far from it. I do not necessarily agree with the way he goes around at dead of night, killing baby chicks with his bare teeth. Personally, that is not the way I would go about it. But let's not be Little Englanders. We must recognise the overwhelming need for those from different cultures to exercise a degree of self-determination.

In this spirit, Monsieur Reynard and I have enjoyed a productive and civilised relationship for a great many years. It is a relationship based on mutual respect and understanding. He prefers to go around killing baby chicks: on the whole, I would prefer he didn't go around killing baby chicks. So after a great deal of friendly negotiation, we reached a compromise appropriate to both parties: he was allowed to kill baby chicks, and I was allowed to express the need for a more satisfactory alternative.

That's the way one should go about these things.

Regrettably, that's something my successor as Leader of the Conservatives (let's not name names) never understood. Incidentally, Monsieur Reynard and I still exchange Christmas cards. I don't imagine he sends one to HER!!!!!

Nicky Haslam: So, so common! Foxes are so common! No one should wear a tail in public, and as for whiskers they are very, very, VERY common.

It's terribly common to be chased by hounds. Where do you end up? Either getting desperately dirty down some dreadfully cramped little hole – or ripped to shreds! And – pah! – there is nothing commoner than getting ripped to shreds.

I avoid celebrity foxes like the plague. Basil Brush is the absolute pits. That awful throaty laugh! Common, common, common! Has he never heard of lozenges? What of the other foxes? Sam Fox is terribly passé, dear. Appearing topless on Page Three of the *Sun* is common. As for Charles James Fox, it's very common to oppose William Pitt. Edward Fox wasn't common until he played the man who tried to assassinate de Gaulle, which was really very, very common indeed. And Liam Fox is a little common, too: it's common to be in Opposition.

The Rt Hon John Prescott: Let's free bank about this. I don't remain not firmly unopposed to shunting and hooting. I don't blame anyone for staking a hand. But let no one claim that this Labourised governmentable hasn't backed over bentwards to preserve our countryside with its hows and courses. On the other hand in question, let's not forget the people of the clowns and titties. They have their tights rue, you know.

Iain Duncan Smith: Let's be absolutely clear about one thing. Two things. One and a half things. I know exactly where I stand on this issue. I stand full square behind it, marching shoulder to shoulder, leading from the front. Let's not push it to one side. And let me add one more thing. Two more things. The way ahead has never been more clear. Let's turn around, close our eyes for one minute and take a long, hard look at it. As a party, we support the right of those who want to do something about the sort of thing we should be doing to support those who are demanding the right to support what they believe in. Decisive leadership: most people feel that may well be a good thing, in the long run.

Nineteen Things You Didn't Know About Glastonbury

Drugs have always played a part in the Glastonbury festival, however hard the police have tried to crack down on them. Even in the comparatively carefree days of the 1950s and early 1960s, drugs were already in circulation. Many who attended the legendary performance by the Black and White Minstrels on the main stage in 1958 remember a large amount of Vick inhalers being passed around, along with an unknown number of Strepsils; in 1961, Frank Ifield's headlining performance of "I Remember You" was marred by three arrests for suspected possession of cherry-based Tunes.

2 Even in the height of summer, the English climate can prove variable, but dedicated Glastonbury festival-goers will let nothing deter them. The freak tidal wave that hit Glastonbury in the wet June of 1978 claimed more than 8,000 festival-goers from the low-lying areas of the site, but it did nothing to stop bill-topper Joe Cocker from completing a memorable set, with additional encores. "Joe always sings with his eyes shut," explained his manager. "The first he knew about the disaster was on the evening news."

3 The festival is organised by legendary farmer Michael Eavis, who began life as bass-player with the chart-topping band the Wurzels. One of the problems he must tackle each year is what to do with his displaced farm livestock for the duration of the festival. Eavis generally deploys the horses as roadies and the chickens and geese as sound engineers, while some of the senior cows are happy to help out in the Frisbee Field, demonstrating throwing techniques to intermediate classes.

4 Five summers ago, one of Eavis's billy goats volunteered to step in when the drummer with Oasis was taken poorly. All went well until he insisted upon performing a lengthy drum solo in the middle of "Roll With It". Lead singer Liam Gallagher furiously ordered him offstage, adding that he needed "a good thumpin'". The dejected billy goat was replaced on drums by an aggressive Welsh collie, who proceeded to round up the remaining members of the group. He then led them offstage and into a waiting truck, where they were sheared and, where necessary, castrated.

5 In 1997, for the very first time, the Glastonbury festival was officially included in the English Social Season, after Wimbledon and just before Henley. To qualify for this honour, a number of minor changes had to be made, including the addition of a Royal Box adjacent to the Pyramid Stage. In 1998, HM the Queen Mother watched the Stone Roses from the box, accompanied by

the Earl of Wessex on tambourine. This year, Princess Michael of Kent is hosting a finger buffet in the Royal Box, attended by Sir Cliff Richard, Sir Elton John, Sir Mick Jagger, Sir Paul McCartney and Sir Blobby.

6 In line with Glastonbury's new social status, before the festival debutantes are instructed by Lady Elizabeth Anson on the correct way to blag a roach, followed by a lecture with slides on the Art of Getting Totally Out of It by a former bass guitarist with Blodwyn Pig.

7 This would have been veteran disc jockey John Peel's forty-eighth Glastonbury festival. "In the early days," he reminisced in his autobiography, "the stage was an upturned tea chest, the Edgar Broughton Band were the headliners, there was just the single toilet for 10,000 fans, and someone called Banana ran the medical tent, naked. But now Paul McCartney is appearing on the Pyramid Stage, each festival-goer is guaranteed his or her own ensuite bathroom, only paid-up Bupa members are admitted to the medical tent, and everyone is invited to the Conservative Party coffee morning fundraiser hosted by Mike Ancram in the marquee next to the Mercedes showroom. You know, the kids these days – they don't know what they're missing."

8 Over the past ten years, the Glastonbury site has suffered from increasingly ingenious attempts at breakouts, leading to ever-higher fencing. In 1997, while headliners the Prodigy were playing, a group of six young people decided that they couldn't take it any more. They attempted to make a bid for freedom by constructing a makeshift aeroplane from old tent pegs and flying it over the festival fence, but their plane was shot down by security, and they were forced to watch the remaining five numbers, including a twelve-minute version of "Smack My Bitch Up" complete with drum solo.

9 In 2000, two festival-goers executed a daring escape during a Hawkwind reunion by donning long beards and disguising themselves as members of top American blues-rock trio ZZ Top and slipping out through the artistes' exit. But within less than three hours, they were tracked down by festival security using helicopters fitted with the latest infrared tracking devices. Amnesty International is at present campaigning for their release.

This year, the fencing alone is said to have cost £1 million. "There were no reports of successful escapes," says festival organiser Michael Eavis. "It was money well spent."

10 In recent years, critics claim Glastonbury has become a good deal less "alternative", the cost of tickets – this year over £100 – discriminating against the less well-off. But as one of the Duchess of Devonshire's party maintained yesterday, the general spirit remains much the same. "There's still a tremendously easy-going, democratic atmosphere at Glastonbury, with even some of the more minor public schools being allowed to slip in," says Sir Roy Strong, former head of the Victoria and Albert Museum, "and I'm simply delighted that cravats are now permitted as a smart/casual alternative to ties. Let's face it, in this warm weather they are SO much easier on the neck."

11 For the past five years, the Rees-Mogg family has taken a box in the dress-circle at Glastonbury, alongside boxes taken by corporate sponsors British Telecom and Prince and Princess Michael of Kent. "My memories of Glastonbury now stretch back nigh-on thirty years, and by now I should feel confident of mastering its traditions," writes Lord Rees-Mogg. "But the question continues to haunt: how much should one tip the lead guitarist?"

12 To the Healing Field and the Craft Field was this year added the Stock Field, where members of the audience can deal direct with leading brokers on the international commodity market.

13 The problem of identifying exactly who is performing 500 yards away in the distance was finally solved this year. For a modest fee, members of the audience may now receive regular text messages informing them of artiste and song, and a further message telling them when to applaud, and for how long.

14 The longest drum solo was by Rik Dobson of Hawkwind in 1971, during a performance of their epic "In Search of Space". It began in the early evening of July 11 and ended shortly before lunchtime on July 16, by which time the rest of the band were onstage in Rome. Dobson always performed with his eyes shut "for maximum concentration". When he finally opened his eyes, he found that the festival had closed, and that he was drumming in a fenced-off corner of the annual Berkshire County Show. The

complete drum solo is now available in a sixty-six-CD Box Set, *The Legendary Dobson*, on the Dobson Label.

15 The only senior Conservative politician ever to have performed live at a rock festival is Sir Malcolm Rifkind, who was the replacement bass player with Deep Purple when they played at Knebworth in 1967. Best-known back then by his nickname "The Rif", Sir Malcolm went onstage in white semi-flared loon pants and a scoop-neck tie-dye T-shirt. But even in his youth, he preferred the less radical approach. "The other members of the band had smiley badges that said, 'Make Love Not War'," he recalls, "but my own smiley badge had a more purposeful expression on its face, and wore glasses, and its slogan said 'Best Get Married First'."

16 The alternative tents at Glastonbury this year included the Lucy Clayton Manners and General Deportment Tent, where festival-goers could go to improve their vowels and posture. "Liam Gallagher dropped in on Saturday morning," says the principal of the college, Dame Dorothy Agnew, "and when he left us in the evening he was standing with a lovely straight back saying 'Thanks awfully' to the Festival porters."

17 Traditionally, festivals have a strongly egalitarian ethos. "There's no snobbery at Glastonbury," explains veteran festival-goer Kate Moss. "Just so long as no one thinks they can just walk past security and stray into the VIP area."

18 Few major painters have immortalised a rock festival on canvas, though many experts believe that Picasso's *Guernica* was based largely on his experiences at Glastonbury in the late 1960s.

19 Since 1997, Glastonbury has included a special staff tent, where those in service to leading rock stars can change out of their livery in order to mingle with ordinary festival-goers in their time off from their duties. "Mr Sting is a most gracious employer, most gracious indeed," says his butler, Geoffrey. "This year he permitted us to nip out for the White Stripes just as soon as we'd finished on the silver."

Eight Anti-Social Animals

(I) THE FIDGETY MONKEY

Robert Cusack, forty-five, has been found guilty of attempting to smuggle endangered species into America.

When customs officials at Los Angeles airport opened Mr Cusack's suitcase, a tropical bird fluttered out. This prompted them to take their investigations a step further. When they ordered Mr Cusack to drop his pants, they discovered two ten-inch pygmy monkeys. They had, it emerged, been stuffed into Mr Cusack's underpants throughout his 8,200-mile flight from Thailand. "The little critters were in surprisingly good condition," commented the prosecutor, Joseph Johns.

Bad enough to be born a ten-inch pygmy monkey, you might think; still worse to be a ten-inch pygmy monkey stuffed for seventeen hours into Mr Cusack's underpants. If I were a Buddhist, I might wonder what sort of disgraceful behaviour these creatures had got up to in a previous life.

One feels sorry, too, for whoever was sitting next to Mr Cusack throughout the long flight from Thailand. We have all experienced the nuisance of fellow passengers who can't sit still and are always wriggling this way and that. But imagine the horror of glancing down at one's neighbour's trousers only to see them jiggle about of their own accord, possibly accompanied by sinister squeaking and scratching noises. Worse still if a tiny little hand were to pop out through the fly buttons, perhaps in search of a selection of sugared almonds or some other in-flight snack. This truly is the stuff of nightmares.

In these tense times, Mr Cusack was lucky to have got away without being set upon by his fellow passengers. Given the choice of sitting next to Richard Reid, with his exploding shoes, or Mr Cusack with his vivacious underpants, most of us would plump for Mr Reid. Of course, the worst-case scenario would be a pair of exploding underpants, but let's not put ideas into people's heads.

(October 12, 2002)

(II) THE KIND RAT

The rat population of Britain has increased by nearly a third in the past four years, according to the National Pest Technicians Association. Rats are now believed to outnumber human beings.

Rats have little to recommend them. Speaking for myself, I particularly dislike their tails. Their supporters would no doubt argue that the poor rats were born with them, and should not be criticised for something they cannot change. But if I were a rat, I would make the effort to cover my tail in cotton wool and act like a squirrel. It would be the least I could do.

The rat explosion has led to a number of unpleasant articles against them, full of incriminating details. Their teeth are apparently harder than aluminium or copper, allowing them to gnaw through cables. They can squeeze through holes no bigger than a man's thumb, and are able to swim up the U-bends of lavatories. They also have sex twenty times a day, and urinate eighty times a day, which must make them a nightmare on long car journeys.

With all these fresh revelations, rats must now be the most unpopular animals on the planet. It can only be a matter of time before their appointed representative is spotted knocking on the door of Mr Max Clifford. For an agreed fee, Mr Clifford will then drum up headlines such as "Rat Saves Drowning Tot", "Cilla: I Cried On Kind Ratty's Shoulder" and "Brave Rat Condemns Sicko Perverts". Then we will all like them once more, though I for one will still not welcome them popping unannounced through the U-bend of my lavatory.

(January 23, 2003)

(III) THE WANNABE WALLABY

Mr and Mrs Tony Meeghan were surprised to discover bloodstains near the basement window of their home in Henley-on-Thames in Oxfordshire. Naturally, they suspected that a burglar had cut himself when trying to force his way in. However, tests on the blood indicate that the intruder was a wallaby. Apparently, the creature bounced into the sunken area in front of the basement window, and was then unable to get out.

There have been a number of other sightings of wallabies in the area. Jane Martin, who lives at Lower Assenden, says she was driving along a country road when she was overtaken by a wallaby hopping past her on the verge. "It must have been going at almost thirty miles per hour," she reports.

People who know about these things suggest the Meeghans's wallaby is one of many. They claim that Oxfordshire is home to a colony of wallabies who have escaped from wildlife parks and zoos.

This seems an unlikely explanation. These sightings of strange animals in the Home Counties – cheetahs, penguins, sharks, the yeti and so forth – are frequent, but they always come to nothing. I believe there is a far more likely explanation which the Thames Valley Police would do well to consider.

The former deputy prime minister, Michael Heseltine, lives in the area, at Thenford House, on the Oxfordshire-Northamptonshire border. He has not been spotted for some time, but it is said that he spends his days hopping back and forth around the fancy arboretum he created for himself in its 400-odd acres.

Lord Heseltine has always been very bouncy, and might easily be mistaken for a wallaby. He is now best remembered for whirling the mace around his head in the chamber of the House of Commons in 1977. As far as I can remember, no one was seriously injured during the incident, and so no blood samples were taken. But it now seems likely that there is a high percentage of wallaby in the Heseltine make-up.

Perhaps a great-great-grandfather enjoyed a brief romance at nearby Whipsnade. Tellingly, Lord Heseltine has always kept the side-quiffs in his hair very long. This suggests he is covering up long furry ears which twitch at the first sign of alarm. Also, *Who's Who* reveals that his middle name is Dibdin. This must surely be a clue of some sort.

Thankfully, we live in enlightened times. There is, of course, nothing wrong with being a member of the wallaby family. Quite the opposite. They have much to contribute to our society. Britain could certainly do with some of their tremendous energy and positive, can-do attitude. Indeed, it is greatly to the credit of the Conservative Party that they were prepared to raise a wallaby to high office.

But this should not blind us to the fact that honest, decent home-owners such as Tony and Jean Meeghan and law-abiding motorists such as Jane Martin are owed protection against untoward behaviour by even the most distinguished wallaby.

Retirement is always a difficult period for former Cabinet ministers. If Lord Heseltine has nothing better to do with his time than to hop boastfully past lady drivers on country roads, he must be given something to keep him out of trouble. A banana and skipping rope might do the trick.

(June 15, 2002)

(IV) THE HUNGRY PYTHON

Tracy, an eleven-foot Burmese python, weighing four stone, escaped from her glass tank in a garage in Wincobank Lane, Sheffield, last Sunday. She has not been seen since.

Tracy is normally fed on guinea pigs, rats and rabbits, but her owner, Mr Paul Tomlinson, is worried that she might now be tempted to give cats and dogs a go. But I wonder if she will leave it at that?

Like all pythons, Tracy has upper and lower jaws that can detach, enabling her to swallow prey five times her body diameter. I am no expert, but I imagine that Tracy could polish off not just cats and dogs but any lean human being, particularly if one of them happened to be lying down rather than standing up straight.

Happily, these days there are precious few lean Britons around. A new book, *Fat Land: How the Americans Became the Fattest People in the World*, maintains that Britons will soon match the 20 per cent of American citizens who are clinically obese.

The only truly thin person in public life at the moment is Mr John Redwood, MP. The poor man has long maintained the unnaturally dignified air of someone who hopes one day to sacrifice himself for the greater good. At present, he is kicking his heels on the Conservative back benches, appreciated by no one. The time has surely come for him to board the first train to Sheffield. Once there, he can make his way to Wincobank Lane, get down on all fours, and make little squeaky noises, like a guinea pig.

(June 26, 2003)

(V) THE LOW-FLYING GOLDFISH

Worthing Borough Council has banned fairground operators from presenting goldfish as prizes. This decision follows a number of unfortunate episodes elsewhere in the country.

In New Bolsover, Derbyshire, for instance, a goldfish was spotted eighteen feet up a tree. It emerged that youngsters had attached its little plastic bag to six helium balloons. The goldfish was finally rescued by RSPCA inspectors, and now resides at an undisclosed address.

Needless to say, the RSPCA is calling for a nationwide ban on goldfish being offered as fairground prizes, arguing that it causes them stress. Yet there is no proof whatsoever that Goldie (name changed to protect identity) did not thoroughly enjoy his balloon trip. These little fellows seldom get a chance to see the world, and now this Branson among goldfish has a memory to cherish for ever.

Or, if not for ever, at least for two or three seconds. Goldfish are well known for their limited memory span. To put this into perspective: were a goldfish to be reading this piece, by the time he had reached this exact spot – X – he would have totally forgotten the name of Worthing Borough Council; ask him who the Prime Minister is, and he'll look back at you with a blank expression on his face.

This means that even if Goldie was upset at the outset of his balloon flight – and few of us are entirely relaxed at take-off – then by the time he had come to rest in his branch he would have had no memory of having once been earthbound. In short, he would have thought he had always been a bird, and that the tree was his natural habitat. One can only imagine his distress at the sight of a team of burly RSPCA inspectors climbing up to his perch, asking him to come quietly.

(July 10, 2003)

(VI) THE FORMER WATER VOLE

A belief in the reincarnation of the soul is common to many ancient religions and philosophies, among them Buddhism, Hinduism and Jainism, as well as the teachings of Pythagoras and Plato. It will act as a great shot in the arm for those listed above that Mr Noel Gallagher of the pop group Oasis has now lent his backing to their belief.

"The thing is, I'm a great believer in karma. I'm always preaching that everything happens for a reason, man. What you give is what you get," he says.

He was recently involved in a head-on collision with another car in Indianapolis. "I'm thinking, 'But I'm a really good person. Why is this happening to me? My life's been a celebration. Shit goes wrong. Sometimes there's a disturbance in the force. But this is my destiny'."

If I understand him correctly, he feels that he is being rewarded for all his good deeds in a past life by being given the identity of "Noel Gallagher". It is a curious feature of celebrities who believe in reincarnation that they are all sure they are someone else's reward, the first prize in the donkey derby of a previous life.

This raises various philosophical and theological questions. If it becomes widely known that being Noel Gallagher is virtue's finest reward, which of us is going to go to all that effort? It may well be, of course, that in a previous life Mr Gallagher was an extremely virtuous small, furry mammal, who now regards being Noel Gallagher as a definite step up. By an extraordinary coincidence, a report earlier this week confirms that the water vole is dying out in the British Isles. Many people mistake them for rats, and kill them. It would be strange indeed if as a consequence the *Top of the Pops* studios began to fill up each week with an increasing number of former water voles on lead guitar.

(October 17, 2002)

(VII) THE NOSY PARROT

A Cardiff hypnotherapist (not a combination one comes across very often) has taken to employing a parrot.

Stressed Cardiff businessmen are reportedly flocking to a clinic owned by Raymond Roberts, 40, to have therapy with his parrot Jessie, 3. "By chatting to the parrot, blood pressure lowers, resulting in a general feel-good factor," says Mr Roberts. "Those who have tried it swear it's helped them enormously."

The patients simply lie on a couch while Jessie looks on. Mr

Roberts believes that they share secrets with Jessie that they would be reluctant to confide in a fellow human being.

"By using a parrot as a therapist those in stressful jobs can come here to pour out what's troubling them," says Mr Roberts, whose Capital Therapy Centre is handily situated above an electrical shop. "With that burden lifted, they feel so much better able to cope." Mr Roberts charges £30 for a half-hour session with the parrot. It is not known how much he keeps for himself, and how much he passes on to Jessie.

Oddly enough, Jessie never answers back, or repeats anything, as she is unable to talk. This guarantees a degree of confidentiality which her clients must find most appealing. On the other hand, there are plenty of readily available household objects – a paperweight, for instance, or a carriage clock – that are, by all accounts, just as tight-lipped, and don't need feeding.

Frankly, I wouldn't trust Jessie for one second. Apart from anything else, her eyes are too close together. If I had to unburden myself to any living thing, it would be to a goldfish, as they are notoriously forgetful. Parrots, on the other hand, remember absolutely everything and can live for thirty or forty years.

One's most immediate concern, is that, far from being mute, Jessie is slowly learning the rudiments of the English language, and inwardly digesting all the most painful secrets of the Cardiff business community. For the time being, she is, like Mrs Currie, content to bottle it all up. But how long will it be before she decides to "set the record straight", and makes a bee-line for the nearest publisher?

(October 19, 2002)

(VIII) THE HORNY DOLPHIN

The actress Demi Moore has suffered an unfortunate experience with a dolphin. According to the *New York Post*, Miss Moore was visiting Siegfried and Roy's Secret Garden and Dolphin Habitat in Last Vegas, accompanied by her three children and her former husband, Bruce Willis.

Among the entertainments on offer was a swim with the dolphins. Many people believe that swimming with dolphins has a marvellously therapeutic effect on human beings, so Miss Moore must have plunged into that pool with high hopes. Imagine her astonishment, then, when one of the dolphins – a male – found her well-known sexual magnetism hard to resist, even though Miss Moore was wearing a swimsuit at the time.

Who knows? Perhaps the dolphin (name withheld) had sat through the otherwise poorly attended film *Striptease*, in which Miss Moore can be seen for a good few minutes dancing around an upright pole wearing nothing but a frown.

"Dolphins are sexually aggressive," an anonymous source told the *New York Post*, "and one went after Demi in a big way." Apparently, the actress screamed for help after the dolphin began to rub his body against her, at which point a trainer came to the rescue.

Earlier this year, I, too, swam with dolphins. I am pleased to report that they were all extremely well mannered, at a given signal making squeaky noises, performing jaunty little dances and even propelling me through the water with their noses. At no point did I feel that they were undressing me with their eyes. Yes, the trainer asked one of them to kiss me, and it was happy to oblige. But the dolphin in question did not try to take advantage, nor did it imagine that its modest peck might lead to anything more serious or long term. But then I have never appeared nude in a major motion picture, now widely available on DVD and video. Even though the movie was released some time ago, dolphins are said to have remarkable memories, and there is every reason to believe that the image of Ms Moore remained vivid in his dolphin mind. If this is the case, Ms Moore must surely take some of the blame for "leading him on".

Anyway, Las Vegas is no place for a young dolphin. Small wonder if some of them grow morally tainted. Doubtless many Las Vegas dolphins end up spending their spare time squandering their hard-earned salaries on the fruit machines, or tipsily singing along to Engelbert Humperdinck while supping pina coladas.

Coincidentally, the day after Demi Moore was accosted by her louche dolphin, friends of Liza Minnelli announced that the noisy singer was splitting up with her husband of fourteen months, Mr David Gest. Or is it such a coincidence? I have no means of judging whether or not Mr Gest is, in biological terms, a dolphin, but he certainly looks very odd, and moves from A to B in a very rubbery sort of way.

On a recent television documentary, he spent a great deal of time making squeaky noises and rubbing his body up against Miss Minnelli's in a most uncalled-for manner. If, as I suspect, Mr Gest's hair turns out to be a toupee, it can only be a matter of time before someone pulls it off. Anyone in the vicinity when this occurs should seize the opportunity to take a closer look at his scalp. Should they spot a small circular breathing hole embedded in the centre, they should immediately alert the relevant authorities, so that he can be returned to Siegfried and Roy's Secret Garden and Dolphin Habitat in Las Vegas forthwith.

Pet Conjugations

My dog is a character
Your dog is a nuisance
His dog is a menace.

My tortoise values his privacy
Your tortoise has nothing to say for itself
His tortoise is dead.

My dog is trying to tell me something
Your dog is making his presence felt
Why can't his dog stop that awful whining?

My cat explores
Your cat strays
His cat will cause an accident.

My dog's not fussy
Your dog will eat anything
His dog has a lump of shit in its mouth.

My budgie chatters
Your budgie chirrups
His budgie never shuts up.

My goldfish is well behaved
Your goldfish is dull
His goldfish is floating.

Our pug looks like Winston Churchill
Your pug looks like Phil Mitchell
His pug has just been run over.

My hamster enjoys the exercise
Your hamster likes to keep himself occupied
His hamster has nothing better to do.

My puppy plays with me
Your puppy plays with you
His puppy plays with itself.

My labrador is cuddly
Your labrador is roly-poly
His labrador is morbidly obese.

My dog is protective
Your dog is aggressive
Why can't he keep his dog under control?

My owl is wise
Your owl doesn't move much
His owl is stuffed.

My dog can say sausages
Your dog can say ggssggsss
Why's Esther got her hands round his dog's throat?

My dog is just saying hello
Your dog is upset about something
His dog should be muzzled.

My puppy is just being friendly
Your puppy is a little forward
His puppy should have had the operation.

My Vietnamese pot-bellied pig makes me interesting
Your Vietnamese pot-bellied pig gives you something
to talk about
He is Dave Lee Travis.

Bovine Thoughts from Abroad
(with apologies to Robert Browning)

Oh, to be Abroad
Now that April's there
And whoever wakes in England,
Sees, some morning, unaware,
That the unborn lamb and the woolly sheep
Shuffle in line to be put to sleep
While the vet takes aim and kills the fearful cow
In England – now!
Hark, where the distant pyre doth crackle
A weekday roast of upturned cattle;
Deepest trenches are dug to tackle
The virus, triumphant through each battle,
Lest you should think it could never recapture
That first fine deadly rapture!
Hark, at the newest country sounds:
Ministers bleating contrary lines –
"The countryside is out of bounds"
"Under control" "Hopeful signs"
And after April, when May follows,
The dead stock builds, and Tony swallows!

The beaming politician, he chirps his song
"Close your eyes; see: nothing's wrong!"
Just hold your noses to the smouldering pong
And the reason every voter will mark us is
(Though the fields are strewn with carcasses)
If it's raining now, it won't get wetter
And remember: things can only get better
And there'll be sunshine after the plague
And your only alternative is William Hague.
Oh, to be Abroad
Now that April's there,
And whoever wakes in England.
Sees, each morning, Tony Blair.

                                              (March 31, 2001)

Four Unusual Friendships

(I) FIGURES recently released show that the number of British motorists caught by speed cameras exceeded a million for the first time last year. It is predicted that the figure will rise above three million by the year 2004, when there will be three times as many cameras on the roads as there are now.

These days, it is hard to go anywhere without being filmed. Even the most humble village store sports livid notices informing customers that their every movement is being recorded by closed circuit television cameras, invariably at a most unflattering angle.

With all these cameras about, it is hard not to shed a tear for Mr Stanley Balderson, aged eighty-one, from Nomini Grove, Virginia.

After his local police force had received complaints from nosy neighbours, they set up a series of hidden surveillance cameras in a nearby meadow. Mr Balderson was then captured on camera running around the meadow wearing a T-shirt, tennis shoes and sunglasses. Nothing illegal about that, of course – but he had abandoned every last shred of trousers and underwear, the better to engage in "lewd activities" with a herd of cows. Captured on film, Mr Balderson was convicted on a charge of bestiality. The farmer said that he knew Mr Balderson personally, "but I never gave him permission to be in the field or to go anywhere near my cows". Mr Balderson has been given a two-year suspended sentence and placed on probation.

In this country, the government has decreed that speed cameras must be painted bright yellow, so that motorists are able to take an informed decision as to whether or not to speed. It seems only fair that the police in Virginia should be forced to do the same with their rural surveillance cameras.

I am not saying this would necessarily deter Mr Balderson. He is obviously a feisty, determined sort of fellow. I suspect he may be one of those people for whom the promise of appearing on film acts less as a deterrent than an incentive.

(II) MEANWHILE, in Glasgow, Mrs Jean Curtis, forty-seven, has filed for divorce, claiming she found her husband, Ian, forty-two, enjoying what would be best described, in modern parlance, as "a relationship" with a frozen chicken on the sofa.

"My jaw just dropped," Mrs Curtis told the *Sun*. "I said, 'You dirty bastard – that's my Sunday lunch.' He was calm as you like and said 'We can still eat it.'" But Mrs Curtis was not persuaded. "I kicked him out."

Where this sort of tale is concerned, it is the little details that stick in the mind, often blocking out the bigger picture. In the case of Curtis v Curtis, the presence of the sofa is bizarre enough, suggesting an unlikely element of romance, but it is the adjective "frozen" that refuses to go away. We are obviously now sailing through uncharted waters, but one would imagine that the already limited sex appeal of a dead chicken is further reduced by the act of freezing.

A visit to Waitrose will never be the same again. I already watch with rather too much interest as the goods of the person in front are rung up by the checkout lady, but now my eyes will be out on stalks. No one will be above suspicion. Perhaps the Home Secretary will introduce CCTV in all freezer cabinets in a bid to reduce similar incidents.

My own Neighbourhood Watch will certainly be placed on red alert: those caught dawdling for too long by the poultry section will have only themselves to blame when they are grabbed in a half-nelson and placed under citizen's arrest.

(September 3, 2002)

(III) FOLLOWING my earlier reports of Mr Stanley Balderson, eighty-one, from Nomini Grove, Virginia, who has recently been convicted of lewd activity with a herd of unnamed cows and Mr Ian Curtis, forty-two, from Glasgow, who has been accused by his wife, Jean, forty-seven, of engaging in lewd activity with a frozen chicken, I am sorry to have to report that an Edinburgh man is alleged by the police to have engaged in lewd activity with a traffic cone in the city's Calton Hill area.

I suppose that, given the choice of a frozen chicken, a cow, or a traffic cone, most of us would opt for the traffic cone. Or am I speaking out of turn? I wouldn't say that a traffic cone is necessarily more attractive than the others, but I feel there would be less of a taboo to a lewd encounter with one; at very least, one would remain immune to accusations of bestiality.

It seems years since the then prime minister, John Major, set up his Traffic Cone Hotline, whereby ordinary members of the public could dial an agreed number and complain of an excess of cones on any given stretch of road. At the time it was billed as Mr Major's great and lasting contribution to civilisation; and so, alas, it proved to be.

But there will always be a danger of these initiatives backfiring. The pages of the gaudier Sunday newspapers are full of advertisements featuring pouting young lovelies wearing next to nothing, encouraging readers to ring this "hotline" or that. Small wonder if one or two people pick up the wrong end of the stick, and develop an unrequited passion for a traffic cone.

Perhaps there should now be two sorts of Cone Hotline, one for those who want to see fewer of them and another for those who want to get to know them better. But the people of Edinburgh should be made aware that the open road is no place to conduct a mutually fulfilling relationship. Edinburgh is now blessed with a selection of wine bars, bistros and restaurants to suit every pocket. I have never dined out with a traffic cone, but they tell me it is surprisingly inexpensive, particularly if you stick to the set menu.

(September 7, 2002)

(IV) IN 1839, Charlotte Brontë and her friend Ellen Nussey enjoyed a holiday at Easton House Farm, two miles inland from Bridlington (or Burlington, as it was then known). When the two ladies walked over the fields to Bridlington, Charlotte was so overcome at her first sight of the sea that she burst into tears and had to sit down. "Our visit to Easton was extremely pleasant," she was to recall. Ten years later, she returned there to write her novel *Shirley*. Sadly, a recent report suggests that the overland trip to Bridlington now lacks much of the grace and serenity of those far-off days.

When a packed train from Hull to Bridlington stopped at signals, the *Sun* newspaper reported, "dozens of passengers stared out in amazement. In seconds, police switchboards were jammed as horrified commuters used their mobiles to report what they had seen." Apparently, Stephen Hall, twenty-three, an unemployed chef, had lassoed a grazing goat with his belt. He had then proceeded to strike up what might best be termed a full relationship with it, in full view of the commuters.

Caution was obviously not high on Mr Hall's agenda that fateful morning. Some will argue that he could never have predicted the sudden change of signals that caused the Hull-Bridlington train to stop right alongside him and his unnamed goat. But he might at least have cast his eye over the surrounding fields for any sign of sightseers. He has only himself to blame that a man out walking his dog also saw him, and made a 999 call to Humberside police.

Two further members of the public were also at hand, jumping on Mr Hall and pinning him down while, according to the *Sun*, "a stream of officers raced to the scene". It all goes to show that where goats are concerned, passion should always take second place to discretion.

This case raises so many issues for those of us in the media that it is hard to know where to begin. Doubtless, a team from ITN has already bustled the poor goat into a studio to ask her in silhouette how she will pick up the pieces of her shattered life. Over on Radio 4's "Thought for the Day", some sensitive soul will even now be struggling to give this topical news story a more permanent spiritual dimension.

Meanwhile, Mr Murdoch's newspapers will be togging the poor

goat up in high heels and suspenders for a television advertisement ("Read my horrific story – only in tomorrow's *News of the World*"). Mr Michael Buerk and his *Moral Maze* team will be sorting out their positions For and Against, and Channel Five will be offering Mr Hall a job presenting a late-night current affairs programme.

At these times, one can only do one's best. So here goes. First, the good news: the example of the Hull-Bridlington express proves that there are still trains in this country with windows clean enough to see through. It is to the credit of Arriva Trains Northern that dozens of passengers were able to pinpoint a man and a goat. In the south, Mr Hall might have had his way with the full range of farm-yard animals and still got away scot-free.

Second, the incident provides an insight into the proliferation of the mobile phone. Not only did dozens of commuters jam the police switchboards, but even the man out walking his dog had a mobile phone at hand. One need only think of the trouble Miss Marple went through to track down the strangler glimpsed on the 4.50 from Paddington to realise what a boon the mobile can be in these unsavoury times.

Mr Hall is due to be sentenced in March. But what of the goat, whose identity remains a closely guarded secret? A vet who examined her described her as "subdued", but then goats often are. British Transport Police Detective Inspector Dave Crinnion said: "I saw the goat the next day – it did not seem to be upset, but it is difficult to tell."

There is no mention in the report as to how Det Insp Crinnion set about determining whether or not the goat was upset. Goats are notoriously po-faced creatures, with cold, impenetrable eyes. They give nothing away, and tend to bottle up their emotions. Even when standing on their hind legs butting one another, their expressions remain utterly impassive, even bored. Det Insp Crinnion must have had to employ every trick in the book – a cigarette, a shoulder to cry on – to get anything out of her. Small wonder he emerged from the interrogation room with barely a scribble on his notepad.

Most bizarrely of all, the *Sun* reports that Mr Hall said after the hearing: "My friends have been giving me a lot of stick. They are all joking with me about it." Such jocularity suggests that, where our four-legged friends are concerned, Bridlington is Liberty Hall. If ever I travel on the Hull-Bridlington express, please remind me to draw the curtains. It is all a far cry from the glorious summer of 1839.

(February 2, 2002)

Department of Media

A Hero for Our Time: Max Clifford

THERE IS, of course, a long tradition of blustering dictators issuing glowing biographies of themselves, with titles like *Kim Jong Il – A Hero of Our Times* or *Mao: Beloved Father of A Grateful Nation*. But until this book* came along, I had never come across the same technique used by sleaze merchants.

"Max Clifford is the image-maker and breaker of the twenty-first century," we are informed on page one. The gush of tributes never stops flowing for the next 250-odd pages. The index offers a flavour. Under "Clifford, Max, character and attributes", you will find page references for Ambition and drive/ Bureaucracy, anathema to/ Confidence/ Desire to help people/ Enjoyment of sex/ Generosity/ Honesty/ Keeps secrets/ Love of sport/ and so on, and on, and on.

His birth is treated with the reverence usually accorded to a new Messiah. "Maxwell Frank Clifford" we are told "was born on Tuesday April 6, 1943 at Kingston Hospital, Surrey, weighing 6lb 4oz". His sister recalls that "His arrival was quite wonderful ... he was a very good baby" and, moreover, that it "shone a bright light in those dark times". The only surprise is that the opposing sides in the Second World War forgot to call a twenty-four-hour ceasefire in honour of the great event.

From Day One, Max is a hero. On his first day at school, he saves a weaker lad from a bully. "I've always hated bullies ... in fact, I have always helped people and supported the underdog," he boasts. This is the man who went on to support such well-known underdogs as Frank Sinatra, James Hewitt, Mohamed Fayed, O J Simpson and Simon Cowell, not to mention the swaggering youths

---

Max Clifford – Read All About It by Max Clifford and Angela Levin

charged with the murder of Stephen Lawrence. If these are the underdogs then who on earth are the overdogs?

Oddly enough, most of Clifford's tales of his own generosity, heroism, integrity, etc, etc, seem to change with each telling. Take, for instance, his vivid tale of his first day at school, when he bravely stood up for the weaker lad. In an interview with the *Sunday Telegraph* in 2000, he told another story, equally heroic, but completely different. "I hated arrogance and pomposity. I had my first experience of it on my first day at junior school. I was kicking a ball about and this boy began speaking to me in a very affected voice, telling me to clear off, so I hit him. He turned out to be the headmaster's son."

What is true and what is false? The more one carries on ploughing through this smug, creepy 250-page inventory of self-adulation, the more one realises that Clifford is either unable or unwilling to tell the difference, often swinging between the two without noticing.

For instance, in his recounting of how the headline "Freddie Starr Ate My Hamster" came to be written, he at first acknowledges that it was invented not by him but by Freddie Starr's ghostwriter's girlfriend. "She, not Max, as legend has it, contacted a friend who was working on the *Sun* newspaper, and, in a moment of inspiration or spite, offered him the fabricated story that Freddie had eaten her hamster," records his shameless hagiographer Angela Levin. But a page later, Clifford is taking all the credit for himself. "A few weeks later Freddie claimed the whole thing was his idea. Max didn't care. 'Everyone knew it had come with me.'"

The book is jam-packed with tributes to this man among men, this heroic genius, this champion of the poor and downtrodden. Many of these tributes, it is true, come from his own lips. One minute, he is Martin Luther King ("I've always had a compassionate side, a powerful social conscience, and find helping others hugely rewarding"), and the next minute he is Casanova, or at least Swiss Tony from *The Fast Show* ("knowing a woman is enjoying herself enhances my own enjoyment and I have taken a personal pride in giving women pleasure").

In true Stalinist show-trial form, many are thrust centre stage to offer dutiful speeches in praise of his honesty, his vision, his love of all mankind. "He is a true man of the people, a charismatic person who understands the human condition," says – ahem – Valerie Harkness, the woman who shopped Alan Clark to the *News of the World*. "He is a great public relations guy, efficient, communicative, human and sincere," says – ahem, ahem – Mohamed Fayed.

Even his next-door neighbours are roped in to join the worship. "Marjorie Cunningham, a former neighbour now in her eighties, tells of his generosity ..." begins one sentence. Another reads, in full: "Ann Pritchard, who with her husband John and three children lived next door but one to Max when he and Liz lived in Raynes Park, describes him as 'a diamond. You can't fault Max as a neighbour.'"

Might that be the most boring sentence ever written? Some would argue that it is not even the most boring sentence in this book. It certainly has strong rivals on the domestic front, including, "Max is very houseproud and likes everything to be kept clean and tidy" and "When he recently bought a new iron in the local shops, he paid over two hundred pounds for one with more options than a washing machine."

Has anyone ever devoted so much time and space to not boasting about their charity work? Chapter Eight, which is called "Charity Began at Home", only just stops short of printing the receipts from every charity Clifford has ever given money to. "Max doesn't publicise what he does, or how much he gives," it says, before publicising what he does, and how much he gives ("Max is particularly generous at Christmas time ... he's paid for first-class flights from the USA for parents of a very sick baby," etc, etc).

Clifford has the instinct of the natural bully to imagine himself on the moral high ground even when standing up to his forehead in the sewer. Thus he will huff and puff against the iniquity of Alan Clark, Sir Peter Harding, David Beckham et al for committing adultery while at the same time bragging of his own extra-marital affairs. Again, at one point he boasts of his need to "protect and help those most in need" and at another he boasts of the "legendary" sex parties he would arrange in Colliers Wood in the 1970s, at which he would introduce young actresses desperate for the Equity cards to agents "who would issue false contracts for sexual favours". Is this what he calls protecting those who are most in need?

Under "Sense of humour" in the index, you will see numerous references (99, 100–104, 112, 128, 130–1) but when you look them up you will find precious little that is funny or even mildly amusing. Much is made of "Max's roguish sense of humour" and his "insatiable appetite for practical jokes", but most of what he calls his "pranks" are strangely cold and joyless, even sadistic.

On a beach, he puts a dead fish into a stranger's handbag. At a flower show, he upsets a pillar of the community by pretending that he is fielding a call from a journalist who is threatening to expose her. Working as a PR for the Sixties crooner Solomon King, he frightens him by pretending his homosexuality is about to be exposed in the press. If some of his "pranks" are excusable, it is only because they simply don't ring true: he claims he has sometimes adopted a false identity, and "phoned a woman who has shown a romantic interest in me, and said that the way to make me jealous was to have sex with one of my friends. I've then told the friend and left it up to the two of them to take advantage of it or not. Certain friends have enjoyed themselves a lot."

If you believe that, you'll believe anything; and if you believe anything, you may well want to read the biography of Max Clifford. He is, after all, the most saintly, the kindest, the most brilliant, the most powerful man in all the world, the man who helped put Bob Dylan, Frank Sinatra, the Beatles and Jimi Hendrix and countless others on the map. Oddly enough, you could search through a whole library of books about them, and still not find a single reference to Max Clifford. Could he by any chance be a figment of his own imagination?

Peter Bazalgette's Diary

There has been an epoch-making moment in this season's *Big Brother*, or so my Endemol production team informs me.

The seat of the lavatory, or toilet, as the contestants prefer to call it (nothing wrong with that – it's hugely important in the twenty-first century that we, or rather they, should be permitted to call it toilet, if that's what they jolly well want!) was extensively "soiled" by one or other of the "housemates".

Television historians will wish to know the exact sequence of events. The soiled seat was discovered by "Science", one of the livelier of our *Big Brother* "housemates" of recent years. Science, I am told, declared "Someone's left poo-poo on the toilet seat!" whereupon Roberto claimed total innocence, insisting he had left the seat in question as clean as he had found it.

At this, Makosi pointed the finger at Roberto, saying he was the last person to have used the "toilet". Unprompted, Anthony spluttered, "I did a shit, I flushed and washed my hands." Some of the housemates then seized on this as an admission of guilt. "Everything is filmed in the toilet so the one who's been shitting will be named and shamed!" said Roberto.

A magic moment. On numerous occasions, *Big Brother* has been bombarded with snobbish criticisms by the middle-class elite. Many of their complaints have centred on the need to place television cameras in the lavatory. These elitists have got on their high horses, saying, "Why is there a camera in the lavatory, or the toilet, as it were?"

I tell them it's all about access – access by the people, for the people. And now my point is proven. If viewers had been denied access to the lavatory, they would have had no way of making up their own minds as to which housemate had soiled that seat. Are we, as television makers, really allowed to deny the public their right to know? Why should this knowledge be restricted to a privileged cabal?

It all reminds me of the 1930s, when only those in the social elite knew that King Edward VIII was conducting a liaison with a married woman. If only Lord Reith had installed BBC cameras in the King's lavatory, the general public would have had a much better idea of what was going on – and, today, with interactive TV, they would have been able to vote on whether it was His Majesty or Mrs Simpson who had left a "poo-poo" in the Royal lavatory.

The days are now long gone when the cultural middle-class hegemony could stick their noses in the air and say, "We don't believe poo-poos on a lavatory seat are good for you – so we're not going to give them to you."

And thank goodness for that. We live in a more democratic age, thank God. Nowadays, the viewer is in charge. If he or she wants poo-poo on a lavatory seat, then poo-poo on a lavatory seat is what we'll give them. It's all about choice.

For me, there's something very, very positive about the whole soiled seat phenomenon, both in terms of the zeitgeist, and in terms of the future of broadcasting. Our highly professional Endemol psychologists confirm that one can tell an extraordinary amount about someone's inner personality by the way in which they tackle the whole issue of going to the lavatory. For this reason, we are investing in an extra camera, with a special waterproof lens, to be placed deep inside the very bowl of the *Big Brother* lavatory. This will give the viewer unique access to the workings of every single bowel evacuation.

Even the so-called "classic" documentaries, such as Kenneth Clark's *Civilisation* (yawn!) or David Attenborough's *Life on Earth* (double yawn!) couldn't claim to have used these opportunities to extend democracy in the home. So, please let's not be too pious about "the good old days". Sadly, so-called "proper" documentaries haven't been performing very well. I'm sorry, but viewers no longer want to watch men just walking around talking about "elitist general knowledge" with their trousers on.

It's a terrifically exciting and challenging new development in the whole *Big Brother* concept. By using their red button, by next year digital viewers will be able to tune into a live *Biggie Brother* relay, providing them with permanent access to the livecam in the lavatory, so that the second a housemate "goes" they will be able to see it on their screen, the very moment it happens.

Meanwhile, our resident team of psychologists, social scientists, top entertainers and experts will be at hand to analyse each effort. Viewers will then be able to make up their own minds by voting on the best of the day's output – and at the end of each day the lovely Davina will carry the winning stool in a specially designed perspex box out to the cheering public, who will be able to get "up close and personal" with it.

The immortal Jade Goody will be at hand with analysis and personal anecdote. *Big Brother* experts and historians will ask her how she used to "go" in the *Big Brother* house, and viewers will then be encouraged to text in their questions on just how regular she was. At last, the barriers are coming down! As we at Endemol say, "There's excitement in excrement!" The ordinary viewer can no longer be denied access to other people's poos – and that must surely be good news for our culture as a whole.

I'm proud to be part of the expanding universe of successful stool-based TV formatting.

Our growing portfolio of modern, forward-looking, shit-oriented, interactive programming will incorporate cutting-edge formulae such as *Celebrity Biggie Brother*, with James Hewitt, Tony Blackburn and Amanda Platell on the toilet 24/7, in a race to see who can "go" first; *Stool for Stars*, in which Sharon Osbourne, Rebecca Loos, David Starkey and Bez pick the lucky finalist who, in their opinion, has what it takes to "run and run"; and *Celebrity Flush Pots* with Johnny Vegas, in which discredited former celebrities like Neil Hamilton, Edwina Currie and Major Charles Ingram stand knee-deep in a cess-pit, wearing only their underpants, while up-to-the-minute, cutting-edge, sexually aware young viewers urinate and excrete all over them!

This represents bold, innovative programming for a multi-cultural creative environment – and an exciting new interactive emotional challenge for the twenty-first century.

Fourteen Things You Didn't Know About I'm A Celebrity – Get Me Out of Here!

1 THE FIRST *I'm A Celebrity* programme was broadcast by the BBC exactly forty years ago. It was originally titled *I'm a Distinguished Commentator – It Is My Considered Belief That I Have Every Reason To Remain Here!*

2 The original contestants were Mr Quintin Hogg, Dame Edith Sitwell, Dr Bodkin Adams, Mr John Osborne and Margaret,

Duchess of Argyll. The five of them were marooned on a desert island off the coast of Panama for just over three weeks. The programme was compered by Mr Gilbert Harding.

3 Things got off to a rocky start when Osborne interrupted Dame Edith's "Celebratory Pageant" by hurling abuse at all and sundry for being "decaying cavities in a mouthful of misshapen teeth". Dame Edith failed the first "bush tucker challenge" of wrestling with an alligator. "The wretched beast has no manners whatsoever," she complained, while Dr Adams sewed her left thumb back on. After the first day, 53 per cent of viewers voted for the alligator to stay.

4 The atmosphere darkened considerably when the alligator revealed that Dr Adams had been passing him secret notes suggesting the best possible lines of attack. "I'm not speaking to you," said Dame Edith in freeform verse, "to whit, to woo."

5 Denying all charges, Dr Adams then fell out with the alligator. Sadly, the alligator succumbed to an unknown bug and died later the same day. In an unexpected twist, it was then revealed that the alligator had changed its will at the last moment, bequeathing a surprised and delighted Dr Bodkin Adams all his worldly possessions.

6 On day two, Mr Quintin Hogg began to irritate his fellow contestants by incessant ringing of his handbells. Some accused him of rabble-rousing techniques. "I am simply appealing over your heads to the viewers at home," he responded. "Unlike you, I have every confidence in the democratic process."

7 In the first series, contestants were expected to wear dinner jackets and full evening dress. This severely hampered Margaret, Duchess of Argyll's attempts at wrestling with eels in her first bush tucker trial. The rule was not relaxed until 1973, when, following a chitty from his doctor, the Earl of Lichfield was permitted to wear a lounge suit and a polo neck.

8 The only member of the present Royal Family to have appeared on *I'm A Celebrity* is the Earl of Wessex. In 1989, he entertained his fellow contestants with a pre-rehearsed one-man all-singing all-dancing show wearing a variety of amusing hats. The following day, he was evicted from the programme with a record-breaking 93 per cent of the vote.

9 In the 1995 series, celebrity contestant Michael Winner was faced with the prospect of standing beneath a shower of maggots. At the last moment, television bosses shelved plans following official protests from the maggots.

10 Experts suggest that the word "celebrity" derives from ancient Turkish "cellar briddi". It translates literally as "he who must be kept locked in a dark cellar".

11 The recent winner, Tony Blackburn, had been plotting his comeback since 1978, when he last appeared on British television. For twenty-four years, he lived anonymously in an Australian rainforest, eating woodlice and grubs, in the hope that he would one day be selected as a contestant. Tony now intends to set up a jungle-based training school for former celebrities who wish to revive their careers. "We've already had 300 applications," he says, "including thingy who was once married to wotsit, and that one who used to be on *The Onedin Line*, you know, the one with the beard."

12 1992 saw the first *I'm An Animal Celebrity – Get Me Out Of Here!* Contestants included former television straight-man Perky; Freda, the *Blue Peter* tortoise; Flipper; Kes; Fred Barker, from the *Five O'Clock Club*, and Clarence the Cross-Eyed Lion. Sadly, after repeated on-set bickering between contestants, viewers voted off Clarence the Cross-Eyed Lion, who was rumoured to have eaten Freda. The eventual winner was Flipper, who received the largest male vote after wearing no swimming costume for her afternoon swim.

13 The only members of the same family ever to have appeared together on the show are novelist sisters A S Byatt and Margaret Drabble, who were among the contestants in the 1994 *I'm A Leading Celebrity Novelist – Get Me Out of Here!*, compered by Melvyn Bragg. Drabble was later to use her experience of mud-wrestling with her sister in *The Limits of Persecution* (1996), while Byatt is widely believed to have used Drabble as the model for Jessica, the spoilt and demanding tree-grub in *Bugs and Insects* (1999).

14 All hell broke loose in 1979, when top musician Joseph Cooper, renowned for his regular appearances on BBC2's *Face the Music*, was found to have broken the rules by smuggling his trade-mark dummy keyboard into the jungle. At first, he pretended he had personally constructed the keyboard from kindling found around the

campsite, but his fellow contestant top model Norman Scott blew the whistle on him, with the result that Cooper was disqualified from further participation, and buried up to his neck in sand.

Mr Pandy: An Apology

AT THE WEEKEND, we may have inadvertently implied that the former television celebrity Mr Andy Pandy, fifty-eight, is experiencing trouble in his bid to re-establish his career as a children's entertainer.

Following a letter from Mr Pandy's lawyers, we are happy to correct this impression. Now wishing to be known only as Andrew Pandy, he is pursuing a successful career in the public relations industry in Ruislip and surrounding areas. Contrary to what we may have suggested, Mr Pandy has not donned his distinctive blue-and-white-striped suit with matching floppy hat for more than thirty-five years. He now wears only a sober two-piece suit and tie. He would also like us to make it clear that he has severed all contact with his former partner, Ms Looby Loo, 54.

SIR – I have been instructed by my client, Mr Ears, to refute implications in your newspaper column.

Mr Ears has managed to put his past as a character in children's fiction behind him, and is now a well-respected figure in his local community. He has thus been greatly distressed by references to him as "Big" Ears. The continued use of such an epithet constitutes an unjustified smear on his hard-won reputation.

He wishes to make it clear that "Big" Ears was the name first forced on him by the late Enid Blyton in 1949 without consultation. Ms Blyton made no attempt to respond to Mr Ears's repeated complaints at the time.

Since Ms Blyton's death, Mr Ears has undergone extensive surgery. He is now known in the local business community as Mr Medium Ears, which is the name under which he presently trades.

Additionally, he wishes to make it clear that for fifteen years he has severed all contact with his former ward "Noddy".

The Diaries of Piers Morgan

MONDAY: Over dinner, I tell Tony and Gordon to shut the f— up while I tell them what to do about running the f—— country. Blimey! The two of 'em have been in Downing Street for – what? – only a few years, but the way they rabbit on, you'd think they were in charge.

But I've gotta hand it to those guys. By the end of my wide-ranging advice – order the fat cats to get their snouts out of the bloody trough, tell the so-called President of the USA where to get bloody off, and, let's face it, there's a crying need for sexier story-lines on *EastEnders* – they're both stunned by what I have to say, listening to me with a reverential silence.

I know what they're thinking: thank God there's someone who's not afraid to tell it like it is – and, yes, we truly admire him for it.

Nice blokes, incidentally – but are they up to the job?

TUESDAY: Took Campbell for lunch at the Savoy. Discussed my new current affairs TV series, where I interview top pin-up Jordan on serious issues such as the NHS vis-à-vis bust enlargement.

"It was very interesting," says Campbell. "You're a TV natural, Piers – and highly intelligent with it."

I tell Alastair about the high degree of sexual tension between myself and Jordan. "Blimey, Alastair, the lady was undressing me with her eyes," I confess. "Just like the Princess of Wales, Cherie Blair, Naomi Campbell, Her Majesty, the Spice Girls, Nana Mouskouri and the rest of them. But as the editor of the *Daily Mirror*, I can't afford to compromise, mate."

Campbell sympathises. He says he's had a tough week, too, advising the President of the USA on how to do his job. "Those people think they bloody know it all," he says, polishing off his pork tenderloin. "You think he's listening to you but then he turns round and does the exact opposite of what you told him. Who does he f—— think he f—— is? Bloody prat!"

I tell Alastair he should get my new mate Jordan on to the government's side over the whole Iraq wotsit.

"She's got a head on her shoulders, mate," I say. "And she's got a f—— strong following in the country. Make her a junior defence minister for starters, give her a week or two to see how she shapes up, then kick Hoon out and give her his job. She'd carry the country right behind her, mate. And it's not just me who thinks that. Top rocker Noel Gallagher thinks so too – and so does GMTV's Eamonn Holmes."

Alastair is obviously impressed, but he says that first he's got to tell Tony which bits of Iraq to bomb. Apparently, Tony doesn't have a clue. Amanda Platell in the *Daily Mail* has been advising one thing, Peter Hitchens in the *Mail on Sunday* another. He doesn't know who to go with.

Luckily, TV's Vanessa Feltz has been secretly advising Downing Street that it's best to bomb just here and there, and not all over the bloody shop, and she's got Tony's ear. I had lunch with Vanessa last week. She fancies me something rotten.

WEDNESDAY: Breakfast with Henry Kissinger. The guy claims he's a bloody doctor. Oh yeah? When I tell him I've got a bit of a tickle in my throat, he doesn't have the foggiest.

He starts to go on about international co-operation to reduce something or other, blah, blah, blah, and how the United Nations must resist the temptation to blah, blah, blah, and I'm falling asleep in my fried egg. Lighten up, mate! I think – and I interrupt him.

"'Kissing-'er'? Great name for pulling the birds, mate!" I laugh uproariously. "Is that the full tongue sandwich, then – or just a bit of a snog?!!!!"

Henry's actually very good fun, and loves my lively and provocative sense of humour, brilliantly managing to keep a straight face throughout. What a guy!

As we say our ta-ras, I get him to sign my autograph book, on the same page as top singer Billie Piper, top *Big Brother* finalist Jade Goody, and top crime icon Reggie Kray. Nice bloke, Henry, but on the way back to the office I wonder if he has much of a moral compass.

THURSDAY: Dinner at Mo Mowlam's. The sexual tension is highly charged.

"Piers," she says. Like everyone in government – Tony, too – she loves rolling my Christian name around her mouth. "Piers," she says, "this is strictly between ourselves, but I hate Peter and Peter hates Gordon and Gordon hates Robin and Robin hates Geoff and Geoff hates David and David hates Jack and Jack hates Peter and Peter hates Gordon – or did I already say that?"

I reassure Mo that her secret's safe with me. When I get home, I jot it down in my diary and send it to the publishers, for safe-keeping.

FRIDAY: Lunch at Harrods with my old mate Mohamed Fayed. Mohamed's a great guy with a terrific sense of humour. Over vintage champagne and a 1911 Château d'Yquem, we agree on how frankly morally repugnant it is that so many top people in the government and the media are prepared to stuff themselves with other people's drink.

SATURDAY: Mohamed gives me a top-secret scoop about how Prince Philip and Tony Blair have ordered the SAS to pay off the yeti. Apparently, the yeti found out that Princess Anne was behind the BrinksMat robbery, and there's been this huge cover-up involving Lord Lucan and MI6. We decide to splash with the story on Monday. There have been far too many lies coming from this Blair government, and it's about time someone had the guts to tell the truth for once.

SUNDAY: To some sort of outdoors "do" at the Cenotaph. I went along to get regally drunk, but everyone was standing stock still, and saying f— all.

As per usual, it fell to yours truly to liven things up a bit, so I told the one about Diana Dors and the elephant. When I'd finished, I roared with good-natured laughter. But I was reckoning without them all having left their senses of humour at home. What a lot of stuffed shirts.

So I turned round and said: "Hey, lighten up, you guys!" Someone had to say it, and I was the only one there with a) the courage and b) the sheer bloody sense of occasion.

The Institute of the Crashingly Obvious

FOR SOME TIME NOW, the pressure of being a humorist has been getting to me. The production of jokes, day in, day out, can grind a man down. When I look through the other pages of any newspaper, I envy those who have only to go to a football match, or a crime scene, or a fashion parade, or a war, in order to find their material. After twenty-five years, I have begun to feel there must be something less demanding than always taking a sideways look at life's lighter side. How I yearn for the time I can start taking a frontways look at life's darker side.

So just imagine how heartened I was to get a call from a head-hunting agency a few days ago. The lady on the other end of the phone seemed very excited. She told me it was all very hush-hush, but she had a client who was looking for someone just like me, someone who yearned for the straightforward. The job wouldn't require the production of a single joke – in fact, quite the opposite. Needless to say, I leapt at the opportunity, and the very next day I found myself reporting to the front desk of a smart office in Park Lane. It turned out to be the worldwide headquarters of an organisation of which I had never previously heard: the ICO.

While waiting to be collected from the foyer, I passed the time leafing through the most recent copy of their in-house journal, ICO Bulletin. The main headline was: "It's Official! – Eating Out More Expensive Than Eating In".

The accompanying story went on to explain that, surveying 25,000 couples over a five-year period, a top team of ICO researchers had come up with "conclusive proof" that couples who ate out regularly in restaurants, brasseries or bistros spent "considerably more" over the course of a year than similar couples who restricted themselves to eating at home.

The other two front-page stories were "Old Folk Die Sooner", which reported the "shock news" that recent ICO studies demonstrated that people aged over eighty could expect to die before those currently in the twenty to thirty age bracket, and "Crisp-Only Diet Bad for You, Say Top ICO Nutritionists", which maintained that people who lived only on potato crisps were likely to be less healthy than those who maintained a balanced diet.

"The occasional packet of crisps does no harm," stated their top medical adviser, "but just eating crisps and nothing else could well have long-term effects on your health."

It was all so absorbing that I didn't notice when a young woman in a neat black suit ("Mr Brown? This way!") arrived to escort me upstairs. "We're on the nineteenth floor, so the lift will be quicker than the stairs," she said, as we waited for the lift to arrive. "Here it is," she added, as the lift doors opened. We walked into the lift. She pushed a button and explained: "If I press nineteen, that should take us to the nineteenth floor."

I was soon shaking hands with the Managing Director of the ICO. "Welcome," he said, "to the Institute of the Crashingly Obvious." He began with a few informal observations ("So you found your way here all right?!") to set me at my ease. He then bade me sit down – "take the weight off your feet" – and got down to business.

The Institute of the Crashingly Obvious had, he explained, been set up ten years ago with the aim of conducting extensive research for media organisations the world over. "Our very first story hit the headlines big time. You can't have missed it. It took six months' research, and put us firmly on the map – 'Official – 90 per cent of Britons Don't Trust Confidence Tricksters'. We polled over 10,000 ordinary Britons and came up with the surprising news that whereas dentists get a 75 per cent approval rating, and firemen a massive 93 per cent, only 10 per cent of ordinary Britons approve of confidence tricksters."

He passed me photostats of other headlines of which the Institute had been particularly proud:

Driving With Eyes Shut Causes Accidents
Dinosaurs Extinct Claims Top Scientist
*Jumping from Aircraft without Parachute "Unsafe", Warns
    Aviation Expert*
Supermarkets Unlikely On Moon "For Years"
Eating Too Much Is Major Cause of Obesity
*Top Expert's Shock Claim: Toys "More Fun for Children than for
    Adults"*

Poll Shows Cats Well Ahead of Ferrets As Nation's Favourite Pets
Tories Must Regain Popularity to Win Next Election, Polls
    Confirm
Sweets Bad For Teeth, Warns Dentist
Gypsies Overlooked for Top Jobs in City, Survey Reveals
Survey Reveals Life's Never Simple
Icebergs Even Bigger Below Water, Warns Expert

It was, I had to admit, a singularly impressive list of major news stories, and one that had kept the British media in business for many years. And now I had been offered the opportunity to join this top team. I looked the Director straight in the eyes. "You know," I said, "a chance in a lifetime doesn't come along every week."

"And I want you to head the survey that proves it," he replied.

The Startling Truth Behind *Today*

The remarkably frank autobiography of Sue MacGregor, presenter of Radio 4's Today *programme for the past forty-five years.*

CHAPTER ONE

I SHALL never forget the day John Humphrys spilt his coffee – and it nearly landed on my lap!!

It was a day that began like any other. We had all arrived in the *Today* studio on the dot of 4am. John had been drinking from a cup of hot coffee, and had just replaced it in the saucer – when he nudged it with his left elbow and spilt it over the table!

Luckily, it only went over the daily newspapers – but another few inches and it might have gone straight over my lap! But I was always the consummate professional, and I went on reading the news – even though I realised that the coffee had been spilt on the table.

John – who, let me make it clear, is a tremendously dedicated journalist and valued colleague – will never live it down! Not that the "spilt coffee" episode in any way detracts from his reputation as a serious radio presenter. Far from it: it was no more than a chance incident – though highly amusing in retrospect!

Over the past forty-five years, the *Today* programme has given rise to a huge amount of similarly hilarious anecdotes. People are always asking me, for instance, whether it is really true that I once inadvertently said "Good Afternoon" to a leading government minister (who shall remain nameless!) – when it was still 8.00 in the morning!

I am able to reply in all honesty that in fact this incident did not happen to me at all. In fact, it happened to my predecessor Jack de Manio, back in 1954. But, needless to say, I have often dined out on it!

CHAPTER TWO

AS AN experienced broadcaster, I have made it a golden rule never to conduct an interview without first paper-clipping my questions together. It was a method that became known in the office as "the paper clip method" or "PCM". It had worked for me over many years but shortly before interviewing the Junior Minister for Transport I had lost my paper clip – and now the thought of conducting a major interview without the famous "PCM" sent a shiver down one's spine!

Colleagues still talk about how I initiated a frantic search for that paper clip. But I am a true professional, and with only two minutes to go before our interview went "on air", I had decided to go ahead and try to conduct the interview without it. Fifty seconds to go, and our studio guest was being led into the studio when Brian Redhead turned to me and said: "Is this by any chance your paper clip, Sue?"

He then passed me the paper clip. Yes, it most certainly was my paper clip! I had inadvertently dropped it on the studio floor!!

A white-knuckle day, to be sure – but, thanks to our sheer professionalism, our audience never guessed the tense drama that took place on the other side of the microphone that February morning!

After thirty-five years, one can look back on this extraordinary drama with a wry smile. In fact, I have been "dining out" on it ever since! But, on a more serious level, I can assure you it made me distinctly uncomfortable at the time.

CHAPTER THREE

I SHALL never forget the day leading politician Stephen Byers asked me if he could have a second cup of instant coffee.

This was the sort of thing that made every day different for those of us who worked on the legendary *Today* programme. One day, a leading politician would ask for no cups of coffee – and the very next day another would ask for two!!

I trust I'm letting no secrets out of the bag when I reveal that the *Today* programme always prided itself in supplying a full range of hot beverages to its guests. Not only coffee but tea as well.

There was always a lot of talk about coffee in the legendary *Today* studios. John Humphrys liked his with milk but no sugar, but Jim Naughtie preferred his black. In the old days, the legendary Brian Redhead used to prefer tea. It was typical of the man.

On a personal note, I liked mine with just a touch of milk. Strangely, I never saw John stir his coffee – but then he probably had no need to. As I have already exclusively revealed, he didn't take sugar.

CHAPTER FOUR

AND SO to my Stephen Byers "second cup" anecdote.

I had just finished cross-questioning him for the usual three minutes fifty seconds – allowing ten seconds for traffic updates to take us up to the 8 o'clock news – when he pointed at his empty cup.

"Would there be any chance," he said, "of a second cup?"

"Oh lawks!" I said. "I think we've just run out!"

But – luckily for the *Today* team! – there were still two teaspoonfuls left in the old jar – and someone had remembered to buy a new jar too!

We all breathed a collective sigh of relief – and then, like true professionals, got on with the job. And as for our loyal listeners, bless 'em – they honestly didn't suspect a thing!

A Storm in a Teacup

John Humphrys: A tidal wave of disbelief and outrage spread across Britain yesterday at unconfirmed reports of a storm in a teacup. I have with me Home Office Minister Ron Turning. Mr Turning, could you confirm that a storm is indeed raging in the teacup in question?

Ron Turning: Good morning, John –

John Humphrys: But that's not the question, is it?

Ron Turning: I was only saying good morning, John.

John Humphrys: But a lot of our listeners will be saying to themselves, yes, that's just what he would say – why can't he just simply answer the question?

Ron Turning: To answer your question, John –

John Humphrys: At last!

Ron Turning: We do not believe that there is a storm in that particular teacup, no.

John Humphrys: Well, that's not what we're hearing. Far from it. Our reporter was told by a reliable source that, and I quote, "I've never seen such a huge storm in a single teacup. A storm was raging through that teacup, causing vast waves to spread across the surface of the tea." And it doesn't end there. He went on to say, "A significant portion of the tea in question ended up spilling over the side of the teacup – and has now come to rest in the saucer." So what do you say to that, Mr Turning?

Ron Turning: Well, if what you're saying is true, John, I'd honestly say it's just a storm in a teacup.

John Humphrys: "JUST a storm in a teacup!" By the sound of it you're not taking these reports very seriously! A number of our listeners will be left wondering whether you would feel the same if it was your teacup that was experiencing this sort of massive disruption. Yes or no?

Ron Turning: You're raising a number of different points.

John Humphrys: Yes or no?

Ron Turning: The storm isn't taking place in my teacup, so it's purely hypothetical.

John Humphrys: Yes or no?

Ron Turning: I – I – I – we mustn't get it out of proportion.

John Humphrys: You see, Mr Turning, our listeners will be saying to themselves, "This government was elected in the belief that it would reduce the number of storms in teacups. But every day we switch on our radios and we hear more and more reports of tea whipped up into tsunamis, tea spiralling into potentially fatal whirlpools, and even, on some occasions, tea spilling over the rim of the cup and into the saucer." And you know what they're saying to themselves, don't you, Mr Turning? They're saying, "Faced with catastrophes like these, when is this government going to keep its promises, for crying out loud?"

Ron Turning: But this is just a storm in a teacup, John –

John Humphrys: Will you be resigning?

Ron Turning: Certainly n –

John Humphrys: I'm going to have to stop you there, Mr Turning. And now over to Charlotte Green for the latest news headlines.

Charlotte Green: The news headlines. In an interview for the *Today* programme, Home Office Minister Ron Turning refused to resign over the storm raging in a teacup. A spokesman for the Teacup Storm Prevention Association said its members were disappointed by the minister's intransigence, and called for more government resources to prevent further outbreaks in future.

I Was Horrified:
Letters of Complaint

SIR – Was no one involved with the making of *The Lost Prince* aware that neither Edward VII nor anyone else would have shot pheasants while the sycamore and oak trees were in full leaf? Needless to say, I watched the programme with my magnifying glass firmly in hand. Imagine my horror, then, upon noticing that the laces on His Majesty's shoes in one scene were double-knotted – a practice quite alien to the court at that time.

~ **Wallace Arnold CBE, the Garrick Club**

SIR – Was no one involved with the making of *The Lost Prince* aware that neither Prince John nor anyone else above servant level would have pronounced the "g"s in the phrase "good morning"?

At that time, it was considered vulgar, and rightly so, for the well bred to enunciate this ugliest – or uliest – of letters. Had one of the young princes encountered Edward VII over the breakfast table, he would have bowed low and said, "Ood mornin randpa", to which the reply would have come: "Ood mornin randson". It is high time television actors were taught the correct way to pronounce this most basic of greetings, or reetings.

~ **Simone Heffer (Miss), Barking, Essex**

SIR – I watched *The Lost Prince* with mounting horror. For all her faults, and they were many, Queen Mary treated everyone she encountered with the utmost courtesy. She would never – never – have struck her fist on a table, downed a half-pint of ale in a single gulp, burped, and screamed, "You're right out of order," before taking a lunge at a complete stranger.

It was only when the programme had been under way for a good twenty minutes that it was pointed out to me by a friend "in the know" that I was not watching *The Lost Prince* but a programme called *EastEnders* on another channel.

Surely it is time television manufacturers cleared up this confusion and made it absolutely clear to viewers exactly which programme it is they are watching. Not since last week, when I viewed *Ready Steady Cook* under the firm impression that it was David Attenborough's *Life of Mammals* have I been so dreadfully upset.

~ **Dickie Hart, Isle of Man**

SIR – May I add to the growing list of complaints concerning the grotesque solecisms in the recent BBC TV production of *The Lost Prince*?

I was frankly astonished to hear Queen Mary enunciating the word "teapot". In those circles, it was, of course, considered dreadfully vulgar to use that word. In those days, "teapot" carried the secondary meaning of "ankle sock", and would never have been employed in polite society. Queen Mary would have avoided its use on

pain of death. I need hardly add that the double "f" in "coffeepot" remained silent until long after the outbreak of the Great War.
~ **The Hon Eileen Dover, Wittering**

SIR – Am I alone in noticing one glaring historical inaccuracy in the recent film *Gosford Park*? In one scene, three-quarters of the way through the film, Robinson, the under-valet, places his left hand to his mouth while clearing his throat in early March.

This would, of course, have resulted in his immediate dismissal. In all the smarter country houses, under-valets were required when clearing their throats to place their right hands to their mouths in any month containing the letters "h" or "c".

As March is unique in containing both, the correct procedure for an under-valet was always to place his right hand over his mouth, then to affect a further throat clearance, this time employing his right elbow as a protective shield.

We surely need no further indication of the disastrous drop in standards in the film industry – and, alas, beyond.
~ **Simone Heffer (Miss), Barking, Essex**

SIR – Further to Miss Heffer's letter, I wish to share my very real sense of horror and disgust in the early "below stairs" scene in *Gosford Park*.

A maid is seen spreading butter over a piece of toast for her master from left to right – an action that would, of course, have resulted in her immediate dismissal. In those more civilised times, bread was spread from left to right – but toast was spread from right to left.

In another scene, the washerwoman is glimpsed walking forwards along a corridor. Honestly! As is well known, washerwomen were trained to walk backwards down corridors, so that if they dropped any laundry they would spot it at once.
~ **Tim Erity, London SE11**

SIR – *Gosford Park* contains a howling error hitherto unnoticed. When the guests assemble in the drawing room after dinner on the first night, one can just glimpse a Jimi Hendrix record on the coffee table – yet Jimi Hendrix was not to enter the hit parade for another thirty-odd years!

Furthermore, at one point Lady Drainbrough turns to Sir Archibald McSwallow and mutters something under her breath. After repeated attempts at lip reading, I am as certain as I possibly can be that what she actually says is, "Should Transport Secretary Stephen Byers resign?" – yet, as your readers will no doubt be aware, Byers was not even born in 1934, let alone in a position to resign!

Might I also point out that the British aristocracy in the first half of the 1930s would never have employed First World War heavy artillery for a pheasant shoot?

~ **Frank O'Pinion, Wittering, Berks**

SIR – Your recent correspondents should be aware that there is also a glaring error in the Walt Disney movie *Snow White and the Seven Dwarfs*. The idea of a responsible young woman choosing to live with seven dwarfs, some of them over twice her age, will strike many as far-fetched. Furthermore, there is no historical evidence that such an event ever took place.

~ **Ann Teak, Mull**

SIR – In casting valuable light on Disney's disgraceful *Snow White and the Seven Dwarfs*, your correspondent Ann Teak misses one fact. My great-grandmother was at school with the so-called Wicked Witch. They remained firm friends throughout their lives. My great-grandmother maintained that far from being the unpleasant harridan of Disney's warped imagination, the Wicked Witch was a philanthropic lady, and that in her self-serving recounting of her side of the tale, Snow White was motivated by common greed.

~ **Cornelius Hook, (Capt, Retd), Great Ham**

SIR – Was I alone in noticing a two-door red E-type Jaguar parked discreetly behind a hedge in the middle distance in the opening scene of Franco Zeffirelli's *Romeo and Juliet*?

~ **Jessica Wheatcroft (Miss), Bickering**

SIR – I can reassure Miss Wheatcroft that she was certainly not alone. Close inspection of the scene also reveals that on the back shelving of the Jaguar in question there is a plastic dog with a nodding head – yet these novelty items for the vehicle were almost certainly not available in sixteenth-century Verona.

~ **Peter Out, Wilts**

SIR – During a recent edition of BBC1's *EastEnders* drama series, I caught a brief glimpse of Lord Nelson's great flagship *Victory* sailing around Albert Square.

Quite apart from the fact that the ship in question is now moored in Portsmouth Harbour, there is little likelihood of any ancient seagoing vessel sailing around the streets of London. Present traffic restrictions expressly forbid it.

~ **Patrick A. Cake, Boreham**

SIR – Further to your lively correspondence concerning anachronisms and inaccuracies in *Gosford Park*, am I alone in noticing an open umbrella being held above the head? Until 1948, it was considered fearfully bad manners to keep an umbrella open over the head: etiquette dictated that, in the teeth of pouring rain, one should keep one's umbrella firmly closed, and at right angles to the body. An open umbrella would only ever be employed upside down, and then solely as a tomato soup container convenient for large shooting parties.

Incidentally, in the grander country houses, tomato soup was not officially recognised as a soup until 1938. Until then, it was employed solely to ward off midges. Household staff would douse all shooting hats with tomato soup prior to the first drive, driving midges quite mad, though, of course, it had the unfortunate side-effect of attracting wasps and bees.

It must also be admitted that soup dripping from the hat down the forehead and into the eyes sometimes ruined a good day's sport. To this day, I maintain that Lord Rumbelow's tragic death from gunshot wounds need never have occurred had not Viscount Budgen's valet been so profligate when filling his deerstalker with tomato soup.

~ **Wallace Arnold, the Travellers Club, SW1**

The 2006 Teddy Bears Picnic

1.

If you go out in the woods today[i]
You're sure of a big surprise.
If you go out in the woods today[ii]
You'd better go in disguise.[iii]
For every bear that ever there was
Will gather there for certain[iv], because
Today's the day the teddy bears have their picnic[v]

(i) The woods have recently been renamed the Tesco Leisure and Fun Park. Car parking is free for two hours maximum to customers of the local Tesco. Unauthorised cars will be clamped.

(ii) The woods are in fact closed until September 2007 for wholesale repairs and safety paving. "Many of the trees were unsuitable for small children to play on, so have had to be removed," explains a Health and Safety Officer. "And following a great many complaints about the unevenness of the floor of the wood from parents and guardians of small children, we are also undertaking an extensive resurfacing operation. The whole-sale tarmacing of the ground will make it much easier for the disabled and infirm to move freely around the wood without encountering holes, bumps or logs.

(iii) Though from 2009 onwards, national identity cards will of course be compulsory throughout the British Isles.

(iv) Local police have in fact been instructed to disperse all groups of bears over twelve in number with immediate effect, in order to avoid a public affray.

(v) Arrangements for picnics and/or barbecues involving over six people and/or animals must be made twenty-eight days in advance with the parks department. Warning: the dropping of litter may carry an immediate fine of up to £1,000.

2.

Picnic time for teddy bears,
The little teddy bears are having a lovely time today.
Watch them, catch them unawares[vi]
And see them picnic on their holiday.
See them gaily dance about[vii]
They love to play and shout[viii]
And never have any cares.[ix]
At six o'clock their mommies and daddies[x]
Will take them home to bed
Because they're tired[xi] little teddy bears.

(vi) In recent weeks, there have been reports of unauthorised person(s) loitering in the woods in a truly sickening attempt to catch the little teddy bears unawares. If any member of the public should detect inappropriate behaviour from such person(s) they must inform the police or parks department immediately. Do not approach the offender: he or she may well be dangerous.

(vii) A free Department of Health Leaflet ("Gaily Dancing About: The Risks to You and Your Partner") is available from the kiosk situated by the toilet area in the Wood Visitor Centre.

(viii) Permissible in public areas of low density housing, but only within the strict guidelines laid down by the Noise Abatement Act.

(ix) Time and time again, surveys have shown that the vast majority of teddy bears do in fact have cares. They may like to seek help for any cares they may have at the Teddy Bear Trauma Counselling Centre. "For many years I was hugged and petted," says one bear, who has asked to remain anonymous. "Then overnight I was thrown out and abandoned in the bottom of a forgotten cupboard. It frankly knocked the stuffing out of me." This is the sort of tale we hear all too often at the TBTCC.

(x) Or legal guardians.

(xi) Is your teddy bear on drugs? This is a problem faced by many parents or guardians. Sluggishness or drowsiness are often the early signs of an incipient drug problem. If in doubt, call the police.

3.

If you go out in the woods today,
You'd better not go alone[xii]
It's lovely out in the woods today[xiii]
But safer to stay at home[xiv]
For every bear that ever there was[xv]
Will gather there for certain, because
Today's the day the teddy bears have their picnic
(to chorus)

(xii) By law, children below the age of fifteen who go into the woods must be accompanied at all times by an adult. Failure to do so may result in a fine or detention.

(xiii) Though statistics clearly demonstrate that being struck by lightning while sheltering in woods accounts for up to 207 deaths a year worldwide.

(xiv) Official Department of Health figures would appear to tell a different tale. Accidents in the home constitute a significant proportion of deaths and injuries among people of all ages. For the free leaflet "Thirty-five Ways to Reduce Terror and Misery in Your Home" please write to The Rt Hon Patricia Hewitt MP at the Department of Health.

xv) Reminder: large and/or unruly gatherings of teddy bears may be dispersed and/or moved on without prior warning under new powers given to the security services by the Prevention of Terrorism Act.

4.

Every teddy bear that's been good[xvi]
Is sure of a treat today
There's lots of wonderful things to eat[xvii]
And wonderful games to play[xviii]
Beneath the trees, where nobody sees[xix]
They'll hide and seek as long as they please
Today's the day the teddy bears have their picnic[xx]

(xvi) Teddy Bears that have not behaved in a conventional manner are likely to be suffering from Attention Deficit Disorder. Apply to your GP for the appropriate drugs to ensure your teddy bear meets the required standards of interpersonal behaviour on future occasions. Or send a stamped addressed envelope to your local Advice Centre for the leaflet, Coping with Your Problem Bear.

(xvii) Wonderful games in the new Teddy Amusement Centre situated near the edge of the wood include Ram Raider III, Bloodlust: The Final Countdown *and* Kill Nan.

(xviii) Patrons are reminded that smoking is strictly forbidden in all public areas. Also, please clear up after your teddy bear with the scoopers provided.

(xix) Inaccurate. These premises are in fact guarded by 24-hour CCTV.

(xx) Cancelled until next year due to leaves on the ground.

Anne Diamond's Diary

I'd been crying all night. Sobbing my heart out, strewing sodden Kleenexes all over the floor. But I fought back from despair.

It took all the courage I could muster to appear before those breakfast television cameras all bright and breezy, the nation's favourite girl next door.

To millions of ordinary viewers, I was the most famous and glamorous person in the world, bigger than Marilyn Monroe, who anyway some argued was dead.

But inside, I was hurting.

Men! They were always letting me down. Bubbly Steve from "Good Morning Cornwall", who'd romanced me royally – before going back to his wife. Smashing Damian from "Have Another Biscuit, Berkshire" who'd smothered me with flowers and kisses – before going back to his wife. Handsome Geoff from "Elevenses from Edinburgh", who bought me designer lingerie from a top store in London's fashionable Old Kent Road before (you've guessed it!) going back to his wife.

One minute I would be romancing top Hollywood hunks, dating politicians and rock stars and lunching with royalty – the next I would be fighting back from despair as yet another man went back to his wife.

So when a deeply dishy guy – a former prime minister who I will never name but who was a silver-haired bachelor with a yacht, a grand piano and a contacts book to die for, and who had been literally huge in the Seventies – phoned and invited me to fight back from despair with him over a candlelit dinner for two at his multi-million-pound designer mansion in Salisbury, I accepted in a jiffy.

"Champagne, smoked salmon, all the trimmings – and hang the expense! How does that sound?" he asked, seductively. Yes, he certainly knew how to treat a lady.

I arrived at his front door looking a million dollars in a Prada dress that would have given my poor bank manager the proverbial nightmares!

The former prime minister who I'll never name – he once confided to me in his deep voice that he'd faced two elections in a single year! – opened the door barefoot, wearing nothing but a designer bathrobe and a huge grin. "I've just had a sensuous, relaxing power shower," he purred. "Come on in, darling – the Moet is on ice. And – by the way, Anne – you look gorgeous."

Over champagne, we discussed politics, world affairs, Europe. He told me how he was fighting back from despair after being dreadfully let down by a woman who'd run off with his job. I told him that to the rest of the world I may look brilliantly successful, with the looks and the charm to match, but inside I was fighting back from despair.

We cried a lot, and laughed a lot, and then fell into each other's arms. "Now, my darling," he said, leading me up the designer stairs, "let's put you first for once." He then scooped me into his arms, carried me to his bedroom and treated me to a reading from his collected speeches, 1970–74.

In the wee small hours of the morning, we kissed and said good-bye. I pulled on my designer heels and teetered away. It had been a wonderful night, and now I could return to the TV-AM sofa, feeling every inch a top-rated celebrity, ready to sparkle and delight the nation as always.

I may have made it look easy, but presenting the top-rated *Wakey Wakey Britain* was acknowledged as one of the toughest jobs in the whole world.

One minute, I would have to ask top singer Vince Hill about his fabulous new album – and the next I would be quizzing top politician Fred Mulley about his smashing new policy initiative. It was vital I didn't mix the two guys up, or their answers might come out all muddled.

If ever there was a major natural disaster – an earthquake or a plane crash, with many hundreds feared dead – I'd have to remember not to smile so much, out of respect for the families. But, then again, if the disaster was particularly dreadful, I'd sometimes smile just that little bit more, to help put a bit of sunshine back in their lives. Then every few minutes I would have to look at the right camera and say, "We'll be back with more – after the break." And if we were due for the weather from Trish, I'd have to remember to say, "And now over to Trish – for the weather."

The pressure was unbearable, and don't let anyone kid you it wasn't. Presenting *Wakey Wakey Britain* was like rescuing over three hundred innocent men, women and children from a burning house under sustained enemy fire every single day – then going back with a wounded leg and blood pouring from your head to rescue three hundred more. And all the time having to wear a sunny smile.

Looking back, I should have twigged that Mike Hollingsworth was married the moment he said he had a wife. But it truly never crossed my mind.

Life with Mike was a roller coaster. One minute, I was in despair. The next minute, I was fighting my way back from despair. And the next minute, I was in despair again.

I first met him when I was presenting the *Time for a Nice Cuppa* slot on ATV's top-rated *Start the Day in Birmingham* programme. The chief presenter, Carol, had sadly broken her leg after falling over a banana skin that had fallen accidentally out of my handbag. I was desperate to help her out by stepping into her shoes, so she wouldn't be missed.

That very morning, a colleague introduced Mike to me as our new producer. When he touched my face I felt an instant surge, like a bolt of electricity. It turned out he always used a cattle prod on his presenters. He said it got the best out of them. I knew then and there that here was a man I'd follow anywhere.

Two years later, I was married to Mike and we were living the Hollywood dream at our home in Edgbaston. A true professional, Mike was 100 per cent committed to making ITV's *A Nice Natter with Anne and Nick* a huge success, so imagine my excitment when, over champagne and lashings of smoked salmon, he told me he'd had a great idea for improving it. "From now on, we're going to rename it, *A Nice Natter with Carol and Nick* he said, "It's got a friendlier sort of ring to it."

I thought nothing of it at the time. But six months later I discovered that, for the past year, I'd been presenting the programme from our living room every morning – and none of the cameras had been switched on. It meant only one thing: from now on, I would be fighting back from despair.

Where Are They Now? Number 241: Snow White and the Seven Dwarfs

THE SEVEN DWARFS first shot to stardom alongside Snow White in 1937 in the hugely successful Walt Disney film *Snow White and the Seven Dwarfs*. There followed a well-publicised break-up with Snow White, in which "irreconcilable artistic differences" were cited.

"Snow White always considered herself so much bigger than the rest of us," complained Grumpy at the time. Some dwarfs claimed, off the record, that her high-pitched voice had been hard to live with; and there were repeated rumours that without the make-up her famous complexion was notably rubicund.

Sadly, in 1941, Snow White's cleaner-than-clean image took a sharp downturn when top columnist Hedda Hopper revealed that for a year she had been living *à deux* with controversial star Cruella de Ville. For the next few years, White struggled to re-establish her goody-two-shoes image in a series of Hollywood B-movies such as *Song of Snow White* and *The Swiss Family White*, but they proved unpopular with the general public. During the 1950s, she battled with alcohol; her brief marriage to Hollywood hellraiser Tony Curtis was to end in divorce.

In the 1960s, her attempts to re-invent herself as Grey Slush met with only limited success. Nowadays, she can occasionally be spotted on a leading shopping channel in the Miami area, giving her celebrity endorsement to the Snow White Collection – a range of health-giving potions in a choice of green, mauve or pink, for you to imbibe in the comfort of your own back garden, garage or luxury under-stairs cupboard.

Some commentators noted with amazement her youthful looks when she appeared as a guest on the *Richard and Judy Show* just over a month ago. But she snapped back: "Don't tell me Mother Teresa never had a facelift."

However hard they tried, the seven dwarfs, who starred opposite White in the 1937 Disney classic, were never to find such a perfect co-star again. Their 1943 follow-up *Rin-Tin-Tin and the Seven Dwarfs* proved a box-office flop, as did its sequel, the *Keystone Cops and the Seven Dwarfs*, which some critics described as "over-crowded". Their success in the 1977 made-for-TV movie *Jaws 4: the Seven Dwarfs* also proved short-lived.

Individual projects undertaken by original members of the group have met with mixed fortunes. Three-times-divorced Grumpy is a regular in the courtrooms of five continents. In particular, he has devoted much of his life pursuing litigation against his neighbours and his neighbours' neighbours. He is at present a leading member of the Noise Abatement Society. Until last year, he was also secretary to the Ramblers' Association, but last year he departed under a cloud, announcing that he was unwilling to let them walk all over him. He is no longer on speaking terms with the other six dwarfs, which he blames on them.

His former colleague Sleepy can sometimes be heard talking on Melvyn Bragg's award-winning radio programme, *In Our Time*, but only when he can be bothered. He also works half-time as the forward planning director of Railtrack, and runs a public relations company, whose clients presently include Anthea Turner, Piers Morgan and former Iraqi president Saddam Hussein.

The self-styled leader of the seven dwarfs, Doc, was struck off by the GMC in the early 1970s after an investigation revealed his qualifications to be fraudulent. He now writes a medical column for a Sunday tabloid, and dispenses health advice on television and radio, as well as appearing as an expert witness for the plaintiff in cases involving compensation.

Happy is believed to have completed a book detailing his experiences on Prozac, and is at present auditioning for a post as a children's television presenter. He currently co-runs a media advisory service with former newscaster Martyn Lewis. Among their clients is Defence Minister Geoff Hoon.

Happy's former colleague Sneezy is a founder member of London's fashionable Groucho Club, and is regularly to be seen disappearing into the back rooms for private discussions with business contacts. Colleagues comment on his extraordinary drive and energy, but sadly few of his recent projects have got off the ground.

For many years, Dopey found it hard to break into the elitist world of broadcasting, but the rise of reality TV has given him the opportunity he always needed. He is now creative director of Endemol, with responsibility for the creation of more than 2,000 new celebrities over the next six months. "Jordan is keen to break into current affairs, which could do with a bloody good modernise," he says. "And we have Simon Cowell lined up to replace Jon Snow on Channel 4 News, which is to my mind way too elitist at the moment."

At the time of going to press, nothing is known of the whereabouts of Bashful.

The End

Way to Go

(1) STEPHEN BYERS – A STATEMENT

"Thank you very much for coming this afternoon. I am not going to make a personal statement. Some people will no doubt maintain that I just said that I was not going to make a personal statement. They are, I'm afraid, labouring under a misapprehension. What I actually said was that I am NOW going to make a personal statement.

"I wrote it myself, without any assistance. Actually, that's not what I said. What I actually said is that I may or may not have had assistance in the writing of my personal statement. That is a departmental matter. Any assistance I had was purely to assist me in the making of my personal statement, and therefore cannot in the strictest sense be regarded as assistance.

"Yesterday afternoon, I asked to see the Prime Minister. Consequently, I went to see him yesterday morning. I see no contradiction in those two statements. It is purely a matter of emphasis and interpretation. In this rapidly changing world of which I am proud to be an inhabitant, it is perfectly possible to see someone in the morning having asked to see him in the afternoon.

"When I saw him at twelve noon precisely, the Prime Minister informed me that I have decided to leave the government of my own accord.

"I am leaving because I have at all times tried to behave honourably and with the interests of the British people at heart. For this reason, I have become a distraction from what the government is trying to do. Key policy issues are being distorted by my involvement.

"The people who know me best know that I am not a lion. That is not what I said. I said they know I am not a liar. The people who know me best know that, if I was a liar, which I am not, I would not automatically lie about the fact that I was not a liar, as that might

425

reveal me as a liar, which means that when I say that I am not a liar I am not necessarily lying.

"I have been kept going by the overwhelming support I have received from parliamentary colleagues, Labour Party members and members of the public. I have had letters of support from literally millions of ordinary rail-travellers the world over who tell me they are convinced that I am just the right man for the job and they know I would never lie.

"At this point, I would like to offer my apologies for my failure to apologise for the apologies I might have made had I done anything for which I needed to apologise. Which fortunately I have not.

"I now intend to return to the backbenches to argue the case for the things I have always believed in. At this moment in time, I do not intend to say what these things may or may not be. I am not prepared to get bogged down in hypotheticals.

"I look forward to going back to represent the interests of my constituents in North Tyneside. I shall, of course, be travelling by train. That's not what I said. What I in fact said was that I would be travelling by train if a car was, or might seem to be, unavailable. It's all a matter of interpretation.

"Finally, I can confirm that, contrary to media speculation, I have not just offered my resignation. I was merely spelling out a series of options."

(II) TONY BLAIR – A STATEMENT

"As I have said many times in the past few months, when it comes to important policy questions, Steve has always taken the right decisions for the future. His resignation from government today totally supports me in this belief.

"I am convinced that Steve has always had a great future. But now it is time to put Steve's great future behind us. Steve can be proud of the part he has played in delivering on the government's agenda. His achievements are without end. I will waste no time in trying to remember them.

"When he came to see me on Monday, he was clear that, in the interests of the government, it was Tuesday.

"I struggled to convince him it was Monday. He finally agreed with me, saying that it was merely a matter of emphasis, and he had always maintained it was Monday. He added that anyone who knew him would know he would never have said it was Tuesday when, strictly speaking, it wasn't, and that Tuesday was just one of seven options he had been considering. I understand and respect that decision.

"Steve has endured a huge amount of criticism. When he came to see me on Sunday, I told him that I was convinced that some of it was deeply unfair. He suggested that all of it was deeply unfair, but he agreed to settle for most. So I am pleased today to stand shoulder to shoulder behind Steve and confirm that at least some of the criticism that has been levelled at him was very slightly unfair.

"Meanwhile, he has continued to face up to difficult policy decisions. Masterminding the deterioration of a national rail network is never easy, but Stephen met the challenge with commitment and conviction. And I have no doubt whatever that, in the fullness of time, his commitment will, indeed, lead to his conviction.

(May 30, 2002)

Tony Blair's Speech to the Labour Party Conference, October 2005

LOOK, I DON'T have to do this job, y'know.

It's not something I do for my own amusement.

Frankly, I've got much better things to do with my time.

Looking after the kids. Enjoying a spot of gardening. Relaxing with a good book.

Kicking a ball about.

So why do I persevere? That's the question. Why do I keep on at this job of being Prime Minister when everyone here today would prefer that I did something else?

I'll tell you why. Because you – every one of you here today, and many millions more decent, hardworking people out there in the country at large – you all deserve me.

So what now? The world is on the move again. Yes it's always spun around on its axis – that's something the excellent science departments in our excellent centres of learning continue to teach us, and we should be very grateful to them for it. But now it's spinning faster than ever.

And – let's be clear about this – if we don't spin with it, we'll only get dizzy.

And fall over. Flat on our faces.

Opportunity for the man.

Sorry, the many.

Opportunity for the many, not the few.

Our values. Unity. Tolerance. Respect. Strong communities, working as one. For shared goals. Shared values.

And to those who do not share these values, I say this.

Out! Now! Stewards! Police! Take them away!

And to those remaining, I say this.

May that be a lesson to you all.

Y'know, values don't change. That's the way they are. But times do.

And when times change, well, you've got to take those values to one side, and you've got to look those values straight in the eye, and then you've got to say to those values, loud and clear: "Look, I respect your point of view. You've got every right to be stubborn and remote and outdated and utterly ridiculous, if that's what you want. But look, chum – don't ask me to tag along with you!"

New Labour. New Challenges. New Visions. New Age. New Town. New Order. New Penny. New Year. New Avengers. New York, New York. New Stock Just In. New Roadworks Ahead.

So what is the challenge? This is the challenge. The challenge is this. The challenge is our challenge. And it is up to each of us to meet that challenge. And challenge that challenge. And to say to that challenge: yes, you are a challenge. And that's a challenge. But you are a challenge worth making.

And yes: you are worth that challenge!

I hear people, good people, who say we have to stop and debate globalisation. Typical! Next, they'll be telling us we've got to stop and debate Iraq!

Well, there's always one or two in every crowd. And to them I say this. I want to apologise, to sincerely apologise, for what you have just forced me to do. I've said I'm sorry.

So – stewards! Take them away!

* * *

Some things really get to you. Believe me. Look, I've never told anyone this before. But I once saw a duck crossing a busy road. A duck with all her little ducklings behind her. And, d'y'know what? She was counting all those little ducklings – one, two, three, four, five, six – safely to the other side.

Even the smallest one.

The fluffy one with the limp.

And I tell you what.

That Mummy Duck was doing the right thing. Because, for her, it was the right thing to do.

Or what about the little child I met last week? In hospital. Desperately ill. Looked me straight in the eye. Little tear running down her cheek. Said: "You're the best, Tony – and don't let anyone tell you otherwise."

And then gently passed away.

Y'know, I've never said this before. But an elderly man came up to me the other day. Lovely bloke. Wobble in his voice. Not well off. Scraping to make ends meet. Salt of the earth. Tears in his eyes. And you know what this lovely old bloke said to me?

He said: "You're standing on my toe."

Then he looked me deep in the face, this weepy old bloke. And he said: "I want you to keep standing on my toe, Tony. Because I know you're a decent kinda guy, and I know you know what you're doing."

And – I haven't told anyone this before – but as I stood there, standing on his toe, I thought: the cynics may never understand why I'm standing on the toe of this senior citizen. But he understands. And that's good enough for me.

And I think of little Rachel, aged eleven, from Warminster, suffering from nothing too serious, thank goodness, but with a bit of a sniffle, what with winter coming on. Little Rachel wrote to me last week. And you know what she said? She said that, though she profoundly disagreed with me over Iraq, she thought I'd done the right thing. And then she sent her love.

And her little puppy, Patch – he sent his love, too.

And don't believe anyone who tells you they don't feel choked up when they receive letters like that. Sorry, guys. You'll have to excuse me for one second. (Pulls out handkerchief. Blows. Continues.)

* * *

Did you miss me, when I went away? Did you hang my picture on your wall?

Hello. Hello. It's good to be back! Back with a focus on what really matters.

And you know what really matters? I'll tell you what really matters.

What really matters – that's what really matters.

I said no complacency in 1997. I said no complacency in 2001. And so I think to myself, it seemed to work then – so why not say it again now?

Where we have lost support, we go out and win it back.

Where we have made mistakes, we say so.

So thank goodness we haven't.

People are thinking. Do we go back with the Tories? Or forward with New Labour? And I say to them this.

Forwards, not backwards. Up, not down.

In, not out. Big, not little. Hot, not cold.

Start, not stop. Fortnum, not Mason.

Callard, not Bowser. Torvill, not Dean. Pinky, not Perky.

Y'know, I understand why some people feel angry. Not just over Iraq, but over many of the difficult decisions we have made and which they haven't appreciated because they frankly can't be bothered to do their homework and see things through my eyes.

Yes, I've had it up to here.

And, as ever, a lot of it is about me. It's not a bad idea to think of it in terms of it being like any relationship. You, the British people. Me, the Prime Minister. First, you loved me, you really loved me. And I didn't even notice you. Then you stopped noticing me.

And that's when I really got interested.

So we got married, and we had our baby. We were over the moon. But then it wouldn't stop crying. Sleepless nights. Tempers frayed. The mood changes.

It's your turn, not mine. No, I did it last night. And then, all of a sudden, there you are, the British people, thinking, you're not listening, and I'm thinking, you're not hearing me, and you're thinking, when's it going to stop, he's stretching this metaphor to breaking point.

And before you know it, you raise your voice. I raise mine. Some of you throw crockery. So I say, right, that's it, I'm in charge, I've just about had enough, you're under house arrest, it's not your bloody country, it's mine, I'll deport you if you say another word and it's ID cards for the rest of you.

* * *

But now I want to move back in with you. And not just back. But forward.

Forward and back. Back and forward.

I believe in you, the British people, as much as ever. And I know that you, the British people, believe in me.

We go well together. Everyone says so. We always have done. And I'm different now. I've changed.

You see, I don't know how to put this. But, well, I think I love you. So what am I afraid of? I'm afraid that I'm not sure of. A love there is no cure for.

I think I love you. Isn't that what life is made of? Though it worries me to say. That I never felt this way. Before.

* * *

Look, I've learnt a tough lesson over these past years. And the lesson I've learnt is that, look, I've learnt a tough lesson.

This job may be a harsh teacher. But it is a wise one.

I learnt that, however pleasant popularity is, being "all things to all people" never lasts long. No, you can't be all things to all people. You have to be lots of different things to lots of different people.

As I struggled with the levers of power, saw with genuine urgency the challenges a new world was thrusting on Britain, I was determined to do the right thing. But if you're not careful, there's a danger you become enslaved to empty slogans and childish phrases.

So that's why I started the Big Conversation, and now Forward, Not Backwards.

I went back out, and instead of talking at people, I listened at them.

And I learnt.

And what I learnt was this.

I learnt I still have a lot of teaching to do.

* * *

So today I present you with Six Pledges.

Pledge number one.

To make a further five pledges. And – I promise you this – that's up to and including the sixth pledge.

Pledge number two.

No stinting on pledges.

Pledge number three.

Pledges free on the point of delivery.

Pledge number four.

Your children receiving their fair share of pledges.And your children's children too.

Pledge number five.

Your pledges safer in our hands.

Pledge number six.

More pledges for you, your family and friends.

Pledge number seven.

A seventh pledge for nothing. Why?

Because you're worth it.

* * *

On Friday in Newcastle, I talked to a patient suffering from a broken leg, a collapsed lung, and facial scarring.

And you know what he told me?

He told me a senior Tory had done it to him.

And I thought: how dare these right-wing Tories strut around causing ordinary, decent men and women serious injury.

The same night, back in my own constituency, a woman came over to me, limping badly, in desperate need of a knee operation. And she told me who had kicked her repeatedly in the knee.

John Redwood.

How backward. How aggressive. How typical. I never want that sort of right-wing philosophy in charge of our country. Not now. Not ever.

* * *

London. London is a truly great city. A world-beating city. A city with a past. But also a city with a future. A city of buildings, yes – but also a city of people. Many millions of people. Every single one of them hard-working and decent and innovative and multi-cultural.

It is a privilege to be Prime Minister of a country with such a capital city.

London. It's so great you say it once.

London. A London with pride in its past, but with eyes fixed to the future.

A London that says to the world: we're proud of our diversity. Proud to be an open, dynamic, outward-going city. Proud to take centre stage at the party, holding out its glass for a bit of a top-up, yes – but at the same time remaining within easy reach of the nibbles.

London. The city of the Olympic Games for Britain in 2012. And let me tell you what won that bid. I'll tell you what won that bid. I'll be honest.

I won that bid.

There were others, too nameless to mention. Yes, it was all about teamwork. Teamwork by me.

* * *

Wishing and hoping.
And thinking and praying.
And planning and dreaming.
His kisses will start...
That won't get you into his heart.

* * *

Y'know, if there's one thing I've learnt while being Prime Minister, it's this. Once a dam has burst, there's no point trying to plug it with a cork. Because by that time the water's already gone everywhere, the whole place is soaking wet, and the cork probably won't fit back in anyway.

And if there's another thing I've learnt while being Prime Minister, it's this.

A stitch in time saves nine.

Put it this way, if you've got a rip on your trousers, perhaps a bit of a tear, there's no point in delaying. Far from it. In fact, you're much better off giving them a stitch straight away.

Far better that than to leave it and let the rip get bigger and bigger.

Because then you might have to give it anything up to nine stitches in all.

And I'll tell you something else.

A rolling stone gathers no moss.

Y'know, when I became Prime Minister, I took a decision. And the decision was this. You mustn't take the wrong decision, even if it is at the right time.

And you can't take the right decision if it's at the wrong time, because that doesn't work either.

You've got to take the right decision.

At the right time.

It's all about leadership.

Not his leadership. Mine.

Today, the past is waving us goodbye.

The future is ahead of us. And it's my job. To make sure. I'll still have one. When it arrives.

New Labour Manifesto 2005: Britain Forward, Back, Then a Bit to the Side

AFTER TWO SHORT terms of New Labour, the sooty chimney sweep of only eight or nine years of age, sent shinning up tall chimneys by ruthless employers, is a thing of the past.

Britain forward not back.

No longer are the streets full of rickety old carts filled with the disease-stricken corpses of victims of the Black Death.

Britain forward not back.

No longer are hard-working senior citizens, who should have earned the right to respect in their old age, marched to the gallows and subjected to the indignity of being hanged as witches before a baying crowd.

Britain forward not back.

New Labour has banished the twin demons of serfdom and press gangs.

Under New Labour, half the population of rural England is no longer consigned to personal servitude to a lord and master. Young men with their lives ahead of them aren't swept up off the streets and forced against their wishes into the Navy.

And open sewers – which used to flow through our city streets, spreading typhoid among our close-knit, hard-working communities – are a thing of the past.

No going back to a Britain filled with mothers weeping as their sons and daughters wave a tearful farewell.

No going back to a Britain in which children as young as three are dressed in rags and made to polish the shoes of hoity-toity aldermen.

Going forward to a stronger, fairer, merrier country. A Britain of maypoles and travelling jesters.

Going forward to a colourful world of thrilling jousts, free grazing on the village green – and buxom wenches with come-hither looks serving ale aplenty.

Balancing work and family

Streamling grassroots.

Responding to challenges.

Allowing grassroots to flourish at a local level.

Taking major strides.

Providing a framework for flexibility.

Abolishing the burden of grassroots at a local level.

Balancing frameworks.

Tackling frameworks.

Creating a long-term platform for grassroots in the arts.

Taking tough decisions on the whole grassroots question – and providing a solution to benefit not only those who can afford to pay for it but the community as a whole.

A great country

Britain is a great country.

Older people make a great contribution.

So do younger people.

And let's not forget the tremendous contribution shown by men and women in their middle years.

Tough choices

We do not duck tough choices. Far from it. To deal with tough choices, we have set up ToughChoice Direct – a wide-ranging nationwide information service to help tackle the whole issue of tough choices.

Today, our country faces some tough choices. We believe the British people have the capacity to make those tough choices.

Or not – as the case may be.

Children – young now, but tomorrow a day older

Children are our future. In a decade or two, they'll be adults, just like us.

They deserve the best.

We believe every child should have a clean pair of shorts at least once a week.

Boys like model railways – whereas girls prefer a dolly with a pretty pink dress.

We believe children are happiest when smiling. Children who

pinch are not to be encouraged. We believe that pinching is not clever – and it is not nice. Our new PinchStop Action Direct programme provides a complete information service to hard-working parents wishing to crack down on pinching in the home.

Education – a great way to learn

We believe that teaching provides the best means towards education.

Transport – the best way to get from A to B

Transport is a source of pride. Cars and lorries go on roads, whereas trains are better suited to railway tracks. Aeroplanes fly in the sky. We will continue to provide sky access for aeroplanes, and will maintain our commitment to all forms of transport.

Iraq

Iraq is a country in south-west Asia. It covers an area of 167,881 square miles. Its capital city is Baghdad. That's all you need to know.

The future in front of us

We want clean hospitals, free of infection. We want to preserve hospitals as places where people come to get better, not go to get worse. We believe the British people have a great capacity to get well soon.

We want a new partnership in our hospitals with a ten-year strategy on innovation and commitment.

Since 1997, up to 95 per cent of hard-working Britons have not suffered from MRSA. This is great news for New Labour – and for the hard-working people of Britain.

Our ambition

Our ambition is to eliminate death, and provide eternal life for all the people of Britain, regardless of race, colour or creed. To help meet this target, we will introduce ID cards, including biometric data, backed by a national register.

A personal message from Tony

So now I fight my last election as leader of my party and Prime Minister of our country. My call is a passionate one: let's deal with the challenge, let's tackle insecurity, let's forge bonds and crack down on the divisions of the past.

When I visit communities in Southampton and Darlington, Blackpool and Middlesbrough, a lot of decent, hard-working families come up to me and ask me what it's all about.

And to them I say this.

Britain in.

Britain out.

Britain shake it all about.

Do the hokey-cokey.

And you turn around.

Yes.

That's what it's all about.

Appendix

Those Key Marginals

Bagshot
Braun, E
Close, G
Gandhi, I

Barking
Bjork
Fayed, M
Redwood, J
Thatcher, Lady M

Barnet
Beethoven, L van
Bragg, M
Einstein, A
Fawcett-Majors, F
Heseltine, Rt Hon M
Karadzic, R

Bath
Baddiel, D
Gallagher, N
MacGowan, S
Rasputin, G
Swampy

Berks
Burrell, P
Hewitt, Major J

Rooney, W
Wisdom, N

Bickering
Blunkett, D
Fortier, K
Quinn, S

Blandford
Ball, M
Clooney, G
Como, P
Frostrup, M
Stewart, E
Williams, A

Boreham
Barlow, K
Bono
Duncan Smith, Rt Hon I
Sting
Toynbee, P

Bray
But-Dim, T N
Grosman, L
Harry, Prince
Palmer-Tomkinson, T

The Broads
Greer, G
Jordan
Osborne, S
Parker Bowles, C

Bucks
Beckham, D
Byng, S
Grant, H
Walliams, D

Burley
Clarke, Rt Hon K
Jupitus, P
Moore, M
Prescott, Rt Hon J

Bushey
Darwin, C
Healey, D
Kahlo, F
Laden O bin
Williams, Rt Rev R

Cardigan
Deedes, W F
Doonican, V
Palmer, G
Titchmarsh, A

Chatham
Finnegan, J
Madeley, R
Ross, J
Skinner, F

Cheshire
Blair, C
Harriot, A
Henry, L
Lama, Dalai
Punch
Wildenstein, Jocelyne

Chippenham
Aldrin, B
Eccleston, C
Martin, Rt Hon M
Moyles, C
Reid, J
Wessex, E

Clapham
Carey, M
Mosley O
Stalin, J
Tse-tung, M

Conwy
Archer, J
Ingram, Mr and Mrs C
Morgan, P
Whittock, T
Wyatt, Lord

Cookham
Blanc, R
Craddock, F
Lawson, N
Ladenis, N
Rhodes, G

Cornwall
Blackburn, T
Dunn, C
Goldsboro, B
Harris, R
O'Connor, D

Deal
Blaine, D
Gordon-Cumming, W
Jay, R
Sharif, O

Dedham
Bobby, G
Dracula, Count
Hirst, D
Stokes, D
von Hagen, G

Diss
Callow, S
Campbell, A
Robinson, A

Effingham
Allen, K
Fayed, M
Osborne, O
Pinter, H
Street-Porter, J

Fakenham
Anderson, A
Chatterton, T
Irving, C
Keating, T
Leeson, N

Fawler
Campbell, N
Corbett, R
Eagle, E
Kinnock, N

Goring
Cordobes, L
Paxman, J
Skinner, D
Sugar, Sir A

Great Ham
Berkoff, S
Blair, T
Blessed, B
Hardy, R
Sinden, D

Ham Common
Black, C
Blethyn, B
Gordon, N
Keith, P
Nesbitt, J

Hanger Lane
Bush, G W
Jeffreys, Judge
Pierrepoint, A
Taylor, T

Hipswell
Bunter, W
Crosby, D
Diamond, A
Soames, N

Huffington
Carey, M
Gallagher, L
John, Sir E
Nott, J
Wessex, E

Leatherhead
James, S
Kilroy Silk, R
Krueger, F
Neil, A.
Noriega, M
Parkinson, M

Legs Cross
Peg, J T
Stone, S

Littlehampton
Amis, M
Askey, A
Duncan, A
Redford, R
Thumb, Gen. T

Little Snoring
Bear, D, M and B
Howe, G
Mulley, F
van Winkle, R

Lustleigh
Ashdown, P
Bloom, H
Cook, R
Mellor, D
Parkinson, C

Maida Vale
Best, G
Church, C
Gascoigne, P
Kennedy, C
Reed, O
Smith, D
Vegas, J

Maidenhead
Arc J of
Elizabeth, R
Widdecombe, A

Masham
Ladenis, N
Ramsay, G
White, M P

Middlesex
Clary, J
Everage, Dame E
George, B
Hambling, M

Mole Valley
Blunt, A
Burgess, G
Maclean, D
Philby, K

Much Hadham
Argyll, M, Duchess of
Bankhead, T
Emin, T
Gabor, Z Z
Kensit, P
Loos, R

Muck
Clifford, M
Levy, G
Morgan, P
Murdoch, R

Mull
Biggs, R
Crusoe, R
Heath, E
Hess, R
Stylites, S

New Cross
Livingstone, K
Starkey, Dr D
Wales, Prince of

Oval
Dickson-Wright, C
Dumpty, H
French, D
Margolyes, M

Plumpton
Brando, M
Kay, P
Pollard, V
Smith, Sir C
Weidenfeld, Lord

Probus
Aitken, J
Clinton, B
Gilligan, A
Stonehouse, J
Vaz, K

Pulham
Casanova, G
Clark, A
Stewart, R
Stringfellow, P

Sandwich
Nicolson, Sir H
Sackville-West, V
Trefusis, V

The Scillies
Caplin, C
Dodd, K
Mallet, T
Ono, Y
Strong, Sir R

Selby
Beckham, V
Campbell, Sir M
Edmonds, N
Evans, C
Frost, Sir D
Fukuyama, F
Glitter, G
Kerry, Senator J
King, J
Rushdie, S

Staines
Emin, T
Jackson, M
Lewinsky, M
Macbeth, Lady
Patterson, Sir L

Stopham
Dixon, G
Gillick, V
Plod, PC
Whitehouse, M

Tooting
Clarkson, J
Ears, B
Montagu, Lord
Thatcher, Lord M
Toad, Mr

Wapping
Bindon, J
Flynn, E
Geldof, B
Jones, T
Proby, PJ

Wigan
Bosanquet, R
Curtis, T
Daniels, P
Fabricant, M
Savage, L
Wogan, T

Wilts
Dee, S
Feltz, V
Halliwell, G
Holden, A

Wittering
Cooper, J
Fawlty, S
Goody, J
Ogden, H
Sherrin, N